ASSEMBLY LANGUAGE for the PDP-11

Charles Kapps
Robert L. Stafford
Temple University

A Joint Publication in Computer
and Management Information Systems

Prindle, Weber & Schmidt
CBI Publishing Company, Inc.
Boston, Massachusetts

© Copyright 1981 by Prindle, Weber & Schmidt, 20 Providence St., Boston, MA 02116, and CBI Publishing Company, Inc., 51 Sleeper St., Boston, MA 02110.

All rights reserved. No part of this book may be reproduced or transmitted in any form or by any means, electronic or mechanical, including photocopying, recording, or any information storage and retrieval system, without permission in writing from the publisher.

Prindle, Weber & Schmidt is a division of Wadsworth, Inc.

Second printing: July, 1981

Library of Congress Cataloging in Publication Data

Kapps, Charles
    Assembly language for the PDP-11.

    Includes index.
    1. Assembler language (Computer program language)
2. PDP-11 (Computer)--Programming.   I. Stafford, Robert L., joint author.   II. Title.
QA76.73.A8K36   001.64'24   80-39985
ISBN 0-87150-304-2

Cover design and text art by Julie Gecha. Text design and production by Nancy Blodget. Composed on a Compugraphic Editwriter in Times Roman by A & B Typesetters. Cover printed by New England Book Components, Inc. Text printed and bound by Haddon Craftsmen.

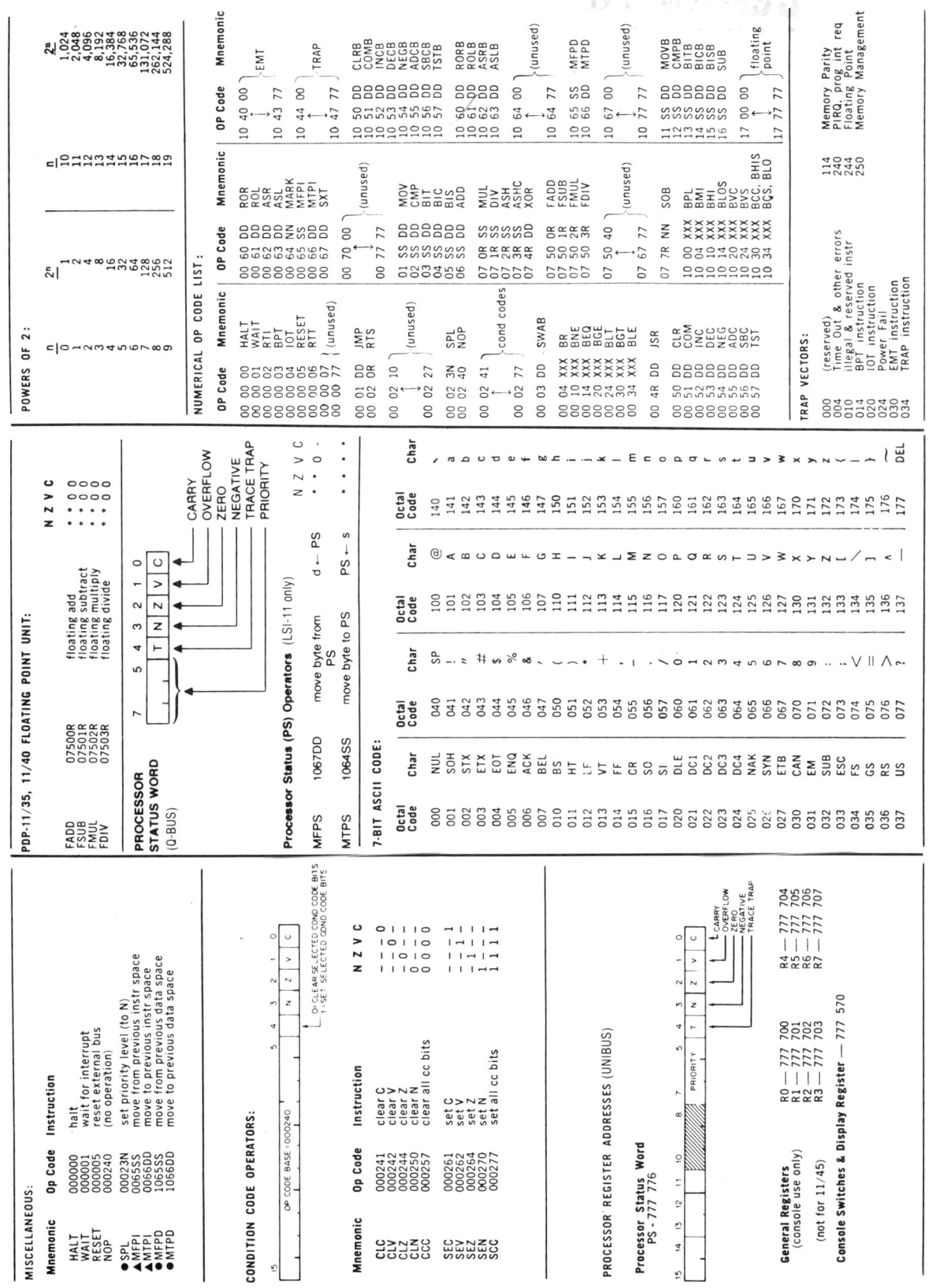

We dedicate this book to:
Christianne
Judy
Marcia
Sarah

The Authors

Charles Kapps received his Ph.D. in Computer Science from the University of Pennsylvania in 1970. He has published papers on programming languages and automated theory of large-scale integrated circuits, and has co-authored *Introduction to the Theory of Computing,* published by Charles Merrill. In addition, he has worked on the Apollo Moonlander Project as a numerical analyst under a contract to Raytheon. Most recently he has worked with Integrated Circuits Systems on the development of design processes for Very Large-Scale Integrated Circuits. He is currently an Associate Professor of Computer Science at Temple University.

Robert L. Stafford received his Ph.D. in Industrial Administration from Yale University in 1969. He has done research in the area of picture processing and has taught at the Pennsylvania State University and the University of Pittsburgh. His current position is Associate Professor of Computer Science at Temple University.

The Computer and Management Information Systems Series

- Barry Bateman and Gerald Pitts/*JCL in a System 370 Environment*
- Charles Kapps and Robert L. Stafford/ *Assembly Language for the PDP-11*
- Jud Ostle/*Systems Analysis and Design*

SERIES FOREWORD

This book is part of the Computer and Management Information Systems Series from Prindle, Weber & Schmidt and CBI Publishing Company, Inc. As publishers we recognize the impact that computer technology has on the academic community, the business world, and the computer industry itself. Recent rapid advancements in hardware and software have created a need to communicate new developments to the varied audiences who teach, implement, and initiate these new technologies. We have designed this series of books as a timely, educational vehicle for the interchange of these ideas.

Traditional college textbooks that emphasize the theoretical aspects of computer science are frequently used by industry professionals and business executives. Conversely, books that reflect a more practical, "state-of-the-art" presentation are used by colleges and universities as texts. By merging the resources and efforts of our two companies, we have made a commitment to facilitate an interchange among the audiences mentioned above. We believe this multi-market potential for books in Computer and Management Information Systems is crucial to the exciting developments in computer-related fields.

It has long been our publishing philosophy that the needs of an audience are best served by concentrating on those areas of study where the publishers' editorial, marketing, and production specialists have their greatest expertise. Our companies are uniquely suited to implement this philosophy. CBI is a well-known and established publisher of professional and reference books; Prindle, Weber & Schmidt publishes exclusively in the computer and mathematical sciences for the academic community. Together, we focus our full editorial and marketing efforts on publishing books which can be utilized by academics, business executives, and industry professionals. We welcome your comments on this text, and any inquiries into our joint publishing venture in Computer and Management Information Systems.

PREFACE

This book is designed for a one-semester course in assembly and machine language programming for the PDP-11 family of computers. It is assumed that people using this book will have some familiarity with computer programming, most likely in a higher level language such as FORTRAN or BASIC. However, minimal assumptions have been made in this regard, and the basics of machine organization are covered very thoroughly. Our motivational philosophy is to knit theory and practice firmly together. Every effort has been made to develop a conceptual understanding of the PDP-11 architecture while leading the student to early hands-on experience on the machine. This approach should also be ideal for individuals who wish to use the text as a self-study guide for learning the assembly and machine language of the PDP-11 family.

The PDP-11 was chosen not only because of its popularity, but also because we believe that the architecture is ideal for learning. The organizational consistency makes the PDP-11 an extremely easy computer to program in machine or assembly language. The richness of the machine language makes it easy to use the assembly language for complicated problems. This richness also makes the PDP-11 ideal as a stepping-off point for learning the architecture of other machines. By focusing on a single computer family, we are able to include advanced topics such as floating point operations, hardware level input and output, interfacing to a high level language, and operating system functions. These topics extend the scope of the book into the larger field of computer science.

Our major goal is to make the book both accessible and relevant for the reader and the instructor. For example, the PDP-11 programming card is printed on the inside front cover for easy reference. In the early chapters, methods are shown which enable students to run simple programs on the computer. Later, the reader is shown how to perform input and output both with a bare machine and by using the RT-11 operating system. Appendices show how to run PDP-11 machine language programs using ODT, and assembly language programs using RT-11 both on line and with batch. Basic use of the PDP-11 on-line editor is also explained. Although the appendices are centered around use of the RT-11 operating system, most of the examples in the text are not tied to any operating system, and therefore this book is appropriate for use with any PDP-11 system.

The organization of the chapters is as follows: Chapters 1 and 2 contain background information for persons who may have had limited experience with computers. Chapters 3, 4, and 5 introduce the basic concepts of machine language and assembly language on the PDP-11. By the end of Chapter 5 the use of processor registers and simple subroutines has been covered so that the students can start running fairly complex programs using input/output routines shown in the appendix. Chapters 6, 7, and 8 present intermediate material that focuses on the manipulation of data. This includes more sophisticated operations with numbers, the processing of alphabetic information, and arrays. Chapters 9–12 present the advanced topics of subroutines and global symbols, macros and conditional assembly, hardware level input/output, and floating point operations. These chapters can be covered in any order or omitted. Chapter 13 ties together the advanced topics to form an introduction to operating systems and systems programming.

Chapters 1–7 are intended for use in the order presented. The order of the remaining chapters can be varied according to the following graph of chapter dependencies.

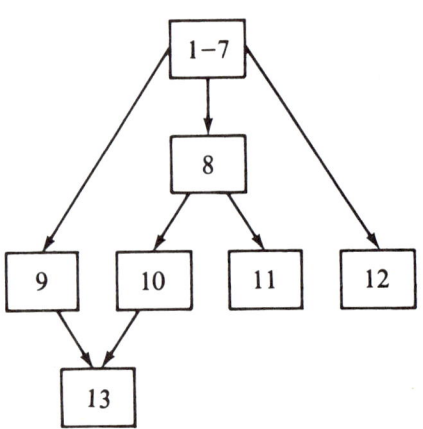

We extend sincere appreciation to our students who provided us with many suggestions during the preparation of this material. James Gips of Boston College also class-tested the manuscript and provided many valuable comments. George Gorsline of Virginia Polytechnic Institute and State University deserves special mention for his advice and detailed insights at several stages during the development of the manuscript. We benefited from the comments of the following people who reviewed all or parts of the manuscript: Clifford Anderson, California State University, Los Angeles; Donald Cooley, Utah State University; Paul Jalics, Cleveland State University; William Lau, California State University, Fullerton; and Michael Lutz, Rochester Institute of Technology.

We would also like to acknowledge the following people who helped us in preparing the manuscript: Patricia DeSpirito, Maryaurelia Lemmon, and Judy Lennon.

Special thanks are due to our production editor, Nancy Blodget.

Charles Kapps
Robert L. Stafford

TABLE OF CONTENTS

CH. 1	INTRODUCTION	
1.1	History	1
1.2	Developments in Computer Software	4
1.3	The PDP-11 Family of Computers	7
CH. 2	**NUMBERS, COUNTING, AND LOGIC IN A COMPUTER**	
2.1	Number Systems	15
2.2	The Decimal and Octal Number Systems	17
2.3	Binary Numbers	20
2.4	Octal Encoding	23
2.5	Two's Complement Arithmetic	26
2.6	Boolean Logic	28
2.7	Hexadecimal Encodings	30
2.8	Other Encodings	30
CH. 3	**MACHINE LANGUAGE PROGRAMMING**	
3.1	Digital Computers	33
3.2	Memory Representation on the PDP-11 Computer	34
3.3	Processor Use of Memory	39
3.4	Machine Language Programs	42

Table of Contents

3.5	The Use of a Memory Cell	44
3.6	Writing Machine Language Programs	52
3.7	Memory Structure of Other Computers	56

CH. 4 ASSEMBLY LANGUAGE PROGRAMMING

4.1	Introduction	63
4.2	Developing an Assembly Language Program	64
4.3	The Assembly Process	69
4.4	Examples of Errors in the Assembly Process	71
4.5	Programs in the Computer	78
4.6	Running a Sample Program	82

CH. 5 PROGRAM CONTROL FEATURES

5.1	Introduction	87
5.2	Looping	88
5.3	Single-Operand Instructions	91
5.4	Machine Language Coding of the Branch Instructions	95
5.5	Other Instructions	97
5.6	Machine Language Operation Codes	102
5.7	Processor Registers	105
5.8	Subroutines	111
5.9	Stopping Your Program if Using RT-11	115

CH. 6 PDP-11 ARITHMETIC

6.1	Introduction	119
6.2	Signed and Unsigned Numbers	119
6.3	Multiplication and Division	129
6.4	Multiple-Precision Arithmetic	137

CH. 7 ARRAYS

7.1	Introduction and Review	143
7.2	Indexing	146
7.3	Other Addressing Modes	151
7.4	Full Set of Addressing Modes	154
7.5	Multiply-Dimensioned Arrays	160

CH. 8 ALPHABETIC INFORMATION—BYTE INSTRUCTIONS

8.1	Representing Alphabetic Information	165
8.2	Manipulating Characters	172
8.3	Simplified Input and Output	179
8.4	Bit Manipulation Instructions	183
8.5	Other Character Representations	190

CH. 9 SUBROUTINES

9.1	Introduction	197
9.2	Calling a Subroutine	197
9.3	Independent Assembly—Global Symbols	206
9.4	Interfacing Assembly Language with FORTRAN	209
9.5	Recursive Subroutines	214

CH. 10 MACROS AND CONDITIONAL ASSEMBLY

10.1	Repetitive Blocks of Code	219
10.2	Symbolic Expressions	223
10.3	Macros	229
10.4	Conditional Assembly	232
10.5	Nesting and Recursion	234

CH. 11 INPUT AND OUTPUT

11.1	Introduction	239
11.2	Device Polling	239
11.3	Other Input/Output Devices	247
11.4	Interrupts	252
11.5	Other Considerations	260

CH. 12 FLOATING POINT NUMBERS AND EXTENDED INSTRUCTIONS

12.1	Introduction	265
12.2	Fixed and Floating Point Numbers	265
12.3	Floating Point Operations	269
12.4	PDP-11 Floating Point Numbers	275
12.5	Extended Instruction Set Operations	281

CH. 13 ADVANCED ASSEMBLY LANGAUGE TOPICS

13.1	Introduction	289
13.2	Program Format	290
13.3	Object Code	296
13.4	Load Files	302
13.5	Program Execution	304

APPENDIX A Running Machine Language Programs with On-Line Debugging Technique — 309

APPENDIX B Routines for Reading and Printing Numbers — 313

APPENDIX C

| C.1 | Running Assembly Language and FORTRAN Programs Using RT-11 Batch | 319 |
| C.2 | Notes for the Instructor | 322 |

APPENDIX D Running Assembly Language and FORTRAN Programs from the Console Typewriter with the RT-11 System

D.1	Communicating with the RT-11 System	325
D.2	Files	326
D.3	Running a Program	327

APPENDIX E Using the RT-11 Editor

E.1	Function of the Editor	331
E.2	Creating a Program	332
E.3	Correcting Errors	333
E.4	Inserting and Locating the Pointer in a Line	334
E.5	Combining Commands	335
E.6	The Search Command	336
E.7	Terminating the Edit Run	336
E.8	Editing a Preexisting Program	337
E.9	Immediate Mode Editing	338

Glossary 341

Index 349

CHAPTER 1

INTRODUCTION

1.1 HISTORY

The Early Days

The history of automatic computers goes back much further than many people realize. In the 1830s and 1840s, an English mathematician by the name of Charles Babbage attempted to build an automatic computer based on gears and punched cards. Unfortunately, Babbage was never able to complete his analytic engine. Later in the century, however, an American named Herman Hollerith developed a punched card tabulating system that was used with the 1890 U.S. census.

Punched card tabulating equipment based on Hollerith's designs came into extensive use in the early part of the twentieth century. This equipment, which came to use the initials EAM for Electronic Accounting Machinery, was made of electrical and mechanical parts (motors, switches, solenoids, relays, gears, clutches, ratchets, and so forth). Although modern equipment is considerably different from the early EAM equipment, the original Hollerith standards are still used for punched cards. (See page 190 for more detail on Hollerith codes.)

One major drawback to the EAM equipment was that it consisted of a conglomeration of special purpose machines, card duplicators, tabulators, sorters, and collators. These were all hard-wired or designed to perform specific tasks. Any variability in the system was accomplished by wiring configurations through plug boards. These plug boards allowed the user to route data and control information in much the same way that a switchboard operator routes telephone calls.

The next big step in computing came around 1940, when a more general and convenient method for controlling computations was developed. This appeared in the form of the Mark I computer developed by Howard Aiken at Harvard University. The Mark I computer was essentially a cross between a giant adding machine and a player piano. The entire control of the machine was "programmed" by punching appropriate patterns of holes in several player-pianolike scrolls.

Electronic Computers

Like its predecessors, the Mark I computer was electromechanical. In other words, electricity was only used to move mechanical parts. These moving parts, in turn, activated switches that controlled the electric currents. At best such mechanical operations require about one one-thousandth of a second, and often may require much more. The solution to such relative slowness was to replace the mechanical switches with electronic switches. An **electronic switch** is one that has no moving parts. The switching is accomplished by applying electrostatic or magnetic fields to the materials or empty space where the electrical conduction is taking place. In 1940, the available active element for an electronic switch was the vacuum tube.

Shortly after the Mark I was in operation, Presper Eckert and John Mauchly built the first electronic computer, called the ENIAC, at the University of Pennsylvania. Because a vacuum-tube switch is capable of operating in one one-millionth of a second, the ENIAC had the potential of being 1000 times faster than the Mark I. As computers became faster, they began to tax people's ability to make use of the speed. In fact, one of the early computer scientists was reputed to have said that six ENIAC's would keep all the mathematicians in the country busy forever, just finding problems for them to solve.

In order to perform a given computational process on the ENIAC, it was necessary to plug in a large number of wires in a certain configuration, a time-consuming process. The next innovation was the idea that a computational process should be specified by a **computer program** that resides in memory along with the data. In addition to making computers easier to use, an **internally stored program** makes it possible for the computer program to modify itself as it executes. (Although this was important with early computers, modern computers have been designed with instruction sets so that modification is no longer necessary or even desirable.)

In the past, many people have credited John von Neumann of Princeton University for developing the idea of the internally stored program. However, recent evidence indicates that Eckert and Mauchly deserve at least as much credit as von Neumann. In any case, the computer field owes a great debt to all three individuals.

The Solid-State Era

In the late 1950s and early 1960s, transistors began to replace the vacuum-tube switches in computers. Transistors have five distinct advantages over vacuum tubes: they are smaller, they consume much less energy, they are faster, they are less expensive, and they are more reliable.

Although there is no fundamental difference between transistor computers and vacuum-tube computers, the five advantages of transistors have a tremendous economic impact leading to two opposed trends in computer design:

1. First, it became feasible to build very large and powerful "supercomputers." Early examples of these were the IBM 7094, CDC 6600, and DEC PDP-6.*

2. It also became feasible, for the first time, to build small, inexpensive "minicomputers." These computers were low enough in cost so that small laboratories could afford to have them for dedicated use, so that one user could have the computer all to him/herself. (The large computers were so expensive that use had to be scheduled and shared.) Early examples of minicomputers were the IBM 1620, Royal McBee RPG 4000, and DEC PDP-5.

The proliferation of both kinds of computers started the extensive use of computers, and computers began to become better understood. Consequently the architecture and organization of later computers reflect an improved understanding; however, the organization principles have remained basically unchanged since the days of the first general purpose machines.

Integrated Circuits

Transistors are made by implanting small amounts of impurities in a semiconductor crystal such as silicon. Early transistors were all individually packaged in a small metal or plastic container with contact leads protruding. Because the actual transistor was much smaller than its package, much space was wasted. Integrated circuits, on the other hand, are made by forming many transistors on the surface of a silicon wafer. Wiring is then photographically applied right on the surface of the wafer. This allows extremely complex circuits to be constructed in a very small space. (At present, it is possible to have 70,000 transistors on a "chip" less than 1 cm^2 in area.)

The advent of integrated circuits completely revolutionized the economics of computers. Large computers have become less expensive and minicomputers have become more sophisticated, so that now it is sometimes difficult to dis-

---

*Some people may argue the appropriateness of the term "supercomputer" for these examples. However, in the early to mid 1960s, they were pretty "super."

tinguish one from the other. We also have the so-called microcomputers in which an entire computer is placed on a single silicon chip that can be sold for only a few dollars. Originally, microcomputers were rather crude, but recent advances have blurred the distinction between microcomputers and minicomputers.

At present, integrated-circuit technology is rapidly developing, and one can only guess where the future will lead.

Other Hardware Advances

The physical components that make up a computer system are collectively referred to as **computer hardware**. The previous subsections primarily dealt with advances in processor design and implementation. Paralleling this, though perhaps not so dramatic, have been advances in other hardware devices such as memories and peripheral equipment.

Memory design has followed a similar history from electromechanical designs to integrated circuits. On the other hand, peripheral devices such as printers, card readers, magnetic tape units, disks and drums, and so forth have not improved as much. As a result, peripheral devices are by far the most expensive parts of most computer systems.

1.2 DEVELOPMENTS IN COMPUTER SOFTWARE

Machine and Assembly Language

To build a computer, designers first select a particular set of orders or instructions and then construct a machine that will carry out or execute programs comprised of these orders or instructions. The instructions or orders are called **machine-language instructions** and the resulting programs are called **machine-language programs**. Notice that the machine-language instructions of one machine may be totally different from the machine-language instructions of another machine.

Machine languages are usually numerical languages that are awkward for human beings to use. For example, the PDP-11 machine-language instruction to add the contents of one memory cell (in this case the memory cell called 001000) to another memory cell (called 002000) can be written as:

$$063737 \quad 001000 \quad 002000$$

where 063737 is the numerical operation code for a particular kind of addition.

In the early 1950s, assembly languages were developed to ease the burden on programmers. In an **assembly language**, names are substituted for numbers.

For example, the preceding PDP-11 machine-language instruction might be rewritten in assembly language as follows:

                ADD   BONUS,SALARY

The advantage of using names instead of numbers should be obvious.

Before an assembly-language program can be executed, it must be translated into machine language. This translation is basically a clerical process that involves substituting the correct number for each of the names (that is, substituting 063737 for ADD in the previous example). However, this is exactly the kind of problem that is easily solved with a computer. Therefore, the designer of an assembly language creates a program, called the **assembler**, that will input a users' assembly-language program and translate it into machine language.

Higher-Level Languages

In the mid 1950s, the first higher-level languages were developed. Unlike an assembly language, a higher-level language is not associated with any particular machine language. Instead, the designer of a higher-level language concentrates on developing a language that is convenient for solving a certain class of computing problems. Then the designer builds a translator* called a **compiler** to translate a users' program into a given machine language. If it is desired to use the high-level language on a computer with a different machine language, a second translator is constructed. Thus the user of a high-level language does not have to know the machine language of the computer being used. In addition, it is possible to transfer a program written in a high-level language from one computer to another without rewriting the program (assuming that the necessary translators are available).

The difference between assembly language and higher-level languages can also be described in terms of the translation process. Each assembly-language instruction is generally translated into one machine-language instruction. In contrast, each statement in a higher-level language may be translated into many machine-language statements.

In the late 1950s and throughout the 1960s, a variety of high-level languages became popular. The first of these was FORTRAN (FORmula TRANslation) which was developed by a group headed by John Backus at IBM. FORTRAN was designed to help people solve *scientific problems* where a large number of calculations are required as opposed to *data-processing problems* where a large number of input and output operations (such as reading and printing) are necessary. In order to solve data-processing problems, COBOL (Common Business Oriented Language) was designed by a committee spon-

---

*Some higher-level languages are **interpreted,** which is a step-by-step translation during program execution.

sored by the Department of Defense. In 1960, an international group of computer experts met to develop a new language for scientific problems. (The original specifications for FORTRAN were written in 1954, and a great deal had been learned about language design in the intervening years.) The result was the programming language ALGOL 60 (ALGOrithmetic Language). In the mid 1960s IBM developed the language PL-1 (Programming Language 1) which was designed for both scientific programming problems and data-processing applications. At about the same time, John Kemeny and Thomas Kurtz at Dartmouth College developed BASIC (Beginners' All purpose Symbolic Instruction Code). Although BASIC resembles a simplified version of FORTAN, it was specifically designed to be used from an interactive time-sharing terminal. Other languages that are now in common use include APL (A Programming Language), which is also designed to be used from a time-sharing terminal, and PASCAL, which resembles a simplified version of ALGOL. It should be noted that this list of programming languages is far from exhaustive. There are literally hundreds of programming languages. Many are specialized languages designed for a particular class of problems such as simulation.

Why Study Assembly Language?

Higher-level languages are easier to use than machine or assembly language. In addition, higher-level languages can generally be transported from one computer system to another without rewriting the program. Why then should people still write programs in machine or assembly language?

In some cases, a user may wish to use features of a computer that are not accessible from available higher-level languages. This situation often occurs in developing operating-system software, especially in the portions involving input, output, and other machine-dependent resources. In such cases it becomes necessary to use machine and assembly language for at least some sections of the program.

For some applications, a carefully written assembly-language program to solve a given problem will be more efficient (in terms of running time and/or memory space used) than a carefully written program in a higher-level language. This often overrides the fact that assembly-language programs may require more programmer time to write, debug, test, and modify than an equivalent program written in a higher-level language. The selection of a language is an economic question, and the various costs for the particular application must be examined in order to make a rational decision. With current costs, it appears that higher-level languages will be the correct choice in the majority of applications but that assembly language is still appropriate for a significant number of applications.

In addition, there are important reasons for knowing (as opposed to programming in) machine and assembly language. To a large extent, the purpose of a higher-level language is to "hide" the complexity of machine language from the average programmer or user. However, the higher-level language is generally not completely successful in burying the complexity. As a result, the higher-level language may produce unexpected results such as arithmetic overflow, and apparently simple changes in a higher-level language program may result in large changes in running time or memory usage. A knowledge of machine language is useful for understanding and predicting these results. Such knowledge is particularly useful when a higher-level language program is transported from one machine to another. Finally, computer scientists should know machine and assembly languages for a variety of reasons, particularly if they are to develop more effective higher-level languages.

EXERCISE SET 1

Exercise questions marked by an asterisk (*) will require outside reading.

1. Identify the following persons, and name their major accomplishment:
   (a) Herman Hollerith
   (b) Howard Aiken
   (c) Presper Eckert
   (d) John Mauchly
   (e) John von Neumann

*2. Using reference material other than this text, write a short (one page or so) biography of any of the persons named in question 1.

3. Vacuum-tube computers have been completely replaced by solid-state computers. This is true to the extent that there are very few if any vacuum-tube computers in practical operation anywhere in the world today. To account for this, name as many disadvantages of vacuum-tube computers as you can.

*4. One of the important names in the founding of computer science is Grace Hopper. What is she best known for? And how do her accomplishments differ from those referred to in question 1?

1.3 THE PDP-11 FAMILY OF COMPUTERS

Overview

The first PDP-11 computers were introduced at the end of the 1960s. These computers were intended to replace the PDP-5/PDP-8 family of minicomputers that were then becoming obsolete. The PDP-11's used integrated circuits that allowed considerable sophistication at a reduced price. As a result, the PDP-11 became a very popular minicomputer.

Early PDP-11's were used primarily with paper tape operating systems. This means that programs are stored in the form of a punched paper tape that can be read into the computer. All programs are stored this way, both user programs and system programs. As a result, use of such a machine was rather slow and awkward. Fortunately inexpensive forms of magnetic media (tapes and disks) have been developed. These are much faster and more convenient to use and are within the economic reach of most users.

As a consequence, most PDP-11's now have rather sophisticated operating systems that use mass-storage media (disk or magnetic tape). These systems can store many user programs and provide the user with a number of system functions. One of these functions is to provide the user with a variety of languages in which to write programs. These include assembly language, FORTRAN, and BASIC. Full-blown systems will also include COBOL, APL, PASCAL, and other languages. With the operating systems provided, these languages are easily accessible to the user.

The PDP-11 Processors

The PDP-11 is designated a **16-bit** minicomputer. The 16-bit designation means that most operations in the processor deal with a unit of information that consists of sixteen binary digits. (See Chapters 2 and 3.) This is also called the **word size** of the processor. To a certain extent, the word size determines the speed at which the processor can operate. It also tends to determine the price. While a 32-bit machine may be twice as fast as a 16-bit machine, it *may* also be twice as expensive because it needs parts that are at least twice as complicated.*

Although the basic architecture and primary operations are the same on all PDP-11's, many different models have many different features. Some differences are based on changes in technology that have occurred in the years since the first PDP-11's appeared on the market. Other differences are based on how much a customer is willing to pay for a faster or more powerful computer.

The least expensive processors in the PDP-11 family are the so-called LSI-11's (see Figure 1.1). The name comes from the fact that the bulk of the processor resides on a few Large-Scale Integrated-circuit chips. An LSI-11 processor board can be bought for well under $1000. This processor has all the power of the basic PDP-11 instruction set. In packaged form, this processor forms the 03 series of models, such as the PDP-11V03. The 03 series of PDP-11's are the least expensive, but they are comparatively slow, limited in the amount of memory, and limited in the selection of peripheral equipment (see Figure 1.2).

A new version of the LSI-11 is called the PDP-11/23. This version is about twice as expensive, but is much faster and allows four times as much memory. It also allows for the operation of sophisticated peripheral devices. (See Chapter 11.)

*Note the word *may*; the bit-price ratio may vary because different technologies may cause radical cost and speed differences.

The full-scale PDP-11 processors use a high-speed parallel connection to the outside world called the UNIBUS©. At the present time, in order to have access to all of the available peripheral devices such as high-speed printers and card readers, large-capacity disks, and magnetic tape, it is necessary to have a UNIBUS© machine. The most popular machine with a UNIBUS© at present is the PDP-11/34 (see Figure 1.3). The model 34 is somewhat faster than the model 23 and has the added capability of the UNIBUS©. The cost is somewhat higher, but is well within the reach of dedicated laboratory use.

The PDP-11/50 and 11/70 (see Figure 1.4) are larger, faster, and more powerful PDP-11 computers that may be too big to be called "minicomputers" (although most people do). They share the machine language of the other PDP-11's but have added features that entitle them to be classified as full-scale computers. These computers are normally used in a **multiuser** environment, which means that the computer is servicing a number of users during the same general time period.

The VAX-11/780 is an even more powerful machine that can execute PDP-11 machine-language programs. However, it is really a 32-bit machine instead of a 16-bit machine, and it normally uses a different machine language.

Figure 1.1 LSI-11 Computer (Courtesy of Digital Equipment Corp.)

Figure 1.2 PDP-11/03 Computer (Courtesy of Digital Equipment Corp.)

Figure 1.3 PDP-11/34 Computer System (Courtesy of Digital Equipment Corp.)

Figure 1.4 PDP-11/70 Computer System (Courtesy of Digital Equipment Corp.)

Systems Software

Although it would be possible to enter one's own programs into a machine without an operating system, various areas such as input, output, file management, and language translation would require much programming effort. As a result, virtually all computer users purchase a packaged set of programs for their computer for running the system. This is **systems software.**

Systems software falls into several categories:

1. Monitors—these programs coordinate and direct the execution of all other programs.
2. Utility programs—these programs are used for creating, copying, deleting, and updating files and operating systems themselves.
3. System subroutines—these allow user programs to perform system functions as described in item 2.
4. Language processors—these enable the user to write programs in various languages: assembly language, FORTRAN, BASIC, and so forth.
5. Special library packages—these allow one to use special mathematical functions, statistical functions, graphics control, and so forth.

An **operating system** normally contains programs in categories 1 through 3, and user-selected features of 4 and 5. Since systems software requires a considerable development effort, one must pay a license fee to use an operating system. The cost of these licenses may be thousands of dollars for PDP-11 systems (and even more for full-sized computers).

The most frequently seen operating systems for the PDP-11 are RT-11, RSTS (pronounced "Ristiss"), RSX-11, and paper tape systems. RT-11 is a fairly simple operating system that services a single user at a time, although one mode of operation allows two programs to execute at the same time. The intent is to allow program development at the same time that the computer is controlling laboratory equipment. While RT-11 has many sophisticated file and language features, it is streamlined so that it is fast and uses a minimal amount of memory. Most small PDP-11's operate under the control of the RT-11 operating system.

RSTS is a multiuser system that was originally designed as a BASIC only system but now allows other languages such as assembly language and FORTRAN. The intended purpose of the RSTS is to service terminal users.

RSX-11 is a large, complex, general-purpose system. It allows many users access to the machine at many levels. Because of the sophistication of RSX-11, it requires much memory and much input/output activity. As a consequence, RSX-11 is used on most of the larger PDP-11's. The PDP-11/34 and 11/23 seem to be the dividing line. Larger computers use RSX-11; smaller ones use RT-11, and model 34 and 23 users are split.

Paper tape systems had just about disappeared until the advent of inexpensive "home" versions of the PDP-11 such as the Heathkit© H-11. With a paper tape system, the user purchases a supply of paper tapes, each of which contains a system program that must be manually loaded using a paper tape reader.

Peripheral Devices

Without peripheral devices, a computer would have no way of receiving or giving out information. Peripheral devices are any input or output or external data-storage devices. The PDP-11 computer can accommodate a large variety of peripheral devices. These include teletypewriters, cathode-ray-tube (CRT) displays, card readers, punched paper tape readers, and punches and various kinds of magnetic media (tapes and disks).

Originally minicomputers such as the PDP-5 and later the PDP-8 and then the PDP-11 had rather meager input and output facilities. This is because the cost of peripheral equipment tends to be much greater than the cost of the computer. Therefore, most early minicomputers only had a teletypewriter that was equipped with a paper tape reader/punch. With such a system, it was not unusual for a program to require thirty minutes time to be read into the machine.

Later machines had some rudimentary tape and disk capability. And now it is possible to outfit a PDP-11 with the most sophisticated magnetic tapes, multiplatter disks, high-speed printers, card readers, and more specialized devices. The powerful, high-speed peripheral equipment found its way to the PDP-11's by two routes. First, there are the big PDP-11's that need the high-speed equipment to operate effectively. Second, PDP-11's are used as input/

output controllers for some larger computers such as the DEC System 20 and the VAX-11/780.

On the other hand, recent hardware developments have brought many medium-speed devices within reach of the user with limited resources. Perhaps the most significant of these at present is the **floppy** disk system. The floppy disk is a small circular disk made of flexible plastic coated with magnetizable iron oxide. The disk resides in a cardboard envelope from which it is never removed. There are apertures in the cardboard that allow access to the rotating disk by the read/write mechanism. Floppy disk systems are inexpensive, moderately fast, and can store a fairly large amount of data. As a result, many small systems are configured with a teletypewriter or a CRT along with a dual floppy disk. Such a system would be considered minimal by today's standards for practical use.

The next step up from a floppy disk system would be a single-platter hard disk. Such systems are somewhat more expensive, but are much faster and can store more data.

EXERCISE SET 2

Exercise questions marked by an asterisk(*) will require outside reading.

1 Identify the following PDP-11 processors. What are the main characteristics and main applications?

   (a) PDP-11/03

   (b) PDP-11/23

   (c) PDP-11/34

   (d) PDP-11/70

*2 Identify the following peripheral devices that can be attached to the PDP-11. What purposes do they serve? What is their data-handling capacity?

   (a) CR-11   (b) LA-180

   (c) DX-01   (d) LA-34

   (e) LP-11   (f) RP-11

   (g) VT-100   (h) VT-11

*3 What does DEC mean by "traditional product line"? Name several traditional products and state how they were superceded.

CHAPTER 2

NUMBERS, COUNTING, AND LOGIC IN A COMPUTER

2.1 NUMBER SYSTEMS

Historical Aspects

Throughout history, people have devised many and varied methods for reckoning or counting. Even today we can still find people using such primitive methods of counting as placing stones in a bag or carving notches in a stick. In contrast with the primitive schemes, we can find the elaborate Roman numeral system which is now used mostly for show. However, the number system with which all of us are most familiar is the decimal or Arabic system.* Figure 2.1 shows some examples of numbers represented in various systems.

One thing that is common to all these systems is that they use a physical event or phenomenon such as a pile of stones, a carving, or a configuration of ink on paper, to *represent* a number. Note the word *represent*. Numbers are not physical objects but are abstract concepts which are used to answer the question "How many?" The objects or shapes which we build or write down are often referred to incorrectly as *numbers*. In reality they are *representations of numbers*.

---

*Arabic numerals were introduced to the European culture in the twelfth century by means of a Latin translation of a book by the Arabic mathematician Muhammad ibn-Musa al-Khwarizmi (ca. A.D. 780–850). A corruption of al-Khwarizmi's name gives us the word **algorithm,** meaning a well-defined, step-by-step process for solving a problem.

15

Figure 2.1 Several Systems of Number Representation

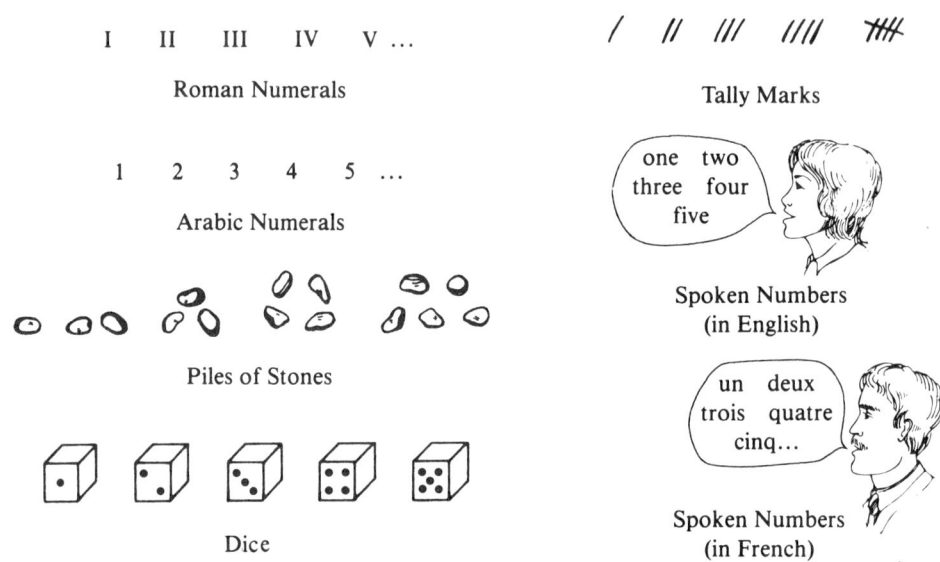

Decimal Notation

Another feature of most of the traditional number representation systems is that the schemes of representation tend to use groupings of fives and tens. This causes us to regard 5, 10, and their multiples and powers as extremely important numbers with almost magical properties. After all, it is very easy to multiply or divide a number by 10. It is not so easy to do those same operations with 8, 9, 11, or 12.

The fact is that the only reason that the numbers 5 or 10 have any special properties is because the numbers' representations are based on 10s. As we shall soon see, number representations can be based upon numbers other than 10. There is really no particular advantage to a ten-based system. The only reason that fives and tens received such importance in number representation is that humans are endowed with ten fingers (five per hand), and long before any written forms of counting were developed, people counted on their fingers. Since computers do not have five-fingered hands, there is no special advantage to fives or tens in a computer. In fact, the contrary is true. Computers can be built to operate more efficiently if they operate using number-representation systems based on numbers other than 10.

2.2 THE DECIMAL AND OCTAL NUMBER SYSTEMS

Counting

As we introduce other number systems, we will review the basic concepts of the decimal system. This includes counting, addition, and subtraction, as well as the interpretation of number representations. In the **decimal system,** numbers are expressed in the form of a string of symbols chosen from a collection of ten **digits:** 0, 1, 2, 3, 4, 5, 6, 7, 8, and 9. Counting is performed by starting with 0, and writing down successive digits, that is, 0, 1, 2. When we get up to 9, we have used every digit, and thus continue by going back to 0 and placing a 1 to the left to get 10, 11, 12, and so forth. When we get to 19, we bring the 9 back to 0 and count once with the digit on the left to get 20, and so on. When a sequence of 9s occurs on the right, they all go back to 0 and a count, or carry, is propagated to the left. Thus, after 3999, we get 4000.

As stated in the preceding section, there is nothing sacred about the number 10, nor is there any magic about using a set of ten digits. Suppose there were only eight. This might be the number system we would be using if people had four fingers on each hand rather than five. As it turns out, we are doing more than just an intellectual exercise here because the base eight, or **octal,** number system is extremely useful when dealing with some computers.

In the octal number system, we have eight digits: 0, 1, 2, 3, 4, 5, 6, and 7. Counting is basically the same in octal as in decimal, except that since there are no 8s or 9s, we must revert to 0 and produce a carry when 7 is reached. Thus, the next number after 7 is 10, after 17 we get 20, and after 277 we get 300. Table 2.1 shows a sequence of counting, both in octal and decimal. (For the moment, ignore the columns labeled binary and hexadecimal). Note the octal and decimal correspondences. For example, the table shows that the decimal number 30 is equivalent to the octal number 36.

Addition and Subtraction

Addition and subtraction of numbers is an extension of the counting process. In effect, you are performing counting for addition and backward counting for subtraction. As we all learned in our early education, such counting becomes quite tedious when dealing with large numbers. To avoid this, we were all taught a shortcut method for addition and subtraction. This method required that we memorize tables that give the results for adding or subtracting any combination of one-digit numbers. We then add or subtract the numbers digit by digit. If the result of simple digit operation is greater than 9 or less than 0, we **carry** a 1 into or **borrow** a 1 from the next digit to the left.

Addition and subtraction in the octal number system are basically the same processes except that the tables are different. Since there is no 8 or 9, the carrying takes place when a sum goes over 7.

TABLE 2.1 **COUNTING IN DECIMAL, BINARY, OCTAL, AND HEXADECIMAL**

Decimal	Binary	Octal	Hexa-decimal	Decimal	Binary	Octal	Hexa-decimal
0	0	0	0	32	100000	40	20
1	1	1	1	33	100001	41	21
2	10	2	2	34	100010	42	22
3	11	3	3	35	100011	43	23
4	100	4	4	36	100100	44	24
5	101	5	5	37	100101	45	25
6	110	6	6	38	100110	46	26
7	111	7	7	39	100111	47	27
8	1000	10	8	40	101000	50	28
9	1001	11	9	41	101001	51	29
10	1010	12	A	42	101010	52	2A
11	1011	13	B	43	101011	53	2B
12	1100	14	C	44	101100	54	2C
13	1101	15	D	45	101101	55	2D
14	1110	16	E	46	101110	56	2E
15	1111	17	F	47	101111	57	2F
16	10000	20	10	48	110000	60	30
17	10001	21	11	49	110001	61	31
18	10010	22	12	50	110010	62	32
19	10011	23	13	51	110011	63	33
20	10100	24	14	52	110100	64	34
21	10101	25	15	53	110101	65	35
22	10110	26	16	54	110110	66	36
23	10111	27	17	55	110111	67	37
24	11000	30	18	56	111000	70	38
25	11001	31	19	57	111001	71	39
26	11010	32	1A	58	111010	72	3A
27	11011	33	1B	59	111011	73	3B
28	11100	34	1C	60	111100	74	3C
29	11101	35	1D	61	111101	75	3D
30	11110	36	1E	62	111110	76	3E
31	11111	37	1F	63	111111	77	3F
				64	1000000	100	40
				65	1000001	101	41
				...			

Small octal numbers can be added using Table 2.1. Using the table you can convert the octal numbers to decimal, perform the addition in decimal, and then use the table to convert the sum to octal. Instead of using the table, it is possible to add two octal digits using the following rule: Add the two digits as though they were decimal digits. If the resulting sum is 7 or less, it represents the correct octal sum. If the sum is greater than 7, add 2 more to the decimal sum to get the correct octal answer. Thus 3 + 3 is 6 in decimal, which is less than or equal to 7. Therefore 3 + 3 is 6 in octal. Similarly, 4 + 5 is 9 in decimal, which is greater than 7. Therefore, add 2 to get 11. Thus 4 + 5 is 11 in octal. (The reason that 2 is added is to skip over the decimal digits 8 and 9 which do not appear in the octal system.) Analogous techniques can be developed for octal subtraction.

Figure 2.2 shows several examples of octal addition and subtraction. Note that octal arithmetic behaves like decimal arithmetic in that it is never necessary to carry or borrow more than once from any given digit position. (This is based on the assumption that just two numbers are added at a time, that is, no column additions.)

Figure 2.2 Examples of Octal Addition and Subtraction

Addition		Subtraction	
4 + 3 — 7	*carry* 5 + 4 — 11	5 − 3 — 2	*borrow* 13 − 6 — 5
43 + 21 — 64	*carry* 53 + 16 — 71	46 − 23 — 23	*borrow* 53 − 27 — 24
carry carry carry 1 7 4 3 2 + 5 6 7 1 6 ——————— 7 6 3 5 0		*borrow borrow borrow* 7 5 6 4 3 − 4 7 7 0 5 ——————— 2 5 7 3 6	
carry carry carry carry 7 7 4 3 5 + 5 0 6 ——————— 1 0 0 1 4 3		*borrow borrow* 5 7 2 3 4 − 5 6 4 6 0 ——————— 0 0 5 5 4	
carry carry carry carry carry 5 7 6 4 2 + 7 7 7 7 7 ——————— 1 5 7 6 4 1		*borrow borrow borrow borrow borrow* 1 5 7 4 4 3 − 7 7 7 7 7 ——————— 5 7 4 4 4	

Octal to Decimal Conversion

The numbers computed in Figure 2.2 may seem bewildering. For example, what do the octal numbers 23, 554, or 25736 represent? This raises the whole question of interpretation of numbers. One method of interpretation is to count until you get there. For example, if Table 2.1 is examined, it is easy to see that 23 octal is equal to 19 decimal. If the table were extended, larger octal numbers could be interpreted. However, the counting method would be almost useless for large numbers such as 25736. To handle these numbers, we must treat them just as we do multidigit decimal numbers. The respective digits of a decimal number going from right to left are designated the **units, tens, hundreds,** and **thousands,** and so on, columns. This means that the value of the number is determined by multiplying the value of each digit by 1, 10, 100, and 1000, and so on, and adding the products together. In other words, the decimal number 3469 is equal to $(9 \times 1) + (6 \times 10) + (4 \times 100) + (3 \times 1000)$.

The same principle applies to the octal number system. The only difference is that the multipliers are powers of eight rather than powers of ten. Thus, the octal number 23 represents the number $(3 \times 1) + (2 \times 8) = 3 + 16 = 19$ (decimal). This is the same result we obtained by counting in Table 2.1. Similarly, the octal number 554 represents $(4 \times 1) + (5 \times 8) + (5 \times 64) = 4 + 40 + 320 = 364$ (decimal). Finally, the octal number 25736 can be converted as is shown in Figure 2.3.

Figure 2.3 Octal to Decimal Conversion

$$25736 \text{ (octal)} = \begin{matrix} 6 \times 8^0 \\ 3 \times 8^1 \\ 7 \times 8^2 \\ 5 \times 8^3 \\ 2 \times 8^4 \end{matrix} \quad \begin{matrix} 6 \times 1 \\ 3 \times 8 \\ 7 \times 64 \\ 5 \times 512 \\ 2 \times 4096 \end{matrix} = \begin{matrix} 6 \\ 24 \\ 448 \\ 2560 \\ 8192 \\ \hline 11230 \text{ (decimal)} \end{matrix}$$

2.3 BINARY NUMBERS

The Need for Binary Numbers

In the previous section, the octal number representation system was introduced as an example of a system other than the decimal system. We will later see that the octal system is extremely important for programming the PDP-11 computer. However, in the meantime we will consider a number system that is even more important for computers, the **binary system.**

Recall that our use of the decimal number system is based upon the

Sec. 2.3 Binary Numbers

primitive practice of counting on our fingers. In other words, the original human hardware available for counting was fingers. Since fingers are used in a ten-state fashion, we perceive the base 10 number system as natural for human use. The use of base 5 and base 20 (the score) by some societies has a similar origin.

The question now is, "What is natural for the computer?" Clearly, computers do not have fingers and thus would have no propensity toward using the decimal system. What is natural for computers is dependent upon the kinds of operations that occur within the various parts of a computer. As we look at the workings of a digital computer, virtually every operation consists of one or more events that either happen or fail to happen. If you look at a certain region of a punched card, that area can either have a hole punched through it or it can fail to have a hole punched through it. There are just two alternatives and no others. A hole cannot be half-way punched. A physical event that can only occur in one of two ways (such as a hole either existing or not existing) is called a **binary** event.* Table 2.2 lists several different binary events.

TABLE 2.2 BINARY EVENTS

Event	States
Hole in punched card	Can be *punched* or *not punched*
A toggle switch	Can be *on* or *off*
A light bulb	Can be *lighted* or *dark*
A wire	Can have *high voltage* or *low voltage*

Because the design of most digital computers consists of combinations and collections of two-state events, it is reasonable for computer designers to find it natural to use base 2. As a consequence, the number system that is *natural* for the computer is the base 2, or binary number representation system.

Binary Counting

The binary number system operates in much the same way as the decimal or octal systems, except that there are only two digits, 0 and 1. When you count, you start at 0 as usual. The next number is 1, but you cannot go further since there are no more digits. Therefore, you must go back to 0 and carry a 1 to the next place, giving us 10 for two. The second column of Table 2.1 (page 18) illustrates binary counting.

---

*Readers may note that it is possible for events such as hole punches to be multistate rather than just two-state. For example, three or four or more differently shaped holes could be punched. However, for computer design, this is not usually practical because the construction of a device capable of reliably recognizing several different hole shapes would be considerably more expensive than a device that merely has to recognize the presence or absence of a hole.

Binary Arithmetic

Binary addition and subtraction follow the same scheme shown in the previous section for octal arithmetic. First, a rule is needed for adding together two binary digits. Although techniques analogous to those used with octal digits could be used, it is easier simply to memorize the following table:

$$0 + 0 = 00 \text{ (zero with no carry)}$$
$$0 + 1 = 01 \text{ (one with no carry)}$$
$$1 + 0 = 01 \text{ (one with no carry)}$$
$$1 + 1 = 10 \text{ (zero with a carry)}$$

A similar set of rules can be developed for subtraction. Figure 2.4 shows some sample binary calculations.

Figure 2.4 Binary Calculations

```
         Addition                    Subtraction

a.         1 0 1              d.         1 1 0
         + 1 0                         -   1 0
         -------                       -------
           1 1 1                         1 0 0

               carry carry carry                    borrow borrow
b.         1 1 0 1 0           e.         1 1 0 0 1
         +   1 0 1 1                    -   1 1 0 1
         ---------                      ---------
           1 0 0 1 0 1                    1 1 0 0

       carry carry carry carry carry       borrow borrow borrow borrow borrow
c.         1 1 1 1 1           f.         1 0 0 0 0 0
         +       1 0 1                  -     1 0 1 1
         ---------                      -----------
           1 0 0 1 0 0                    1 0 1 0 1
```

Binary numbers can be interpreted in much the same way that octal or decimal numbers are interpreted. Since there are just two digits, the value of each digit is weighted by a power of 2. Thus, the binary number 11010 is equal to $(0 \times 1) + (1 \times 2) + (0 \times 4) + (1 \times 8) + (1 \times 16) = 2 + 8 + 16 = 26$. Similarly, $1011 = (1 \times 1) + (1 \times 2) + (0 \times 4) + (1 \times 8) = 1 + 2 + 8 = 11$. And finally, $100101 = (1 \times 1) + (0 \times 2) + (1 \times 4) + (0 \times 8) + (0 \times 16) + (1 \times 32)$. This is $1 + 4 + 32 = 37$. Note also that $37 = 11 + 26$, as might be expected from example b in Figure 2.4. A list of the powers of 2 is shown on the endsheets at the back of the book.

2.4 OCTAL ENCODING

Purpose for Encoding

It may be noted that the lower the base of the number system, the fewer possible values for a single digit: 10 for decimal, 8 for octal, and 2 for binary. Because there are fewer possibilities for each digit, the digits carry less information. As a consequence, numbers represented in the octal system tend to require more digits than the same numbers represented in decimal. For example, 10000 octal represents the same number as 4096 in decimal. The problem is even more severe with binary numbers. For example, the number 71230, as expressed in decimal, comes out as 10001011000111110 in the binary system. There are more than three times as many digits in the binary representation of this number as there are in the decimal representation. This is usually the case.

A single binary digit contains the smallest possible amount of digital information and is usually referred to as a **bit** for *b*inary dig*it*. Because binary numbers tend to be very long, they are very difficult for humans to deal with. Consider your seven-digit telephone number. If it were translated into binary, it would have around twenty-one binary digits or bits. How many people would be able to remember their own telephone number, much less dial a string of twenty-one 1s and 0s without making a mistake? It turns out that even professional computer programmers who have been practicing for many years are not usually capable of dealing with large binary numbers very well. How then can people and machines communicate?

Method for Encoding

One solution comes in the form of **octal encoding.** Octal encoding operates as follows: A large binary number is split into groups of three bits starting from the right. For the number discussed in the previous section, this would be done in the following manner:

```
                    1 0  0 0 1  0 1 1  0 0 0  1 1 1  1 1 0
                    ⏟    ⏟     ⏟      ⏟      ⏟      ⏟
Extra 0     ⟶      010   001    011    000    111    110
added
```

Note that since the original number contains 17 bits and since 17 is not a multiple of 3, it was necessary to pad the left end of the number with a 0 to fill out the leftmost group of three. Note that this does not change the number because appending 0s to the left of the number does not change the number.

The next step is to consider each group of three bits as a three-bit binary number. Three bits can be arranged in 2^3 or 8 ways. However, a single octal digit can also be arranged in 8 ways. In this sense, one octal digit is equivalent to three binary digits because they both represent a particular setting of an 8 position switch.

The next step is to replace each group of three binary digits with the equivalent octal digit (see Figure 2.5). Applying this rule to the binary string produces the following:

```
                 1 0  0 0 1  0 1 1  0 0 0  1 1 1  1 1 0    Binary number
                 ‾‾‾  ‾‾‾‾‾  ‾‾‾‾‾  ‾‾‾‾‾  ‾‾‾‾‾  ‾‾‾‾‾
Extra 0 ⟶ 010   001    011    000    111    110       After grouping
added      ↓     ↓      ↓      ↓      ↓      ↓
           2     1      3      0      7      6           Octal encoding
```

Thus the octal representation of the binary string is 213076.

It is important to notice that this procedure actually converts the binary number into the equivalent octal number. For example, if the binary number and the octal number above are both converted to decimal, the result will be 71,230 (decimal) in both cases. The reason that the conversion from binary to octal (or from octal to binary) is so simple is that the octal number system weights its digits by powers of eight, but eight is a power to two, namely 2^3. Consequently, it is not surprising that there is a simple relationship between binary and octal.

The octal representation not only looks somewhat like the numbers with which we are all familiar, but it has one-third the number of digits as the binary number, and therefore it is much easier for humans to deal with. In addition, if one wishes to examine the original binary number, it is easy to convert the octal representation back to binary by using Figure 2.5 in reverse. For this reason, throughout the remainder of this text, we will usually deal with binary numbers in their octal encoded form.

Figure 2.5 Encoding of Binary Groups

Binary Grouping	Octal Encoding
0 0 0	0
0 0 1	1
0 1 0	2
0 1 1	3
1 0 0	4
1 0 1	5
1 1 0	6
1 1 1	7

EXERCISE SET 1

1. Making use of information available in dictionaries and encyclopedias, describe three historical number systems other than the Roman and Arabic. How do these number systems compare in:
   (a) ease of learning   (b) use for computational purposes
   (c) use for representing large numbers

2. Continue the octal counting sequence shown in Table 2.1 until you reach the equivalent of 200 decimal.

3. Perform the following octal additions:

   (a) 573   (b) 674   (c) 777
      + 132   + 326   + 123

   (d) 2146   (e) 2173   (f) 5723
      + 3704   + 3442   + 2710

   (g) 71426   (h) 716534   (i) 7713642
      + 53402   + 61244   + 65413

4. Perform the following octal subtractions:

   (a) 573   (b) 674   (c) 521
      − 132   − 326   − 123

   (d) 3704   (e) 3442   (f) 2345
      − 2146   − 2173   − 1346

   (g) 71426   (h) 716534   (i) 10067134
      − 53402   − 61244   −   67253

5. Give the decimal equivalent for the following octal numbers:
   (a)   53   (b)   146   (c)   632
   (d) 742   (e) 1675   (f) 1777
   (g) 43721   (h) 53462   (i) 52717

6. Continue the binary counting process shown in Table 2.1 until you reach the equivalent of 100 decimal.

7. Perform the following binary additions:

   (a)   101   (b)   110   (c)   101
       + 11   + 101   + 101

   (d) 10111   (e) 11011   (f) 11101
      + 1010   + 1001   + 101

   (g) 1011011   (h) 110101101 (i) 110101100011
      + 101101   + 10110010   + 101100011010

8 Using the same pairs of numbers as in exercise 7, perform binary subtraction rather than addition.

9 Give the decimal equivalent of the following binary numbers:
   (a) 101   (b) 11010   (c) 111010
   (d) 101110   (e) 110011   (f) 1011101
   (g) 1100011   (h) 1101111   (i) 11100101
   (j) 1110101011   (k) 101110100001   (l) 11001010101110

10 Give the octal equivalents of the binary numbers shown in exercise 9.

2.5 TWO'S COMPLEMENT ARITHMETIC

Fixed Register Arithmetic

Our discussion so far has treated numbers assuming that there are no size limitations on the numbers. However, in a computer, arithmetic is generally performed in devices called **registers.** A **register** is a device which contains the representation of a number. A familiar example of a register is the automobile odometer, which registers the accumulated mileage traveled. The odometer is made of wheels with digits around them which can be rotated to display any number from 0 through 99999 miles. It is important to note the fixed upper bound. Most registers in computers have a fixed number of parts and, therefore, there is a fixed upper bound to the size of the number that can be represented. For example, most operations in the PDP-11 are limited to sixteen binary digits. As a result, you can get some strange results as happens when an old automobile has gone more than 100,000 miles and registers a very "low" mileage.

It actually turns out that this property can be useful. Consider a small machine with 5-bit binary registers. We will look at what happens when we add 11101 or decimal 29 to various numbers such as 7, 8, and 9. Figure 2.6 shows this arithmetic in binary. It should be noted in each case that a carry is lost off the answer because we are restricted to five bits.

Figure 2.6 *Addition in a 5-Bit Register*

```
    11101 = 29         11101 = 29         11101 = 29
  + 00111 =  7       + 01000 =  8       + 01001 =  9
    00100 =  4         00101 =  5         00110 =  6
```

Negative Numbers

Examining the results in Figure 2.6, we can see that when we add 11101 to the binary representation of either 7, 8, or 9, the result is 3 less than the original number. It is as if we had subtracted 3. This works for other examples as well. As a result, in a 5-bit system, 11101 can be thought of as a negative 3. Similarly, 11111 behaves like -1, 11110 behaves like -2, and so on. Figure 2.7 shows all 32 possibilities of 5-bit numbers with their appropriate signed decimal equivalent. To divide the number representations so that approximately half are positive and half are negative, the leading digit is used to designate the sign: 1 means negative, and 0 means positive. Note that this means that numbers like 11101, which look as if they were large positive numbers, are in fact negative. It should also be noted that there is a -16 but no $+16$. This is to make up for the fact that there is a positive 0 but no negative 0.

Figure 2.7 5-Bit Two's Complement Numbers

10000	-16	11000	-8	00000	0	01000	8
10001	-15	11001	-7	00001	1	01001	9
10010	-14	11010	-6	00010	2	01010	10
10011	-13	11011	-5	00011	3	01011	11
10100	-12	11100	-4	00100	4	01100	12
10101	-11	11101	-3	00101	5	01101	13
10110	-10	11110	-2	00110	6	01110	14
10111	-9	11111	-1	00111	7	01111	15

Representing negative numbers in this way is called the **two's complement** system. The name derives from the fact that the negative of a number is obtained by subtracting the number from the power of 2 which is just too large to fit in the register. For example:

$$\begin{array}{r} 100000 \\ -00011 = 3 \\ \hline 11101 = -3 \end{array}$$

Another way of computing the two's complement of a number is to change all of the 0s in the number to 1s and vice versa, and then add 1. For example:

00011	= 3
11100	Interchange 0s and 1s
11101	Add 1 to get -3

One's Complement

Some computers negate numbers more rapidly by eliminating the step of adding 1. Thus 11100 would be the representation of -3. This system is called the one's complement system because negatives are obtained either by interchanging 1s and 0s, or by subtracting the number from all 1s. For example:

$$\begin{array}{r}11111\\-00011=3\\\hline 11100=-3\text{ in one's complement}\end{array}$$

Of particular note in the one's complement system is that there are two representations of 0. They are 00000 and its complement 11111. The two representations of 0 may require programmers to be cautious if they are checking to see if a result is 0. The arithmetic operations of addition and subtraction as well as multiplication and division must be modified somewhat if one's complement notation is used. However, since very few computers* use one's complement arithmetic, these topics will not be discussed here.

Nevertheless, one's complementing is important to note because it is used for logical as well as numerical operations as can be seen in the next section.

2.6 BOOLEAN LOGIC

Values and Operations

In the nineteenth century, an English mathematician named George Boole developed algebraic methods for dealing with the logical values of true and false. In computers it is quite useful at times to interpret the binary one and zero as the **Boolean values** of true and false.

In order to manipulate the Boolean value, it is necessary to have **Boolean operations.** The Boolean operations are AND, OR, and NOT. The AND and OR combine the truth values of two sentences together in much the same way that is done in English. For example, a AND b is true if and only if both a and b are true. Similarly a OR b is true when a or b is true or if both a and b are true. The NOT operation reverses the truth value; thus, NOT a is true if a is false, and NOT a is false if a is true. Figure 2.8 shows all of the possible combinations

Figure 2.8 Boolean Operations

0 AND 0 = 0	0 OR 0 = 0	NOT 0 = 1
0 AND 1 = 0	0 OR 1 = 1	NOT 1 = 0
1 AND 0 = 0	1 OR 0 = 1	
1 AND 1 = 1	1 OR 1 = 1	

*The CDC Cyber computers are notable examples of one's complement machines.

of operations for the three Boolean operators. As is done in most computer usage, TRUE is represented as 1 and FALSE as 0.

Tables of a Boolean operation such as the one shown in Figure 2.8 are called **truth tables** and can be used to define any Boolean operation other than the basic three just shown. For example, another commonly used Boolean operation is the exclusive OR. This is defined as the same as OR but false when both operands are true. The truth table for exclusive OR is:

$$0 \text{ exclusive OR } 0 = 0$$
$$0 \text{ exclusive OR } 1 = 1$$
$$1 \text{ exclusive OR } 0 = 1$$
$$1 \text{ exclusive OR } 1 = 0$$

It turns out that any Boolean operation can be formed from the basic three; AND, OR, and NOT. For example:

$$a \text{ exclusive OR } b = (a \text{ OR } b) \text{ AND NOT } (a \text{ AND } b)$$

Multibit Operations

Computers are usually designed with registers that contain a string of bits. Because of this, Boolean operations in computers are often extended to operate in a bit-by-bit fashion across corresponding bits in a pair of registers. For example, with 16-bit registers such as in the PDP-11, we could have the following operation:

```
     1011011111001010
  OR 0010010101010011
     1011011111011011
```

Note that each bit of the result is the OR of the two corresponding bits above it. There are operations other than purely logical ones that can make use of Boolean operations this way. For example, the following use of AND could be used to mask out the leading bits of a string:

```
      1011011111001010  string
  AND 0000000011111111  mask
      0000000011001010  result
```

Finally note that if the NOT operation is applied to the bits of a string, it will invert each bit, or change each 1 to a 0 and each 0 to a 1. Note that this is the definition of one's complement given in the previous section. As a result, the terms NOT and "one's complement" are used interchangeably.

2.7 HEXADECIMAL ENCODINGS
(Optional Section)

The manufacturer of the PDP-11 computer has published all its PDP-11 literature using octal encoding for binary numbers, which is why we have given so much attention to the octal system. Some other manufacturers (IBM in particular) prefer to use the **hexadecimal** or base 16 number system for encoding, the basic difference being that binary numbers are split up into groups of four bits rather than three.

Because four bits can be arranged in 2^4 or 16 different ways, the hexadecimal system requires 16 different digits. The 10 decimal digits are augmented with the first six letters of the alphabet. A is 10, B is 11, C is 12, D is 13, E is 14, and F is 15. Since F is the last single digit, adding 1 to F causes a carry; that is 1 + F = 10. The fourth column of Table 2.1 shows hexadecimal counting from 1 through 65.

When converting from hexadecimal to binary, each digit is converted to a 4-bit binary string using the table of Figure 2.9. When converting back, the binary number is split into four-bit groupings and converted back using the table. Thus, the hexadecimal representation of the binary number 0001 0001 0110 0011 1110 is 1163E.

Figure 2.9 Hexadecimal Encoding of Binary Groups

Binary Grouping	Hexadecimal Encoding	Binary Grouping	Hexadecimal Encoding
0 0 0 0	0	1 0 0 0	8
0 0 0 1	1	1 0 0 1	9
0 0 1 0	2	1 0 1 0	A
0 0 1 1	3	1 0 1 1	B
0 1 0 0	4	1 1 0 0	C
0 1 0 1	5	1 1 0 1	D
0 1 1 0	6	1 1 1 0	E
0 1 1 1	7	1 1 1 1	F

2.8 OTHER ENCODINGS

Numbers can be represented in other ways as well. For example, four bits can be used to represent a decimal digit in the following manner: Four bits can, of course, be arranged in 16 different ways. If six of these possibilities are considered to be "illegal," the remaining ten "legal" arrangements result in a ten position switch that can represent a single decimal digit. With this system, the string of binary digits

0001 1000 1001 0010 0000 0100

represents the decimal number 189204 (where 0000 represents the decimal digit 0, 0001 represents the decimal digit 1, and so on). This representation is called **binary coded decimal**. Another representation that is based on scientific notation is called **real** or **floating point** representation. It is similar to the exponent notation used to represent large numbers in more expensive calculators (such as 3.84536E + 08).

Finally, the emphasis on representing numbers may give a reader the impression that computers are mainly used to perform arithmetic computations. This is simply not true. Strings of binary digits can be used to represent any physical event that can be detected. For example, many computer terminals are capable of printing 95 separate characters (including the blank space). Seven bits of information can be arranged in 2^7 or 128 ways. Thus seven bits are sufficient to represent any one of the 95 printable characters with 128 − 95 or 33 combinations that can be used to represent the special function keys such as RETURN or TAB. Indeed, Chapter 8 will use such a 7-bit code in order to process strings of characters. Using these coding techniques, it is possible to write programs for analyzing literary works.

Similarly, there are 88 keys on a standard piano. Seven bits of information could therefore be used to designate the pressing of a particular key. (Additional bits may, of course, be required to indicate such things as the time at which the key was pressed, the velocity at which the key was struck, and the length of time that the key was depressed.) With such coding techniques, it is possible to write programs for analyzing music or even composing music.

As a final example, it is possible to represent pictures in terms of strings of bits. To do this, a grid pattern with perhaps 1000 rows and 1000 columns is drawn on top of a photograph. From each of the 1 million square areas on the photograph, the amount of light that is reflected is measured and the result converted to a binary number. [If 64 different shades can be detected, the light reflected from each square might be converted to a 6-bit number where 000000 (base 2) represents white, 111111 (base 2) represents black, and the other combinations represent various shades of gray.] The picture has now been converted into a form that can be processed by computer. Photographs from satellites and certain kinds of X-ray images are regularly processed by computers using similar encodings.

EXERCISE SET 2

1 Continue the hexadecimal counting sequence shown in Table 2.1 until you reach the equivalent of 200 decimal.

2 Give the hexadecimal equivalents of the binary numbers shown in exercise 9 on page 26.

*3 Show how to count to the equivalent of 200 decimal in the base 7 number system. In the base 7 system, how can you tell even numbers from odd numbers? Is there a simple rule, as in decimal?

4 Add the following pairs of 5-bit two's complement numbers. Show the signed number equivalents of both numbers and the result in decimal with each problem.

(a) 00011
     00101

(b) 01011
     11100

(c) 11101
     11010

(d) 11100
     11111

(e) 00111
     11011

(f) 11101
     00101

5 Repeat exercise 4 but subtract the second number from the first instead of adding.

6 Show the signed decimal equivalents for the 64 binary combinations in a 6-bit two's complement number system.

7 For the pairs of binary numbers shown in exercise 4, show the results of the multibit Boolean operations, AND, OR, and exclusive OR.

*8 Give an algorithm for converting a number in any base to any different base.

CHAPTER 3

MACHINE LANGUAGE PROGRAMMING

3.1 DIGITAL COMPUTERS

System Blocks

Figure 3.1 illustrates the important parts of a digital computer: an input device, an output device, a memory, and a central control unit. The **input device** permits us to get information into the computer. The input device might be as simple as the buttons on an electronic calculator or as complicated as a card reader. The **output device** allows us to get results back from the computer. The output device might be as simple as the lighted numerals on an electronic calculator or as complicated as a high-speed line printer. The **memory** is used for storing information. Generally, memory consists of a set of boxes or **cells,** each of which contains a number. The input device, the output device, and the memory are all connected by electrical wires to a central control unit called the **processor.** By sending electrical signals on these wires, the processor can:

1. Ask the input device to get or **read** a number and make that number available to the processor or memory.
2. Ask the output device to **print** a particular number.
3. Ask memory to save or **store** a particular number in a particular memory cell.
4. Ask memory to retrieve or **fetch** the number that was previously stored in a particular memory cell.

Figure 3.1   A Simple Computer

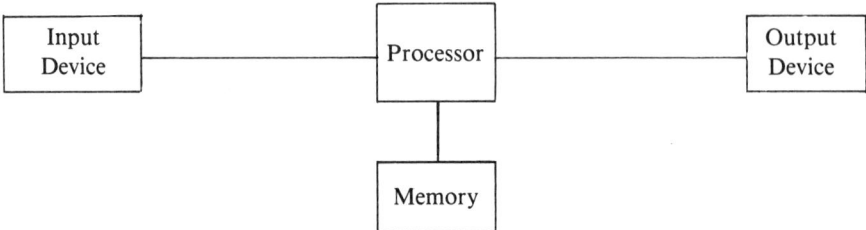

In this simple computer, the input device, the output device, and the memory are passive devices. They do not do anything unless they are told to do something by the processor. The processor is the active device that controls the shuffling of numbers between itself and the other devices. The sequence of operations that the processor performs is determined by a set of **instructions** that form a **computer program.** The job of a programmer is to set up an appropriate set of instructions that direct the processor to perform the necessary operations to solve a particular problem.

3.2   MEMORY REPRESENTATION ON THE PDP-11 COMPUTER

Memory as a Collection of Bytes

Memory on the PDP-11 computer can be viewed as a large number of boxes or **memory cells,** each of which contains an 8-bit binary number. For example, the following illustrates a memory cell that contains the 8-bit number 00110101.

00110101

An 8-bit binary number is called an **8-bit byte,** or simply a **byte.** Since each memory cell can contain an 8-bit byte, we will refer to the contents of each memory cell as a **memory byte.**

Each memory byte is identified by a number called the **address.** The address of a memory cell identifies it as a specific physical device, and can be thought of as being analogous to the street address of a building. A street address allows you to find or identify a particular building; a memory address allows you to find or identify a particular memory cell.

On the PDP-11 computer, an address is a 16-bit binary number. Notice that two numbers are associated with each memory byte—the address, which is 16 bits long, and the contents, which is 8 bits long. The following example shows that the memory byte with address 0000111100001111 contains 00110101:

Sec. 3.2   *Memory Representation on the PDP-11 Computer*   35

                       Address   *Contents*
               0000111100001111 | 00110101 |

     Since 16 binary digits can be arranged in 2^{16} or 65,536 different ways, a PDP-11 computer may have up to 65,536 different memory cells. The first byte in memory has an address of 0000000000000000 (binary) and the last byte has the address 1111111111111111 (binary). Since each of the 65,536 memory cells can contain an 8-bit byte, the total storage capacity can be as high as 65,536 times 8 or 524,288 bits. Figure 3.2 illustrates the first 10 bytes of memory.

Figure 3.2   *Byte Representation of Memory*

Binary Address	*Binary Contents*
0000000000000000	01010011
0000000000000001	11010101
0000000000000010	00001010
0000000000000011	00000000
0000000000000100	11111111
0000000000000101	11010001
0000000000000110	00000001
0000000000000111	11100000
0000000000001000	00000000
0000000000001001	00000000

Memory as a Collection of Words

Although 8 bits is a convenient amount of information for some purposes, it is inconveniently small for others. For example, 8 bits can only be arranged in 2^8 or 256 different ways. If an 8-bit byte is used as a counter, it is only possible to count from 0 through 255 (decimal).

     To avoid this problem, memory on the PDP-11 combines two bytes to form a 16-bit word. This situation is illustrated in Figure 3.3.

Figure 3.3   *Byte/Word Representation of Memory*

Binary Address	*Binary Contents*		*Binary Address*
0000000000000001	11010101	01010011	0000000000000000
0000000000000011	00000000	00001010	0000000000000010
0000000000000101	11010001	11111111	0000000000000100
0000000000000111	11100000	00000001	0000000000000110
0000000000001001	00000000	00000000	0000000000001000

Notice that the contents of the 10 bytes in Figure 3.3 are identical to the bytes in Figure 3.2. The position of the bytes has simply been rearranged. The 16-bit *word* beginning at memory cell 0000000000000000 consists of the 8-bit byte in 0000000000000000 along with the 8-bit byte in memory cell 0000000000000001. Similarly, the 16-bit *word* beginning at memory cell 0000000000000110 consists of the 8-bit byte in memory cell 0000000000000110 along with the 8-bit byte in memory cell 0000000000000111. A **word** in memory always consists of the contents of an even-numbered byte on the right, along with the contents of the next successive byte on the left. For example:

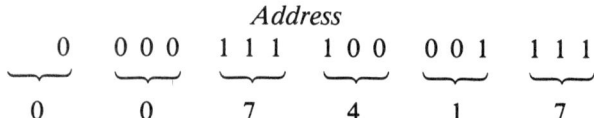

Because of this, the address of a word must be an even number. In binary, this means that the address of a word must end with a zero.

Octal Representation of Words

Dealing with binary numbers is awkward for human beings. To avoid this problem, memory is usually represented using the octal number system. As shown in Chapter 2, converting from binary to octal is accomplished by replacing three binary digits with one octal digit using Figure 2.5 (page 24). For example, a 16-bit address is converted to octal as follows:

Address

$$0 \quad 0\,0\,0 \quad 1\,1\,1 \quad 1\,0\,0 \quad 0\,0\,1 \quad 1\,1\,1$$
$$0 \qquad 0 \qquad 7 \qquad 4 \qquad 1 \qquad 7$$

In converting from a 16-bit binary address to a 6-digit octal address, the leftmost bit must be treated as a special case. (Six octal digits would normally represent 3 times 6 or 18 binary digits.) The conversion is made by assuming that there are two binary zeros immediately to the left of the 16-bit address. This is the same as in decimal; adding zeros to the left of a number does not change it. For example, the following shows the conversion of the largest legal word address from binary to octal:

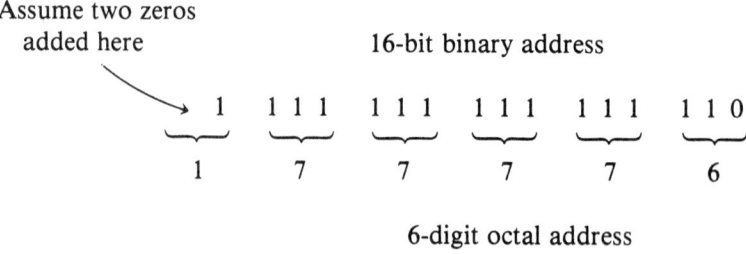

Notice that the largest legal word address is 177776.

Just as a 16-bit address can be represented in octal, the contents of a 16-bit word can be represented in octal. For example, the contents of the word beginning at memory cell 000000 is represented in octal as follows:

16-bit binary word

| 1 1 0 1   0 1 0   1 0 1   0 1 0   0 1 1 |

  1   5   2   5   2   3

6-digit octal word

As when converting addresses, it is necessary to add two binary zeros at the left of the 16-bit binary word. If all of the 16-bit words in Figure 3.3 are converted to octal, the result is Figure 3.4. Notice that Figure 3.2, 3.3, and 3.4 specify identical memory contents. These figures represent different ways of describing the contents of the first 10 bytes (or the first 5 words) in memory.

Figure 3.4 Word Representation of Memory

Octal Address	Octal Contents
000000	152523
000002	000012
000004	150777
000006	160001
000010	000000

In using the octal representation of words, it is important to remember three things. First, a 16-bit word is composed of two 8-bit bytes. Second, the byte with the even (and lower) address forms the *right* half of the word and the byte with the odd (and higher) address forms the *left* half of the word. Finally, the address of a word must be even. (In octal, this means that word addresses must end in either 0, 2, 4, or 6.)

Addresses versus Contents of Memory

It is important to avoid confusion between the address of a memory word and the contents of a memory word. In Figure 3.4, for example, we might describe memory word 000004 in any of the following ways:

1. The memory word with address 000004 contains 150777.
2. Memory word 000004 contains 150777.
3. 000004 contains 150777.
4. The contents of memory word 000004 is 150777.*

*The word "contents" is often used in computer jargon as a singular noun meaning "the number contained in some location."

In each of these cases, 000004 is the address, and 150777 is the contents. It is possible to change the contents of a memory word but never its address. In other words, the contents of a memory word is variable but the address of a word in invariable.

In the vast majority of cases, we will consider memory to consist of 16-bit words as shown in Figure 3.4. Indeed, when reference is made to the contents of memory, it should be *assumed that we are referring to 16-bit words, not to 8-bit bytes*. Furthermore, most of the PDP-11 operations will be described in terms of the octal representation. This is possible because, in many instances, the octal representation and the binary representation give equivalent results. For example, with addition:

	Binary Encoding	*Octal Encoding*
	0 000 000 010 110 011	000263
+	0 000 000 001 101 110	000156
	0 000 000 100 100 001	000441

The sum of the octal encodings, 000263 and 000156, is 000441, which is the octal encoding of the binary answer.

As we proceed, octal encodings will be used for just about everything—so much so in fact that there is a tendency to start thinking that the PDP-11 is an octal computer rather than a binary computer. This is not the case, however, since there are a few operations in the PDP-11, such as shifting*, which can most easily be understood in terms of the actual binary representation. However, for a vast majority of the PDP-11 operations, it is quite acceptable to think in terms of the much more compact octal representation.

EXERCISE SET 1

1 Convert each of the following binary words to octal:
   (a) 0 111 000 111 000 111
   (b) 1 111 111 111 111 111
   (c) 0 000 000 011 111 111
   (d) 1 111 111 100 000 000
   (e) 0 001 010 011 100 101
   (f) 1 110 101 100 011 010

2 The contents of memory words 000000 through 000010 is represented below as five words, each of which consists of six octal digits. Represent

---

*Shifting a binary number left has the effect of multiplying it by 2; that is, 110 (base 2) is 6 (base 10) and 1100 (base 2) is 12 (base 10).

the memory contents in terms of 10 bytes, each of which consists of 8 bits. (In other words, specify the contents of bytes 000000 through 000011 in binary.)

Address	Contents
000000	177776
000002	000377
000004	176000
000006	123456
000010	000777

3 Each of the following octal words represents an unsigned number. Give the decimal equivalent.

(a) 000001

(b) 000010

(c) 000100

(d) 000064

(e) 000144

3.3 PROCESSOR USE OF MEMORY

Fetch and Store Operations with Memory

Memory is controlled by the processor. The processor can either ask memory to **fetch** the contents of a particular memory cell, or to **store** a particular number in a particular memory cell. A fetch does not change the contents of the designated memory location but a store does. In order to perform a fetch, the processor sends memory the address of the desired memory location, and memory responds by sending the processor the contents of the addressed cell. For example, using the data from Figure 3.4, if the processor asked memory to fetch the contents of memory cell 000004, memory would respond by sending the number 150777 back to the processor. Memory cell 000004 would still contain 150777.

In order to perform a store, the processor sends memory the address of the desired memory cell along with a number that is to be placed in the designated cell. Again using data from Figure 3.4, assume that the processor asked memory to store the number 123123 in memory cell 000004. The old contents of memory cell 000004 would be lost or destroyed, and 123123 would become the new contents. There would be no record of the fact that memory cell 000004 ever contained 150777. If the processor subsequently asked memory to fetch the contents of memory cell 000004, memory would respond by sending back the new contents, 123123.

The fetch and store operations are the only operations that memory can perform. (Memory cannot perform an addition, for example.) However, memory can perform the store and fetch operations quite rapidly (typically more than 1 million operations in a single second).

Not all addresses are legal addresses. As previously noted, the memory address of a 16-bit word must be an even number. The use of an odd address during a fetch or store operation will cause an error, called an **addressing error,** to occur.

Second, it is possible to purchase a PDP-11 computer with less than the maximum amount of memory. For example, it is possible to purchase a memory that only contains, and thus only responds to, memory addresses 000000 through 017777. An attempt to fetch or store from an address outside this range, such as 040000, also causes an addressing error to occur.

Finally, memory addresses between 160000 and 177777 are reserved for special purposes on many PDP-11 computers. Certain of these locations control input/output devices and are described in Chapter 11. Using these memory locations may produce unpredictable results.

The ADD Instruction

As previously noted, the processor is the active device that controls the shuffling of numbers back and forth between itself and the other devices that form the computer, such as memory. The programmer, in turn, controls the processor by writing a set of instructions, called a program, that the processor executes. For example, the following instruction will cause the processor to add the 16-bit word contained in memory cell 000026 to the 16-bit word contained in memory cell 000032, and place the 16-bit result in memory cell 000032:

ADD THE CONTENTS OF 000026 TO 000032

Note that this instruction does *not* cause the processor to add 26 (octal) to 32 (octal) to get 60 (octal). Rather, this instruction causes the *contents* of memory cells 000026 and 000032 to be added, and the sum to be placed in memory cell 000032. The processor executes this instruction in four steps:

Step 1: Fetch the contents of memory cell 000026.
Step 2: Fetch the contents of memory cell 000032.
Step 3: Add the numbers fetched during steps 1 and 2.
Step 4: Store the resulting sum in memory cell 000032.

Notice that instructions such as ADD THE CONTENTS OF 000027 TO 000032 are illegal. *Word addresses must be even numbers.*

The SUBTRACT, MOVE, and HALT Instructions

The MOVE and the SUBTRACT instructions are similar to the ADD instruction. To execute the instruction:

SUBTRACT THE CONTENTS OF 000040 FROM 000050

the processor performs the following steps:

Step 1: Fetch the contents of memory cell 000040.

Step 2: Fetch the contents of memory cell 000050.

Step 3: Subtract the number fetched in step 1 from the number fetched in step 2.

Step 4: Store the resulting difference in memory cell 000050.

To execute the instruction:

MOVE THE CONTENTS OF 000070 TO 000060

the processor performs the following two steps:

Step 1: Fetch the contents of memory cell 000070.

Step 2: Store the number fetched during step 1 in memory cell 000060.

A program is simply a sequence of instructions. For example, the following will set the contents of memory cell 000032 equal to the sum of the numbers that are contained in memory cells 000024, 000026, and 000030.

Instruction 1: MOVE THE CONTENTS OF 000024 TO 000032

Instruction 2: ADD THE CONTENTS OF 000026 TO 000032

Instruction 3: ADD THE CONTENTS OF 000030 TO 000032

Instruction 4: HALT

The processor executed these instructions one after the other. The HALT instruction causes the processor to stop executing instructions. Figure 3.5 shows the effect of each instruction on the contents of memory locations 000024 through 000032.

Figure 3.5 *Memory Contents During Execution*

Address	Original Contents	Contents after Instruction 1	Contents after Instruction 2	Contents after Instruction 3	Contents after Instruction 4
000024	000003	000003	000003	000003	000003
000026	001000	001000	001000	001000	001000
000030	000200	000200	000200	000200	000200
000032	000000	000003	001003	001203	001203

3.4 MACHINE LANGUAGE PROGRAMS

Machine Language Codes

One question that should arise at this point is where the computer program physically exists. In our previous description of the computer, there was one place for holding information, the memory. The memory therefore can be used for storing computer programs. However, since the memory cells are only capable of storing binary strings, the specific processor instructions must be encoded using a binary code. The following table shows the operation codes for the instructions MOVE, ADD, SUBTRACT, and HALT. Each 6 digit octal number in the table represents a 16-bit binary operation code.

Operation Name	Operation Code
MOVE	013737
ADD	063737
SUBTRACT	163737
HALT	000000

It should be noted that these codes can be broken down into significant pieces. For example, the operation code for MOVE is really 01. The 37s are addressing mode codes that indicate which of several ways there are for accessing the data. The addressing modes are described in more detail in Chapters 5 and 7.

Forming a Program

Substituting the operation code for each operation in the previous program would produce the following numerically encoded program:

Numerical Encoding			English Meaning
1. 013737	000024	000032	Move the contents of 000024 to 000032
2. 063737	000026	000032	Add the contents of 000026 to 000032
3. 063737	000030	000032	Add the contents of 000030 to 000032
4. 000000			Halt

Instructions in the all-numerical format are called **machine language instructions.** While this encoding is quite inconvenient for human beings, it is the language computers "understand." In order to determine what the program does, it is necessary to know that 013737 is the code for a MOVE operation, 063737 is the code for an ADD operation, and so on. The preceding program consists of 10 numbers, each of which consists of 6 octal digits. These 10

Sec. 3.4   Machine Language Programs   43

numbers can be placed in memory cells 000000, 000002, 000004, ..., 000022, to produce the program shown in Figure 3.6.

Figure 3.6   A Simple Machine Language Program

Address	Contents	Meaning
000000	013737	⎫
000002	000024	⎬ Move the contents of 000024 to 000032
000004	000032	⎭
000006	063737	⎫
000010	000026	⎬ Add the contents of 000026 to 000032
000012	000032	⎭
000014	063737	⎫
000016	000030	⎬ Add the contents of 000030 to 000032
000020	000032	⎭
000022	000000	Halt
000024	000003	The octal number 000003
000026	001000	The octal number 001000
000030	000200	The octal number 000200
000032	000000	

A program in this format is called a **machine language program.** If the processor is told to execute the program that begins at memory cell 000000, the processor will execute instructions in sequence as follows:

a. Execute the MOVE instruction that begins at memory cell 000000.

b. Execute the ADD instruction that begins at memory cell 000006.

c. Execute the ADD instruction that begins at memory cell 000014.

d. Execute the HALT instruction in memory cell 000022.

As the result of executing these four instructions, the sum of the numbers in memory cells 000024, 000026, and 000030 will be placed in memory cell 000032.

Although a program might reside almost anywhere in memory, the numeric operation codes are 16 bits long and therefore must be located at even-numbered addresses.

The Program Counter

The way that the processor keeps track of what it is doing as it executes a program is by use of a special register called the **program counter.** The program counter contains a 16-bit number that is the address of the next instruction to be executed. Every time an instruction or part of an instruction is fetched from memory, the processor adds 2 to the program counter. In the previous example, the program starts in memory location 000000. Therefore to start our program, we must somehow set the program counter to 000000. (This can be done manually with the switches on the machine if need be.)

The MOVE instruction at the beginning of the program requires three words of memory: one for the operation code and one for each data address. As each of these words is fetched, the program counter has 2 added to it. It will therefore have a value of 000006 when the operation is complete. Note that since 000006 is the address of the beginning of the next instruction, the processor is all set to start the next instruction in sequence.

The execution of a given instruction can be divided into a **fetch cycle** during which the instruction is fetched and an **execute cycle** during which the instruction is actually executed. For example, consider the move instruction that begins in address 000000. Since this instruction occupies memory words 000000, 000002, and 000004, the fetch cycle requires three fetches from memory. In order to achieve the move, it is necessary to fetch the contents of memory cell 000024 and store the result in memory cell 000032. Thus the execute cycle requires one fetch operation and one store operation. (Chapters 5 and 7 will describe the fetch and execute cycles in a somewhat different way.) In total, the MOVE instruction requires four fetch operations and one store operation. The reader should be able to determine that an ADD instruction requires a total of five fetch operations and one store operation—three fetches for the fetch cycle and *two* fetches and one store for the execute cycle.

3.5 THE USE OF A MEMORY CELL

As was just stated, the contents of a memory cell can be interpreted or used in a variety of different ways. In Figure 3.6 for example, the contents of some memory cells were treated as operation codes, others were treated as numbers. It is not possible simply to examine the contents of a memory cell and determine how the contents should be interpreted. If a given memory cell contains 000000, the contents could be interpreted as either the number 0, the address of the first memory cell, or a HALT instruction. To make the classification, it is necessary to see how the processor uses the contents of the memory cell.

Consider the following machine language instruction that moves the contents of memory cell 000024 into memory cell 000032:

Address	*Contents*	*Use*
000000	013737	Operation code
000002	000024	Address
000004	000032	Address
. . .		
. . .		
000024	000003	Operand
. . .		
. . .		
000032	000000	Operand

Sec. 3.5   *The Use of a Memory Cell*   45

When this instruction is executed, a total of five memory cells are involved. The contents of 000000 is treated as an operation code, the contents of 000002 and 000004 are treated as addresses, and the contents of 000024 and 000032 are treated as **operands.** (An operand is simply data that is operated on by the processor.)

Operation Codes

It is important to distinguish between operation codes, addresses, and operands because different rules apply to each. The operation code directs the processor to perform some operation such as MOVE, ADD, SUBTRACT, or HALT. Only certain operation codes are legal or valid. For example, 000100 is an illegal operation. If memory cell 000000 contained the (illegal) operation code 000100 and the processor were directed to execute the program beginning in memory cell 000000, an error would occur and execution of the program would terminate. Only four legal operation codes have been discussed: 013737 (MOVE), 063737 (ADD), 163737 (SUBTRACT), and 000000 (HALT).

Addresses

Just as there are legal and illegal operation codes, there are legal and illegal addresses. As noted previously, addresses of 16-bit words must be even numbers. In addition, computers that have less than the maximum amount of memory will have an upper limit on legal addresses.

Signed and Unsigned Numbers

Finally, any octal number from 000000 to 177777 is a legal operand. As noted in Chapter 2, the binary digits that are represented by these octal encodings can be interpreted in a variety of ways. For the moment, our discussion will be limited to two interpretations—unsigned numbers and signed numbers.

Table 3.1 shows how octal numbers between 000000 and 177777 can be interpreted as unsigned or signed numbers. As shown in the table, unsigned numbers range from 0 to 65535 (decimal) with 000000 (octal) representing 0 and 177777 (octal) representing 65535 (decimal). For signed numbers, the two's complement representation is used (see page 26 of Chapter 2). Signed numbers range from -32768 (decimal) to 32767 (decimal). Note that 100000 (octal) represents -32768 (decimal), 177777 (octal) represents -1, 000000 (octal) represents 0, and 077777 represents 32767.

It is important to realize that only one ADD instruction is required. For example, if 177774 and 000003 are added, the result is 177777. With the unsigned interpretation, this corresponds to adding 65532 to 3 to get 65535 (see Table 3.1). With the signed interpretation, this corresponds to adding -4 to 3 to get -1.

TABLE 3.1 THE RANGE OF SIGNED AND UNSIGNED NUMBERS IN OCTAL WITH DECIMAL EQUIVALENTS

Octal Contents	Unsigned Interpretation	Signed Interpretation
000000	0	0
000001	1	1
000002	2	2
000003	3	3
000004	4	4
000005	5	5
000006	6	6
000007	7	7
000010	8	8
000011	9	9
000012	10	10
000013	11	11
⋮	⋮	⋮
077774	32764	32764
077775	32765	32765
077776	32766	32766
077777	32767	32767
100000	32768	−32768
100001	32769	−32767
100002	32770	−32766
100003	32771	−32765
⋮	⋮	⋮
177774	65532	−4
177775	65533	−3
177776	65534	−2
177777	65535	−1

Overflow errors are possible with either interpretation; for example, the sum of 177777 and 000003 is 000002 (what would normally be the correct sum, namely 200002, will not fit in a memory cell). For signed numbers, this is correct because the sum of −1 and 3 is 2. However, for unsigned numbers, the result is incorrect because 65535 plus 3 is certainly not equal to 2, and we say that **unsigned overflow** has occurred. Similarly, the sum of 077776 and 000004 (octal) is 100002. In this case, the unsigned result is correct (32766 + 4 = 32770) but the signed result is incorrect (32766 + 4 is not equal to −32766), and we say that **signed overflow** has occurred. Obviously, either kind of overflow condition indicates that an arithmetic operation may have produced an incor-

Sec. 3.5   *The Use of a Memory Cell*   47

rect result. However, the processor does not treat overflow as an error, and it is the programmer's responsibility to ensure that overflow does not produce wrong answers. Chapter 6 discusses how to test for overflow.

Multiple Interpretations

Let us now look at some ramifications of the fact that it is possible to interpret the contents of a memory cell in more than one way. The contents of a given memory cell might be interpreted or used as an operand, an address, and an operation code at different times. Assume, for example, that the processor is told to execute the program shown in Figure 3.7 beginning at memory cell 001000. This program appears to consist of three instructions—a SUBTRACT instruction in memory cells 001000 through 001004, a SUBTRACT instruction in memory cells 001006 through 001012, and a HALT instruction in memory cell 000014. However, the first instruction directs the processor to subtract the contents of memory cell 001000 from memory cell 001006. Since both cells contain 163737, executing this instruction causes the contents of memory cell 001006 to be set to 000000. In effect, the SUBTRACT operation code in memory cell 001006 has been changed into a HALT operation code. When the processor executes this instruction, it halts.

The program shown in Figure 3.7 obviously does not accomplish anything useful. In fact, most programmers consider instruction modification of this sort to be extremely bad style. However, there are important applications where it is necessary to treat a memory cell in more than one way. In order to translate

Figure 3.7 A Self-modifying Program

Before executing the instruction in memory cells 001000 to 001004:

Address	Contents	Apparent Interpretation
001000	163737	Subtract the contents of memory cell 001000 from memory cell 001006
001002	001000	
001004	001006	
001006	163737	Subtract the contents of memory cell 002000 from memory cell 002000
001010	002000	
001012	002000	
001014	000000	Halt

After executing the instruction in memory cells 001000 to 001004:

Address	Contents	Interpretation
001000	163737	Subtract the contents of memory cell 001000 from memory cell 001006
001002	001000	
001004	001006	
001006	000000	Halt
001010	002000	Unused
001012	002000	
001014	000000	

a computer program written in one language into another language, it is necessary to treat operation codes and addresses as numbers. In order to process tables or arrays, addresses are frequently interpreted as numbers.

The processor uses very simple rules to decide whether the contents of a memory cell will be interpreted as an operation code, an address, or an operand. These can be illustrated by describing the sequence of steps the processor goes through to execute the program in Figure 3.7:

Step 1: Fetch the first instruction (fetch cycle). Because the program counter was initially set to 001000, the processor fetches and interprets the contents of that location as an operation code. Because 163737 is an operation code for a subtract instruction that occupies three memory cells, the processor fetches the contents (001000) of memory cell 001002 and the contents (001006) of memory cell 001004 as well, increasing the program counter to 001006.

Step 2: Execute the first instruction (execute cycle). At this point, the processor has been instructed to subtract the number in memory cell 001000 from the number in memory cell 001006. (The processor is totally unaware of the fact that it just interpreted the contents of memory cell 001000 as an operation code.) To execute the instruction, the processor (a) fetches the number (163737) contained in memory cell 001000; (b) fetches the number (163737) in memory cell 001006; (c) subtracts the two numbers to obtain 000000; and (d) stores the result (000000) in memory cell 001006. As the result of executing this instruction, memory cell 001006 now contains 000000.

Step 3: Fetch the second instruction (fetch cycle). Since the program counter now contains 001006, the processor fetches the operation code (000000) in memory cell 001006. (The processor is totally unaware that the previous instruction modified the contents of memory cell 001006.)

Step 4: Execute the second instruction (execute cycle). The operation code 000000 causes the processor to halt.

As this example implies, the processor executes a program by blindly fetching then executing instructions. This process continues until either (a) a HALT instruction is executed, (b) an illegal operation code is encountered, (c) an illegal address is encountered, or (d) the computer operator manually stops the computer.

Some Additional Instructions

The MOVE, ADD, and SUBTRACT instructions have a similar format. Each of the instructions occupies three memory cells. The first memory cell contains a 16-bit operation code, the second word contains the first 16-bit address, and

Sec. 3.5 *The Use of a Memory Cell* 49

the third word contains the second 16-bit address. Consider the following MOVE instruction:

Address	Contents	Interpretation
001000	013737	Operation code (Move)
001002	002000	First address (the address 2000)
001004	003000	Second address (the address 3000)

This instruction will, of course, cause the contents of memory cell 002000 to be moved to memory cell 003000. The contents of memory cell 002000 is the source of the operand that is moved, and memory cell 003000 is the destination of the operand. For this reason, the first address is called the **source** and the second address is called the **destination.**

The MOVE, NUMBER, ADD NUMBER, and SUBTRACT NUMBER instructions are very similar to the MOVE, ADD, and SUBTRACT instructions with one major exception: the second word of the instruction is a number rather than an address. (In other words, the second word of the instruction is the operand rather than the address of the operand.) Consider the following MOVE NUMBER instruction:

Address	Contents	Interpretation
001000	012737	Operation code (MOVE NUMBER)
001002	002000	Source (the number 002000)
001004	003000	Destination (the address 003000)

Note that the operation code for the MOVE NUMBER instruction is 012737 while the operation code for the MOVE instruction is 013737. Executing the MOVE NUMBER instruction causes the *number* 002000 to be placed in memory cell 003000. The contents of memory cell 002000 is not involved in the execution of this instruction in any way. In a similar manner, the ADD NUMBER instruction can be used to add a number to the contents of a memory cell. For example, the following instruction will add the octal number 000001 to the contents of memory cell 001400. The operation code for the ADD NUMBER instruction is 062737.

Address	Contents	Interpretation
001000	062737	Operation code (ADD NUMBER)
001002	000001	Source (the number 000001)
001004	001400	Destination (the address 001400)

In the last example, notice that the source is an odd number. This is legal because the source is a number rather than an address. In a similar manner, the SUBTRACT NUMBER instruction with an operation code of 162737 can be used to subtract a number from the contents of a memory cell.

Recall that executing a MOVE instruction requires a total of four fetch operations and one store operation. Three memory fetch operations are required during the fetch cycle to fetch the instruction, and one fetch and one store are required during the execute cycle. In contrast, the MOVE NUMBER instruction only requires a total of three fetch operations and one store operation. The fetch cycle still requires three fetch operations. However, the execute cycle requires only a store operation. The reader should be able to verify that the ADD NUMBER and SUBTRACT NUMBER instructions require a total of four fetch operations and one store operation. The seven instructions described up to this point are summarized in Figure 3.8.

Figure 3.8 List of Seven Operation Codes

Instruction	Operation Code	Source	Destination	Fetch Operations	Store Operations
HALT	000000	None	None	1	0
MOVE NUMBER	012737	Number	Address	3	1
MOVE	013737	Address	Address	4	1
ADD NUMBER	062737	Number	Address	4	1
ADD	063737	Address	Address	5	1
SUBTRACT NUMBER	162737	Number	Address	4	1
SUBTRACT	163737	Address	Address	5	1

EXERCISE SET 2

1 Assume that memory cells 001200 through 001236 contain the following:

Address	Contents	Address	Contents
001200	000001	001220	000037
001202	000777	001222	177776
001204	123456	001224	001200
001206	177777	001226	000004
001210	001000	001230	001234
001212	177775	001232	000003
001214	001214	001234	000006
001216	077777	001236	100000

What will be the effect of executing each of the following instructions? That is, what memory cell will be changed by each instruction, and what will be the new contents of the memory cell?

(a) 013737
     001202
     001230

(b) 012737
     001202
     001224

(c) 063737
     001200
     001202

(d) 162737
     001210
     001214

(e) 062737
     000002
     001206

(f) 063737
     001216
     001232

Exercise Set 2

(g) 163737
001234
001236

(h) 163737
001204
001204

(i) 012737
000000
001220

(j) 163737
001216
001222

2 Assume that you are using a PDP-11 with 4096 decimal words (10000 octal words) of memory, so that the largest legal memory address is 017776. Which of the following instructions will execute without error?

(a) 013737
001234
012345

(b) 012737
020000
020202

(c) 163737
000000
000000

(d) 062737
062737
001000

(e) 000000

(f) 162737
013737
013736

(g) 063737
017772
016744

(h) 163737
000001
001000

3 Each of the following programs will modify zero to three memory cells and then terminate, either by executing a HALT instruction or encountering an illegal operation code or address. Assume that any operation code other than the seven that have been discussed is illegal. Assume that the largest legal address is 017776. Six question marks (??????) mean that the contents of the memory cell is not known. For each program, list the new contents of any memory cell that is modified, and describe the way in which the program terminates.

(a) Address   Contents
     001000   012737
     001002   000020
     001004   001014
     001006   062737
     001010   177760
     001012   001014
     001014   ??????

Execute beginning at 001000.

(b) Address   Contents
     002000   012737
     002002   012737
     002004   002012
     002006   000000
     002010   000000
     002012   000000

Execution begins at 002000.

(c) Same as (b) except execution begins at 002002.

(d)
Address	Contents
002000	062737
002002	000001
002004	002010
002006	163737
002010	002016
002012	002016
002014	000000
002016	??????

Execution beginning at 002000.

(e)
Address	Contents
001000	163737
001002	001200
001004	001200
001006	012737
001010	000001
001012	001200
001014	000000

Execution begins at 001000.

(f)
Address	Contents
004000	012737
004002	012737
004004	004006
004006	000000
004010	000000
004012	004014
004014	??????

Execution begins at 004000.

3.6 WRITING MACHINE LANGUAGE PROGRAMS

Using the seven machine language instructions currently available, it is possible to implement very simple computer programs. In this section, the FORTRAN and BASIC programs shown in Figure 3.9 will be manually translated into machine language.* These programs are identical in the sense that, when the

---

*Strictly speaking, there is no integer data type in BASIC, therefore the BASIC example is perhaps somewhat erroneous. It is given here because some readers may know BASIC but not be familiar with FORTRAN. Consequently, for this and other examples to follow, the reader should assume that we are dealing with an "integer only" version of BASIC. Such versions of BASIC do indeed exist and are implemented on some small microcomputers such as those based on the National Semiconductor-based Nibbler.

Figure 3.9 *A Simple FORTRAN and BASIC Program*

A Simple FORTRAN Program	*An Identical BASIC Program*
INTEGER J,K,L,M	
J=3	10 LET J=3
K=J+4	20 LET K=J+4
L=K-J	30 LET L=K-J
M=K-L+J	40 LET M=K-L+J
STOP	50 STOP
END	60 END

STOP statement is reached, memory cell J will contain 3, K will contain 7, L will contain 4, and M will contain 6.

It is important to regard a variable name, such as J, K, L, or M, as the symbolic name of a memory cell rather than the contents of a memory cell. For example, the statement K = J + 4 tells the computer to add 4 to the number in memory cell J and place the resulting sum into memory cell K. It does *not* tell the computer to set the number K equal to the number J plus 4. Although this may seem like a minor semantic point, it is really the difference between the name of a memory cell and the contents of a memory cell. To emphasize this distinction, we refer to variable names such as J, K, L, and M in the preceding programs as **symbolic addresses.** They are symbols that represent the name (rather than the contents) of a memory cell.

The machine language program is to occupy consecutive memory cells beginning at memory cell 001000. This area of memory must contain space for the variables J, K, L, and M as well as the machine language instructions. Creating the program is easier if space for the variables is allocated first as shown in the following table:

Symbolic Address	*Memory Address*	*Contents*
J	001000	??????
K	001002	??????
L	001004	??????
M	001006	??????

A table such as this, which shows the relationship between symbolic addresses and actual memory addresses, is called a **symbol table.** Note that we are not concerned with the contents of these memory cells. At this time, therefore, question marks have been used to indicate the contents. The machine language program will place numbers into these memory cells during execution. It is now quite easy to implement each of the FORTRAN or BASIC statements as follows:

1. J = 3

    Since J is the symbolic name for memory cell 001000, the instruction can be implemented in machine language by a MOVE NUMBER instruction that moves the number 000003 into memory cell 001000. Since memory cells 001000 through 001006 have already been allocated, this instruction can be placed into memory beginning at memory cell 001010:

Address	Contents	Comment
001010	012737	J = 3
001012	000003	
001014	001000	

2. K = J + 4

J is the symbolic name of memory cell 001000, and K is the symbolic name of memory cell 001002. We can implement this instruction by (a) moving the contents of memory cell 001000 to 001002, and then (b) adding the number 4 to the contents of memory cell 001002. In effect, the complex FORTRAN statement, K = J + 4, is replaced by two simple FORTRAN statements, K = J and K = K + 4. The machine language implementation is:

Address	Contents	Comment
001016	013737	K = J
001020	001000	
001022	001002	
001024	062737	K = K + 4
001026	000004	
001030	001002	

3. L = K − J

This FORTRAN statement is also implemented with two machine language instructions, MOVE and SUBTRACT. In effect, the FORTRAN statement, L = K − J, is being replaced by two simpler statements, L = K, and L = L − J.

Address	Contents	Comment
001032	013737	L = K
001034	001002	
001036	001004	
001040	163737	L = L − J
001042	001000	
001044	001004	

4. Similarly, M = K − L + J can be simplified to M = K, M = M − L, and M = M + J.

Address	Contents	Comment
001046	013737	M = K
001050	001002	
001052	001006	
001054	163737	M = M − L
001056	001004	
001060	001006	
001062	063737	M = M + J
001064	001000	
001066	001006	

Sec. 3.6 *Writing Machine Language Programs* 55

5. STOP

This statement is implemented with a HALT instruction:

Address	Contents	Comments
001070	000000	STOP

The complete program is shown in Figure 3.10. Note that the processor should begin executing instructions at memory cell 001010, not 001000.

Figure 3.10 Machine Language Simple FORTRAN Program

Address	Contents	Comments
001000	?????	Memory cell J
001002	?????	Memory cell K
001004	?????	Memory cell L
001006	?????	Memory cell M
001010	012737	J = 3 (Move the number 000003
001012	000003	to memory cell 001000)
001014	001000	
001016	013737	K = J (Move the contents
001020	001000	of 001000 to 001002)
001022	001002	
001024	062737	K = K + 4 (Add the number 000004
001026	000004	to memory cell 001002)
001030	001002	
001032	013737	L = K (Move the contents of
001034	001002	001002 to 001004)
001036	001004	
001040	163737	L = L − J (Subtract the contents
001042	001000	of 001000 from 001004)
001044	001004	
001046	013737	M = K (Move the contents of
001050	001002	001002 to 001006)
001052	001006	
001054	163737	M = M − L (Subtract the contents
001056	001004	of 001004 from 001006)
001060	001006	
001062	063737	M = M + J (Add the contents of
001064	001000	001000 to 001006)
001066	001006	
001070	000000	STOP

The process of manually translating FORTRAN programs into machine language can be viewed in the following manner. The machine language instructions MOVE, MOVE NUMBER, ADD, ADD NUMBER, SUBTRACT, and SUBTRACT NUMBER can each implement a certain type of FORTRAN or BASIC expression. These are shown in Figure 3.11.

Figure 3.11 FORTRAN to Machine Language Correspondence

Sample FORTRAN Statement	Machine Language Implementation
J = 5	MOVE NUMBER instruction
J = K	MOVE instruction
J = J + 5	ADD NUMBER instruction
J = J + K	ADD instruction
J = J − 5	SUBTRACT NUMBER instruction
J = J − K	SUBTRACT instruction

In order to implement any FORTRAN statement that does not match one of the six types shown, it is necessary to decompose the statement into simpler statements that do match. For example, the statement N = 5 − N can be decomposed into

Decomposed Statement	Type
T = 5	Figure 3.11 line 1
T = T − N	Figure 3.11 line 6
N = T	Figure 3.11 line 2

Notice that temporary storage cells, such as T in the preceding example, may be necessary to implement a given FORTRAN statement.

3.7 MEMORY STRUCTURE OF OTHER COMPUTERS *(Optional Section)*

We are primarily concerned with the organization and structure of the PDP-11 family of computers. However, in various sections in the text, the similarities and differences between the PDP-11 and other computers will be discussed. Although these sections are not required in order to understand the PDP-11, they are very useful for someone who wants to gain a general knowledge of computers.

One of the most obvious ways that computers differ is in the structure of memory. The three most important factors in describing memory are (1) the size of a memory cell, (2) the size of a word, and (3) the size of an address. The size of a memory cell is usually referred to as **the unit of addressable storage.** On the PDP-11, the unit of addressable storage is an 8-bit byte. It is simply the quantity of information that is contained in each memory "box" or memory cell. (If the processor fetches the contents of memory byte 000123, the result is an 8-bit byte.) On all of the computers to be mentioned here, the unit of addressable storage is a certain number of bits. This, however, is not true of all computers. Computers have been built in which the unit of addressable storage is a ten-digit decimal number.

The range of addresses is sometimes called the **address space** and indicates the maximum number of memory cells that a program can access. On the PDP-11, an address is 16 bits long. Since 16 bits can be arranged in 2^{16} or 65,536 different ways, there are a maximum of 65,536 bytes of memory on the PDP-11 computer. For the computers to be described here, the size of an address is a certain number of binary digits. However, other arrangements, such as decimal addresses, are possible.

On many computers, the processor manipulates quantities of information that are larger than the unit of addressable storage. For example, the processor on the PDP-11 manipulates 16-bit quantities. This larger quantity of information that the processor can manipulate is called a **word**. Typically, the size of a word on any processor is some multiple of the unit of addressable storage.

Many small computers, called microcomputers, have a memory structure that is very similar to the PDP-11 memory structure. That is, the size of an address is 16 bits and the unit of addressable storage is 8 bits. However, on many of these computers, the word size is only 8 bits. That is, the ADD instruction can only add two 8-bit numbers. If longer additions are required, a series of several instructions must be used. Such processors are called 8-bit microprocessors, and computer systems built with these processors are called 8-bit microcomputers. Processors in this category include the 8085 (Intel Corporation), the Z80 (Zilog Corporation), the 6800 (Motorola), and the 6502 (MOS Technology). Computer systems based on these processors include the TRS 80 (Radio Shack) the APPLE (Apple Computer), and the PET (Commodore).

Many of these computer systems use base 16 (hexadecimal) rather than octal to represent memory. As shown in Chapter 2, the hexadecimal system uses 16 "digits"—0, 1, 2, 3, 4, 5, 6, 7, 8, 9, A, B, C, D, E, and F. Since each hexadecimal (hex for short) digit represents four bits, a 16-bit address is represented with four hex digits, and an 8-bit byte is represented with two hex digits. The contents of memory might be illustrated as shown in Figure 3.12.

A variety of minicomputers* have an addressing structure that is identical to the PDP-11. That is, the unit of addressable storage is 8 bits, the size of an address is 16 bits, and the size of a word is 16 bits. Examples of such computers include the TMS 9900 (Texas Instruments) and the Series 1 (IBM Corporation). In most instances, memory is represented in terms of 16-bit words instead of 8-bit bytes, as in the PDP-11. However, hexadecimal numbers are often used instead of octal numbers. Thus, memory is represented as shown in Figure 3.13.

---

*Computers used to be classified into three approximate sizes based on their cost—small, medium, and large. When computers were developed that were far less expensive than small computers, they were called minicomputers. When even less expensive computers were developed, they were called microcomputers. The PDP-11 is generally considered a minicomputer. However, very small PDP-11's, like the LSI-11, are often classified as microcomputers, and very large PDP-11's, like the PDP-11/70, are too large to be called minicomputers.

Figure 3.12 *Hexadecimal Memory Representation for 8-Bit Computer*

Address (in hex)	Contents (in hex)
0000	13
0001	4A
0002	00
0003	FF
0004	B0
...	...
...	...
4099	03
409A	E3
409B	52
409C	19
409D	AA
409E	3C
409F	73
40A0	C2
...	...
...	...
FFFD	59
FFFE	DF
FFFF	01

Figure 3.13 *Hexadecimal Memory Representation for 16-Bit Word Computers*

Hex Address	Hex Contents
0000	0135
0002	2A4F
0004	56B3
0006	537D
0008	AB2E
000A	FFFF
000C	0012
000E	0000
0010	B3BC
...	...
...	...
FFFC	1234
FFFE	6ABC

International Business Machines Corporation (IBM) has produced and installed a large number of medium- and large-scale computers. The IBM 360 series of computers was introduced in the mid-1960s. The 370 series was introduced in the early 1970s and the 303x and 43xx series were introduced in the late 1970s. Each of these series represents a family of computers that vary in capacity (and price). For example, the 303x series is currently available in three models: 3031, the 3032, and the 3033. All of these computers are compatible in that they have the same basic set of machine language instructions and thus form an "extended family." (Several additional instructions and features were added to the later series.)

On all of these computers, the unit of addressable storage is an 8-bit byte. The hexadecimal (base 16) system is used, so that a byte is specified with two hexadecimal digits. An address is 24 bits long, which means that memory may contain up to 2^{24} or 16,777,216 bytes. However, most installed systems have much less memory than this. In addition to manipulating bytes, the processors can manipulate 16-bit, 32-bit, 64-bit and longer quantities. These quantities of information are given the following names:

Name	Number of Bits	Number of Bytes
Halfword	16	2
Word	32	4
Doubleword	64	8

Notice that the length of a word on this machine is 32 bits or 4 bytes. In other words, a word consists of 4 consecutive bytes in memory. (On some machines, the address of a word must be divisible by 4 while other machines do not have this restriction. Analogous comments apply to halfwords and doublewords.)

Figure 3.14 shows a section of memory that contains a variety of bytes, halfwords, words, and doublewords. The 24-bit addresses are represented as six hexadecimal digits.

Figure 3.14 Sample Memory Contents for Large IBM Computers

Address	Contents	Quantity of Information
0A3B0	3A63CD55AA12335F	Doubleword
0A3B8	05BC3894	Word
0A3BC	F53E16C3	Word
0A3C0	3E	Byte
0A3C1	82	Byte
0A3C2	5AE6	Halfword
0A3C4	98F320E4	Word

All of the computers described to this point are examples of byte addressable machines. On such machines, the unit of addressable storage contains a small number of bits, such as 8. In contrast, many computers have a unit of addressable storage that contains larger quantities of information, such as 36, 48, 60, or 64 bits. On these machines, the word size is generally the same as the unit of addressable storage. For example, a variety of computers manufactured by Control Data Corporation (CDC) have a 60-bit word as the unit of addressable storage. The contents of a memory cell is generally represented as 20 octal digits. On these machines, addresses are 18 bits long and are usually represented with 6 octal digits. Figure 3.15 shows how the contents of memory is represented.

Figure 3.15 Sample Memory Representation for the CDC Cyber Computers

Address	Contents
303627	572634337162635 40536
303630	036130274512003 53011
303631	533746200253233 25536
303632	362644726133020 04520
305633	472677735300253 42302

The computers with large word lengths tend to be expensive. They are generally designed to perform scientific calculations very rapidly. Computers with a small word size, such as an 8-bit byte, tend to be less expensive and slower. However, this is only a crude rule of thumb. One of the problems is that we have described memory as the programmer sees it. If one looks at the electrical components and circuits inside a computer, it is possible to reach quite different conclusions. Consider the problem of fetching a byte from memory on a PDP-11 computer. The processor actually fetches a 16-bit word and then "throws away" 8 of the bits to leave an 8-bit byte. This process is totally transparent to the programmer. However, an electrical engineer looking at circuit diagrams might well conclude that the unit of addressable storage on the PDP-11 was 16 bits rather than 8 bits.

EXERCISE SET 3

1 Beginning in memory cell 001000, write a machine language program that is equivalent to the following FORTRAN program. (Remember to convert the decimal numbers to octal.)

```
        INTEGER J,K,L
        J=15
        K=22
        L=J-K+9
        STOP
        END
```

2 Beginning in memory cell 001000, write a machine language program that is equivalent to the following:

```
        INTEGER J,K
        J=27
        K=-J
        STOP
        END
```

Exercise Set 3

3 Translate the following FORTRAN program into a machine language program that begins at address 001200. Notice that multiplication can be achieved with successive addition. (Your program should use a temporary memory location to store the sum of J and K. When your program halts, J and K should still contain 5 and 9, respectively.)

```
INTEGER J,K,L
J=5
K=9
L=3*(J+K)
STOP
END
```

4 Translate the following FORTRAN program into a machine language program beginning at address 001000. (*Hint:* K can be computed from J with fewer than 10 additions.)

```
INTEGER J,K
J=5
K=J*32
STOP
END
```

5 Solve exercise 4 assuming that K=J*23. (*Hint:* Express 23 decimal in binary. Each 1 represents a multiple of J that must be added to K.)

6 Solve exercise 1 assuming that the machine language program is to begin at address 000000 instead of 001000. What numbers change when a program is relocated? Can you easily change the program so that it begins at address 002000?

CHAPTER 4

ASSEMBLY LANGUAGE PROGRAMMING

4.1 INTRODUCTION

Programming in machine language is difficult for a programmer. For example, in order to add a quantity called TAX to a quantity called TOTAL, a programmer would have to write a machine language instruction such as:

Operation Code	Source	Destination
063737	002000	003000

In creating this instruction, the programmer must remember that (a) 013737 is the operation code for addition, (b) TAX is the symbolic name for memory cell 002000, and (c) TOTAL is the symbolic name for memory cell 003000. In order to appreciate the problems that face a programmer, it is worth noting that the PDP-11 contains several hundred different operation codes. Furthermore, it is not unusual for a computer program to use several thousand memory cells.

Assembly languages relieve some of the demands on a programmer's memory by using **symbolic names** instead of numbers. For example, the preceding machine language instruction could be written in assembly language as:

Operation Code	Source ↓	Destination ↓
ADD	TAX,	TOTAL

63

A computer program, called the **assembler,** translates the assembly language program into machine language by substituting appropriate numbers for the symbolic names. For the preceding assembly language statement, the assembler should substitute 063737 for ADD, 002000 for TAX, and 003000 for TOTAL.

In addition to allowing the programmer to use symbolic names, the assembler also performs computational services such as converting numbers from one base into another. Typically, each type or model of computer has its own assembly language. Indeed, there are sometimes different assembly languages for a given type or model of computer. The assembly language to be described for the PDP-11 computer is called MACRO-11.

4.2 DEVELOPING AN ASSEMBLY LANGUAGE PROGRAM

Mnemonic Operation Codes

In order to understand the assembly process, it is useful to see how an assembly language program could be developed from a machine language program. In this section, the machine language program presented in the previous chapter (Figure 3.10) will be converted to assembly language. For convenience, this program is reproduced as Figure 4.1. Notice that the format has been altered however. For instructions that occupy three memory cells, only the address of the operation code is listed. Source and destination are obviously contained in the next two memory cells. In addition, the location for J, K, L, and M have been moved to the end of the program so that execution will begin at location 001000. In Figure 4.1, memory cell 001000 contains the operation code 012737, memory cell 001002 contains the operand 000003, and memory cell 001004 contains the address 001062.

Figure 4.1   Machine Language Program

Address	Op Code	Source	Destination	Comments
001000	012737	000003	001062	J=3
001006	013737	001062	001064	K=J+4
001014	062737	000004	001064	
001022	013737	001064	001066	L=K−J
001030	163737	001062	001066	
001036	013737	001064	001070	M=K−L+J
001044	163737	001066	001070	
001052	063737	001062	001070	
001060	000000			STOP
001062	??????			MEMORY CELL J
001064	??????			MEMORY CELL K
001066	??????			MEMORY CELL L
001070	??????			MEMORY CELL M

Sec. 4.2   Developing an Assembly Language Program   65

The first step in converting this program is to substitute names for the operation codes, using Figure 4.2. Notice that some of the symbolic operation codes are abbreviated. For example, the MOVE operation code is shortened to MOV, and the MOVE NUMBER operation code is written as MOV #. (The programmers who created the MACRO-11 assembler chose these abbreviations. These abbreviations are often called **Mnemonic** op codes. Mnemonic refers to a human memory aid that uses association.) Substituting symbolic operation codes for the numerical operation codes in Figure 4.1 produces Figure 4.3.

Figure 4.2 Seven Operation Codes

Symbolic Operation Code	Numerical Operation Code
ADD	063737
ADD #	062737
HALT	000000
MOV	013737
MOV #	012737
SUB	163737
SUB #	162737

Figure 4.3 Machine Language Program with Symbolic Op Codes

Address	Op Code	Source	Destination	Comments
001000	MOV	#000003	001062	J=3
001006	MOV	001062	001064	K=J+4
001014	ADD	#000004	001064	
001022	MOV	001064	001066	L=K−J
001030	SUB	001062	001066	
001036	MOV	001064	001070	M=K−L+J
001044	SUB	001066	001070	
001052	ADD	001062	001070	
001060	HALT			STOP
001062	?????			MEMORY CELL J
001064	?????			MEMORY CELL K
001066	?????			MEMORY CELL L
001070	?????			MEMORY CELL M

Symbolic Addresses

Just as numerical operation codes can be replaced with mnemonic operation codes, numerical addresses can be replaced with symbolic addresses. Figure 4.4 is a **symbol table** that lists the numerical addresses along with the symbolic addresses that the authors have chosen. The first entry indicates that every occurrence of the numerical address 001000 should be replaced by the symbolic address START.

Figure 4.4 A Symbol Table

Symbolic Address	Numerical Address
START	001000
J	001062
K	001064
L	001066
M	001070

Using this symbol table, each numerical address of importance in Figure 4.3 can be replaced by a symbolic address. Performing this series of substitutions produces the partially converted program shown in Figure 4.5.

Figure 4.5 Program with Symbolic Op Codes and Addresses

Symbolic Address	Op Code	Source	Destination	Comments
START	MOV	#000003	J	J=3
	MOV	J	K	K=J+4
	ADD	#000004	K	
	MOV	K	L	L=K−J
	SUB	J	L	
	MOV	K	M	M=K−L+J
	SUB	L	M	
	ADD	J	M	
	HALT			STOP
J	?????			MEMORY CELL J
K	?????			MEMORY CELL K
L	?????			MEMORY CELL L
M	?????			MEMORY CELL M

Symbolic addresses such as J and START in Figure 4.5 are also called **symbolic names** or **labels.** Symbolic addresses such as J, K, L, and M are analogous to variable names in FORTRAN or BASIC. They are the names of memory cells that contain "numbers" which are manipulated by the program. Symbolic addresses such as START are analogous to statement labels in FORTRAN and BASIC. They are the names of memory cells that contain (machine language) instructions. Higher-level languages such as FORTRAN or BASIC clearly distinguish between variable names and statement labels. The statement label 10 is very different from the variable name J. Other higher-level languages, such as PL/1, do not make this distinction so clearly. In machine language or assembly language, however, this distinction does not really exist. A symbolic address is the name of a memory cell, regardless of whether the contents of the memory cell is a number or an instruction.

Sec. 4.2 *Developing an Assembly Language Program* 67

The partially converted program in Figure 4.5 is certainly much easier to understand than the machine language program in Figure 4.1. However, the conversion process has not altered the *meaning* of the program in any way. Figures 4.1 and 4.5 are really just two different representations for the same program.

The Syntax of Assembly Language

The final step in conversion is the addition of some punctuation so that the program satisfies certain **rules of syntax** required of assembly language programs. The complete assembly language program is shown in Figure 4.6.

Figure 4.6 Assembly Language Program

Label	Op Code	Operands	Comments
	.TITLE	SIMPLE PROGRAM	
	.ENABL	AMA	;SEE TEXT
START:	MOV	#3,J	;J=3
	MOV	J,K	
	ADD	#4,K	;K=J+4
	MOV	K,L	
	SUB	J,L	;L=K-J
	MOV	K,M	
	SUB	L,M	
	ADD	J,M	;M=K-L+J
	HALT		;STOP
J:	.BLKW	1	;MEMORY CELL J
K:	.BLKW	1	;MEMORY CELL K
L:	.BLKW	1	;MEMORY CELL L
M:	.BLKW	1	;MEMORY CELL M
	.END	START	;SEE TEXT

The assembly language program consists of four columns or **fields.** The first field contains symbolic addresses, the second field contains operation codes, the third field specifies operands, and the fourth field is for comments. Each of these fields will be described in greater detail.

The label field contains labels or the names of symbolic addresses. Each label is the name of a memory cell. (Generally, the remaining fields on each line specify the contents of the memory cell.) Labels are composed of one to six letters and numbers. In addition, the first character must be a letter. Thus A, Z123, and SUNDAY are valid, but 52, AB?CD, and TUESDAY* are illegal. A

---

*Names that are too long do not produce error messages, but the extra characters are ignored, and thus confusion could occur between TUESDAY and TUESDAQ, which would be indistinguishable. Additionally, periods and dollar signs can be used in names as if they were letters of the alphabet. However, since they are frequently used in systems programs, their use in non-systems programs is not recommended.

colon (:) must immediately follow a label. A label may begin anywhere on a line, but by convention they are normally typed beginning in column 1.

The operation code field contains mnemonic operation codes such as MOV, ADD, SUB, and so on. In addition, however, it may contain things like .TITLE, .ENABL, .BLKW, and .END, which are definitely *not* operation codes. These are called **assembly directives** (with some assemblers, they are called pseudo-operations). It is easy to distinguish operation codes from assembly directives because MACRO-11 assembly directives always begin with a period (.). The .BLKW 1 indicates that a word of memory is to be reserved without specifying its contents. In other words, it is equivalent to our writing six question marks (??????). In Figure 4.6, .BLKW 1 simply indicates that J, K, L, and M are the names of four memory cells (16-bit words) whose contents are not known. Specifically .BLKW means "block of words." The number following .BLKW is called an **argument** and indicates the number of words in the block. The .TITLE, .ENABL and .END assembly directives are described further on. Operation codes and assembly directives may begin in any column, but by convention they are usually typed beginning in column 9.

The contents of the operand field on a given line depends on the contents of the operation code field. A HALT op code must not have any operands, an .END directive in this context should have one operand, and a MOV op code requires two operands. When two operands are required, they *must* be separated by a comma with *no spaces* between the two operands. Notice that leading zeros on numbers may be eliminated, so that #000003 may be typed as #3. By convention, the operand field begins in column 17.

A comment must start with a semicolon (;). Anything after the semicolon is ignored in the sense that it is not considered to be part of the assembly language program. Comments can begin anywhere on a line after the operands (or after the op code or assembly directive if there are no operands). It is possible to make an entire line a comment by placing a semicolon in column 1.

The .END, .ENABL, and .TITLE directives still have to be described. The .END directive is analogous to the END statement in FORTRAN or BASIC. .END, which must appear on the last line of an assembly language program, simply marks the physical end of the program. The operand following .END is called an argument and specifies the symbolic address where execution is to begin.

The function of the .ENABL directive is more difficult to explain. There are two slightly different versions of the operation code table. The directive .ENABL AMA is a message to indicate that the operation code table shown in Figure 4.2 is being used. The PDP-11 has two memory addressing schemes: **relative** (discussed later) and **absolute.** In absolute, the actual numerical address is used in the instruction. Enabling AMA tells the assembler to use the easier to understand *absolute memory addressing* wherever possible. The .TITLE directive is simply for identification purposes. It has a message in the operand field that is printed at the top of every page of assembly language listing. Therefore, each listing page for this example would say SIMPLE PROGRAM in the upper

Sec. 4.3   The Assembly Process   69

left hand corner. The .TITLE directive is not necessary to the program and has little more effect than a comment. However, its use is important for the proper documentation of the program.

Another commonly used assembly directive that was not used in the example is .WORD. This directive is used to place one or more numbers into consecutive memory locations. For example, .WORD 57,34,171 would cause three words to be inserted into the program:

$$
\begin{array}{c}
000057 \\
000034 \\
000171
\end{array}
$$

4.3 THE ASSEMBLY PROCESS

The PDP-11 Assembler

In order to create machine language programs for the PDP-11, programmers typically write assembly language programs such as the one in Figure 4.6. The assembly language program is input data to another computer program called the **assembler** which translates the assembly language program into machine language. The assembler to be described here is called MACRO-11. MACRO-11 was written by the manufacturer of the PDP-11, Digital Equipment Corporation.

Simple Translation

If the symbol table and the operation code table are available, the assembly process is simple. Consider, for example, the assembly language program in Figure 4.6. Using the symbol table (Figure 4.4), replace each symbolic address with the equivalent numerical address. Using the operation code table (Figure 4.2), replace each symbolic operation code with the equivalent numerical operation code. Remove the punctuation characters, and the result is the machine language program shown in Figure 4.1.

The previous description assumed that (a) the operation code table is available, and (b) the symbol table is available. The operation code table does not vary from one program to another. That is, the symbolic operation code HALT is always replaced with the numerical operation code 000000. For this reason, the operation code table is built in to the program called MACRO-11 that translates assembly language programs into machine language.

In contrast, the symbol table varies from program to program. It would be possible to require the programmer to construct the symbol table and give the table to MACRO-11. However, creating the symbol table is almost as difficult as creating the machine language program directly. A much better

Creating a Symbol Table

MACRO-11 creates the symbol table by assuming that *numbers are to be placed in consecutive memory cells*. For example, suppose that MACRO-11 has determined that START in the following program segment is the symbolic name of memory cell 001000:

```
START:  MOV     #3,J
        MOV     J,K
```

Since the instruction MOV #3,J is a three-word instruction, it will occupy locations 001000, 001002, and 001004. The next available location is 001006. Therefore, the second MOV instruction will be located starting at 001006. Since it also requires three words, locations 001006, 001010, and 001012 will be used, and the next available location will be 001014.

Using this technique, the assembler can determine the exact address of each instruction or data location in the program. Since some of these lines in the program contain a label, the labels can be identified with addressses to form a symbol table. For example, this allows us to determine that J would be location 001062, K would be 001066, and so on. The assembler can then use these addresses to fill in the addresses of such instructions as MOV #3,J.

Let us now review the method that MACRO-11 uses to construct the symbol table. MACRO-11 keeps track of a single quantity—the address of the next available memory cell. This quantity is called the **location counter**. MACRO-11 scans the assembly language program from beginning to end using the following rules:

Rule 1: When MACRO-11 encounters a symbol followed by a colon (such as START:, A:, or ZONK:), a symbolic address is being defined. MACRO-11 inserts the symbolic address into the symbol table along with the current value of the location counter. The value of the location counter is not changed.

Rule 2: When MACRO-11 encounters a symbol in the operation code field, MACRO-11 adds an appropriate quantity to the location counter as shown by the following table:

Op Code Field	Appropriate Quantity	Op Code Field	Appropriate Quantity
ADD	6	SUB	6
ADD#	6	SUB#	6
HALT	2	.BLKW	2 times the argument
MOV	6	.ENABL	0
MOV#	6	.END	0

It should be noted that the location counter is to the assembler what the program counter is to the processor during execution. Although producing a symbol table is crucial to the assembly process, the primary objective of the assembler is to produce a machine language program. Let us now examine the problems associated with producing machine language.

Examining the program in Figure 4.6, we can see what the assembler "sees" during the translation process. The first thing is the .ENABL AMA line. As described earlier, this directive does not generate any machine language code, but merely sets a mode switch in the assembler. The next line, however, is START: MOV #3,J. This line causes much to happen. First the symbol START is entered in the symbol table with the starting address of 001000. Next the MOV # instruction is encountered. The assembler searches the table in Figure 4.2 to determine that MOV # is a 6-byte or 3-word instruction and the location counter is modified. Finally, we would like to produce the three words of the instruction, 012737, 000003, and 001062. However, there is a problem. The last of these words, 001062, is the address of J. But how can the assembler "know" the address of J since it has not yet "seen" the line J: .BLKW 1 where J is defined.

Two-Pass Assembly

To solve this problem, the PDP-11 assembler uses two passes. (Chapter 13 mentions other possible solutions to this problem.) This means that the assembler reads through the assembly language program *twice*. The first time, no machine language code is generated because address definitions are missing. However, addresses can be determined as the program is read, and the symbol table is generated. Then in a second pass through the program, the assembler will have all the addresses defined in the symbol table, and the machine language code is produced.

The process of constructing the symbol table by scanning the assembly language program is called **pass 1** of the assembly process. The machine language program is produced during **pass 2**. During pass 2, MACRO-11 scans the assembly language program a second time and, using the operation code table and the symbol table, substitutes numbers for symbolic names to create the machine language program.

4.4 EXAMPLES OF ERRORS IN THE ASSEMBLY PROCESS

Kinds of Errors

Two distinct steps are required to execute an assembly language program. First, the assembly language program is given to the MACRO-11 assembler which translates the assembly language into machine language. Second, the machine language program is executed. Errors can occur during either one of these steps. The errors that may be generated during each step are quite different.

The errors generated during the assembly step are generally either **syntax** errors or **undefined symbols.** In order to translate an assembly language program into machine language, MACRO-11 must be able to find the label field, the op code field, and the operands field on each line of the assembly program. In order to make this possible, the assembly program must contain appropriate punctuation, such as a colon after a symbolic address. Syntax is the set of punctuation and other grammar rules, and if the punctuation is incorrect, a syntax error will be produced. An undefined symbol occurs when MACRO-11 encounters a name that is not contained in either the operation code table or the symbol table. This will occur if the operation code MOV is misspelled as MOVE, or if the .END directive is misspelled as END. This error will also occur if the programmer forgets to define a symbolic address. (Symbolic addresses are defined by placing the name in the label field, followed by a colon.) It is also possible to generate an error by defining the same symbolic name twice.

It is important to understand that errors such as syntax errors and undefined or multiply defined symbols are the only kinds of errors that MACRO-11 detects. In particular, MACRO-11 does *not* check the validity of the machine language program that it produces *in any way*. MACRO-11's only function is to substitute numbers (such as operation codes and addresses) for names. It is the programmer's responsibility to ensure that the result is a valid machine language program.

Once the assembly process is completed, the machine language program can be executed. The errors that occur during execution include such things as illegal addresses and illegal operation codes. In addition, of course, the program may simply produce incorrect answers.

Examples of Errors

To illustrate these points, a series of assembly language programs and their machine language translations are described next. Each example consists of eight columns. The assembly language program is contained in columns 2, 3, and 4, with column 2 containing the label field, column 3 containing the operation code, and column 4 containing the operands, if any. Column 1 contains the numerical addresses, so that columns 1 and 2 represent the symbol table created by pass 1 of the assembly process. The machine language program produced by MACRO-11 is shown in columns 5 through 8. In each case, it is assumed that the location counter is initialized to 001000, so that cell 001000 is the first memory cell used by the program.

Sec. 4.4   Examples of Errors in the Assembly Process

> **EXAMPLE 1** This assembly language program is designed to (a) set the contents of memory cell A to 000003 (octal), (b) set the contents of memory cell B equal to the contents of memory cell A, or 000003, and (c) add the number 000004 to memory cell B, so that its contents become 000007. Notice that we do *not* say that the value of B is 000007. *The value of B is its symbol table entry,* 001026. The value *contained* in memory cell B is 000007.
>
> | | | ASSEMBLY LANGUAGE PROGRAM | | | MACHINE LANGUAGE PROGRAM | | |
> |---------|-------|---------|----------|---------|---------|---------|---------|
> | Address | Label | Op Code | Operands | Address | Op Code | Operand | Operand |
> | | | .TITLE | EXAMPLE #1 | Program title | | | |
> | | | .ENABL | AMA | Use the op code table in Figure 4.2 | | | |
> | 001000 | ST: | MOV | #3,A | 001000 | 012737 | 000003 | 001024 |
> | | | MOV | A,B | 001006 | 013737 | 001024 | 001026 |
> | | | ADD | #4,B | 001014 | 062737 | 000004 | 001026 |
> | | | HALT | | 001022 | 000000 | | |
> | 001024 | A: | .BLKW | 1 | 001024 | ?????? | | |
> | 001026 | B: | .BLKW | 1 | 001026 | ?????? | | |
> | | | .END | ST | | | | |
>
> During pass 1 of the assembly process, the symbol table is constructed. ST becomes the symbolic name for memory cell 001000, A becomes the symbolic name for memory cell 001024, and so on. During pass 2, the machine language program is created. Finally, the machine language program is executed beginning at memory cell 001000. When the program halts at memory cell 001022, memory cell 001024 will contain 000003, and memory cell 001026 will contain 000007.

> **EXAMPLE 2** The second example is similar to example 1 except that the programmer has forgotten the .BLKW directive on the fifth and sixth lines of the program. The omission of .BLKW does *not* cause an assembly error. Recall that the only function of the .BLKW directive is to add 000002 to the location counter during pass 1 of the assembly process. Because .BLKW is omitted, A and B are both symbolic names for memory cell 001024. (MACRO-11 simply assumes that the programmer wishes to refer to memory cell 001024 by two different symbolic names.)
>
> When the machine language program is executed, the MOV # instruction in 001000 replaces the contents in 001024 with the number 000003. The MOV instruction moves the new contents 001024 into 001024, and the ADD # instruction adds 000004 to the contents of 001024. When the HALT instruction is executed, memory cell 001024 will contain 000007. Obviously, this is not what the programmer intended. However, this is a difficult error to find because no error messages are produced.

		ASSEMBLY LANGUAGE PROGRAM		MACHINE LANGUAGE PROGRAM			
Address	Label	Op Code	Operands	Address	Op Code	Operand	Operand
		.TITLE	EXAMPLE #2	Program title			
		.ENABL	AMA	Use the op code table in Figure 4.2			
001000	ST:	MOV	#3,A	001000	012737	000003	001024
		MOV	A,B	001006	013737	001024	001024
		ADD	#4,B	001014	062737	000004	001024
		HALT		001022	000000		
001024	A:			001024	?????		
001024	B:			001024			
		.END	ST				

EXAMPLE 3 Example 3 is identical to example 1 except that the programmer has forgotten the HALT statement. This too will fail to produce an assembly time error. During execution, however, the PDP-11 will eventually execute the ADD # instruction in memory cells 001014, 001016, and 001020. The processor will then try to execute the "instruction" in memory cell 001022 (symbolic address A). By this time, memory cell 001022 contains 000007, which happens to be an illegal operation code. The computer will stop executing the program and print an error message such as:

```
TRAP TO 000010 FROM 001024
```

The TRAP TO 000010 simply indicates that the processor has found an illegal operation code. The address that follows (in this case 001024) is generally one or two memory cells *after* the memory cell that caused the problem.

The programmer in this example was lucky because the machine language program "bombed" immediately. If the contents of memory cell 001022 were a valid machine language instruction, the processor might execute a large number of "garbage instructions" in memory cells 001022, 001024, 001026, 001030, and so on.

If the processor finally encountered an illegal instruction at memory cell 001040, an error message such as:

```
TRAP TO 000010 FROM 001044
```

would be produced. This message is not particularly useful in finding the cause of the error (the missing HALT instruction). A clue is that the value 001044 is the contents of the program counter when the error was detected. However, the value will usually be somewhat higher than the instruction causing the error because the program counter will be incremented some number of times depending upon how many fetches were needed before the error was detected.

Sec. 4.4 Examples of Errors in the Assembly Process

		ASSEMBLY LANGUAGE PROGRAM		MACHINE LANGUAGE PROGRAM			
Address	Label	Op Code	Operands	Address	Op Code	Operand	Operand
		.TITLE	EXAMPLE #3	Program title			
		.ENABL	AMA	Use the op code table in Figure 4.2			
001000	ST:	MOV	#3,A	001000	012737	000003	001022
		MOV	A,B	001006	013737	001022	001024
		ADD	#4,B	001014	062737	000004	001024
001022	A:	.BLKW	1	001022	??????		
001024	B:	.BLKW	1	001024	??????		
		.END	ST				

EXAMPLE 4 This example is identical to example 1 except that the number sign (#) has been omitted from the assembly language instruction MOV #3,A. Recall that the number sign is really part of the operation code. Omitting the number sign changes the operation code in memory cell 001000 from 012737 to 013737. The rest of the machine language program is unchanged. Since MACRO-11 was able to substitute a number for each symbol in the program, no error message is generated.

When the machine language program is executed, however, the MOV instruction beginning in memory cell 001000 instructs the processor to move the contents of memory cell 000003 into memory cell 001026. Because 000003 is an illegal (odd) address, the program will "bomb" with an error message such as TRAP TO 000004 FROM 001004.

A quite different result would occur if the number sign were omitted on the instruction ADD #4,B in example 1. The assembly language instruction ADD 4,B generates a machine language instruction that tells the processor to add the contents of memory cell 000004 to memory cell B (001026). Since the contents of memory cell 000004 has not been specified, it must be assumed to contain garbage. When the machine language program halts, memory cell B (001026) will contain garbage.

		ASSEMBLY LANGUAGE PROGRAM		MACHINE LANGUAGE PROGRAM			
Address	Label	Op Code	Operands	Address	Op Code	Operand	Operand
		.TITLE	EXAMPLE #4	Program title			
		.ENABL	AMA	Use the op code table in Figure 4.2			
001000	ST:	MOV	3,A	001000	013737	000003	001024
		MOV	A,B	001006	013737	001024	001026
		ADD	#4,B	001014	062737	000004	001026
		HALT		001022	000000		
001024	A:	.BLKW	1	001024	??????		
001026	B:	.BLKW	1	001026	??????		
		.END	ST				

EXAMPLE 5 The previous examples have emphasized errors that may occur when a machine language program is executed by the processor. The following example illustrates the kinds of errors that will be detected by MACRO-11 during the assembly process.

Label	Op Code	Operands	Error
	.TITEL	EXAMPLE #5	.TITLE IS MISSPELLED
	ENABL	AMA	ENABL IS UNDEFINED (MISSING PERIOD)
ST;	MOV	#3,A	ST IS UNDEFINED (";" TYPED FOR ":")
	MOV	A,B	B IS UNDEFINED (SEE BELOW)
	ADD	#4,B	B IS UNDEFINED (SEE BELOW)
	,HALT		ILLEGAL SNYTAX (ADDED COMMA)
B	.BLKW	1	B IS UNDEFINED (MISSING COLON)
A:	.BLKW	1	
	.END	ST	ST IS UNDEFINED (SEE ABOVE)

Some of these errors deserve greater explanation. On the third line, the programmer has inadvertently typed a semicolon (;) instead of a colon (:). As a result, MACRO-11 assumes that ST is in the operation code field and that the remainder of the line is a comment. (ST cannot be in the label field, because arguments in the label field must end with a colon.) MACRO-11 searches the operation code table and the symbol table looking for the symbol ST. In this case, no such symbol is found and an error message is printed. Because of the error, ST is not entered in the symbol table and a second error message is printed with the .END statement because the operand is undefined.

The missing colon on the sixth card produces a similar result. B is undefined and every line that uses B as an operand will be flagged with an error message. A single error can generate a large number of error messages.

EXERCISE SET 1

1. In examples 1 through 4, it was assumed that the location counter was initialized to 001000. Reassemble example 1 assuming that the location counter is initialized to 000000. Does this change affect the content of memory cells A and B when the machine language program halts?

2. Assume that the fourth line in example 1 is modified to read MOV #A,B. (That is, a number sign is added in front of the operand A.) Hand assemble this program assuming that the location center is initialized to 001000. What will be contained in memory cell B when the machine language program halts? (*Hint:* Remember that the number sign just changes the operation code.)

Exercise Set 1

3 Hand assemble the following program beginning at memory cell 001000. What will be contained in memory cell LAST when the machine language program halts? Can you describe what this program does in a few (English) words?

Label	Op Code	Operands
	.TITLE	EXERCISE
	.ENABL	AMA
FIRST:	MOV	#LAST,LAST
	SUB	#FIRST,LAST
	ADD	#2,LAST
	HALT	
LAST:	.BLKW	1
	.END	FIRST

4 Hand assemble the following program beginning in memory cell 001000. What number will be contained in memory cell ANS when the program halts?

	.TITLE	EASY
	.ENABL	AMA
START:	MOV	#10,J
	MOV	#20,ANS
	ADD	J,ANS
	HALT	
J:	.BLKW	1
ANS:	.BLKW	1
	.END	START

5 What effect will each of the following changes have on the program in exercise 4? (The changes are not cumulative.) If the program reaches the HALT statement, either identify the final contents of ANS or indicate the source of the garbage that makes the contents of ANS unknown. If the program executes a garbage instruction, identify the memory cell that contains the garbage instruction.

(a) The number sign is omitted from the third line so that the line becomes START: MOV 10,J.

(b) The line containing the HALT instruction is omitted.

(c) A number sign is added to the fifth line so that the line becomes ADD #J,ANS.

(d) The assembly directive, .BLKW is omitted from the seventh line so that the line contains only the label definition J:.

4.5 PROGRAMS IN THE COMPUTER

Multiple Programs in Memory

The memory of a modern computer typically contains more than one machine language program. Figure 4.7 illustrates a computer system in which memory contains two programs labeled A and B.

Figure 4.7

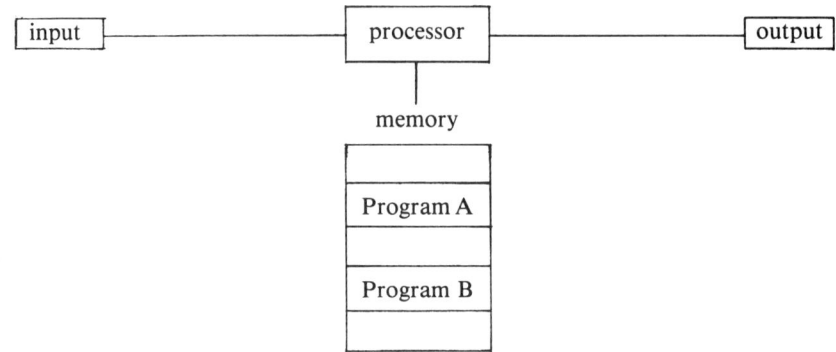

At any point in time, only one program is actually being executed by the processor. However, there are special machine language instructions that cause the processor to stop executing one program and start executing another. There are several reasons why it is desirable to have more than one program in memory. Some of these are described next.

Modular Programs

Debugging one large program is usually much more difficult than debugging several small programs. As a result, good programmers usually break up a large problem into two or more small programs. In Figure 4.7, for example, programs A and B might be two programs, written by the same programmer, that were designed to solve a single complex problem. When a problem is split up in this fashion, the first program (in this case program A) is called the **main program.** The other programs (in this case B) are called **subprograms** or **subroutines.** There are two instructions in the PDP-11 for calling subroutines and returning from them: JSR and RTS. The JSR instruction (Jump to SubRoutine) can be used to tell the processor to temporarily stop executing the main program and start executing the subroutine. The RTS instruction (ReTurn from Subroutine) can be used to stop executing the subroutine and resume execution of the main program. These instructions will be described in more detail in the next chapter.

It is even possible for the programs to be written in different languages. In Figure 4.7, program A could be the machine language translation of an assembly language program, while B could be the machine language translation

Sec. 4.5   *Programs in the Computer*

of a FORTRAN program. By breaking a large problem into smaller subproblems, the programmer can select the best language for solving each subproblem.

Even if the programmer writes a single program with no subroutines, there is usually another program in memory. In Figure 4.7, program A could be a user's program, while program B could be part of the RT-11 operating system. The user program can use the RT-11 operating system to obtain various services such as input or output operations. These services are obtained by placing an EMT instruction (EMulate Trap) in the user program. The EMT instruction stops the execution of the user program and starts executing the RT-11 operating system. For example, if you are using RT-11, you should use an EMT 350 instruction to terminate your program rather than a HALT instruction. EMT 350 simply informs RT-11 that your program has finished executing. RT-11 can then load the next user's program into memory and execute it.

Relocation

Because there are multiple programs in memory, it is important to be able to move or **relocate** a program from one area of memory to another. (It would be very unfortunate if a user accidentally placed a machine language program in memory cells that were already occupied by the RT-11 operating system.) One way of relocating an assembly language program is to reassemble the program.

Figure 4.8 contains the same assembly and machine language program that previously was shown in example 1 (page 73). This example assumed that the location counter was initialized to 001000. During pass 1 of the assembly process, the following symbol table was generated:

Symbolic Address	Numerical Address
ST	001000
A	001024
B	001026

During pass 2, the machine language program on the right side of Figure 4.8 was generated. During execution, this program resides in memory cells 001000 through 001024.

Figure 4.8

	ASSEMBLY LANGUAGE PROGRAM			MACHINE LANGUAGE PROGRAM			
Address	Label	Op Code	Operands	Address	Op Code	Operand	Operand
		.TITLE	EXAMPLE #1	Program title			
		.ENABL	AMA	Use the op code table in Figure 4.2			
001000	ST:	MOV	#3,A	001000	012737	000003	001024
		MOV	A,B	001006	013737	001024	001026
		ADD	#4,B	001014	062737	000004	001026
		HALT		001022	000000		
001024	A:	.BLKW	1	001024	??????		
001026	B:	.BLKW	1	001026	??????		
		.END	ST				

Figure 4.9

```
              ASSEMBLY LANGUAGE
                  PROGRAM                          MACHINE LANGUAGE PROGRAM
Address  Label   Op Code   Operands        Address   Op Code   Operand   Operand
                 .TITLE    RELOCATION
                 .ENABL    AMA             Use the op code table in Figure 4.2
000000   ST:     MOV       #3,A            000000    012737    000003    000024
                 MOV       A,B             000006    013737    000024    000026
                 ADD       #4,B            000014    062737    000004    000026
                 HALT                      000022    000000
000024   A:      .BLKW     1               000024    ??????
000026   B:      .BLKW     1               000026    ??????
                 .END      ST
```

The assembly language program in Figure 4.9 is identical to the one in Figure 4.8. However, the location counter has been initialized to 000000 rather than 001000. As a result, the symbol table produced from Figure 4.9 is:

Symbolic Address	Numerical Address
ST	000000
A	000024
B	000026

The resulting machine language program, shown on the right side of Figure 4.9, occupies memory cells 000000 to 000026 during execution.

The Relocation Process

Notice that both machine language programs produce the same answer. When either program halts, the contents of memory cell B will be 000007. It should be obvious that the assembly language program can be relocated to any area in memory by initializing the location counter to an appropriate value. If the location counter is initialized to address n, the resulting machine language program will occupy memory cells n through n + 26.

It should also be noted that most of the actual words of both programs do not change when we go from the machine language of one to the other. There are, however, four exceptions. These exceptions are words that contain addresses within the program. In Figure 4.8 and 4.9, the four words that change when the program is relocated have been underlined. Notice that each of the underlined quantities is an address in the program and that the relocation changes each address by the amount of 001000. This result is obvious if the assembly process is considered. The only difference between the two assemblies is the initial value given to the location counter—001000 in the first assembly and 000000 in the second. Changing the location counter by 001000 changes each address by 001000.

This suggests a way of relocating a machine language program: simply add

Sec. 4.5   *Programs in the Computer*   81

the appropriate constant to each address and each underlined word in Figure 4.9. For example, if 001000 is added to each underlined word, the machine language program in Figure 4.8 is produced. If 003000 is added to each number, the following machine language program is produced:

```
Address   Op Code  Source   Destination
          Use the op code table in Figure 4.2
003000    012737   000003   003024
003006    013737   003024   003026
003014    062737   000004   003026
003022    000000
003024    ?????
003026    ?????
```
Execution begins at 003000

During execution, this machine language program will occupy memory cells 003000 through 003026.

In a machine language program, the addresses that must be changed when a program is relocated are called **relocatable addresses** and all other numbers are called **absolute**. In Figure 4.9, for example, the relocatable addresses are underlined, while the absolute, or unchanging, locations are not. The assembler uses a simple rule to distinguish relocatable from absolute quantities. Any word that contains an address within the program is relocatable and must change when the program is moved. For example, the address A is relocatable. On the other hand, data, numerical operation codes or fixed addresses in memory are absolute. The following example shows where a program uses a fixed address in memory:

```
         .TITLE   ABSOLUTE EXAMPLE
         .ENABL   AMA
ST:      MOV      10,A
         HALT
A:       .BLKW    1
         .END     ST
```

This program contains an absolute address (000010) and a relocatable address (A). If the program is relocated to begin at memory cell 004000, then A is the symbolic name of memory cell 004010. In contrast, 000010 is an absolute address. No matter where the program is relocated, the processor will fetch the contents of memory cell 000010 when the MOV instruction is executed. In most assembly language programs, the use of an absolute address is an error, unless it is used for special system purposes.

Modern large computer systems attempt to allocate memory to programs at the last possible moment. This allows the allocation decision to be tailored to the current workload of the computer system. The relocation technique described previously allows the allocation decision to be made after the program is assembled. Some computer systems attempt to delay the decision until the program is actually executing. This involves techniques such as paging, segmentation, and virtual memory, which are beyond the scope of this book. Memory is an important computer resource, and the management of this resource is a fairly complex topic.

4.6 RUNNING A SAMPLE PROGRAM

A Sample Program

As an illustration, the following program will be assembled, relocated, and executed:

```
            .TITLE  SAMPLE PROGRAM
            .ENABL  AMA
    ST:     MOV     #7,A
            MOV     #4,B
            MOV     A,C
            SUB     B,C
            HALT
    A:      .BLKW   1
    B:      .BLKW   1
    C:      .BLKW   1
            .END    ST
```

The first step is to load the MACRO assembler program into memory and execute it. (On a large PDP-11, the MACRO-11 program would almost certainly be stored on a magnetic disk of some kind. On a small system, the user might have to put a paper tape containing MACRO-11 into the paper tape reader).

The MACRO-11 program reads the user's assembly language program and translates it into a relocatable machine language program called an **object program**. (An object program is simply a machine language program in which the relocatable numbers are marked in some way.) During the translation process, MACRO-11 prints the following information for the user:

```
SAMPLE PROGRAM    RT-11 MACRO V03-02B        14:51:11   PAGE 1

    1                                              .TITLE  SAMPLE PROGRAM
    2                                              .ENABL  AMA
    3    000000  012737  000007  000032' ST:       MOV     #7,A
    4    000006  012737  000004  000034'           MOV     #4,B
    5    000014  013737  000032' 000036'           MOV     A,C
    6    000022  163737  000034' 000036'           SUB     B,C
    7    000030  000000                            HALT
    8    000032                          A:        .BLKW   1
    9    000034                          B:        .BLKW   1
   10    000036                          C:        .BLKW   1
   11            000000'                           .END    ST
```

Sec. 4.6   *Running a Sample Program*   83

```
SYMBOL TABLE

A       000032R         B       000034R
C       000036R         ST      000000R

ERRORS DETECTED:  0
FREE CORE:  18096.  WORDS
```

The assembly language program is printed on the right side, and the object program is printed on the left. The first memory cell used is (relocatable) memory cell 000000. The relocatable words in the object program are followed by an apostrophe (').

Below the program listings, MACRO-11 lists the symbol table. In the symbol table, relocatable numbers are followed by the letter R. The symbol table entry for A is 000032R.

Object Output

In addition to the listing, MACRO-11 also outputs a machine-readable copy of the object program to some output device such as a paper tape punch or a disk. The object program that is produced by the assembler contains the following kinds of information.

1. The size of the program
2. Address and contents of each location to be loaded into memory
3. A code of some sort indicating which locations contain relocatable values that must be changed
4. The (unrelocated) address where the program begins

Linking and Loading

The next step is to load and execute a program called LINK (for linker). One of the linker's functions is to relocate programs. To accomplish this, the linker inputs the object program that was created by MACRO-11, adds a constant to all the addresses to relocate the program to an unused area in memory. It then outputs the relocated program, adding the constant to all of the relocatable locations. In addition, the linker prints information such as the following:

```
                SECTION ADDR    SIZE
                . ABS.  000000  001000
                        001000  000040
```

The first line indicates that something is using a section of memory called . ABS. which occupies memory cells from 000000 up to (but not including) memory cell 001000. (The something is the RT-11 operating system which uses memory cells 000000 through 000776 for special purposes.) The second line indicates that an unnamed section of memory occupies memory cells from 001000 up to (but not including) 001040. This is the machine language program that has been relocated to run in memory cells 001000 through 001036. This completes the link step.

The final step is to load and execute the relocated program that was created by the linker. In order to see if the program ran correctly, it is necessary to dump the contents of memory cells 001000 through 001036 after the program halts. The memory dump produces the following:

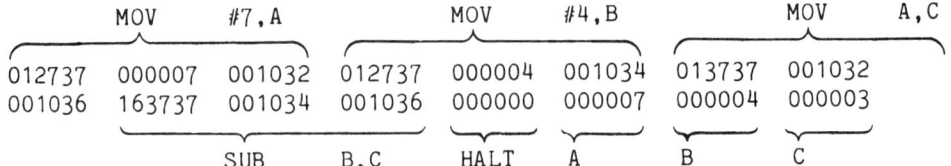

Memory cell C contains 000003 indicating that the program generated an answer that happens to be correct. Notice that the number 001000 was added to the contents of each of the relocatable locations.

EXERCISE SET 2

1 The following FORTRAN programs appeared in the exercises at the end of Chapter 3 (pages 60-61). Translate each program into assembly language.

(a)
```
INTEGER J,K,L
J=15
K=22
L=J-K+9
STOP
END
```

(b)
```
INTEGER J,K
J=27
K=-J
STOP
END
```

(c)
```
INTEGER J,K,L
J=5
K=9
L=3*(J+K)
STOP
END
```

(d)
```
INTEGER J,K
J=5
K=J*32
STOP
END
```

(e)
```
INTEGER J,K
J=5
K=J*23
STOP
END
```

2 In a previous exercise (page 77, exercise 3), the following program was hand assembled beginning at memory cell 001000. Hand assemble the program beginning at memory cell 000000 and then relocate the program so that it begins in memory cell 002000. When the program executes, will the same number be left in memory cell LAST?

```
            .TITLE  EXERCISE
            .ENABL  AMA
    FIRST:  MOV     #LAST,LAST
            SUB     #FIRST,LAST
            ADD     #2,LAST
            HALT
    LAST:   .BLKW   1
            .END    FIRST
```

3 The following is a nonsense program that uses instruction modification. However, the program will terminate normally. Hand assemble this program beginning at memory cell 000000, relocate the program so that it begins at memory cell 001000, and then specify the contents of memory cells 001000 through 001020 when the program halts (and it will halt).

```
             .TITLE  HARD
             .ENABL  AMA
    STRT:    ADD     #101000,BAD
    BAD:     ADD     #NOHOPE,NOHOPE
    NOHOPE:  MOV     BAD,STRT
             .END    STRT
```

CHAPTER 5

PROGRAM CONTROL FEATURES

5.1 INTRODUCTION

As anyone experienced with computers knows, the whole purpose for having high-speed circuitry is so that programs or sections of programs can be executed repeatedly. Repeated sections of programs are called **loops.** In order to have a loop, there must be some way of transferring control from one part of the program to another. In FORTRAN or BASIC, the GO TO statement can be used to achieve this transfer of control. In order to be executed, these statements are translated into **branch** and **jump** instructions that are part of the PDP-11 machine and assembly language.

Another important point of any loop is the determination of how many times the instructions are to be repeated. In order to make such determinations, the computer must have some decision-making capability. The computer can then determine whether to go back to loop again, or to continue on without looping, or even to jump out of the loop from somewhere inside. In FORTRAN and BASIC, this can be done with IF statements. Such statements are translated into conditional branch instructions that are part of the machine language instruction set of the PDP-11.

Another topic discussed in this chapter is the use of **processor registers.** The processor registers are special locations that can hold 16-bit words of data. Because they are faster than memory, their use can improve program speed. In addition, some special operations require using the processor registers.

Finally, this chapter will look at how to write subroutines for the PDP-11.

Although this topic is covered in considerable detail in Chapter 9, we will take a brief look at simple cases of subroutine use. As we shall see, the PDP-11 has instructions to which the CALL or GO SUB statements and the RETURN statement of FORTRAN and BASIC are translated. The reader is shown how to use subroutines to read and print numbers.

5.2 LOOPING

An Example of Looping

Figure 5.1 contains program segments designed to compute the sum of the integers from 1 to 10 (decimal).* After each program segment is executed, memory cell K will contain $1+2+3+4+5+6+7+8+9+10 = 55$ (decimal) or 000067 (octal). Notice that the examples shown in Figure 5.1 are program segments rather than complete programs. It is therefore assumed that certain lines of program precede and follow the segments. For this reason, the STOP and END statements are missing from the BASIC and FORTRAN segments. Similarly, the HALT instruction and all of the assembly directives (.ENABL, .BLKW, and .END) are missing from the assembly language segment.

Figure 5.1   Simple Loop

BASIC	FORTRAN	Assembly Language	
20 LET K=0	K=0	MOV	#0,K
30 LET J=10	J=10	MOV	#12,J
40 LET K=K+J	40 K=K+J	LOOP: ADD	J,K
50 LET J=J-1	J=J-1	SUB	#1,J
60 IF J<>0 THEN 40	IF (J.NE.0) GO TO 40	TST	J
70 ...	70 ...	BNE	LOOP
		AFTER: ...	

Testing and Branching

The last two instructions in the assembly language segment are TST J and BNE LOOP. The machine language translation of these instructions tells the processor to test the value of J, and then branch to (GO TO) statement LOOP if memory cell J does not contain 0. If J contains 0, the processor will execute the next sequential instruction (that is, the instruction contained in memory cell AFTER). The first 11 (octal) times that the branch instruction is executed, J will be greater than 0, and the processor will branch to LOOP to repeat the loop

---

*Again we are assuming an "integer only" form of BASIC, and integer variables in FORTRAN.

again. On the twelfth (octal) time, J will be 0 and no branch will occur. Instead, the processor will execute the next sequential instruction which begins in memory cell AFTER.

The process of performing a conditional branch involves two separate processes that require two separate instructions. First, a value must be tested, and then a conditional branch can occur based upon the value tested. In this case, the instruction TST J tests the value of J. Then, the BNE LOOP instruction branches to location LOOP if the tested value is *not equal to* 0. Note that the BNE instruction itself does not state what is being compared with 0. The assumption is that this instruction will be preceded by a test such as TST J.

Several other things about Figure 5.1 should be mentioned. First, notice that the octal number 12 was used on the second line of the assembly language segment. When FORTRAN or BASIC programs are converted to assembly language, decimal constants should be converted to octal constants. Notice that symbolic addresses (statement labels) in BASIC or FORTRAN must be numbers, while symbolic addresses in assembly language must begin with a letter. It is strongly recommended that assembly language programmers select meaningful names for symbolic addresses. Such names can be a very important aid in understanding and debugging an assembly language program. Most BASIC dialects require a symbolic address (statement label) on each line. FORTRAN and assembly language do not have this restriction. Finally, each BASIC or FORTRAN statement in Figure 5.1 was translated into one or two lines of assembly language. It frequently requires many lines of assembly language to implement a single BASIC or FORTRAN statement.

Additional Instructions

The BR (for BRanch) instruction is an unconditional branch instruction. It is analogous to the GO TO statement in FORTRAN or BASIC.

BASIC	FORTRAN	MACRO-11	
40 GOTO 80	40 GO TO 80	OLDADR: BR	NEWADR

The operation code is BR. The operand NEWADR is the symbolic address to which the processor branches. The machine language instruction that is produced from this assembly language statement causes the processor to fetch its next operation code from memory cell NEWADR. (The processor simply uses the information from the branch instruction to place the desired branch address in the program counter).

The BEQ (for Branch if EQual to 0) instruction is the opposite of the BNE instruction.

BASIC	FORTRAN	MACRO	
		TST	L
30 IF L=0 THEN 90	IF (L.EQ.0) GO TO 90	BEQ	LZERO
40 . . .	40 . . .	NEXT: . . .	

In the MACRO-11 program segment, the number contained in memory cell L is tested. If memory cell L contains 0, the processor will branch to memory cell LZERO. Otherwise, the next sequential instruction (beginning in memory cell NEXT) will be executed.

The Testing Process

As was the case with the BNE and BEQ instructions, each conditional branch requires that a value be tested before the branch can have meaning. In all the previous examples, this was accomplished with the TST instruction. There are, however, a number of other ways to test a value.

One of these ways is to perform an arithmetic operation. Every arithmetic instruction automatically tests its result as it is stored in the destination location. For example, the instruction ADD A,B automatically tests the value being stored in B. The result is almost as if the pair of instructions:

```
        ADD     A,B
        TST     B
```

were executed. Since this is true of all arithmetic instructions, the same applies to ADD #, SUB, SUB #, and (although no computation is performed) MOV and MOV #.

The advantage of this is that many times the TST instruction will be unnecessary. In fact, this happens to be the case in the example shown in Figure 5.1. Note that the instruction SUB #1,J is followed by TST J. Since the instruction SUB #1,J automatically tests the resulting value of J, the instruction TST J is redundant and can be eliminated. As a result, the program segment of Figure 5.1 can be shortened to:

```
                MOV     #0,K
                MOV     #12,J
        LOOP:   ADD     J,K
                SUB     #1,J
                BNE     LOOP
```

The computed result would be exactly the same.

As it turns out, this is not a freak situation. It is *usually* the case that the value being tested by a conditional branch is, in fact, the most recently computed number. Consequently, it is rare that the TST instruction is needed. The following is an example where the TST instruction is necessary:

BASIC	FORTRAN	MACRO	
20 LET K=K-4	K=K-4	SUB	#4,K
30 IF L=0 THEN 90	IF (L.EQ.0) GO TO 90	TST	L
40 . . .	. . .	BEQ	LZERO
		. . .	

5.3 SINGLE-OPERAND INSTRUCTIONS

Program Execution Time

In building computers, it is often inexpensive to add additional machine language instructions. It is significantly more expensive to speed up the processor or to add additional memory. As a result, modern computers typically have in excess of 100 different machine language instructions, many of which are unnecessary in the sense that their functions can be accomplished in other ways. However, these unnecessary instructions generally reduce program execution time and memory requirements. For example, only two of the three branch instructions described up to this point are absolutely necessary. A BNE instruction such as:

```
           TST    THETA
           BNE    GAMMA
NEXT:      ...
```

can always be replaced with a BEQ and a BR instruction. For example:

```
           TST    THETA
           BEQ    NEXT
           BR     GAMMA
NEXT:      ...
```

Both program segments will branch to GAMMA if the number contained in memory cell THETA is not equal to 0. If the number in THETA is 0, the instruction beginning at NEXT will be executed.

The Clear Instruction

In writing a program, it is frequently necessary to set the contents of a memory cell to 0. This can be accomplished with a MOV # instruction. For example:

```
           MOV    #0,ALPHA
```

This method requires a total of four memory operations—three fetches to fetch the instruction, and one store to execute the instruction. The same result can be achieved with a SUB instruction. For example:

```
           SUB    ALPHA,ALPHA
```

However, this approach requires six memory operations—three fetches to fetch the instruction, and two fetches and a store to execute the instruction.

To save time and space, the PDP-11 instruction set includes a CLR (for

CLeaR) instruction whose only purpose is to set a memory cell to 0. For example:

> CLR   ALPHA

will set the contents of memory cell ALPHA to 0. Assuming that the instruction is located at address 001012, and that ALPHA is the symbolic name for address 002000, the machine language translation of this instruction would be:

Address	Contents	Comment
001012	005037	CLR operation code
001014	002000	Address of memory cell to be cleared

This instruction requires only three memory operations—two fetches to fetch the instruction and one store to execute the instruction. In addition, the CLR instruction only occupies two words of memory instead of three, thus saving memory space.

The Increment Instruction

Another common function is adding 1 to the contents of a memory location. The instruction:

> ADD   #1,ALPHA

requires five memory operations—three fetches to fetch the instruction, and one fetch and one store to execute the instruction. This instruction can be replaced by the INC (for INCrement) instruction:

> INC   ALPHA

which increments the contents of ALPHA by 1. Assuming that the increment instruction and ALPHA are located at 001012 and 002000, respectively, the machine language translation of this instruction is:

Address	Contents	Comment
001012	005237	The INC operation code
001014	002000	Address of memory cell to be incremented

This instruction requires a total of four memory operations—two fetches to fetch the instruction, and one fetch and one store to execute the instruction.

Sec. 5.3 Single-Operand Instructions

The Decrement Instruction

Similarly, the DEC (for DECrement) instruction is used to subtract 1 from the contents of a memory cell. For example:

DEC   ALPHA

will decrement the contents of ALPHA by 1. The machine language translation of this instruction is:

Address	Contents	Comment
001012	005337	DEC operation code
001014	002000	Address of memory cell to be decremented

The Test Instruction

To complete the machine language translation for our new instructions of this type, consider:

TST   ALPHA

The machine language translation for this instruction is:

Address	Contents	Comment
001012	005737	TST operation code
001014	002000	Address of memory cell to be tested

Operation Codes

As the following table shows, the operation codes for these new instructions are close together*:

Symbolic Operation Code	Numerical Operation Code
CLR	005037
INC	005237
DEC	005337
TST	005737

*As before, the 37 on each of these operation codes indicates an addressing mode.

These four instructions belong to a group or **family** of instructions called **single-operand instructions.** Instructions in this family consist of a 16-bit operation code followed by a 16-bit address.

Using these instructions, it is again possible to rewrite the assembly language program that sums the integers from 1 to 10 (decimal). The original program is reproduced on the left side of Figure 5.2. The revised version is shown on the right. The machine language translation of the original program requires 15 words, but the revised program requires only 11. This is a significant savings in memory and in execution time.

Figure 5.2 Revised Simple Loop

```
              Original                    Revised

        MOV     #0,K              CLR     K
        MOV     #12,J             MOV     #12,J
LOOP:   ADD     J,K        LOOP:  ADD     J,K
        SUB     #1,J              DEC     J
        TST     J                 BNE     LOOP
        BNE     LOOP
```

Using these instructions, we can now see one of the most common ways for writing a loop for the PDP-11. Imagine a process that we wish to perform N times. The skeleton structure shown in Figure 5.3 is often the simplest way to

Figure 5.3 Common Loop Structure

```
        MOV     N,COUNT          ;INITIALIZE COUNTER
LOOP:   .
        .
        .
        Lines of program needed
        for the process that is
        to be repeated N times
        .
        .
        .
        DEC     COUNT            ;DECREMENT COUNTER
        BNE     LOOP             ;LOOP UNTIL COUNT = 0
```

construct the program. As we can see, the revised program in Figure 5.2 is, in fact, an example of this structure. Many examples to be found later will also follow this form.

5.4 MACHINE LANGUAGE CODING OF THE BRANCH INSTRUCTIONS

One-Word Instructions

Up to this point, no mention has been made of the machine language translation of the branch instructions. One would expect the translation of a branch instruction such as:

        BR   ALPHA

to occupy two memory cells—one for the 16-bit operation code and one for the 16-bit address. However, this is not the case.

It has been found that most branch instructions branch to a nearby memory cell. For example, a branch instruction in memory cell 001000 is much more likely to branch to memory cell 001020 than to memory cell 040000. Because of this, the PDP-11 branch instruction *packs* an operation code and the address into a single 16-bit memory cell. The left eight bits specify the operation code, and the eight bits on the right specify the relative branch address as a two's complement number from -128 to $+127$. The possible branch addresses are restricted so that it is only possible to branch backward up to 127 memory words and forward up to 128 memory words from the branch instruction.

To understand the branch instruction, it is necessary to represent the contents of a memory cell as a 16-bit binary number rather than as a 6-digit octal number. The binary representation of the BR instruction is as follows:

0 0 0 0 0 0 0 1	? ? ? ? ? ? ? ?
Operation Code	Displacement

The 8-bit displacement designates the branch address. The displacement is coded as shown in Figure 5.4. The following branch instruction will cause the processor to branch ahead three memory cells:

0 0 0 0 0 0 0 1	0 0 0 0 0 0 1 0
Operation Code	Displacement

The way this operates is that twice the signed value of the displacement is added to the program counter. The displacement is multiplied by 2 because the program counter must always be an even number. In this example, the signed value of the displacement is 0 0 0 0 0 0 1 0, or $+2$. Therefore $+4$ is added to the program counter. However, the normal instruction fetch has already added 2 to the program counter, so the total increment is six bytes or three words from the location of the branch instruction. In other words, if the branch instruction had been in location 0 0 1 0 0 6, the next instruction executed would be taken from $001006 + 6 = 001014$ octal.

Figure 5.4 Branch Displacement Table

Displacement	Meaning
10000000	Branch backward 127 (decimal) memory words
10000001	Branch backward 126 (decimal) memory words
10000010	Branch backward 125 (decimal) memory words
10000011	Branch backward 124 (decimal) memory words
. . .	
. . .	
11111101	Branch backward 2 (decimal) memory words
11111110	Branch backward 1 (decimal) memory words
11111111	Branch backward 0 (decimal) memory words
00000000	Branch forward 1 (decimal) memory words
00000001	Branch forward 2 (decimal) memory words
00000010	Branch forward 3 (decimal) memory words
00000011	Branch forward 4 (decimal) memory words
. . .	
. . .	
01111110	Branch forward 127 (decimal) memory words
01111111	Branch forward 128 (decimal) memory words

Example of Branch Instructions in Machine Language

Two special cases of the branch instruction should be mentioned. Consider first the instruction 000777 (octal). In octal, it is not clear that this is a branch instruction. To interpret the instruction, it is necessary to convert it to binary:

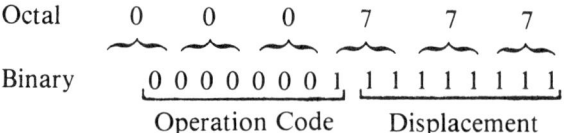

$$\text{Octal} \quad 0 \quad 0 \quad 0 \quad 7 \quad 7 \quad 7$$

$$\text{Binary} \quad \underbrace{0\ 0\ 0\ 0\ 0\ 0\ 0\ 1}_{\text{Operation Code}} \underbrace{1\ 1\ 1\ 1\ 1\ 1\ 1\ 1}_{\text{Displacement}}$$

The binary representation shows that this is a BR instruction that will branch backward zero memory cells. This is because the displacement is 1 1 1 1 1 1 1 1, which is equivalent to -1. Therefore, -2 is added to the program counter, canceling out the $+2$ that was added for the instruction fetch. This puts the program counter back where it started, at the address of the branch instruction. It is equivalent to the following:

BASIC	FORTRAN	MACRO
30 GOTO 30	30 GO TO 30	LOOP: BR LOOP

Neither the assembler nor the processor treats this infinite loop as an error.

The instruction 000400 is represented in binary as:

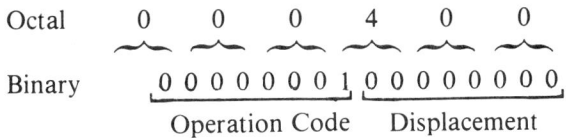

This instruction will branch to the instruction that immediately follows the branch instruction. Here the displacement is 0 so nothing extra is added to the program counter. Therefore, the processor simply proceeds to the next instruction. It is equivalent to:

BASIC	FORTRAN	MACRO
GOTO 30	GO TO 30	BR NEXT
30 . . .	30 . . .	NEXT: . . .

In assembly or machine language, such "do nothing" statements are often called **no-ops** (for no operation).

Because of the way the operation code and the displacement are coded, any instruction between 000400 and 000777 will be an unconditional branch (BR) instruction. Similarly, instructions between 001000 and 001377 octal are BNE instructions, and those between 001400 and 001777 are BEQ instructions.

Relative Addressing

The displacement in any branch instruction tells the processor to branch so many memory cells from the memory cell that contains the branch instruction. This method of specifying an address is called **relative addressing.** In contrast, all of the other instructions described up to this point (such as MOV) use **direct addressing.** That is, the actual 16-bit address is part of the instruction.

Computing displacements for branch instructions is awkward. Fortunately, the assembler will calculate the displacements for the programmer. In fact, the assembly language programmer can ignore the exact coding of the branch instructions if two points are remembered: (1) branch instructions occupy only one memory word; (2) it is only possible to branch backward 127 (decimal) words or forward 128 words from the branch instruction. If the programmer specifies a branch address that is too far away, the assembler will print an error message.

5.5 OTHER INSTRUCTIONS

The JMP Instruction

For long branches where the BR instruction will not reach, the JMP (for JuMP) instruction is used instead. For example, the following statement will cause an unconditional branch to memory cell ALPHA:

                    JMP   ALPHA

The machine language translation of this statement is straightforward. If the instruction and ALPHA are located at addresses 001006 and 002000, respectively, then the machine language translation would be:

Address	Contents	Comment
001006	000137	The JMP operation code
001010	002000	Branch address

For short branches, BR is preferable because it only occupies one word of memory and only requires one memory operation (a fetch). The JMP requires two words of memory and two fetches. To execute the jump instruction, the processor simply copies the branch address into the program counter.

The JMP instruction must sometimes be used for loops. For example, the following segment executes the indicated statements 100 (octal) times:

```
            MOV     #100,COUNT
LOOP:       ...
            Statements to be executed 100 times
            ...
            DEC     COUNT
            BNE     LOOP
```

However, if there are too many statements inside the loop, address LOOP will be more than 127 memory cells from the BNE instruction. In this case, the loop would have to be rewritten as:

```
            MOV     #100,COUNT
LOOP:       ...
            Statements to be executed 100 times
            ...
            DEC     COUNT
            BEQ     ENDLP
            JMP     LOOP
ENDLP:      ...
```

The CMP Instruction

The branch instructions described thus far can only test to see if a memory cell contains 0 or not. Some method is needed to determine if one number is greater than another. That is, an assembly language equivalent of the following statements is needed:

> FORTRAN   IF (J.GT.K) GO TO 50
>
> BASIC   IF J>K THEN 50

The desired result is achieved with the following pair of instructions:

```
              CMP    J,K
              BGT    JGTK
       NEXT:  ...
```

These statements tell the processor to branch to JGTK if the number in memory cell J is greater than the number in memory cell K. If the number in J is equal to or less than the number in K, no branch occurs and the next sequential instruction that begins in NEXT is executed.

The CMP (for CoMPare) instruction is similar to the TST instruction in that its only function is to test something. The instruction CMP J,K causes the processor to test whether (1) the number in J is greater than the number in K, (2) the number in J is equal to the number in K, or (3) the number in J is less than the number in K. The CMP instruction does not alter the contents of J or K. The BGT (for Branch if Greater Than) causes the processor to branch if the first operand of the compare instruction (in this example, J) is greater than the second operand (in this example, K). Numbers are interpreted to be signed numbers in the two's complement number system and are compared in the normal algebraic manner.

Machine Language Translation of the CMP Instruction

The machine language translation of the CMP instruction is straightforward. If the CMP instruction, J, and K are located at addresses 001006, 002000, and 003000, respectively, then the assembly language statement:

```
              CMP    J,K
```

would be translated into:

Address	Contents	Comment
001006	023737	The CMP operation code
001010	002000	Address of the first number
001012	003000	Address of the second number

CMP belongs to the **double-operand family** of instructions that includes such instructions as MOV, ADD, and SUB. Instructions in this family can be identified by the fact that the second octal digit from the left is not equal to 0. (For example, the operation code 043737 has not been discussed. However, the presence of the 04 indicates that this is a double-operand instruction.)

Signed Conditional Branches

The BGT (for Branch if Greater Than) instruction belongs to a family of four **signed branch instructions.** The complete family is as follows:

Symbolic Operation Code	Numerical Operation Code	Description
BGT	003000-003377	Branch if the first operand is Greater Than the second
BGE	002000-002377	Branch if the first operand is Greater than or Equal to the second
BLT	002400-002777	Branch if the first operand is Less Than the second
BLE	003400-003777	Branch if the first operand is Less than or Equal to the second

The machine language translation of each of these instructions is similar to that of the BR instruction. The 16-bit binary instruction consists of an 8-bit operation code and an 8-bit displacement. As a result, it is only possible to branch backward 127 memory words or forward 128.

The preceding four branch instructions can be used after arithmetic instructions such as ADD, INC, TST, and so on. In such cases, the result is compared to 0. For example, the instruction sequence:

```
        TST     X
        BGT     ALPHA
```

will cause a branch to ALPHA if the number in memory cell X is greater than 0.

Similarly, the BEQ and BNE instructions can be used with the CMP instruction to test if the operands of the CMP are equal or not equal. Thus:

```
        CMP     A,B
        BEQ     ALPHA
```

will cause a branch to ALPHA if the contents of A and B are equal.

In addition, several branch instructions can follow a single CMP instruc-

Sec. 5.5   Other Instructions   101

tion. For example, the statements:

                CMP   J,K
                BLT   ALPHA
                BGT   BETA
                BR   GAMMA

will cause the processor to branch to ALPHA, BETA, or GAMMA, depending on whether the number in memory cell J is less than, greater than, or equal to the number in memory cell K, respectively. Notice that the last instruction is a BR instruction. It should be obvious that changing the BR instruction to a BEQ instruction will not affect the result. The choice is really a question of programming style.

Long Branches

For a long branch, a JMP instruction must be used. Assume that the programmer wishes to branch to statement LOWER if the number in memory cell A is less than the number in memory cell B. The programmer would normally write:

                CMP   A,B
                BLT   LOWER

If the memory cell LOWER is too far away, these statements would have to be rewritten as:

                CMP   A,B
                BGE   NOTLO
                JMP   LOWER
        NOTLO: ...

Notice that BGE (not BGT) is the opposite of BLT. BGT is the opposite of BLE.

Order of Comparison

The order of the operands in the CMP instruction is important. That is, the effect of the instructions:

                CMP   A,B
                BGT   ALPHA

is very different from the effect of:

                CMP   B,A
                BGT   ALPHA

The first pair of instructions branches when the number in memory cell A is greater than the number in memory cell B, while the second pair branches when the number in B is greater than the number in A.

Number signs (#) may be used with the CMP instruction. For example:

    CMP #21,A
    BLT ALPHA

will branch to ALPHA if the number 000021 is less than the contents of memory cell A. The presence of the number sign changes the operation code from 023737 to 022737. The number sign may also be used on the second operand. For example, the instruction:

    CMP WAGE,#1000
    BGT GETTAX

will branch to GETTAX if the number in memory cell WAGE is greater than 001000. In this case, the operation code becomes 023727.

These operation codes exhibit an obvious pattern. The presence of a number sign on the first operand changes the middle two digits from 37 to 27. (The compare operation code is changed from 023737 to 022737). The presence of the number sign on the second operand changes the last two digits from 37 to 27. (The operation code 023737 becomes 023727).

5.6 MACHINE LANGUAGE OPERATION CODES

Operand Codes

In point of fact, the different forms of the CMP instruction bring to light a very important fact about machine language codes for single- and double-operand instructions in the PDP-11 computer. The reality is that there is only one CMP instruction. Its machine language representation is 02ssdd. The letters ss (for source operand) represent two octal digits that indicate where the first or source operand can be found. The letters dd (for destination operand) represent two octal digits that specify where the second or destination operand can be found.

The ss and dd values tell the processor how to interpret the contents of the memory cells that follow the operation code. For example, assume that the following CMP instruction begins in memory cell 001006:

Address	Contents
001006	02ssdd
001010	002000
001012	003000

Sec. 5.6   *Machine Language Operation Codes*   103

If ss is 27, the processor treats the contents of 001010 as the number 002000. This is called an **immediate operand** because it is fetched immediately as part of the instruction. If ss is 37, then the contents of 001010 is treated as an address, and the contents of memory cell 002000 is fetched. In a similar manner, the numbers substituted for dd (27 or 37) tell the processor whether to interpret the contents of 001012 as a number (dd replaced with 27) or the address of a number (dd replaced with 37).

Application to Other Instructions

This same coding applies to other instructions as well. For example, the MOV operation code is represented as 01ssdd, and the CLR operation code is 0050dd. It is important to realize that a number of useless instructions can be generated. For example, the assembly language statement:

         CMP   #20,#15

will generate the following machine language instruction:

        Address   *Contents*
        001006   022727
        001010   000020
        001012   000015

This is a useless instruction in the sense that the constant 000020 is always greater than the constant 000015.

Other examples of silly instructions include:

        MOV   X,#24
        ADD   #5,#102
        INC   #1000

Neither the assembler nor the processor treats these silly instructions as errors.

Operand Order

In fact, for all of the instructions discussed so far, except CMP, it usually makes no sense to put a number sign on the second or destination argument. The effect would simply be to store the result on top of the number. On the other hand, when a compare instruction is used with an immediate operand, it may be preferable to make the immediate operand the second (destination) operand. For example, assume that we wish to branch to memory location ALPHA if the number in memory cell X is less than 000020. There are two methods for coding this sequence:

	Method One		Method Two
CMP	X,#20	CMP	#20,X
BLT	ALPHA	BGT	ALPHA

The first method branches to ALPHA if the number in memory cell X is less than 20. The second method branches to ALPHA if 20 is greater than the number in X. Obviously, the effect of the two methods is identical. However, it has been the author's experience that fewer errors are made when the first method is used.

While the loop structure shown in Figure 5.3 is very simple, and perhaps the commonest in the PDP-11, there are some disadvantages. The main disadvantage is that the loop is controlled by a counter that counts backward from N to 0. Often it is necessary to have a variable that increases in value. While this can always be accommodated by adding an extra variable, it may be desirable to write a program in a way that closely mimics the BASIC or FORTRAN FOR or DO loops.

The structure in Figure 5.5 shows how the FOR or DO loop could be mimicked. Note that assembly language does not have the complex loop structures of the higher-level languages. Loops must be constructed with the simple instructions already described.

Figure 5.5 *Forward-Counting Loop Structure*

BASIC	FORTRAN	MACRO	
30 FOR I=1 TO 20	DO 70 I=1,20	MOV	#1,I
.	.	LOOP: .	
.	.	.	
.	.	.	
70 NEXT I	70 CONTINUE	INC	I
		CMP	I,#24
		BLE	LOOP

EXERCISE SET 1

1. Hand assemble each of the following statements. In each case, the resulting machine language instruction should begin in address 001000. Assume that the symbol table entries for the symbolic addresses ALPHA, BETA, and DELTA are 001004, 002000, and 003000, respectively.

   (a) TST   DELTA   (b) CLR   BETA

   (c) INC   DELTA   (d) BR   ALPHA

   (e) BNE   ALPHA   (f) BGT   ALPHA

   (g) JMP   DELTA   (h) CMP   BETA,DELTA

   (i) CMP   #20,BETA   (j) CMP   BETA,#20

2 How many memory fetches and stores are required to execute each of the instructions in (1)? Remember to include the fetches required to fetch the instruction.

3 Extend the entries in Figure 5.4 to show the 8-bit displacements required to branch backward from 3 (decimal) memory words to 20 (decimal) memory words.

4 The following program will compute the sum of the integers from 1 through 10. Hand assemble the program beginning at memory cell 000000 and then relocate the program to memory cell 001000.

```
               .TITLE   SUM
               .ENABL   AMA
     BEGIN:    MOV      #10,COUNT
               CLR      SUM
     LOOP:     ADD      COUNT,SUM
               DEC      COUNT
               BNE      LOOP
               HALT
     SUM:      .BLKW    1
     COUNT:    .BLKW    1
               .END     BEGIN
```

5.7 PROCESSOR REGISTERS

Definition

In the previous sections, we have discussed memory as consisting of a large number of locations where data could be stored. In addition to memory, virtually every computer has a few special locations for storing data. These locations are usually an integral part of the processor, and are called **processor registers.**

Some of the processor registers may perform functions that are not apparent to the programmer, such as temporarily holding data or addresses as they are transmitted to or from memory. Other registers may be accessible to the computer program and used for various purposes. In particular, the PDP-11 has eight processor registers that are designated register 0 through register 7. While registers 6 and 7 serve special purposes, the other six registers, 0 through 5, are for general use and can be used just like memory locations to hold 16-bit binary numbers.

Applications

In later chapters we will see some other uses for the processor registers, but for now we will examine their use as extra places to put data. One might ask at this point what the need is for six extra places to put data when even the smallest PDP-11 memories allow for thousands of locations. The answer is that there is a considerable advantage of using processor registers instead of memory.

The first advantage is that processor registers are much faster. Since they are an integral part of the processor, data can be accessed from them as much as 10 times as fast as from memory.

The second advantage is that since there are only a few processor registers, you do not need a 16-bit address to identify which register you are referencing. Instead, registers can be identified by modification of the operation codes. As a result, while the instruction to move the contents of memory location A to memory location B takes *three* words, a move from one register to another can be done with a *one*-word instruction.

There are two benefits from the shorter instruction size. First your program uses less memory. This may be important for large programs. Second there are fewer memory fetches needed to access the shorter instruction. This gives a further enhancement of the speed advantage. The result is that register-to-register instructions are about four times faster (overall) than memory-to-memory instructions.

Processor Register Instructions

All of the data-handling instructions that we have used so far can be used with processor registers as well as with memory. These instructions are MOV, ADD, SUB, INC, DEC, CLR, TST, and CMP. Recalling the discussion of operands on page 102, these instructions use the code 27 for immediate data, and 37 for an addressed location in memory. Similarly, the code 0n refers to the contents of register n. For example, 03 would refer to register 3. (Note that since one octal digit is used to specify the register, it is possible to choose any of the eight registers.)

Recall that the MOV operation code is represented as 01ssdd. Thus, the operation code 010203 would move the contents of register 2 to register 3. (Note that all registers contain full 16-bit words. Therefore, odd-numbered registers can be used, whereas odd-numbered memory addresses cannot.) To see this example more clearly, let us compare the register move to the memory move:

Register-to-Register Move	Memory-to-Memory Move
010203	013737
	002000
	003000

Note that since the register move does not refer to any memory addresses, it requires only one word instead of three.

Assembly Language Notation

The question that arises at this point is how to designate register operations in assembly language. The answer is that a special character, namely the percent sign (%), is used to designate registers. In other words, %0 means register 0, %1 means register 1, and so on. Therefore, to designate the previous register move, we would use the assembly language statement:

                    MOV   %2,%3

Following this scheme, we can see what the revised program of Figure 5.2 would look like if processor registers 0 and 1 were used instead of memory cells J and K. Figure 5.6 shows the comparison. When this program was originally introduced, we remarked that we had compressed it to 11 words of machine language. By using registers for data instead of memory, the program is reduced to six words of machine language and will execute much faster.

Figure 5.6 Simple Loop Using Registers

Memory Format			Register Format		
	CLR	K		CLR	%1
	MOV	#12,J		MOV	#12,%0
LOOP:	ADD	J,K	LOOP:	ADD	%0,%1
	DEC	J		DEC	%0
	BNE	LOOP		BNE	LOOP

A particular point to notice is that the second instruction, MOV #12,%0, combines an immediate operand with a register operand. This is permissible in virtually every meaningful combination. If this instruction were translated into machine language beginning at address 001200, the result would be as follows:

Machine Language		Assembly Language	
Address	Contents	Op Code	Operand
001200	012700	MOV	#12,%0
001202	000012		

The source operand code, 27, indicates an immediate operand. The destination operand code, 00, indicates register 0. This is a two-word instruction because a word is needed for the immediate operand. In general, instructions require three, two, or one word(s) if there are two, one, or no memory addresses or immediate operands. The examples in Figure 5.7 illustrate the mixing of different kinds of operands, and how many words each instruction required.

Figure 5.7 Various Operand Combinations

```
        MOV    A,B          Three words
        ADD    #12,%0       Two words
        SUB    A,%3         Two words
        MOV    %0,B         Two words
        CMP    %1,%4        One word
        CMP    %1,#23       Two words
```

Standard Notation

A final point to note about register notation is that the use of the percent sign makes the program look a little strange. The reason is probably psychological, but the use of the percent sign seems to make programs confusing and hard to read. Things would be much more understandable if symbols such as R0, R1, R2, and so on were used to indicate the registers. To show this, the example of Figure 5.6 is reshown in Figure 5.8 using these symbols instead of the percent sign symbols.

Figure 5.8 Simple Loop with R Symbols

```
        Percent Signs                          Letters

               CLR    %1                         CLR    R1
               MOV    #12,%0                     MOV    #12,R0
        LOOP:  ADD    %0,%1              LOOP:   ADD    R0,R1
               DEC    %0                         DEC    R0
               BNE    LOOP                       BNE    LOOP
```

The problem with this is that symbols such as R0 and R1 are just ordinary symbols; so the assembler would normally assume they referred to addresses. There is, however, a means of equating these symbols to the registers. At the beginning of the program (or at least before any reference to the symbols), the following lines must appear:

```
        R0=%0
        R1=%1
        R2=%2
```

and so on for whichever registers your program uses. These lines are typed just as they appear, beginning, normally, in column 1. Some assemblers on other computers employ an assembly directive such as EQU to accomplish the task of equating symbols. If you are using the RT-11 operating system, all eight registers can be given symbolic names with the following two lines:

```
        .MCALL   .REGDEF
        .REGDEF
```

.MCALL is an assembly directive that fetches packages of code, called **macros,** from the system library. .REGDEF is a package of eight lines of code that contains the symbol definitions R0 = %0, R1 = %1, and so on. The second line, which is simply .REGDEF, actually causes the fetched code to be inserted into the program. In later versions of the assembler, the symbols R0, R1, and so on, are predefined to refer to the processor registers. Therefore, with these assemblers, there is no need either to define the register symbols or to invoke the .REGDEF macro.

Register 6

Previously we stated that while there are eight processor registers, only the first six are normally put to general use. The reason is that registers 6 and 7 serve special purposes. Casual modification of either of these registers is likely to cause the PDP-11 to produce unforeseen results or even to stop functioning. Although the exact use of these registers is complex and is discussed later in this text, they are introduced here to complete the discussion on registers.

Registers 6 and 7 are both used by the PDP-11 computer as pointers into special areas of memory. Register 6 points into an area of memory called the **stack.** Certain operations in the computer require saving data temporarily. Many of these operations automatically store the data in the stack area. For example, the instruction JSR (which we will see in the next section) saves the return address in the stack. Since the stack is not a fixed area of memory but is under the programmer's control, there must be some way of indicating where the stack is. Register 6 is used for this purpose.

When using the RT-11 operating system, the stack is normally located in the area of memory preceding 001000. That is one reason why RT-11 usually relocates programs to start at 001000 rather than 000000. If you are not using an operating system, it may be necessary for you to set aside your own area for the stack. You would then have to move the stack address into register 6.

Obviously, it would be a very bad idea to place random data in register 6. The next time the system tried to use the stack, it might end up writing data over your program; or worse yet, if register 6 contained an odd number, the system might try to place a word at an odd address. Such an addressing error usually causes a transfer of control to an error routine. However, the transfer of control causes words to be placed in the stack which would cause another addressing error. Therefore, if register 6 is odd, the machine will just halt.

Because of the special use for register 6, it is not normally designated R6 but rather SP for **stack pointer.** This is simply done by the line of code SP = %6. Recall that the names R0, R1, and so on are just ordinary symbolic names, as is SP.

Register 7: The Program Counter

Register 7 is also used as a pointer in memory. However, register 7 is even more important than the SP because register 7 is the program counter. Since register 7 is special, it is not normally referred to as R7 but by the symbol PC (for **program counter**). To do this, the line PC = %7 would have to appear in your program.

Because of its use, the value of the PC must never be haphazardly changed. Any modification of the PC will have the effect of a program jump. In fact, the effect of the instruction MOV #A,PC is exactly the same as JMP A. The latter is preferred, however, because it is more straightforward and therefore less likely to be misunderstood and perhaps lead to strange errors.

The fact that the program counter is accessible as a processor register is quite useful to PDP-11 programming. This will be seen more clearly in later chapters. An example of this is the fact that operand codes 27 and 37 are used for immediate operands and directly addressed operands. In fact, the 7 in each of these codes refers to register 7, the PC. This is because the PC is "pointing" to the word where the data or address is located. This is explained in more detail in Chapter 7.

EXERCISE SET 2

1. Hand assemble each of the following statements. In each case the resulting machine language instruction should begin at address 001000. Assume that the symbol table entry for the symbolic address BETA is 002000.

   (a) CMP   R2,R4   (b) CMP   R3,BETA

   (c) MOV   BETA,R5   (d) TST   R4

   (e) CLR   R3   (f) INC   R0

   (g) DEC   BETA   (h) SUB   #20,R2

   (i) ADD   R3,R1   (j) ADD   R4,BETA

2. How many memory fetches and stores are required to execute each of the instructions in Exercise 1? Remember to include the fetches required to fetch the instruction.

3. The following program will also compute the sum of the integers from 1 through 10. Hand assemble this program beginning at memory cell 000000 and then relocate it to memory cell 001000.

```
                    .TITLE  SUM
                    .ENABL  AMA
        R0=%0
        R1=%1
```

```
          BEGIN:   MOV    #10,R0
                   CLR    R1
          LOOP:    ADD    R0,R1
                   DEC    R0
                   BNE    LOOP
                   MOV    R1,SUM
                   HALT
          SUM:     .BLKW  1
                   .END   BEGIN
```

5.8 SUBROUTINES

Calling and Returning

The whole topic of subroutines is covered in considerable detail in Chapter 10. However, subroutines are being introduced at this point for two purposes. First, subroutines are important for the proper structure of programs, and what follows will enable the reader to write some simple subroutines. Second, Appendix B shows some input/output subroutines that can be incorporated in programs. Using these subroutines will allow the reader to start writing some more sophisticated programs.

There are two problems with subroutines. First, there must be some means of jumping to the subroutine. Second, there must be a means of jumping back to the calling program. In FORTRAN or BASIC, these operations are achieved by the CALL or GOSUB and the RETURN statements, which are translated into the following PDP-11 instructions. To call the subroutine whose name is SUB, the PDP-11 instruction JSR PC,SUB is used. To return, the instruction is RTS PC. (These instructions could be written as JSR %7, SUB and RTS %7.)

The mnemonics JSR and RTS stand for Jump to SubRoutine and Return from Subroutine. The symbol PC stands for the program counter as described in the previous section. As noted there, the line PC = %7 must appear in your program *before* either JSR PC,SUB or RTS PC is used, unless your version of the assembler has PC predefined.

Input and Output

Appendix B contains some input/output subroutines called RNUM and PNUM. Two versions of each subroutine are given. The choice depends upon the operating system being used. RNUM reads one octal number and returns with the 16-bit value in R0. PNUM prints out the octal value of the contents of R0. Therefore, to read a number and store its value in X, execute the instructions:

```
            JSR     PC,RNUM
            MOV     R0,X
```

To print out the value of X:

```
            MOV     X,R0
            JSR     PC,PNUM
```

Of course, the subroutine RNUM and PNUM must be copied from Appendix B and be included as part of your program.

Calling a subroutine is analogous to taking a temporary detour. For example, the following main program segment is designed to read two numbers and place the sum in memory cell SUM:

```
;MAIN PROGRAM SEGMENT
            .
            .
            .
            JSR     PC,RNUM
            MOV     R0,SUM
            JSR     PC,RNUM
            ADD     R0,SUM
            .
            .
            .
;SUBROUTINE RNUM
RNUM:       MOV     R1,-(SP)
            .
            .
            .
            RTS     PC
```

When the processor executes the first JSR instruction, the processor temporarily stops executing the main program and transfers control to subroutine RNUM (see the arrow labeled A). When the processor reaches the RTS instruction at the end of RNUM, control is automatically transferred to the instruction following the JSR instruction, which in this case is a MOV instruction (see arrow B). When the processor executes the second JSR instruction, control is again transferred to subroutine RNUM (see arrow C). Finally the RTS instruction at the end of RNUM transfers control back to the ADD instruction in the main program (arrow D).

The JSR instruction, like the JMP instruction, causes a transfer of control. However, the JSR instruction also provides a mechanism for returning, at some later time, to the statement immediately following the JSR instruction. [As we shall see in Chapter 9, the JSR instruction actually uses the stack pointer (register 6) to save a copy of the program counter (register 7) in the area of memory called the stack.] The RTS instruction uses the information saved by the JSR in order to return.

It is possible for subroutines to be **nested.** For example, a main program could JSR to a subroutine called SUBA which in turn could JSR to a subroutine called SUBB. The RTS instruction at the end of SUBB will return control to SUBA. In turn, the RTS instruction at the end of SUBA will return control to the main program.

Subroutines represent a powerful technique for breaking a large program into more manageable parts. If misused, however, they can lead to errors that are difficult to detect. Assume, for example, that the programmer used the statement JMP RNUM instead of JSR PC,RNUM to transfer control to subroutine RNUM. The subroutine would execute properly until the RTS PC instruction at the end of the subroutine was reached. The RTS instruction assumes that a previous JSR instruction has saved the return address. Because no such address was saved, the RTS instruction will return control to a garbage address, producing unpredictable results. A similar result may occur if the programmer forgets to put a HALT instruction at the end of the main program and drops through the main program into the subroutine.

Subroutine Example

As an example of how to use RNUM and PNUM, and how you might write your own subroutine, let us look at the following problem. The problem is to read in three numbers and print out the largest. Although our method for solving this problem may seem far-fetched or overcomplicated, it is a generalizable technique that will actually simplify larger problems.

From what we have seen previously, we already have subroutines for reading and printing. In addition, we will write a subroutine that finds the larger of two numbers. We will call the subroutine MAX. When MAX is called, it will compare the value of R0 with R1, and put the larger number in R0. Figure 5.9 shows this subroutine. Now, the main program can call RNUM, MAX, and

Figure 5.9 Subroutine to Find the Maximum of Two Numbers

```
;
;SUBROUTINE MAX SETS R0 TO THE MAXIMUM OF R0 AND R1
;
MAX:    CMP     R0,R1           ;IS R0 GREATER THAN R1?
        BGE     MAXR            ;YES, RETURN R0 AS MAX
        MOV     R1,R0           ;NO, THEN R1 IS MAX
MAXR:   RTS     PC              ;RETURN TO MAIN PROGRAM
```

PNUM to read in three numbers and print the largest. Figure 5.10 shows what the main program would look like.

Figure 5.10 *Main Program for Finding the Largest of Three Numbers*

```
;
;THIS MAIN PROGRAM READS THREE OCTAL NUMBERS
;AND PRINTS THE LARGEST.
;
START:  JSR     PC,RNUM         ;READ A
        MOV     R0,R2           ;PUT A IN R2
        JSR     PC,RNUM         ;READ B
        MOV     R0,R1           ;PUT B IN R1
        JSR     PC,RNUM         ;READ C INTO R0
        JSR     PC,MAX          ;R0=MAX(B,C)
        MOV     R2,R1           ;PUT A IN R1
        JSR     PC,MAX          ;R0=MAX(A,R0)
        JSR     PC,PNUM         ;PRINT R0
        HALT                    ;STOP (SEE NEXT SECTION)
```

Finally, Figure 5.11 shows how the main program and the subroutines can be combined to form a single program. Notice that there is only one .END assembly directive and that it is placed after the last subroutine. For the time being, we will combine the main program and its subroutines into a single assembly language program. Later, in Chapter 10, we will see how assembly language programs that are independently assembled can be combined and even included with independently compiled FORTRAN programs.

Figure 5.11 *Complete Program for Finding the Largest of Three Numbers*

```
        .TITLE  LARGEST OF THREE
        .ENABL  AMA
R0=%0                           ;DEFINE REGISTER SYMBOLS
R1=%1                           ;THESE ARE THE ONLY ONES
R2=%2                           ;NEEDED BY THIS
SP=%6                           ;PROGRAM
PC=%7
;
;THIS MAIN PROGRAM READS THREE OCTAL NUMBERS
;AND PRINTS THE LARGEST.
;
START:  JSR     PC,RNUM         ;READ A
        MOV     R0,R2           ;PUT A IN R2
        JSR     PC,RNUM         ;READ B
        MOV     R0,R1           ;PUT B IN R1
        JSR     PC,RNUM         ;READ C INTO R0
        JSR     PC,MAX          ;R0=MAX(B,C)
        MOV     R2,R1           ;PUT A IN R1
        JSR     PC,MAX          ;R0=MAX(A,R0)
        JSR     PC,PNUM         ;PRINT R0
        HALT                    ;STOP (SEE NEXT SECTION)
```

Figure 5.11 *(continued)*

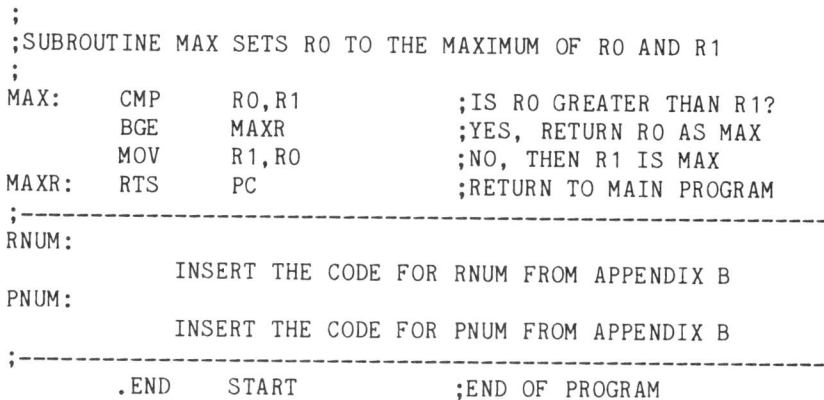

```
;
;SUBROUTINE MAX SETS R0 TO THE MAXIMUM OF R0 AND R1
;
MAX:    CMP     R0,R1           ;IS R0 GREATER THAN R1?
        BGE     MAXR            ;YES, RETURN R0 AS MAX
        MOV     R1,R0           ;NO, THEN R1 IS MAX
MAXR:   RTS     PC              ;RETURN TO MAIN PROGRAM
;-----------------------------------------------------------
RNUM:
                INSERT THE CODE FOR RNUM FROM APPENDIX B
PNUM:
                INSERT THE CODE FOR PNUM FROM APPENDIX B
;-----------------------------------------------------------
        .END    START           ;END OF PROGRAM
```

5.9 STOPPING YOUR PROGRAM IF USING RT-11 *(Optional Section)*

In previous examples, when a program ended, the HALT instruction was used. This instruction does, in fact, *stop* all action on the PDP-11. If you are using an operating system such as RT-11, it is not usually a good idea to stop the computer because subsequent use of the computer then usually requires reloading the whole operating system, reentering the date and time, and other bothersome manual operations. To solve this problem, there is a package of code called .EXIT which should be placed in your program instead of the HALT instruction. This returns the PDP-11 to control of the operating system.

This package of code can be accessed like .REGDEF by using the .MCALL directive (see page 109). Then all HALT instructions should be replaced with .EXIT. Figure 5.12 shows how the program in Figure 5.11 could be rewritten to use the RT-11 system properly. The program consists of a main program and the subroutines MAX, RNUM, and PNUM. RNUM and PNUM contain instructions that have not yet been described. The material in Chapter 8 is required to understand the internal operation of these subroutines. However, RNUM and PNUM may be used without understanding their internal operation.

Figure 5.12 Complete RT-11 Program for Finding the Largest of Three Numbers

```
            .TITLE   LARGEST OF THREE
            .ENABL   AMA
            .MCALL   .REGDEF,.EXIT   ;OBTAINS MACROS
            .REGDEF                  ;DEFINES REGISTERS
;
;THIS MAIN PROGRAM READS THREE OCTAL NUMBERS
;AND PRINTS THE LARGEST.
;
START:      JSR      PC,RNUM         ;READ A
            MOV      R0,R2           ;PUT A IN R2
            JSR      PC,RNUM         ;READ B
            MOV      R0,R1           ;PUT B IN R1
            JSR      PC,RNUM         ;READ C INTO R0
            JSR      PC,MAX          ;R0=MAX(B,C)
            MOV      R2,R1           ;PUT A IN R1
            JSR      PC,MAX          ;R0=MAX(A,R0)
            JSR      PC,PNUM         ;PRINT R0
            .EXIT                    ;EXIT TO RT-11 SYSTEM
;
;SUBROUTINE MAX SETS R0 TO THE MAXIMUM OF R0 AND R1
;
MAX:        CMP      R0,R1           ;IS R0 GREATER THAN R1?
            BGE      MAXR            ;YES, RETURN R0 AS MAX
            MOV      R1,R0           ;NO, THEN R1 IS MAX
MAXR:       RTS      PC              ;RETURN TO MAIN PROGRAM
;
;SUBROUTINE RNUM READS AN OCTAL NUMBER, LEAVING ITS
;BINARY VALUE IN R0
;
            .MCALL   .TTYIN,.TTYOUT  ;GET THE MACRO .TTYIN AND .TTYOUT
RNUM:       MOV      R1,-(SP)        ;SAVE R1 ON THE STACK
            CLR      R1              ;CLEAR ACCUMULATED RESULT
            .TTYOUT  #52             ;TYPE * AS A PROMPT
RNUML:      .TTYIN                   ;READ CHARACTER INTO R0
            CMPB     R0,#15          ;WAS IT CARRIAGE RETURN?
            BEQ      RNUME           ;YES, EXIT
            BIC      #177760,R0      ;NO, CHANGE CHARACTER TO DIGIT
            ASL      R1              ;MULTIPLY ACCUMULATION BY 2
            ASL      R1              ;AND 2 MORE = 4
            ASL      R1              ;AND 2 MORE = 8 (DECIMAL)
            ADD      R0,R1           ;ADD NEW DIGIT TO 8 * ACCUMULATION
            BR       RNUML           ;LOOP UNTIL END OF NUMBER
RNUME:      .TTYIN                   ;DUMMY READ OF LINE FEED
            MOV      R1,R0           ;PUT RESULT IN R0
            MOV      (SP)+,R1        ;RESTORE R1
            RTS      PC              ;RETURN
```

Figure 5.12 (continued)

```
;
;SUBROUTINE PNUM PRINTS OUT THE CONTENTS OF R0 IN OCTAL
;
        .MCALL  .TTYOUT         ;GET THE MACRO .TTYOUT
PNUM:   MOV     R0,-(SP)        ;SAVE R0 ON THE STACK
        MOV     R1,-(SP)        ;SAVE R1 ON THE STACK
        MOV     R2,-(SP)        ;SAVE R2 ON THE STACK
        MOV     R0,R1           ;R1 HOLDS NUMBER BEING PRINTED
        MOV     #6,R2           ;R2 COUNTS DIGITS
        MOV     #30,R0          ;R0 GETS 6 ASCII CODE BITS
        BR      PNUMM           ;FIRST DIGIT HAS ONLY ONE BIT
PNUML:  MOV     #6,R0           ;R0 GETS 4 ASCII CODE BITS
        ASL     R1              ;SHIFT R1 LEFT WITH HIGH BIT
        ROL     R0              ;  GOING TO C BIT AND THEN TO R0
        ASL     R1              ;GET THE SECOND BIT
        ROL     R0
PNUMM:  ASL     R1              ;GET THE THIRD BIT
        ROL     R0
        .TTYOUT                 ;PRINT THE OCTAL DIGIT
        DEC     R2              ;DECREMENT CHARACTER COUNT
        BNE     PNUML           ;AND LOOP SIX TIMES
        .TTYOUT #15             ;THEN OUTPUT CARRIAGE RETURN
        .TTYOUT #12             ;AND LINE FEED
        MOV     (SP)+,R2        ;RESTORE ALL THREE REGISTERS
        MOV     (SP)+,R1        ;FROM STACK
        MOV     (SP)+,R0
        RTS     PC              ;AND RETURN
;-----------------------------------------------------------
        .END    START           ;END OF PROGRAM
```

EXERCISE SET 3

1. Write an assembly language program that reads 20 numbers and prints out the sum of the 20 numbers. Use the read and print routines shown in Appendix B for doing the exercise.

2. (a) Write an assembly language program that reads three numbers. The program then prints out:

   0 if all three numbers are different
   1 if any two of the three are the same
   2 if all three numbers are the same

(b) Write the program so that it loops 20 times printing out the result for 20 sets of 3 numbers.

(c) Write the program so that it reads N, the number of sets of three numbers, and then loops N times.

3 Write an assembly language program that reads three numbers and prints them out in ascending order.

4 Write a program for exercise 3 using a subroutine that takes the number in R0 and R1 and swaps them if necessary so that the contents of R0 will be less than or equal to the contents of R1 upon exit.

5 Write an assembly language program that reads 20 numbers and prints out the largest. Use the subroutine MAX shown in Figure 5.9. Rewrite the program so that it reads N, the number of numbers, and then finds the largest of the N numbers.

6 An inventor constructs a robot whose sole purpose is to construct more robots just like itself. The way that the robot functions is that it spends two days collecting enough raw materials to build three robots. It spends the next three days producing robots, one per day. It then becomes inactive and does nothing more. Each new robot is immediately activated and goes through the five-day building cycle as did the original. Write a PDP-11 assembly language program that prints out the number of robots in existence at the end of each day for 20 days from the activation of the first robot. (*Hint:* Robots behave differently depending upon their age. Keep a tally of how many robots there are in each age group.)

CHAPTER 6

PDP-11 ARITHMETIC

6.1 INTRODUCTION

In previous chapters, we have seen how to add and subtract signed and unsigned numbers, and how to test and compare signed numbers. In this chapter, we will look at more of the properties of signed and unsigned numbers, as well as dealing with overflow, multiplication, division, and multiple precision. We will see more instructions, and see how they can simplify programming. We will also further examine the TST, CMP, and branch instructions and see how they operate.

6.2 SIGNED AND UNSIGNED NUMBERS

Operation and Interpretation

One of the advantages of the two's complement number system is that the same addition and subtraction algorithms can be used for both signed and unsigned numbers. (This is not true of some other signed number systems used in various computers.) Although this result may seem remarkable, it can be illustrated quite easily. For this purpose, it is convenient to use 4-bit numbers rather than 16-bit numbers because the number of combinations is so much smaller.

Figure 6.1 Unsigned Arithmetic

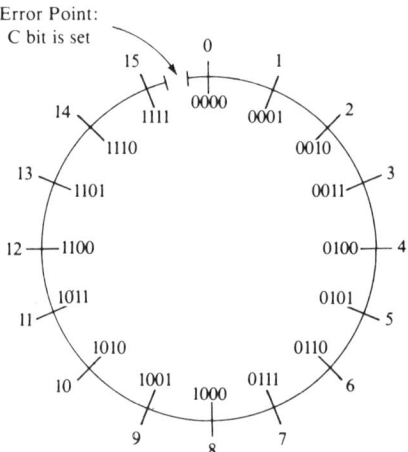

Four bits can be arranged in 2^4 or 16 ways. As shown in Figure 6.1, the 16 combinations can be arranged in a circular pattern to produce something that resembles the face of a 16-hour clock with the binary number 0000 at the 12 o'clock position. A pointer is used to designate one of the 16 binary numbers. Adding 1 to a number is defined as moving the pointer ahead one position. Subtracting 1 is defined as moving the pointer backward one position.

If a 1 is added 16 times in succession, the pointer will make a complete circle and return to its starting position. Mathematicians would call this a **modulo 16** counting system. However, we will call this an error because X plus 16 is obviously not equal to X. In order to make this counting system consistent, it is necessary to agree on an error point somewhere around the clock dial.

For example, it is possible to locate the error point between 1111 and 0000. Whenever 1 is added to 1111 or 1 is subtracted from 0000, an error called **unsigned overflow** has occurred. With the error point specified, the various binary patterns can be given decimal interpretations. If the binary pattern 0000 represents the decimal number 0, it will be found that the pattern 1111 must represent decimal 15. The result is, of course, the unsigned number system.

However, it is possible to place the error point at some other position on the clock face. In particular, the error point can be placed between 0111 and 1000 as shown in Figure 6.2. If 1 is added to 0111 or one is subtracted from 1000, an error called **signed overflow** has occurred. If the binary patterns are now given a decimal interpretation, it is found that the patterns now represent decimal numbers between -8 and $+7$. (Note that if the binary pattern 0000 represents 0, we are compelled by the definition of subtraction to interpret the pattern 1111 as -1.) The result is, of course, the familiar two's complement number system.

Binary numbers on the PDP-11 computer are interpreted in exactly the same way except that 16 bits are used instead of 4. The error point for unsigned

Sec. 6.2   Signed and Unsigned Numbers   121

Figure 6.2 Signed Arithmetic

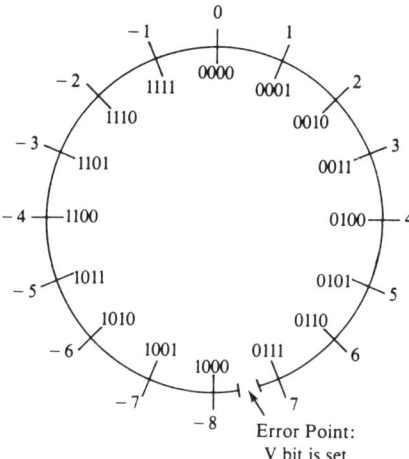

overflow is between 177777 and 000000 (octal) and the error point for signed overflow is between 077777 and 100000 (octal).

The reasons a programmer would choose one system over the other depend on the needs of that particular part of the problem. For example, if addresses are being dealt with, the values may go higher than 32767, but are never negative. Therefore, unsigned numbers should be used. On the other hand, if negative numbers could possibly be generated, then signed numbers should be used.

Detecting Overflow

In order for the programmer to detect the two kinds of overflow, there are two condition switches located in the processor. These are called the C bit and the V bit. The C bit is set (to 1) whenever a Carry is produced out of the high order bit of a word during an arithmetic operation. This is the same as unsigned overflow as shown in Figure 6.1. The C bit is cleared (to 0) if no carry (or unsigned overflow) occurred. The V bit is set if signed oVerflow occurs as shown in Figure 6.2, and is cleared if no signed overflow occurs.

In order for the C and V bits to be useful, there must be a means of testing their state. There are four instructions for doing this:

BCS	Branch if C is Set	(if C = 1)
BCC	Branch if C is Clear	(if C = 0)
BVS	Branch if V is Set	(if V = 1)
BVC	Branch if V is Clear	(if V = 0)

As an example of how these bits are used, the following program segment adds two signed numbers, and then branches to ERROR if the result overflowed, for example, if it was less than −32,768 or greater than +32,767.

```
        ADD     A,B         ;ADD A AND B
        BVS     ERROR       ;EXIT ON OVERFLOW
                .
                .
                .
ERROR:          .           ;PRINT ERROR MESSAGE
```

Note that these four branch instructions are like the other branch instructions and have a limited range of locations to which they can branch, that is, 127 words before the branch or 128 words after. If ERROR were more than 128 words from the BVS instruction, a JMP instruction would be needed. For example:

```
        ADD     A,B         ;ADD A AND B
        BVC     OK          ;IF NO OVERFLOW, CONTINUE
        JMP     ERROR       ;EXIT ON OVERFLOW
OK:             .
                .
                .
ERROR:          .           ;PRINT ERROR MESSAGE
```

Other Condition Switches

We have already seen the use of two condition switches, the C bit and the V bit. There are two other condition switches (collectively known as **condition codes** in the PDP-11): the N bit and the Z bit. The purpose for the N and Z bits is to simplify testing the conditions that result whenever an arithmetic operation is performed. In Chapter 5, we discussed testing and comparing. The following material shows what was really happening with the conditional branches.

The N bit is set whenever the result of an operation is negative. This is true even for such simple operations as MOV. After a MOV instruction, the N bit will be set if the number being moved is negative. The N bit will be cleared if the number was positive. In effect, the N bit will always be the same as the sign bit, or most significant bit of the result. (Recall that 1 means negative, 0 means positive.)

The Z bit is somewhat similar. The Z bit will be set if the result of an operation is zero. It will be cleared if the result is *not* zero. As for the other condition code bits, the N and Z bits can be tested by branch instructions. One slight difference is that the mnemonic operation codes reflect the use of the conditional branch instruction rather than the name of the condition code. The following four instructions complete the list of single-condition code branches:

Sec. 6.2   *Signed and Unsigned Numbers*   123

      BNE   Branch if previous result is *not equal* to zero, that is, if Z is clear

      BEQ   Branch if previous result is *equal* to zero, that is, if Z is set

      BPL   Branch if previous result is *plus* that is, if N is clear

      BMI   Branch if previous result is *minus* that is, if N is set

Note that the BNE and BEQ are the same instructions that were discussed in Chapter 5.

Data-Handling Instructions

With only a few exceptions,* the data-handling instructions cause the condition code bits to be set and cleared according to what is appropriate for the result of the data operation. This is what was referred to as testing in Chapter 5. Data-handling instructions are those which deal with data, such as MOV, ADD, SUB, and so on. These are opposed to control instructions such as JMP, BR, BNE, and so on, which may examine the condition code bits, but do not deal with data, and therefore do not set or clear condition code bits.

Among the data-handling instructions, there are two odd ones, TST and CMP. While these were described partially in Chapter 5, the details of how they work center around the condition codes. TST picks up a piece of data, looks at it, sets condition codes appropriately, and then does nothing else. The data looked at is not modified or used in any other way. The TST instruction will always clear both V and C bits because looking at a number cannot cause either kind of overflow. The N and Z bits will be set appropriately, depending on whether the data looked at are negative or zero.

The CMP instruction is similar. This instruction looks at two pieces of data. That is, the instruction CMP A,B causes B to be subtracted from A. The result is looked at for the purpose of setting condition code bits, and then the result is thrown away. The result is not stored anywhere, and neither A nor B is modified. Of course, this allows the CMP instruction to be used in exactly the way it was used in earlier chapters. For example:

      CMP   A,B
      BEQ   OUT

*There are a number of instructions that do not affect the C bit, thus allowing the test of a previous operation: INC, DEC, MOV, BIT, BIC, BIS, and their byte counterparts. Among extended instructions for the 11/03, 11/34, 11/40, and so on, there are XOR, MFPS, and SXT. SXT also ignores the N bit. Floating point instructions clear both V and C, and SOB does not affect any condition code bits.

Here A − B is computed. If the contents of A = the contents of B, then A − B = 0 and the Z bit is set. The BEQ instruction causes a branch if the Z bit is set. If A ≠ B, then A − B ≠ 0 and Z will be clear and no branch occurs.

It is now possible to look in detail at the BLT, BLE, BGE, and BGT instructions. As an example, consider the following BLT instruction:

```
        CMP     A,B
        BLT     INS
```

It is desired to branch to INS if A < B. The CMP instruction computes A − B, and if A < B, then A − B < 0. Thus the result A − B must be negative. Our first inclination might be that BLT is really the same thing as BMI. However, there is a catch. Overflow may have occurred. Do not forget that A and B are signed, and may in fact have different signs. If A is positive and B is negative, or vice versa, the computation of A − B involves addition, which could result in overflow. When overflow occurs with signed numbers, the sign of the result is reversed. Thus, if overflow occurs, the test should be reversed. Consequently, the BLT instruction is designed to operate as follows:

    Branch if and only if   N is set and V is clear
                   or   N is clear and V is set.

The following examples show how this operates:

```
    CMP  #3,#5
                     000003
                  −  000005
                     ──────
                     177776      Negative result,
                                 no overflow: 3 < 5

    CMP  #3,#-5
                     000003
                  −(−000005)
                     ──────
                     000010      Positive result.
                                 no overflow: 3 > −5

    CMP  #75462,#72531
                     075462
                  −  072531
                     ──────
                     002731      Positive result,
                                 no overflow: 75462 > 72531

    CMP  #75462,#-72531
                     075462
                  −(−072531)
                     ──────
                     170213      Negative result,
                                 with overflow: 75462 > −72531
```

Sec. 6.2   *Signed and Unsigned Numbers*   125

```
CMP #-75462,#72531
```
$$\begin{aligned}&-\ 075462\\&-\ 072531\\&\overline{-\ 170213}\ =\ 007565\end{aligned}$$
                    Positive result
                    with overflow: $-75462 < 72531$

Figure 6.3 shows how all four of these instructions deal with the condition codes.

Figure 6.3 *The Signed Conditional Branches*

Instruction	Condition for Branching
BLT	(N=1 and V=0) or (N=0 and V=1)
BLE	Z=1 or (N=1 and V=0) or (N=0 and V=1)
BGE	(N=1 and V=1) or (N=0 and V=0)
BGT	Z=0 and [(N=1 and V=1) or (N=0 and V=0)]

Note that these instructions should not be used with unsigned numbers. For example, the address 105732 is higher than address 067414; however, a comparison followed by BGT will tell you the opposite because 105732 will be considered a negative number. To solve this, four unsigned conditional branch instructions are provided:

BHI	Branch if HIgh
BHIS	Branch if HIgh or Same
BLOS	Branch if LOw or Same
BLO	Branch if LOw

These four instructions only make sense if used in conjunction with a compare instruction; therefore, the following instructions could be used in order to branch to ALPHA if A is *higher than* (greater than in an unsigned sense) B:

```
CMP   A,B
BHI   ALPHA
```

A curious thing to note is that the BLO instruction is identical to the BCS instruction. The assembler uses the same operation code for both, namely 103400 through 103777. It is left as an exercise for the reader to explain why this works.

Additional Arithmetic Instructions

At this point, three additional instructions are discussed: NEG, which is a new instruction, as well as INC and DEC, which were discussed in Chapter 5. INC and DEC are discussed here because their effect on the condition codes is unusual. A description of three instructions follows:

NEG—This instruction computes the negative value of its operand. Thus, the instruction NEG A causes A to be replaced with −A. It is computed much the same as if A were subtracted from 0, and produces the two's complement negative.

INC—This instruction causes 1 to be added to the operand.

DEC—This instruction causes 1 to be subtracted from the operand.

The INC and DEC instructions can be used with either signed or unsigned numbers. However, one caution must be remembered. These instructions do not affect the C bit. The reason for this is to simplify looping with instructions that use the C bit in the main part of the loop. But because of this, the C bit cannot be used for determining if an INC or DEC caused unsigned overflow. This is not all that bad since there are other simple methods that can be used. For example, if unsigned overflow occurs with INC, the result must be 0. Figure 6.4 shows a list of the appropriate instructions to use with signed and unsigned numbers. Note that in most cases the same instructions are applicable to both kinds of numbers.

Figure 6.4 Signed versus Unsigned Instructions

Signed		Unsigned		
ADD	INC	ADD	INC*	Addition
SUB	DEC	SUB	DEC*	Subtraction
NEG		none		Sign change
CMP	TST	CMP	TST	Comparison and testing
CLR		CLR		Producing zero
BEQ	BNE	BEQ	BNE	Equality or zero test
BPL	BMI	none		Sign test
BVS	BVC	BCS	BCC	Overflow test
BLT	BLE	BLO	BLOS	Relative magnitude
BGE	BGT	BHIS	BHI	

*These instructions do not modify the C bit.

Guidelines for Conditional Branch Instructions

A large number of instructions modify the condition code bits in a variety of ways. In addition, it is easy for beginning programmers to confuse conditional branch instructions that sound similar, such as BPL, BGE, and BHIS. Unfortunately, selecting an incorrect conditional branch instruction can produce errors that are difficult to find. The following guidelines are useful in most situations.

1. A number should be treated consistently. That is, the contents of a given memory cell should not be treated as an unsigned number at one point and a signed number at another point.

2. The six conditional branch instructions that examine the C bit should not be used with signed numbers. The eight conditional branch instructions that examine the N or V bits should not be used with unsigned numbers. The only conditional branch instructions that do not examine the C, N, or V bits are BEQ and BNE which, of course, test the Z bit. Hence, BEQ and BNE are the only instructions that should be used with both signed and unsigned numbers.

3. The only conditional branch instructions that should be used after a CMP instruction are the four signed conditional branches (BGE, BLT, BGT, BLE), the four unsigned conditional branches (BHI, BLOS, BHIS, BLO), BEQ, and BNE. In addition, the unsigned conditional branches (BHI, BLOS, BHIS, BLO) should *only* by used after a CMP instruction.

4. The MOV and TST instructions cannot cause either signed or unsigned overflow. One might conclude that conditional branch instructions that examine the C or V bit would not be useful with MOV or TST. This would leave only BNE, BEQ, BPL, and BMI. However, the designers of the PDP-11 cleverly specified that MOV and TST would set the V bit to 0. As a result, the signed conditional branch instructions (BGE, BLT, BGT, BLE) may also be used. Because the V bit is 0, BGE has the same effect as BPL, and that BLT has the same effect as BMI.

5. When overflow is possible as the result of an ADD, INC, SUB, DEC, or NEG instruction, the programmer should carefully consider the effect of overflow on the behavior of the program. This is particularly true when the signed conditional branch instructions (BGE, BLT, BGT, BLE) are used. As long as signed overflow does not occur, the effect of these instructions is easy to predict. For example, BGE has the same effect as BPL. However, when signed overflow does occur, the situation is more complicated. For example, BGE is then the opposite of BPL. To avoid these problems, it is frequently better to test for overflow directly with a BVS instruction.

6. Addresses should be treated as unsigned numbers. Violating this rule can produce serious errors. For example, it is possible for a program that has run reliably for years to suddenly bomb when it is relocated to a different area of memory.

As long as these guidelines are followed, the effect of the conditional branch instructions is straightforward. However, there are situations where it makes sense to violate these guidelines. In such cases, the programmer should exercise a greater degree of caution.

EXERCISE SET 1

1 Show the decimal equivalents of the following octal numbers interpreted both as unsigned numbers, and as 16-bit two's complement, signed numbers:

(a) 000375   (b) 177775   (c) 077777
(d) 173426   (e) 100000   (f) 100001
(g) 100375   (h) 073125   (i) 067357

2 Show the PDP-11 two's complement negative of each of the numbers in exercise 1. (If there is no answer, state so, and why.)

3 When added, which of the following pairs of octal numbers cause unsigned overflow (carry)? Which cause signed overflow? Show the sums in 16-bit octal.

(a) 000375
     000432

(b) 077754
     065132

(c) 177753
     067135

(d) 177777
     177777

(e) 100001
     077777

(f) 066770
     153667

4 Show what results would occur in the problems of exercise 3, if instead of adding, the second number is subtracted from the first.

5 Show that when signed two's complement overflow occurs, the sign of the result is the opposite of what it should be.

6 Explain why the BLO instruction is the same as BCS. Which unsigned branch instruction is the same as BCC? Explain.

7 Given the following list of possible contents for R0, give the values for the N, C, V, and Z bits after executing the instructions ADD #1, R0, SUB #1, R0, INC R0, and DEC R0. If the value is not knowable from the information given, state why, and what information is needed.

R0 contents:

(a) 077777   (b) 100000   (c) 177777
(d) 000000   (e) 000001   (f) 100001

*8 Write a subroutine that prints out four numbers, which are either 000000 or 000001, indicating the values of N, C, V, and Z bits. (Note, the JSR instruction does not affect the condition codes, nor does any branch or jump. However instructions such as MOV do change them.) Then write a main program that tests this subroutine by doing various calculations and then calling the subroutine after each.

6.3 MULTIPLICATION AND DIVISION

Repeated Addition and Subtraction

Unless you have a PDP-11 with the extended instruction set option (EIS), there are no multiplication or division instructions in the PDP-11. Multiplication and division can be thought of in several ways, including repeated addition or subtraction, shifting operations, or a combination of the two. This is true even if the extended instructions are available. It just means that the shifting and repeated operations are built into the hardware. For this reason, we will spend some time examining how software multiplication operates using more primitive instructions.

The basic mathematical definition of multiplication is based on the idea of repeated addition. Five times 3 means add 3 to 0 five times. Using this notion, it is simple to write a subroutine that multiples A times B and puts the answer in R0. Multiplication of signed numbers must be treated differently from multiplication of unsigned numbers. We will, therefore, restrict our operations to unsigned numbers for the time being. The subroutine shown in Figure 6.5 sets R0 equal to the product of A times B using repeated addition.

Note that the program in Figure 6.5 makes no test for overflow. Note also that the program may take a very long time if A is large. Efficiency could be added to the program by interchanging A and B if B is smaller.

Figure 6.5 Multiplication Program #1

```
        ;SUBROUTINE MULT SETS R0 EQUAL TO A TIMES B
MULT:   CLR     R0              ;R0=0
        MOV     A,COUNT         ;COUNT=A
        BEQ     DONE            ;SKIP OUT IF A.EQ.0
LOOP:   ADD     B,R0            ;ADD B TO R0
        DEC     COUNT           ;DECREMENT COUNT
        BNE     LOOP            ;LOOP UNTIL COUNT.EQ.0
DONE:   RTS     PC              ;RETURN
COUNT:  .BLKW   1
```

A similar method can be used with division. The **quotient** can be defined as the number of times that the **divisor** can be subtracted from the **dividend** without the result becoming negative. Whatever is left after all these subtractions is the **remainder**. Figure 6.6 shows a subroutine that performs division by repeated subtraction. A is divided by B. The quotient is placed in register R0, the remainder is placed in R1. Note that 1 is added to R0 every time B is subtracted from R1. R1 starts out as the dividend when the instruction MOV A,R1 is executed. After repeated subtractions, R1 will be the remainder.

Figure 6.6 Division Program #1

```
;SUBROUTINE DIVD DIVIDES A BY B LEAVING THE QUOTIENT
;IN R0 AND THE REMAINDER IN R1
;DIVISION BY ZERO WILL CAUSE THE SUBROUTINE TO HALT
DIVD:   MOV     A,R1            ;INITIALLY R1=A
        CLR     R0              ;R0=0
        TST     B               ;IF B.EQ.0
        BEQ     ERROR           ;  THERE IS AN ERROR
LOOP:   CMP     R1,B            ;IF REMAINDER IS LESS
        BLO     DONE            ;  THAN DIVISOR, WE ARE DONE
        SUB     B,R1            ;OTHERWISE REM=REM-B
        INC     R0              ;QUO=NUMBER OF SUBTRACTIONS
        BR      LOOP            ;LOOP AND TEST AGAIN
DONE:   RTS     PC              ;WE ARE DONE
ERROR:  HALT
```

Multiplication and Division by Shifting

What the programs in Figures 6.5 and 6.6 have in simplicity is lost in their poor efficiency, especially when dealing with large numbers. Efficiency can often be gained by **shifting** as a method for multiplying or dividing. If a number is shifted to the left, it is in effect multiplied by the base of the number system. For example, in the decimal system, 593 times 10 is 5930. Since the PDP-11 is a binary computer, a left shift has the effect of multiplying a number by 2. Similarly, right shifts can have the effect of dividing a number by 2.

When we look at the shift operations in the PDP-11, it becomes apparent that the PDP-11 is a binary machine and not an octal machine. Twice 000532 is 001264. There is no apparent sense of shifting here unless we look at the binary representations. For example:

$$\begin{array}{lll} 000532 & \text{in binary is} & 0000000101011010 \\ 001264 & \text{in binary is} & 0000001010110100 \end{array}$$

There are four shift instructions in the PDP-11. Each is a single-operand instruction, and each instruction uses the C bit along with the operand almost as if they combined to be a 17-bit register. This will be clearer as each instruction is described as follows:

ASL—Arithmetic Shift Left. The instruction ASL X causes each bit of X to be shifted left one place. A zero is brought into the least significant bit of X and the most significant bit of X is shifted into the C bit. The ASL instruction effectively multiplies by 2. It works for both signed and unsigned numbers. Since the result is usually larger than the original operand, overflow is possible with either kind of number. The V and C bits operate normally for detecting either kind of overflow. The following example illustrates the arithmetic shift left:

Sec. 6.3   *Multiplication and Division*   131

	Binary	*Octal*	*Signed Decimal*	*Unsigned Decimal*
Original Number	0 000 111 000 111 000	007070	3640	3640
Shifted Number	0 001 110 001 110 000	016160	7280	7280

In this case, the unsigned and signed interpretations are the same. In the following example, the unsigned and signed interpretations are different. The shift correctly multiplies the signed number by 2 but produces overflow with the unsigned interpretation.

	Binary	*Octal*	*Signed Decimal*	*Unsigned Decimal*
Original Number	1 111 111 000 111 000	177070	−456	65080
Shifted Number	1 111 110 001 110 000	176160	−912	64624 (Overflow C bit set)

ASR—Arithmetic Shift Right. The instruction ASR X is intended to divide X by 2, where X is a signed integer. (The instruction does not always work with unsigned numbers.) Every bit of X is shifted right one place. The bit that would otherwise be lost off the right end of X is saved in the C bit. (The C bit is not needed for overflow because with a right shift, overflow cannot happen.) The most significant bit of X is not changed, but retains its original value. This bit is the sign bit, and a negative number divided by 2 would still be negative, as the following example indicates:

	Binary	*Octal*	*Signed Decimal*
Original Number	1 000 111 000 111 000	107070	−29128
Shifted Number	1 100 011 100 011 100	143434	−14564

Rounding Off with Division

It is worth noting, at this point, what happens if X is not evenly divisible by 2. One thing that happens is that the low-order bit of X is 1 and this will be shifted into the C bit. Therefore, the C bit contains the remainder of the division. However, another question is, What happens to the quotient? Is it rounded up?

or down? or what? The answer can be seen by looking at some examples. First divide 5 by 2 as follows:

| 000005 is | 0000000000000101 | shifted right this is |
| | 0000000000000010 | which is 2 |

Clearly, fractions seem to be truncated, FORTRAN style. However, before generalizing too far, let us look at another example, -5:

| -5 is 177773 or | 1111111111111011 | shifted right this is |
| | 1111111111111101 | which is 177775 |

but this is -3!

What we have then is not truncation of fractions, but rounding *down* (in the algebraic sense). The next smaller integer from $-2\frac{1}{2}$ is -3. Note what happens when -1 is divided by 2: the result is -1!

The following subroutine could be used if truncation were desired for both positive and negative numbers:

```
;SUBROUTINE TO DIVIDE R0 BY 2 WITH TRUNCATION
HALVE:  ASR   R0      ;DIVIDE BY 2
        BPL   OK      ;POSITIVE NUMBERS ARE OK
        BCC   OK      ;SO ARE EVEN NEGATIVES
        INC   R0      ;ADD 1 TO ODD NEGATIVES
OK:     RTS   PC
```

Rotate Instructions

The remaining two shift instructions are:

ROL - Rotate Left

and

ROR - Rotate Right.

Both of these instructions treat the 16-bit operand and C bit as a 17-bit ring. The bits are either shifted left or right one position around the ring. More specifically, the ROL shifts bit 0 to bit 1, bit 1 to bit 2, and so on, and bit 15 to the C bit, and the original C bit to bit 0 of the operand. The ROR instruction operates in exactly the reverse direction. Figure 6.7 illustrates how these instructions operate. The primary use for the ROR and ROL instructions is in multiple-precision arithmetic, which will be discussed later.

Figure 6.7 ROL *and* ROR *Instructions*

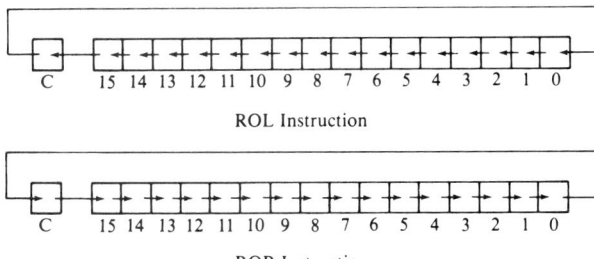

ROL Instruction

ROR Instruction

Efficient Multiplication

Let us now look at an improved algorithm for performing multiplication. The method shown here was allegedly used by a tribe of primitive people. These people knew how to multiply and divide by 2 (presumably by pairing off piles of stones). However, any other numbers required this algorithm. Representations of the two numbers to be multiplied were placed side by side. Then columns were formed by successively dividing the number on the left by 2 and multiplying the number on the right by 2. Fractions are truncated (presumably the tribe did not understand fractions). The process stops when the number on the left has finally been reduced to 1. Figure 6.8 shows how this would operate with the numbers 26 and 36. Now since even numbers on the left contain evil spirits, we cross them out along with the matching number on the right. Finally, summing up the remaining numbers in the right column, we have the product. See Figure 6.9. The product of 26 times 36 is 936.

Figure 6.8 Columns Formed by Halving and Doubling

```
26        36
13        72
 6       144
 3       288
 1       576
```

Figure 6.9 Primitive Multiplication Algorithm

```
-26-      -36-
 13        72
 -6-      -144-
  3       288
  1       576
          ---
          936
```

This algorithm looks quite mysterious and magical unless you write the numbers down in binary. When you do this, the multiplying and dividing by 2 simply represent left and right shifts. Figures 6.10 and 6.11 shows 26 times 36 in binary, performed both in the method just described and in the form resembling decimal multiplication.

Figure 6.10   *Primitive Multiplication in Binary*

```
 11010          100100
  1101         1001000
   110        10010000
    11       100100000
     1      1001000000
            ──────────
            1110101000  =  (936)₁₀
```

Figure 6.11   *Binary Multiplication*

```
    100100
     11010
    ──────
    000000
    100100
   000000
  100100
 100100
 ──────────
 1110101000
```

Now let us write a program for the PDP-11 to implement the primitive multiplication algorithm. Figure 6.12 shows a flowchart of this program and Figure 6.13 shows the assembly language. This program assumes that unsigned numbers are used, and that the result does not overflow 16 bits. This program is clearly much better than multiplication program #1 in Figure 6.6 as far as speed is concerned. In the worst case, the six instruction loop starting with LOOP will be executed 16 times. This adds up to 96 instruction executions. On the other hand, program #1 may go through its three instruction loop as many as 65,535 times, or 196,605 instruction executions, thus taking nearly 2,000 times as long to execute.

Efficient Division

The same techniques used to improve the multiplication algorithm can be used in reverse to obtain a good division algorithm. Division program #1 subtracted the divisor from the dividend as often as it could until all that was left was the remainder. If we shift the divisor left, we multiply it by 2. Then each subtraction would be like two subtractions and our program could run faster. If we shift left more often, each subtraction would have the effect of 4, 8, 16, 32, ... subtractions. The technique in our new algorithm will be to shift the divisor left until it is as big as the dividend. Then we use a process of subtracting and shift-

Sec. 6.3   Multiplication and Division   135

Figure 6.12   *Flowchart of Multiplication Algorithm*

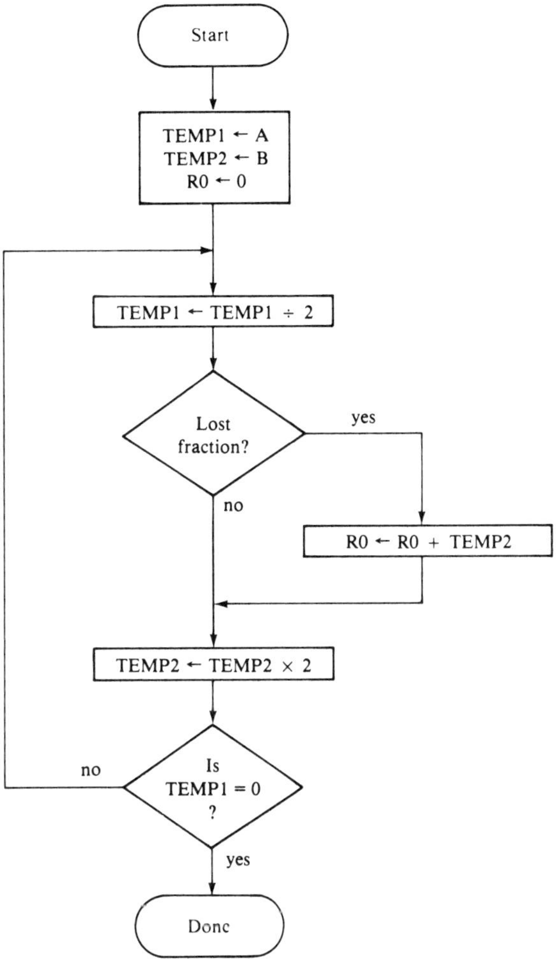

Figure 6.13   *Multiplication Program #2*

```
;SUBROUTINE MULT SETS R0 EQUAL TO A TIMES B
MULT:   MOV     A,TEMP1         ;SAVE A AND B BY WORKING
        MOV     B,TEMP2         ;  WITH TEMP1 AND TEMP2
        CLR     R0              ;CLEAR INITIAL SUM
LOOP:   ASR     TEMP1           ;DIVIDE BY 2
        BCC     NOADD           ;NO ADD IF C IS CLEAR
        ADD     TEMP2,R0        ;OTHERWISE ADD TEMP2 TO SUM
NOADD:  ASL     TEMP2           ;MULTIPLY BY 2
        TEST    TEMP1           ;LOOP UNLESS
        BNE     LOOP            ;  TEMP1.EQ.0
        RTS     PC              ;RETURN
TEMP1:  .BLKW   1
TEMP2:  .BLKW   1
```

ing right in the form of a reverse multiplication. Figures 6.14 and 6.15 show a flowchart and assembly language for this program.

The way this program works, it would be nice if TEMP were a 17-bit register. Since this is not possible in the PDP-11, the program will fail if the dividend (A) is too large. Fixing this problem is not difficult, but it involves a

Figure 6.14 Flowchart for Division Algorithms

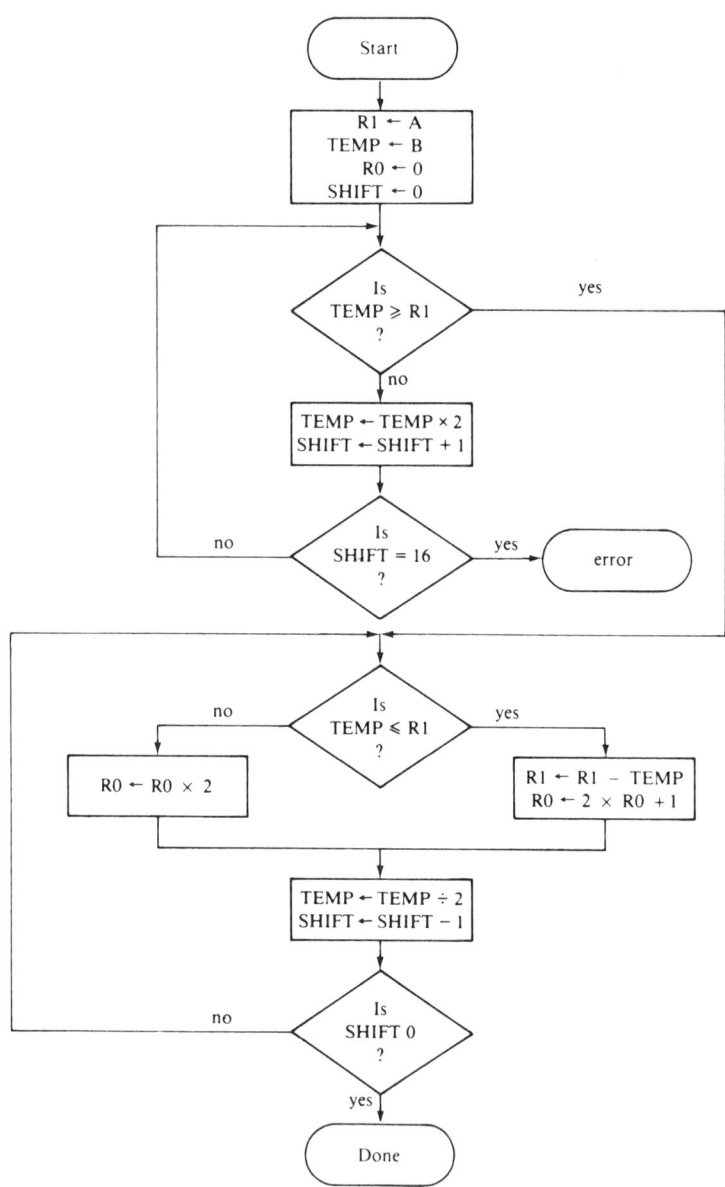

Figure 6.15 Divison Program #2

```
;SUBROUTINE DIVD DIVIDES A BY B LEAVING THE QUOTIENT
;IN R0 AND THE REMAINDER IN R1
;DIVISION BY ZERO WILL CAUSE THE SUBROUTINE TO HALT
DIVD:   MOV    A,R1          ;DIVIDEND IS INITIAL REMAINDER
        MOV    B,TEMP        ;DIVISOR IN TEMP
        CLR    R0            ;QUO=0
        CLR    SHIFT         ;SHIFT=0
LOOP1:  CMP    TEMP,R1       ;LOOP UNTIL
        BHIS   PART2         ;  TEMP.GE.REM
        ASL    TEMP          ;KEEP SHIFTING LEFT
        INC    SHIFT         ;COUNT SHIFTS
        CMP    SHIFT,#20     ;ERROR IF 16 SHIFTS *
        BLT    LOOP1         ;OTHERWISE LOOP
        JMP    ERROR         ;POSSIBLE DIVIDE BY ZERO
PART2:  CMP    TEMP,R1       ;IF TEMP.LE.REM
        BLOS   SUBTR         ;  SUBTRACT
        ASL    R0            ;OTHERWISE JUST
        BR     LPEND         ;  DOUBLE QUOTIENT
SUBTR:  SUB    TEMP,R1       ;REM=REM-TEMP
        ASL    R0            ;DOUBLE QUOTIENT
        INC    R0            ;  AND ADD ONE
LPEND:  ASR    TEMP          ;HALVE DIVISOR *
        DEC    SHIFT         ;DECREMENT LOOP COUNT
        BGE    PART2         ;LOOP UNTIL NEGATIVE
        RTS    PC            ;RETURN
ERROR:  HALT                 ;HALT ON ERROR
TEMP:   .BLKW  1
SHIFT:  .BKKW  1
```

*These instructions may not work if A is initially too large. Fixing this is an exercise for the reader.

thorough understanding of what happens with overflow. This problem is therefore left to the reader to solve.

6.4 MULTIPLE-PRECISION ARITHMETIC

Double-Precision Representation

As mentioned several times earlier, the word size on the PDP-11 computer places a restriction on the magnitudes of the numbers that can be dealt with. Unsigned numbers can be no greater than 65535, and signed numbers may be no greater than +32767 and no less than −32768. Clearly, these magnitudes are relatively small and many scientific and business applications require the use of larger numbers or numbers with more significant digits.

There is only one way to represent a number that will not fit in a single location. That is to use several locations to store the number. The obvious step in this direction is use two locations for a number. This is called **double precision.**

A double-precision number can simply be thought of as a 32-bit number. The 32-bit number can be stored in two words with the upper 16 bits in one word and the lower 16 bits in the second word. It is often easiest to think of this pair of 16-bit words as a single 32-bit word. In doing so, it becomes apparent that both signed and unsigned 32-bit numbers can be represented. All that is necessary is to generalize the concept of two's complement arithmetic to apply to 32 rather than 16 bits. As before, the leftmost bit of the entire number is the sign. This would be the sign bit of the most significant 16-bit word of the pair of words used for representing the number. (Note that the sign bit of the less significant 16-bit word is simply a bit in the middle of the number, and is not related to the sign of the overall number.)

Double-Precision Addition and Subtraction

Of course, the ability to store double-precision numbers is of little use unless it is also possible to perform arithmetic with these larger numbers. Actually, the basic arithmetic processes can be implemented quite simply as can be seen from the following examples. In order to keep these examples simple, we will assume that we are dealing with 6-digit *decimal* numbers in a machine that has 3-digit decimal words.

Now consider the following addition:

```
   | 1 2 3 | | 4 5 6 |
 + | 1 1 2 | | 2 3 3 |    The boxes indicate words
   ─────────────────
   | 2 3 5 | | 6 8 9 |
```

Here we see that the right half of the sum is equal to the sum of the right halves of the numbers being added. Similarly, the left half of the sum is the sum of the left halves.

It should be noted, however, that this is not a general solution, because unsigned overflow can occur when the right halves of the numbers are added together. For example:

```
                1         Overflow carry
   | 1 2 3 | | 7 8 9 |
 + | 1 1 2 | | 5 6 6 |
   ─────────────────
   | 2 3 6 | | 3 5 5 |
```

Sec. 6.4 Multiple-Precision Arithmetic

What has to be done here is to add the overflow carry to the sum of the left halves.

A similar process is used for subtraction:

```
                 1          Borrow
          ┌─────────┐  ┌─────────┐
          │ 2  3  6 │  │ 3  5  5 │
       +  │ 1  1  2 │  │ 5  6  6 │
          └─────────┘  └─────────┘
          ──────────
          │ 1  2  3 │  │ 7  8  9 │
          └─────────┘  └─────────┘
```

Here an unsigned overflow occurs when you try to subtract 566 from 355 because an unsigned number cannot be negative. Because of that overflow, a 1 has to be borrowed from the difference of the most significant halves.

Add and Subtract Carry Instructions

The same methods as just described work when using binary arithmetic with 16-bit registers. In the PDP-11, the C bit indicates the presence of overflow when you add (or subtract) the least significant halves. Therefore all that has to be done is to add (or subtract) the C bit to (or from) the most significant half of the result. You could of course do this by testing the C bit and then either incrementing or decrementing the result register. However, the PDP-11 manufacturers thought that multiple-precision arithmetic was important enough that they provided instructions for the purpose. For addition:

                    ADC   Add Carry

This instruction adds the C bit to the destination. For subtraction:

                    SBC   Subtract Carry

This subtracts the C bit from the destination.

These two instructions could be used along with the other arithmetic instructions to add the 32-bit number A to the 32-bit number B. The numbers A and B will be contained in PDP-11 registers AL, AR, BL, and BR for the left and right halves, respectively. The code for double precision is:

```
        ADD     AR,BR
        ADC     BL
        ADD     AL,BL
```

Similarly, A can be subtracted from B by the following code:

```
        SUB     AR,BR
        SBC     BL
        SUB     AL,BL
```

Either of these programs can be extended to work with triple precision for 48-bit numbers, or even higher precision. However, care must be taken at the next step since either the ADD or the ADC can cause a carry that must be propagated. The same is true of the SUB and SBC.

Multiple-Precision Shifting

Shifting multiple-precision numbers can easily be accomplished using the ROL and ROR instructions along with the ASL and ASR instructions. Recall that ASL and ASR cause the bit that is being shifted out to be saved in the C bit. The ROL and ROR can cause this bit to be picked up in the next portion of the number. As an example of this, see Figure. 6.16

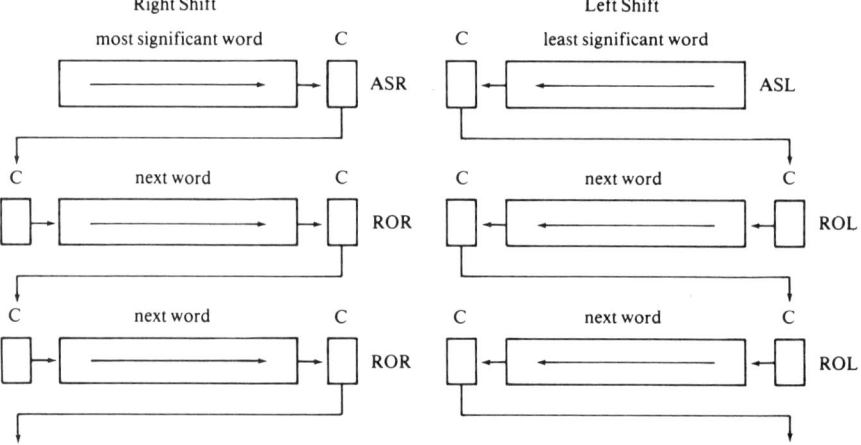

Figure 6.16 Multiple-Precision Shifts

Clearly, all that is needed for shifting multiple-precision numbers is an ASR followed by a succession of ROR's or an ASL followed by a succession of ROL's. Note that Figure 6.16 shows that for a right shift, you must start at the most significant end of the numbers, whereas with a left shift, you must start by shifting the least significant end.

EXERCISE SET 2

1 Multiply the following pairs of octal numbers and show the results as signed and unsigned numbers. Indicate which would result in signed or un-

signed overflow with a 16-bit result.

(a) 000024
     000057

(b) 000374
     000210

(c) 177777
     000001

(d) 177777
     000002

(e) 177777
     177777

(f) 000001
     177777

2. Divide the following pairs of octal numbers and show the quotient and result as signed and unsigned numbers. Indicate any invalid operations. Show the signed remainders with the same sign as the expected quotient.

(a) 000054)006713
(b) 073426)000543
(c) 000000)005614
(d) 005614)000000
(e) 177773)177770
(f) 177775)000144

3. Write a subroutine that multiplies two signed numbers using repeated addition. The result should be a signed 16-bit number following the normal rules of algebra. Your program should exit or stop if the magnitude of the result is too high. Also, write a main program that calls the subroutine several times with a selection of operands, and prints the results.

4. As for exercise 3, write and test a subroutine that performs division of signed numbers by repeated subtraction. There should be two 16-bit results, a signed quotient, and signed remainder. The sign of the remainder should be the same as the expected sign of the quotient. Your program should exit or halt if it cannot compute a valid result. (What are these cases?)

5. Write and test a subroutine as for exercise 3, but make the multiplication more efficient by using shifting, as appropriate.

6. Write and test a subroutine as for exercise 4, but make the division more efficient by using shifting, as appropriate.

7. The programs shown in Figure 6.13 and 6.15 may have some problems when one or more of the operands are too large. Aside from overflow, there may be cases when the result could be stored in a 16-bit word, but the program does not function properly. (For example, a one in the sign bit would fail to shift out on a right shift.) Study these programs carefully, and rewrite them if necessary so that they will operate properly for any pair of unsigned operands that produce a result which fits in 16 bits as an unsigned number. Write a main program that tests your modified subroutine for some extreme cases.

8. Write a subroutine that multiplies two 16-bit, unsigned numbers, and produces a 32-bit, double-precision result. Because no overflow is possible, your program should work for all combinations of input operands. Write and run a main program that tests your subroutine.

9 Write and test a subroutine as for exercise 8 except that it multiplies two 16-bit signed numbers, and produces a 32-bit signed (two's complement) result.

10 Write a subroutine that divides a 32-bit, double-precision, unsigned number by a 16-bit, unsigned number, if possible, to produce a 16-bit quotient and 16-bit remainder. Write and run a main test program for this routine.

11 Do as for exercise 10, except that all numbers are signed, two's complement numbers.

CHAPTER 7

ARRAYS

7.1 INTRODUCTION AND REVIEW

Most readers are already familiar with the concept of an array as used in high-level languages such as FORTRAN or BASIC. The programmer has a collection of data that is to be processed in some related way. Furthermore, the programmer wishes to have the entire collection of data in memory at the same time.

An Example with Sorting

An example of such a problem is sorting a list of numbers or printing them out in increasing order. Since we (supposedly) do not know the actual order of the numbers being input, we cannot print a single number until all of the numbers have been read in. After all, the last number read in could be the smallest, and therefore, the first to be printed out. Figures 7.1a and 7.1b show an example of just such a program written in FORTRAN, and BASIC, respectively. The program reads a list of 20 numbers, sorts them so that they are now rearranged in increasing order, and finally prints the rearranged list. Notice that this program performs three processes: reading, sorting, and printing. These three areas are identified by the comment and remark lines in the programs. The sorting method used in this program is one version of the popular selection sorting technique. If the reader is not already familiar with this method of sorting, it is suggested that the program be examined step by step as an exercise.

Figure 7.1 *Sorting Program*

```
      INTEGER LIST(20),J,K,L,LP1,M
C READ UNSORTED NUMBERS
      DO 10 J=1,20
         READ 100, LIST(J)
   10 CONTINUE
C SORT NUMBERS
      DO 30 L=1,19
         LP1=L+1
         DO 20 K=LP1,20
            IF(LIST(L).LE.LIST(K)) GO TO 20
            M=LIST(L)
            LIST(L)=LIST(K)
            LIST(K)=M
   20    CONTINUE
   30 CONTINUE
C PRINT SORTED NUMBERS
      DO 40 J=1,20
         PRINT 200, LIST(J)
   40 CONTINUE
      STOP
  100 FORMAT(I6)
  200 FORMAT(1X,I6)
      END
```

(a) FORTRAN

```
100 DIM T(20)
110 REM - READ UNSORTED NUMBERS
120 FOR J=1 TO 20
130     INPUT T(J)
140 NEXT J
150 REM - SORT NUMBERS
160 FOR L=1 TO 19
170     LET P=L+1
180     FOR K=P TO 20
190         IF T(L)<=T(K) THEN 230
200             LET M=T(L)
210             LET T(L)=T(K)
220             LET T(K)=M
230     NEXT K
240 NEXT L
250 REM - PRINT SORTED NUMBERS
260 FOR J=1 TO 20
270     PRINT T(J)
280 NEXT J
290 STOP
```

(b) BASIC

Sec. 7.1   Introduction and Review   145

Of special note in both versions of this program is the first statement. This statement is nonexecutable. It simply informs the compiler about the number of memory locations that must be set aside for the array list.

As we have already seen, in assembly language programs, we must make an allocation of every location that is being used for data. This was usually done with the .BLKW 1 assembly directive. In the next section, we will see how locations are allocated for arrays.

Another point to note about these FORTRAN and BASIC programs is that in the various operations in the executable part of the program, the variable identifier LIST or T is used with a **subscript** or **index** which points to the specific location of the array. This is required because we were always referring to a single location and not a whole array. This is usually the case in assembly language. Although there are some machines that have instructions which are capable of moving a whole array, most machine-level operations deal with a single location at a time. Therefore, a means is needed for identifying a single location out of an array. This will be shown in the section on indexing, starting on page 146.

Storage Allocation

As we just saw, some means is needed to allocate or set aside a number of locations when dealing with an array. Although it might be possible to do this in many quite arbitrary ways, the simplest method is to use a contiguous block of memory locations. Successive locations in the block correspond to successive locations in the array.

The way of allocating a block of memory in the PDP-11 assembly language is to use the directive .BLKW. However, as used previously, .BLKW always had 1 in the operand field, indicating the assignment of one word. For an array, a larger number can be used indicating a larger block of memory. The assembler then assigns that number of words at that point in the program. For example, .BLKW 12 would have the effect of allocating 10 words that are placed one after the other (see Figure 7.2). Note that the PDP-11 assembly language normally treats such numbers as octal. Therefore, the number 12 causes *ten* words of memory to be allocated.

Figure 7.2   .BLKW *Directive*

```
        XYZ:    .BLKW    12           XYZ:    XYZ(1)
                                              XYZ(2)
        This directive produces the           XYZ(3)
        allocation on the right.              XYZ(4)
                                              XYZ(5)
                                              XYZ(6)
                                              XYZ(7)
                                              XYZ(8)
                                              XYZ(9)
                                              XYZ(10)
```

Now, in order to be able to refer to the array, there must be a symbolic name. This can be accomplished by placing a label on the .BLKW directive. This causes an entry to be made in the symbol table with the label assigned to the first word of the array.

7.2 INDEXING

Address Expressions

Now that we have allocated space for an array, we are confronted with the problem of accessing a specific location in an array. The first location of the array is really no problem because the name of the array is assigned to the first location. Therefore, we could clear the first location of the array XYZ by executing the instruction CLR XYZ. However, this does not solve the problem of how to access other locations in the array, such as the second, third, or fourth locations.

One solution is through the use of **address expressions.** The address of the second location of the array XYZ is two higher than the address of XYZ. Similarly, the third and fourth locations of XYZ have addresses four and six higher than the address of XYZ. Therefore, we can refer to these addresses symbolically as XYZ+2, XYZ+4, and XYZ+6. And we could thus clear the first four locations of the array XYZ with the following instructions:

```
        CLR     XYZ
        CLR     XYZ+2
        CLR     XYZ+4
        CLR     XYZ+6
```

Note that in assembly language expressions, the symbol XYZ always refers to the address of XYZ and never its contents. This is very important when we consider an instruction like MOV XYZ+2,A. At first glance, this might seem analogous to the FORTRAN or BASIC statement A=XYZ+2. However, this is clearly wrong, because we do not mean the contents of XYZ with two added; we mean the contents of the location two higher than XYZ. Thus, the analogous FORTRAN or BASIC statement would be A=XYZ(2).

Note that address expressions can be used in assembly language just about anywhere an ordinary symbol or number can be used. The expression can be quite complex, but it must be meaningful as an address or a number. This will be covered in more detail in Chapter 10, for the time being, we will just limit ourselves to the most usual case of an address plus or minus a number.

Although the use of address expressions is very important when dealing with arrays, there is a serious limitation. These expressions are evaluated at assembly time, and therefore cannot involve any numbers that would change during execution. This means that although we can refer to specific locations in an array such as XYZ(1), XYZ(2), and so on, we cannot refer to a variable or arbitrary location in an array such as XYZ(J). Consequently, although we could clear out an array with a succession of CLR instructions, we do not yet have a means of writing a loop that would do that.

Index Registers

What is needed is a means of producing the *effect* of an address expression which is computed at the time that the program is being executed. In order to facilitate this, most modern computers have a special instruction mode. A special register called an **index register** is automatically combined with an array address to form an **effective address** that corresponds to a specific location in the array. These effective addresses operate at execution time in much the same way that address expressions operate at assembly time.

In the PDP-11, the eight general-purpose registers, R0, R1, R2, R3, R4, R5, SP, and PC can all be used as index registers. (Because of the special functions of the SP and PC, their use as index registers is usually inadvisable.)

When an instruction such as CLR is used in the index register mode, there is a reference to a **base address** and an index register in the syntax of assembly language which appears as CLR XYZ(R3). Here, XYZ is the base address and R3 is the index register. An effective address is computed by adding the *value* of the base address to the *contents* of the index register. The instruction then operates on the location in memory referred to by the effective address.

Examples of Indexing

As an example, let us see how the instruction CLR XYZ(R3) functions at the machine language level. First the translation of the instruction will require two words, one for the operation code, and the other for the base address, XYZ. (Let us assume that the address XYZ happens to be the location 001500.) The instruction will then assemble as:

005063
001500

The operation code 005063 is really in two parts. First, 0050 is the operation code for CLR. Second, 63 indicates the addressing mode. The 6 is for index register mode, and the 3 indicates that R3 is to be used.

Now, before we can say what this instruction does, we must know the contents of R3. Let us suppose at the time that the PDP-11 is about to execute this instruction, that R3 contains 000014. Then, an effective address is computed by adding the base address, 001500, with the contents of the index register, 000014. The result is 001514. Therefore, the CLR instruction operates on this location, and the contents of location 001514 is cleared to 0.

Note that the computation of effective addresses is performed by the indexing unit inside the processor. Neither R3 nor the instruction itself are modified by the effective-address computation. The only location to be modified is memory location 001514. The instruction locations will still contain 005063 and 001500, and R3 will still contain 000014.

Figure 7.3 shows an example of a program segment that clears an entire array of 50 locations. Several things to note are:

1. The index register starts at 0 as opposed to FORTRAN or BASIC where indices start at 1.
2. Incrementing is by 2 because of even addresses.
3. Similarly, the final value of the index register will be twice the value of the array size.

Figure 7.3   Indexing Example

```
        CLR     R0              ;R0 IS THE INDEX REGISTER
LOOP:   CLR     XYZ(R0)         ;CLEAR ARRAY LOCATION
        ADD     #2,R0           ;INCREMENT INDEX
        CMP     R0,#144         ;TEST FOR FINAL VALUE
        BLT     LOOP            ;LOOP UNTIL REACHED
            .
            .
            .
XYZ:    .BLKW   62              ;ARRAY LOCATION
```

As a final example in this section, the program in Figure 7.1 might be rewritten in assembly language as shown in Figure 7.4. The example does not include input or output, but just the sorting portion in the sixth through fifteenth lines of Figure 7.1.

The style of programming in the example given in Figure 7.4 is essentially the same as that used in Figure 7.3. Consequently, the points to note are essentially the same.

Figure 7.4   Assembly Language, Sorting Problem

```
        CLR     R0                      ;LEFT POINTER=0
LOOP1:  MOV     R0,R1
        ADD     #2,R1                   ;RIGHT POINTER=LEFT+2
LOOP2:  CMP     LIST(R0),LIST(R1)       ;COMPARE LIST(LEFT) AND LIST(RIGHT)
        BLE     NOSWAP                  ;IF LESS OR EQUAL, OK
        MOV     LIST(R0),R2             ;OTHERWISE SWAP
        MOV     LIST(R1),LIST(R0)       ;TWO LIST ELEMENTS
        MOV     R2,LIST(R1)
NOSWAP: ADD     #2,R1                   ;INCREMENT RIGHT POINTER
        CMP     R1,#50                  ;TOO BIG?
        BLT     LOOP2                   ;LOOP UNTIL DONE
```

Figure 7.4 (continued)

```
        ADD     #2,R0           ;INCREMENT LEFT POINTER
        CMP     R0,#46          ;TOO BIG?
        BLT     LOOP1           ;LOOP UNTIL DONE
          .
          .
          .
LIST:   .BLKW   24              ;SPACE FOR ARRAY
```

EXERCISE SET 1

1. Given that general registers R0, R1, and R2 contain the following octal values:

R0	000000
R1	000124
R2	177742

   and that the symbols ABC, PQW, and XYZ correspond to the following addresses:

ABC	001000
PQW	012406
XYZ	177772

   what are the effective addresses of the following clear instructions; that is, what locations would be cleared when they are executed?

(a)	CLR	PQW	(b)	CLR	PQW+24
(c)	CLR	ABC+54	(d)	CLR	PQW(R1)
(e)	CLR	PQW(R0)	(f)	CLR	XYZ+1046
(g)	CLR	PQW(R2)	(h)	CLR	XYZ(R1)
(i)	CLR	ABC+40(R1)	(j)	CLR	XYZ+100(R1)

2. Assemble each of the instructions in exercise 1, in machine language. (Assume the .ENABLE AMA card has been used as usual.)

3. Convert the program segment shown in Figure 7.4 to a complete sorting program. Use the RNUM and PNUM subroutine shown in Appendix B to complete the missing input and output sections. Run the program with sample data.

150   Arrays   Ch. 7

4 The following flowchart describes a sorting algorithm known as the **bubble sort**:

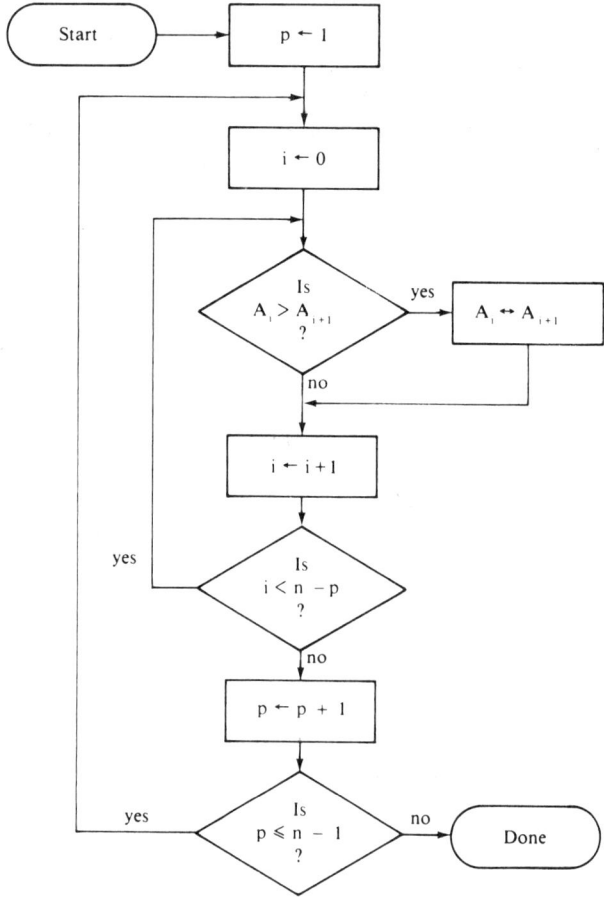

(a) How does this sorting program work? Show an example with four or five elements?

(b) How does this sorting program differ from the selection sort shown in Figure 7.4?

(c) Which method is more efficient, or is there any difference?

(d) What advantages or disadvantages are there, one over the other, if any?

5 Write an assembly language program segment (such as was done in Figure 7.4) for the bubble sort program shown in exercise 4.

6 Write and run a complete bubble sort program adding input and output sections using the subroutines given in Appendix B.

7.3 OTHER ADDRESSING MODES

Register-Deferred Addressing

Because of the importance of arrays in computing, and because of the different ways that arrays are used in programs, the PDP-11 has several ways of dealing with arrays. The method used in the previous examples is the index register mode, where one of the general registers is used as an index register. Another method of accessing elements of arrays is the **deferred-addressing method.** Deferred addressing is the use of an intermediate operand register that contains the address of the real operand. In the PDP-11, the simplest of the deferred addressing modes is the **register-deferred mode.** Here a general register contains the address of the operand. In assembly language, this mode is indicated by placing parentheses around the name of the register. For example, the instruction CLR (R0) would clear the memory location whose address is contained in R0. More particularly, if R0 contains 001244, then this instruction would clear the contents of memory location 001244. The contents of R0 are not affected in any way by this instruction, and would remain at 001244.

Note that register-deferred addressing is in effect a simplified version of index register addressing. In index register addressing, an effective address is computed by adding a base address to the contents of a register. With register-deferred addressing, the effective address is simply the contents of the register —there is no base address to add. Consequently, the instruction CLR (R0) performs exactly the same function as the index register mode instruction CLR 0(R0). There is, however, one main difference. Since the second instruction does have a base address, even though it is zero, it is a two-word instruction, whereas the register-deferred version is a one-word instruction.

In many cases, the effect of adding in a base address can be achieved by adding it to the original value of the register. This is clearer from examining the example given in Figure 7.5. This example gives two versions of a program that adds together the elements of a 20-word array, DATA, and leaves the answer in SUM.

Of special note in the register-deferred version of the program in Figure 7.5 is that the first and fifth instructions use addresses as data. This is very important to the concept of assembly language. Addresses are just numbers, and as such can be treated as data just as any numbers that may represent other things.

Generally, however, both versions are very much alike. If each program is traced, it will be found that instruction executions match one for one. The main difference is that in version (b), the contents of R0 will always be larger by the value of the address of DATA. This takes care of the need for a base address in the third instruction of version (a). Without getting involved in the complex question of the efficiency of specific instructions, it can be said that one version would be about as preferable as the other.

Figure 7.5 *A Program to Add 20 Numbers*

```
            CLR     R0                              MOV     #DATA,R0
            CLR     SUM                             CLR     SUM
LOOP:       ADD     DATA(R0),SUM      LOOP:         ADD     (R0),SUM
            ADD     #2,R0                           ADD     #2,R0
            CMP     R0,#50                          CMP     R0,#DATA+50
            BNE     LOOP                            BNE     LOOP
             .                                       .
             .                                       .
             .                                       .
SUM:        .BLKW   1                 SUM:          .BLKW   1
DATA:       .BLKW   24                DATA:         .BLKW   24
```

    (a) Index Register Version   (b) Register-Deferred Version

The question then arises that if both methods are so similar, why have both? It turns out that the index register method has advantages when dealing with more than one array, because often one index register can serve to point to several arrays if you are pointing to the same place in all of them. However, with the register-deferred method, a separate register would be needed for each array. The advantages of the register-deferred method become clearer when it is used in conjunction with the auto-increment and auto-decrement modes that will be discussed next.

Auto-Increment Addressing

As can be seen from most of the examples given previously, when scanning through an array, it is necessary to update the index register by adding some number every time through the loop. This is true in both of the methods given already. Also, the number added each time is usually 2 since the programs usually step through successive words in an array. In order to facilitate this, and to make many programs much more efficient, the PDP-11 has an addressing mode where this increment takes place automatically. This is called the **auto-increment mode.**

The auto-increment mode operates in essentially the same way as the register-deferred mode in that a register is used to hold the address of the operand. The only difference is that after executing the instructions, the register involved will be increased by 2. For example, the auto-increment instruction:

```
            CLR     (R0)+
```

is much the same as the pair of instructions:

```
            CLR     (R0)
            ADD     #2,R0
```

Sec. 7.3   Other Addressing Modes

There are, however, two notable differences. The first is simply that the auto-increment mode requires fewer instructions. The second is that with auto-increment, the condition codes are determined by the effect of the instruction, not the increment process. Also of note is the assembly language convention of using the plus sign to indicate automatic incrementing.

For an example of how auto-increment can be used, let us look at the example from Figure 7.5b and see how this could be rewritten using the auto-increment mode. See Figure 7.6 for this comparison.

As would be expected from the preceding discussion, the difference between the two programs is that the auto-increment version does not need the instructions ADD #2,R0. This makes the program shorter, clearer, somewhat easier to write, and it requires less memory and is also about 25 percent faster. (Note that the saved instruction is inside a loop.)

Figure 7.6   *A Modified Program to Add 20 Numbers*

```
           MOV    #DATA,R0                    MOV    #DATA,R0
           CLR    SUM                         CLR    SUM
  LOOP:    ADD    (R0),SUM          LOOP:     ADD    (R0)+,SUM
           ADD    #2,R0
           CMP    R0,#DATA+50                 CMP    R0,#DATA+50
           BNE    LOOP                        BNE    LOOP
            .                                  .
            .                                  .
            .                                  .
  SUM:     .BLKW  1                 SUM:      .BLKW  1
  DATA:    .BLKW  24                DATA:     .BLKW  24
```

          (a) Register-Deferred Version   (b) Auto-Increment Version

Auto-Decrement Addressing

In order to deal with the fact that it is often necessary to access the elements of an array in reverse order, the PDP-11 has another addressing mode called the **auto-decrement mode.** The auto-decrement mode is essentially the same as the auto-increment, with the general register being decremented or reduced by 2. Another difference is due to the need for symmetry between the two modes. In the auto-increment mode, the general register is incremented *after* it is used. In the auto-decrement mode, the general register is decremented *before* it is used. This means that the auto-decrement instruction exactly undoes what the auto-increment does. This is important when an array is used as a **stack.** Stacks will be discussed in more detail in Chapter 9. But briefly, a stack is an array where information is added and then used in much the same way that dishes are added to or removed from a stack of dishes.

In assembly language, the auto-decrement mode is indicated as:

    CLR   -(R3)

This instruction would cause R3 to be decremented by 2, and *then* the location that R3 is pointing to would be cleared. Note that the designers of the assembly language require the minus sign in front, whereas in the auto-increment mode, the plus sign is in back. This is to remind programmers that decrementing takes place before use, whereas incrementing takes place after use.

As an example of the use of auto-decrement mode, Figure 7.7 shows a program that copies a 20-word array A to another array B, reversing the order of the words.

Figure 7.7 A Program for Reversing an Array

```
            MOV     #A,R0
            MOV     #B+50,R1
LOOP:       MOV     (R0)+,-(R1)
            CMP     R0,#A+50
            BNE     LOOP
              .
              .
              .
A:          .BLKW   24
B:          .BLKW   24
```

7.4 FULL SET OF ADDRESSING MODES

Review of Op Codes

In the earlier chapters, a bit of subterfuge was used to make understanding machine language simpler. For example, we stated that the operation code for MOV A,B was 013737 and the op code for MOV #5,X was 012737, and so on. From this and from looking at assembly listings, it must seem that there is something special about 27s and 37s on the PDP-11. Among other things, this section should clear up the mystery.

Except for a few special cases of instructions that have restricted or no addressing capability, each operand of an instruction is signified by a 6-bit code. Three of the six bits indicate the addressing mode. The other three indicate the general register involved. For example, mode 6 is index register mode and 3 stands for R3. Therefore, the instruction op code 005063 would be generated for CLR X(R3). (Note all CLR instructions have the 0050XX form of op code.)

Other modes that have already been discussed are shown in Table 7.1.

TABLE 7.1

Mode	Name	Example	Op Code
0	Register	CLR R3	005003
1	Register-deferred	CLR (R3)	005013
2	Auto-increment	CLR (R3)+	005023
4	Auto-decrement	CLR -(R3)	005043
6	Index register	CLR X(R3)	005063 (Address X)

Other Addressing Modes

With three bits used for expressing modes, one should expect eight modes, and only five are shown in Table 7.1. In fact, there are eight modes. Each odd mode is the deferred addressing form of the previous even mode. This can already be seen with modes 0 and 1. Similarly, mode 3 is a deferred version of mode 2. For example, the instruction code 005033 is expressed in assembly language as CLR @(R3)+. (Note that an at sign @ shows deferred addressing.) With this instruction, the contents of R3 are fetched and used as an address. The contents of that location are then fetched, and are also used as an address. The location specified by the second address is then cleared. (The general term for this type of addressing is **indirect addressing**.) Also, after R3 is used, it is incremented by 2.

For example, assume that we have the following contents of R3 and memory:

R3 001046

Memory

Address	Contents
001046	001210
001210	XXXXXX

If the instruction CLR @(R3)+ is executed, the contents of location 001210 will be cleared, and R3 will be incremented to 001050.

For the most part, modes 3, 5, and 7 are used in advanced programming where tables of addresses are used for complex data structures. It should be noted that indirect addressing is an extremely powerful programming technique that often simplifies the solution of difficult problems. Indirect addressing will be used in Chapter 9 when FORTRAN programs and assembly language programs are combined. Table 7.2 shows the complete list of all eight addressing modes.

TABLE 7.2 PDP-11 ADDRESSING MODES

Mode	Name	Example		Op Code
0	Register	CLR	R3	005003
1	Register-deferred	CLR	(R3) or @R3	005013
2	Auto-increment	CLR	(R3)+	005023
3	Auto-increment-deferred	CLR	@(R3)+	005033
4	Auto-decrement	CLR	-(R3)	005043
5	Auto-decrement-deferred	CLR	@-(R3)	005053
6	Index register	CLR	X(R3)	005063
7	Index register deferred	CLR	@X(R3)	005073

Note: Modes 0–5 are one-word instructions; modes 6 and 7 require an extra word for the address of X. As a result, modes 6 and 7 automatically add 2 to the program counter.

Immediate and Absolute Addressing

The most curious use of the addressing modes has to do with how they are used when the designated register is register 7. Recall that register 7 is the program counter usually called PC, and will contain the address of the next instruction word to be fetched from memory. This is an important concept, because it means that the PC is always incremented immediately after a fetch, and before any other kind of use of it contents.

For this reason, the following instructions operate as:

MOV	PC,R0	Moves the address of the next instruction to R0
MOV	PC,X(R3)	Moves the address of the location that contains the address X to R3 locations after X
MOV	(PC),R0	Moves a copy of the next instruction to R0

Of course, it is occasionally useful to deal directly with the program counter, even in a deferred way, but there are four modes that have very special uses. These are modes 2, 3, 6, and 7, and are listed in Table 7.3.

It is now possible to explain the function of the .ENABL assembly directive. In Chapter 3, it was suggested to include the statement .ENABL AMA in your program in order to make the machine language program easier to understand. Without the .ENABL AMA statement, all addresses are normally assembled using mode 67 (relative addressing). Adding the .ENABL AMA statement causes the assembler to use mode 37 (absolute addressing) instead.

Modes 27 and 37 should be very familiar to the reader. Let us now see how these modes actually work. Mode 27 is actually mode 2 or auto-increment

Sec. 7.4   *Full Set of Addressing Modes*   157

TABLE 7.3

Mode	Name	Example		Op Code
27	Immediate	MOV	#4,R0	012700 000005
37	Absolute address	MOV (if AMA	X,R0 is enabled)	013700 (address of X)
67	Relative address	MOV (if AMA	X,R0 is not enabled)	016700 (distance from the instruction to X)
77	Relative address deferred	MOV	@X,R0	017700 (distance from the instruction to X)

mode. The following two instructions are equivalent:

```
MOV     #5,R0               MOV     (PC)+,R0
                            .WORD   5
```

Assume, for example, that the MOV instruction begins in memory cell 001000. Before the instruction is fetched from memory, the program counter will contain 001000.

```
                    Address     Contents
PC 001000 ─────→    001000      012700
                    001002      000005
                    001004      . . .
```

When the processor fetches the instruction, it automatically adds 000002 to the program counter. Thus, after the instruction is fetched (but before it is executed), the program counter contains 001002.

```
                    Address     Contents
                    001000      012700
PC 001002 ─────→    001002      000005
                    001004      . . .
```

The instruction is now executed. Mode 27 indicates that register 7 contains the address of the source operand. The processor therefore fetches the number 000005 contained in address 001002 and places it in register 0. However, mode 27 also specifies that 000002 should be added to the program counter. As a result, after the MOV instruction has been executed, the program counter will contain the address of the next instruction, namely 001004.

	Address	Contents
	001000	012700
	001002	000005
PC 001004 ⟶	001004	...

Note that the absolute-addressing mode (mode 37) works in the same way and the instruction MOV 1024,R0 could be written as:

```
MOV    @(PC)+,R0
.WORD  001024
```

However, here we have deferred addressing, so we do not move 001024 to R0, but what 001024 points to, namely the contents of location 001024. Sometimes the absolute-addressing (37) is preferred for special cases in programs that do not contain the .ENABL AMA directive. In such cases, the instruction can be written as MOV @#X,R0. It should be noted that mode 37 increments the program counter so that the PC will be advanced to the next instruction.

Finally, note that although it is possible to write an instruction that autodecrements the PC, it normally makes no sense to do so. However the reader should consider the effect of the instruction MOV −(PC),−(PC).

Relative Addressing

The relative-addressing mode (67) is the normal addressing mode used by the PDP-11 unless you specifically prevent it by using the .ENABL AMA. Earlier examples in the text suggested the use of .ENABL AMA because it makes the assembly listings easier to understand. As we shall soon see, the relative-addressing mode can be quite mysterious.

In effect, relative addressing is about the same as using register 7 as an index register, for example, CLR X(PC). This means that an effective address is computed by adding the base address X and the PC. For example, if the instruction CLR X(PC) is located at location 001032, and X is 001242, we can determine the effect of the instruction execution. Note that the program counter has just been used to fetch the base address of the instruction in question, located at 001034. Since the PC is always incremented immediately after this fetch, its value during execution will be 001036. This is added to X, or 001242, to obtain an effective address of 002300, which is then cleared.

Consequently, this instruction is simply an instruction to clear location 002300. In other words, it could be replaced with CLR 2300. Figure 7.8 shows how these instructions operate.

Since both instructions require the same number of words and therefore fetches, it would seem that the most straightforward method, namely the absolute-addressing mode would be preferred. Why then does the PDP-11 assembler seem to prefer relative addressing? The answer is that straightforwardness is not really of much consequence. It certainly would be if you were

Sec. 7.4   *Full Set of Addressing Modes*   159

hand assembling your programs and had to compute the rather strange addresses needed in the relative-addressing mode. The MACRO assembler, however, has arithmetic capability that makes these computations trivial and automatic.

The advantage of relative addressing can be seen quite easily by taking the example from Figure 7.8 and redoing it in Figure 7.9 so that all addresses are made 1500 higher. This would be the effect if the same program were to be loaded 1500 higher in memory.

Figure 7.8   Comparison between Modes 37 and 67 Addressing

Address	Contents	Address	Contents	
001032	005037	001032	005067	effective address =
001034	002300	001034	001242	001242 + 001036 = 002300
001036	Next instruction	001036	Next instruction	
.	.	.	.	
.	.	.	.	
002300	Location cleared	002300	Location cleared	
	(a)		(b)	

Figure 7.9   Relocated Comparison between Modes 37 and 67 Addressing

Address	Contents	Address	Contents	
002532	005037	002532	005067	effective address =
002534	004000	002534	001242	001242 + 002536 = 004000
002536	Next instruction	002536	Next instruction	
.	. address	.	.	
.	.	.	.	
004000	Location to be cleared	004000	Location to be cleared	
	(a)		(b)	

When we examine both Figures 7.8 and 7.9, it becomes obvious that there is an advantage to using relative addressing. Moving the program required no modification of the machine language code.

Since most programs must be relocated from the addresses of original assembly, the use of relative addressing reduces the amount of machine language modification that must be made during relocation. In fact, because of 67 addressing and user access to the program counter, it is possible, with extreme care, to write programs that can be loaded into *any* location in memory and run without modification. Programs written in this way are called **position independent code.** This is used for many operating systems programs that must be rapidly fetched and slotted into some available area of memory. This subject is described in more detail in Chapter 13.

The final mode to mention here is the relative-addressing-deferred mode. In effect, this is the same as relative addressing except that addressing is deferred. Figure 7.10 shows the operation of a mode 77 address. (Compare Figures 7.8 and 7.9.)

Figure 7.10 *Mode 77 Addressing*

Address	Contents	
001032	005077	
001034	001242	effective address = 001242 + 001036 = 002300
001036	next instruction	
.	.	
.	.	
002300	003724	but this location is used as a deferred address
003724	location to be cleared	

7.5 MULTIPLY-DIMENSIONED ARRAYS

As experience with FORTRAN or BASIC may have shown, arrays are often needed with multiple dimensions. Most frequently, this is seen in the form of the matrix (see Figure 7.11).

Since the computer memory is organized in the form of a linear string, more complex data structures such as matrices must be mapped or translated into the linear format. For a structure as simple as a matrix, the usual thing to do is to subdivide the matrix into a number of one-dimensional arrays or strings. This can be done either by stringing out the rows of matrix one after the other, or by stringing out the columns. Basically, it makes little difference which way is chosen. However, most FORTRAN systems store matrices columnwise. Since much of the use of assembly language by casual users is to augment FORTRAN, we suggest that unless some other reason overrides, the FORTRAN conventions be followed. Table 7.4 shows how a 5 × 7 matrix of one-word integers might be stored in the PDP-11 in the FORTRAN manner starting at location 003500.

From Figure 7.11, it can be seen that any array element A_{ij} can be accessed by displacing the proper amount from the base address 003500. The displacement amount can easily be derived from the formula $2[i - 1 + 5(j - 1)]$.

Figure 7.11 *A Classical m × n Matrix*

$$A_{11}A_{12}A_{13} \ldots A_{1n}$$
$$A_{21}A_{22}A_{23} \ldots A_{2n}$$
$$A_{31}A_{32}A_{33} \ldots A_{3n}$$
$$\vdots$$
$$A_{m1}A_{m2}A_{m3} \ldots A_{mn}$$

TABLE 7.4 MEMORY MAP OF A 5 × 7 MATRIX

Address	Matrix Element	Address	Matrix Element	Address	Matrix Element
3500	A_{11}	3530	A_{33}	3560	A_{55}
3502	A_{21}	3532	A_{43}	3562	A_{16}
3504	A_{31}	3534	A_{53}	3564	A_{26}
3506	A_{41}	3536	A_{14}	3566	A_{36}
3510	A_{51}	3540	A_{24}	3570	A_{46}
3512	A_{12}	3542	A_{34}	3572	A_{56}
3514	A_{22}	3544	A_{44}	3574	A_{17}
3516	A_{32}	3546	A_{54}	3576	A_{27}
3520	A_{42}	3550	A_{15}	3600	A_{37}
3522	A_{52}	3552	A_{25}	3602	A_{47}
3524	A_{13}	3554	A_{35}	3604	A_{57}
3526	A_{23}	3556	A_{45}		

For example, if the matrix element A_{36} is desired, $i = 3$ and $j = 6$. Therefore, the displacement is:

$$2[3 - 1 + 5(6 - 1)] = 54_{10} = 66_8$$

The resulting address is 003566.

The derivation of this formula is straightforward. The matrix is stored in memory with the first column occupying the first five memory words, the second column occupying the next five memory words, the third column occupying the next five memory words, and so on. Thus the jth column begins $5(j - 1)$ words from the start of the array. The ith word in the column will be located $i - 1$ words from the beginning of the column or $i - 1 + 5(j - 1)$ words from the beginning of the array. (The first element in a column is obviously zero words past the beginning of the column). Multiplication by 2 is necessary because word addresses increase by twos.

The computation of the subscript using the preceding formula involves multiplication, which is not a basic operation on the smaller PDP-11's. Arrays are often scanned by row, column, or diagonally. In these cases, it is often possible to index through these arrays in a much simpler way.

Clearly, if we were going to scan down the matrix columns one after the other, we would be doing the same thing as simple indexing through an array of 35 elements. Therefore, any of the techniques described in previous sections could be used.

Quite often (and this distinguishes a matrix from a one-dimensional array) a special operation must be performed at the end of scanning each column. For example, we might be trying to find the sums of the numbers in each column. This can easily be accomplished by including a second counter that tests for the ends of the columns. Figure 7.12 shows how a program could scan through the columns of the 5 × 7 matrix.

At first glance, scanning across the rows of a matrix may seem more complex than scanning down a column. However, it is in fact not any harder, and with some tricks, may even be easier. To scan across a row merely means incrementing by an appropriate number. Referring back to Table 7.4 we can see that elements A_{11}, A_{12}, A_{13}, A_{14}, and so on are at location 003500, 003512, 003524, 003536, and so on. Each is 12 locations from the previous one. (Octal 12 is decimal 10 or twice the number of rows in the matrix.)

Figure 7.12 A Program for Scanning Down the Columns of a Matrix

```
          MOV      #A,R1
LOOP1:    Any processing for the beginning of a column
          ...
          MOV      #5,R2
LOOP2:    Any processing on the array element (R1)
          ...
          ADD      #2,R1              ;LEFT OUT IF AUTO-INC USED
          DEC      R2
          BNE      LOOP2
          End of column processing
          ...
          CMP      R2,#A+106          ;106 = 2 X 35 IN OCTAL
          BLO      LOOP1
```

Consequently, it is merely necessary to increment our pointer register by 12 each time. The problem is knowing how to initialize the pointer register at the beginning of each row. One method for doing this would be to have a dummy pointer register that scans down the first column. See Figure 7.13 for an example of this kind of approach.

There is, however, a rather simple trick of arithmetic that can make the dummy counter unnecessary. Figure 7.14 shows how this operates. By successively adding 000012 (octal) to the address in R1, the first row of the matrix is processed. Since the matrix has 5 times 7 or 35 elements, each of which uses two addresses, the span of addressess for the matrix is 70 decimal or 106 octal. When the contents of R1 reaches 000106 octal, the first row has been processed. Subtracting 104 octal sets the contents of R1 to 000002, the correct displacement for the first element in the second row.

Figure 7.13 Program to Scan Rows of a 5 × 7 Matrix

```
           MOV      #A,R2              ;SET UP DUMMY POINTER
LOOP1:     Beginning of row processing
           ...
           MOV      R2,R1              ;SET UP REAL POINTER
LOOP2:     Operate on matrix element (R1)
           ...
           ADD      #12,R1
           CMP      R1,#A+106
           BLO      LOOP2
           End of row processing
           ...
           ADD      #2,R2              ;INCREMENT DUMMY
           CMP      R2,#A+12
           BLO      LOOP1
```

Figure 7.14 Improved Program for Scanning the Rows of a 5 × 7 Matrix

```
           MOV      #A,R1
LOOP1:     Beginning of row processing
           ...
LOOP2:     Operate on matrix element (R1)
           ...
           ADD      #12,R1
           CMP      R1,#A+106
           BLO      LOOP2
           End of row processing
           ...
           SUB      #104,R1
           CMP      R1,#A+12
           BLO      LOOP1
```

EXERCISE SET 2

1 Given that R0 contains 001200 and that memory has the following contents:

Address	Contents
001172	001206
001174	001174
001176	001172
001200	001206
001202	001204
001204	001200
001206	001172

what are the new contents of memory and R0 after each of the following instructions? (Assume the above contents for *each* instruction.)

(a) CLR	R0	(b) CLR	(R0)
(c) CLR	(R0)+	(d) CLR	-(R0)
(e) MOV	R0,(R0)	(f) MOV	(R0),R0
(g) MOV	(R0)+,(R0)+	(h) MOV	(R0)+,(R0)
(i) MOV	(R0)+,-(R0)	(j) MOV	-(R0),-(R0)
(k) MOV	@(R0)+,R0	(l) MOV	@(R0)+,@(R0)+

2 Assemble each of the instructions in exercise 1 into machine language.

3 Assume that the following program is loaded into location 2000. What does it do when executed?

```
            PC=%7
    START:  MOV     -(PC),-(PC)
            HALT
            .END    START
```

4 Hand assemble the following program into machine language. Since there is no .ENABL AMA, you should *not* use mode 37, but rather mode 67. Do any locations in the program need to be changed if your program is relocated to a different address? If so, what are they, and how do they change?

```
    START:  MOV     #7,A
            MOV     #3,B
            MOV     A,C
            ADD     B,C
            HALT
    A:      .BLKW   1
    B:      .BLKW   1
    C:      .BLKW   1
            .END    START
```

5 Rewrite the program(s) from exercises 3, 5, or 6 in the previous section of exercises (pages 149–150) so that maximum use is made of the auto-increment or auto-decrement modes.

6 Write a program that reads 35 numbers in the order that they would be if scanning a 5 × 7 matrix across the rows. Print out the numbers in the order they would have if scanning the matrix down the columns.

*7 A two-dimensional array can be scanned by row or by column. What are the corresponding ways that a three-dimensional array can be scanned? Write a program that reads 60 numbers forming a 3 × 4 × 5 array and then print out the 60 numbers in all the different ways that the array can be scanned. (Do not consider all possible reversals of direction.)

CHAPTER 8

ALPHABETIC INFORMATION— BYTE INSTRUCTIONS

8.1 REPRESENTING ALPHABETIC INFORMATION

Introduction

So far in our discussion, we have dealt with how to perform the elementary numeric calculations. Nothing has been said about alphabetic information, even though it should be clear that there must be some way of dealing with alphabetic data. After all, the assembler, the operating system, the FORTRAN compiler, and the BASIC interpreter all deal with statements that are strings of alphabetic characters. Furthermore, since these processors are really just ordinary computer programs, any program should be able to manipulate alphabetic data.

The immediate question is how alphabetic information is represented in the computer. The answer is that character data are encoded as binary numbers that have a unique representation for each character of the alphabet. (This must also include numerals and punctuation.) The actual encoding used is completely arbitrary. In other words, the interpretation of the character code is completely determined by the design of the input/output device used for reading or printing the characters. With the PDP-11, the most frequently used code is the one that is standard for teletypewriters. This code is called **ASCII** which means American Standard Code for Information Interchange. Other codes

165

used with the PDP-11 are Hollerith (punched card code) and RAD50. These will be discussed later.

The ASCII Code System

As just stated, the ASCII code system originated from use with teletypewriters. As such, each code represents the pressing of some combination of keys on a typewriter-like keyboard. (Note that as on most typewriters, pressing more than one key at a time is usually illegal. The exceptions are the SHIFT and CONTROL keys which do not produce a code themselves, but are used in combination with other keys.) With a typewriter, every key you press causes the printing mechanism to do something, that is, type a character, space, carriage return, and so on. Similarly, every implemented ASCII code causes the printing mechanism on the teletypewriter to do such an operation. In order to type a message on a typewriter, you must press the keys in a sequence. For the computer program to type a message on a teletypewriter, the program must provide the teletypewriter with a sequence of ASCII codes.

The full 7-bit ASCII system uses 128 codes, of which 95 are used for printing characters, and 33 are used for control operations such as carriage return and line feed. The 95 printing characters consist of the following:

> 26 Uppercase letters
> 26 Lowercase letters
> 10 Numerals
> 1 Blank space
> 32 Punctuation marks

The 32 punctuation marks are:

> ! " # $ % & ' ( ) * + , - . / < > : ; = ? @ [\ ] _ ~ ` { | } ∼

Note here that some of the less expensive teletypewriters and printers are only capable of printing 64 characters, which are:

> 26 Uppercase letters
> 10 Numerals
> 1 Blank space
> 27 Punctuation marks
> (the marks ` { | } ∼
> are excluded)

Of the 33 control characters, only a few are commonly used; the most common of these are:

Sec. 8.1   Representing Alphabetic Information   167

> BEL—Rings the bell on the typewriter
> BS—Backspaces the typewriter*
> HT—Horizontal tab†
> LF—Line feed, advances the paper one line
> VT—Vertical tab†
> FF—Form feed, advances the paper to a new page*
> CR—Carriage return, moves the print mechanism back to the beginning of the line

At this point, the reader may wonder what the other 26 control characters do. For the most part, with computer equipment, they do nothing. (Many of them are used as control codes for message switching and sending telegrams. In fact, this is what teletypewriters were originally used for.) In most equipment, the unused control characters are ignored. For example, a teletypewriter with no horizontal tab feature will do nothing when sent a horizontal tab character. As a consequence, these characters can be used for software functions. For example, the PDP-11 operating system will replace a horizontal tab with space characters so that the program, in effect, simulates a tab key.

Because there are $128 = 2^7$ ASCII characters, it would require a 7-bit number to cover all the possibilities. Therefore, ASCII is a 7-bit code, where each character is represented as a 7-bit binary number. The first 32 numbers are used for 32 of the 33 control characters, 000 through 037 (octal). Blank space is 040; the decimal digits 0-9 are 060 through 071; uppercase letters occupy 101 through 132; lowercase letters, 141 through 172; punctuation is assigned in an *ad hoc* manner to the otherwise unused codes from 041 through 176. All this leaves one control character to be assigned to 177. This character is called Rub Out or DEL (for DELete) and had a special importance in the days of hand-prepared paper tape. If you make a mistake typing, you can backspace a paper tape punch, but you cannot erase the holes. You can, however, punch more holes. Therefore, a special character was created called Rub Out or DEL with a code of all 1s (177). This character would cause all holes to be punched across the tape, and was generally ignored by the input processors. Because of this traditional usage, the PDP-11 operating system uses DEL or Rub Out as a software backspace to erase mistakes. Table 8.1 shows the entire 128-character ASCII code in octal.

The ASCII Keyboard

Because of the size of the ASCII alphabet (128 characters), it is not usually practical to assign one key for each character. As a consequence, it is normal to use a combination of keys to obtain some of the symbols. For example, a shift

---
*Some equipment is not capable of this function.
†Most equipment is not capable of this function.

TABLE 8.1 THE ASCII CHARACTER SET

000	NUL	040	SP	100	@	140	`
001	SOH	041	!	101	A	141	a
002	STX	042	"	102	B	142	b
003	ETX	043	#	103	C	143	c
004	EOT	044	$	104	D	144	d
005	ENQ	045	%	105	E	145	e
006	ACK	046	&	106	F	146	f
007	BEL	047	'	107	G	147	g
010	BS	050	(	110	H	150	h
011	HT	051	)	111	I	151	i
012	LF	052	*	112	J	152	j
013	VT	053	+	113	K	153	k
014	FF	054	,	114	L	154	l
015	CR	055	-	115	M	155	m
016	SO	056	.	116	N	156	n
017	SI	057	/	117	O	157	o
020	DLE	060	Ø	120	P	160	p
021	DC1	061	1	121	Q	161	q
022	DC2	062	2	122	R	162	r
023	DC3	063	3	123	S	163	s
024	DC4	064	4	124	T	164	t
025	NAK	065	5	125	U	165	u
026	SYN	066	6	126	V	166	v
027	ETB	067	7	127	W	167	w
030	CAN	070	8	130	X	170	x
031	EM	071	9	131	Y	171	y
032	SUB	072	:	132	Z	172	z
033	ESC	073	;	133	[	173	{
034	PS	074	<	134	\	174	|
035	GS	075	=	135	]	175	}
036	RS	076	>	136	∧	176	∼
037	US	077	?	137	_	177	DEL

key is used for distinguishing between upper- and lowercase letters on the 95 (printing) character keyboards. The shift key also serves to distinguish between certain punctuation marks and numerals as is done on most ordinary typewriters. Therefore, a 64-character keyboard has a shift key even though there are only uppercase letters.

In fact, on the 64-character keyboard, the function of the shift key is quite simple. It reverses, or complements, the fifth bit (bit 4 if the least significant bit is bit 0). Therefore, the shift key would change 061 to 041 or would change 056 to 076. From Table 8.1, we see that these are

$$1 \quad ! \quad . \quad \text{and} \quad >$$

respectively. Thus, on most ASCII keyboards, *exclamation point is* "shift *one*" and *greater than* is "shift *period.*" Figure 8.1 shows a typical keyboard for

Sec. 8.1 Representing Alphabetic Information

64-character ASCII. Note that some punctuation appears as shifted letters. The reader may verify that bit 4 is being complemented as stated before.

Note that the 64-character keyboard has very few keys for control characters. Typically carriage return, line feed, escape, and delete are the only ones. The first two are needed because they are typewriter functions that are used just to do ordinary typing. The latter two serve no particular hardware function, but are used extensively for software purposes, as mentioned before for delete.

The reader may well wonder how one might produce other control characters. Note that near the lower left-hand corner of Figure 8.1, there is a key marked CNTL (for control). This key is much like the shift key in that it has no particular function of its own, but is held down while another key is pressed. The basic function of the control key is to force the two most significant bits of the character code to zero. Thus, for example:

> Control @ is 000 or NUL
> Control A is 001 or SOH
> Control B is 002 or STX
> Control C is 003 or ETX

Note that all of the control characters except DEL can be produced this way. This includes carriage return (control M) and line feed (control J). DEL is somewhat odd, being all 1s, and therefore usually is given a separate key. In any case, since the control key forces bits to zero, it could not be used to create DEL.

The 95-character ASCII keyboard is usually quite similar to the 64-character keyboard, except that the shift key must function differently with letters. Here the normal code will be lowercase, and the shift will produce uppercase. This is done by forcing the sixth bit (bit 5) to zero. Thus the character "a" or 141 becomes "A" or 101. In addition, since shifted letters cannot be used for punctuation, separate keys are needed for

Figure 8.1 ASCII 64-Character Keyboard

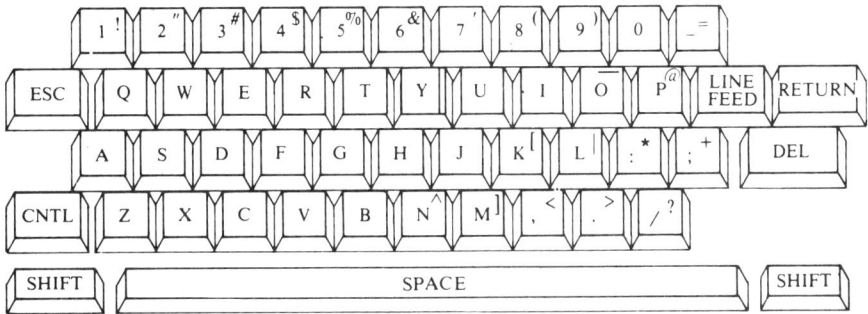

Furthermore, we pick up the additional punctuation

$$\{ \quad | \quad \} \quad \sim \quad \text{and} \quad `$$

However, it can be seen that the shift key will allow these characters to share keys with other punctuation. Many 95-character keyboards also have a special locking key that may be marked ALL CAPS. This key causes the keyboard to behave like a 64-character keyboard. The reason for this is that 95-character keyboards are relatively new, and much of the existing software is not capable of dealing with lowercase letters. Without such a switch, you would have to hold the shift key down most of the time while using such software.

Devices Other than Teletypewriters

The ASCII code is a **serial** (character-by-character) code that was originally designed for use with teletypewriters which are character-by-character typing machines. Even so, the ASCII code is quite useful for such devices as line printers and character display screens (often called CRTs because the major component is a cathode-ray tube).

Even though these devices are designed for high-speed multicharacter operations, information is usually fed to them one character at a time in order to simplify interconnections. Line printers and CRTs usually handle information in units of a line or a page at a time; as such, they do not have a typing carriage to return as does a teletypewriter. However, in order to be compatible with normal ASCII, carriage return and line feed are used to terminate a line and to advance to the next line. Therefore, for the most part, these devices may be treated as if they were ordinary teletypewriters.

There may, however, be some differences, or special ways that these devices must be handled. For example, some line printers must advance the paper in order to print a line; thus it is not necessary to transmit both a carriage return and a line feed.

Some devices have special capabilities. Printers may allow the programmer to advance the paper to the top of a new page. CRTs may have functions such as screen erase, cursor control, and scroll versus page mode. A **cursor** is a flashing marker that indicates where text is to be inserted on the screen. The cursor usually moves to the right as you type, but some CRTs allow the cursor to be repositioned anywhere on the screen. **Scrolling** allows the user to add lines to the bottom of the screen by rolling the remaining text up, losing the top line. These special capabilities usually operate through some protocol of control characters. The particular manual for the device should be consulted for such information.

Storing Characters in the PDP-11

As we have just seen, the basic ASCII code is a 7-bit code. However, on some teletypewriters and other equipment, an eighth bit is added in order to obtain

Sec. 8.1 *Representing Alphabetic Information* 171

error detection. This bit is called a **parity bit** and is set to a 1 or a 0 in order to make the total number of 1s in the 8-bit code an even number. This is called **even parity**. Now, if noise or a malfunction causes one of the 1s to change to a 0, or one of the 0s to change to a 1, the total number of 1s becomes an odd number (**odd parity**), and this error is detectable. (Note: Some machines generate odd parity, and then even parity means there is an error.)

Since parity ASCII is rarely used on the PDP-11, we will not discuss it further now. However, in order to have full generality with parity systems, the ASCII code is usually treated as an 8-bit code. The most significant bit, which would be the parity bit if parity were used, is then either always a 1 or always a 0, depending upon the device being used.

Now, since we have 8-bit codes, and since the PDP-11 has 16-bit words, it stands to reason that the most efficient use of memory will occur when two character codes are **packed** into each word. PDP-11 tradition has the *first* character placed in the *least* significant eight bits, and the *second* character placed in the *most* significant eight bits. As an example of how this works, the message **HELLO!** would be stored starting in location 001000 as follows:

Address	Binary Contents
	E H
001000	0100010101001000
	L L
001002	0100110001001100
	! O
001004	0010000101001111

Note that the order in which characters are packed into words seems backwards. However, aside from being PDP-11 tradition, this method also serves a practical purpose that will be discussed in the next section.

Another peculiarity becomes apparent when we convert the previous binary words to octal, and get:

Address	Contents
001000	042510
001002	046114
001004	020517

Looking at the octal word, it is certainly not obvious what the ASCII character codes are. The reason for this is that octal encoding is based upon dividing a word into multiples of three bits, and the 8-bit ASCII code is not a multiple of three bits. For this reason, most mini- and microcomputer manufacturers have given up octal all together, and use hexadecimal encoding, which divides a word into groups of four bits.

There is really no simple formula for extracting the ASCII codes from the octal encoding of a whole word. The easiest thing to do is probably to translate the word into binary, and split it into its 8-bit character codes. Then translate these back into octal. Figure 8.2 shows how this may be done. Fortunately, the software in the PDP-11 is set up so that you do not have to do this very often. And in any case, after you have done the translation a few times, you tend to get the knack for doing it in your head.

Figure 8.2 Converting Bytes to Words

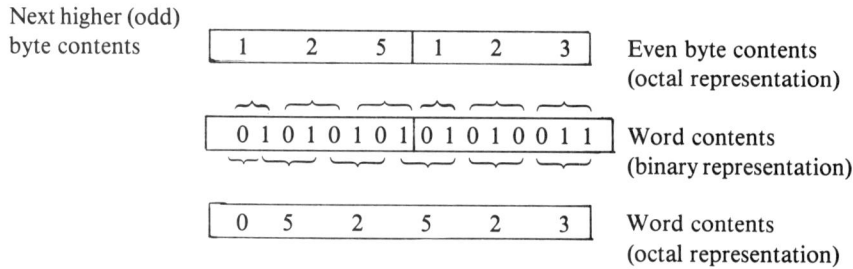

8.2 MANIPULATING CHARACTERS

Bytes and Byte Instructions

Now that we know how to store character codes in the PDP-11, our next step is to see how to write programs to manipulate strings of characters. The first step in that process is to decide how to separate the two character codes in a single word. Clearly, some sort of scheme using the shift instructions discussed in Chapter 6 could be made to work. However, this does not seem to be particularly easy either for the programmer or the computer. Since character processing is so important, instructions are available to accomplish it.

There is a whole special class of instructions called **byte instructions.** The term **byte** is used to refer to a small number (perhaps a mouthful) of bits. A byte is usually smaller than a word, but is large enough for a character code. The actual size of a byte and the number of bytes per word varies somewhat from machine architecture to machine architecture. In the PDP-11, there are eight bits to a byte, and therefore two bytes per word. Thus, in effect, bytes are the same as the character codes described in the preceding section.

Bytes were mentioned briefly in Chapter 3, pages 34–35, but not used after that. Let us now review what was said about bytes, and see how bytes are used. There is something very important about bytes. *Bytes are addressable!* Recall that word addresses must be even numbers. The reason is that odd addresses are reserved for byte operands. The even addresses refer to the low-order eight bits of a word, and the odd addresses refer to the upper eight bits of the word. Note, however, that only *byte instructions* may use odd addresses.

A typical example of a byte instruction is MOVB. This instruction is like

MOV, except that it only moves eight bits rather than sixteen, and it may have either or both of its addresses odd. To see how this works, let us reconsider the example of the message **HELLO!**. As bytes, this message appears as:

Byte Address	Binary Contents	Octal Contents
001000	01001000	110
001001	01000101	105
001002	01001100	114
001003	01001100	114
001004	01001111	117
001005	00100001	041

Now the instruction MOVB 1005,1002, would cause the byte at 001002 to change to what the byte at 001005 contains, namely 041. This would change memory to contain:

Byte Address	Octal Contents
001000	110
001001	105
001002	041
001003	114
001004	117
001005	041

Or equivalently, this would be the encoding of the message **HE!LO!**.

Most of the data-handling instructions that have been described so far have byte instructions as their counterparts. This results in the following list of byte instructions:

CLRB	TSTB	ADCB
NEGB	RORB	SBCB
INCB	ROLB	MOVB
DECB	ASRB	CMPB
	ASLB	

Note specifically that ADDB and SUBB are *missing* from the list. There are *no* instructions for adding or subtracting two bytes.

The operation of the byte instructions is essentially the same as their full-word counterparts except that their effect is limited to eight bits. For example, the instruction INCB 1003 would cause the 114 in byte location 001003 to change to 115. This changes the message to **HE!MO!**.

The operation code for a byte instruction is closely related to the operation code for the corresponding word instruction. The operation codes are identical except that the first bit of the word instruction is 0, while the first bit of the byte instruction is 1. For example, the operation code for MOV is 01ssdd, while the operation code for MOVB is 11ssdd. Similarly, the operation code for CLR is 0050dd, while the code for CLRB is 1050dd.

Bytes can represent signed or unsigned numbers. Since 8 bits can be arranged in 2^8 or 256 different ways, unsigned numbers range from 0 to 255 (decimal), and signed numbers range from -128 to 127 (decimal). The condition code bits operate in the normal manner (see Chapter 6). The error point for signed numbers is between 177 and 200 (octal). Passing this point causes the V bit to be set. Similarly, the error point for unsigned numbers is between 377 and 000 (octal). Passing this point may cause the C bit to be set. (Note that INCB and DECB, like INC and DEC, do not affect the C bit.) The shift and rotate instructions change the C bit in the expected manner. For example, a ROLB instruction moves bit 7 into the C bit in the same way that a ROL instruction moves bit 15 into the C bit. In both cases, the old value of the C bit is placed into bit 0.

Byte Instructions with Processor Registers

A question arises when instructions such as INCB R2 are used. Since the processor registers are 16 bits long, it is not clear which bits of the register are affected by the byte instructions. On the PDP-11, the following convention is followed. All byte instructions except MOVB affect only the 8 low-order bits of a processor register (bits 0 through 7). The high-order bits of the register (bits 8 through 15) are unaffected. For example, if register 2 contains 000377, the instruction INCB R2 will change the contents of the register to 000000. If register 2 contained 177777, the result of the instruction would be 177400.

The MOVB instruction is an exception. When the destination of a MOVB instruction is a processor register, the upper 8 bits of the register (bits 8 through 15) are set equal to the sign bit of the byte (bit 7). For example, if register 2 contains 177777 and the instruction MOVB #144,R2 is executed, the contents of the register will be changed to 000144 because the sign of the byte is 0. If register 2 contains 000000 and the instruction MOVB #234,R2 is executed, the contents of the register will be changed to 177634 because the sign of the byte is 1. Moving a byte to a processor register was defined in this way to allow a programmer to convert a signed 8-bit number into a signed 16-bit number. The reader should verify that 234 is the 8-bit, two's complement representation of -100, and that 177634 is the 16-bit, two's complement representation of -100.

Note that these questions only arise when byte instructions are used with processor registers. These questions do not occur when byte instructions are used with memory because the unit of addressable storage is only 8 bits. An instruction such as MOVB #177,2002 will change the contents of memory byte 002002, but it will have no effect on the contents of bytes 002001 or 002003.

Assembly Language Conventions for Bytes and Characters

As we saw in the previous section, it is somewhat difficult to convert from bytes to words, or vice versa. Because of this, the assembly language has some special assembly directives that facilitate dealing with bytes.

As can be seen from the previous examples, most of the use of bytes is in the form of arrays. Therefore, most of the assembly directives operate with arrays. The first is the .BLKB directive that operates just like .BLKW, except that bytes are allocated instead of words. However, in some cases, just allocating space for bytes is not enough. We would like to be able to specify what is in those locations. For example, we might want to specify that an array of successive bytes is to contain the characters **HELLO!**. One method of doing this is with the .BYTE directive. This directive has .BYTE followed by a number of byte data separated by commas. For example, in order to store the message string **HELLO!**, one could use the following line of code:

```
MESG:   .BYTE   110,105,114,114,117,041
```

The label MESG would identify the address of the first byte of the message. Note that since bytes can occupy odd addresses, it is quite possible that the symbol MESG would be assigned to an odd address. This is perfectly all right, but remember that odd addresses can only be referred to with byte instructions; word instructions *must* have *even* addresses.

There is a companion to .BYTE that can be used to fill a *word* array with data. It is .WORD. Referring back to the example on page 171, the same message could be expressed in the form of words as:

```
MESG:   .WORD   42510,46114,20517
```

Note however, that in this case MESG must be an even address.

After a long sequence of byte data, it may easily become unclear to a programmer whether the next location to be loaded is an odd or an even location. This may not be important if the next location is to be filled with another byte. However, if you are about to insert more instructions or full-word data into the program, you *must be certain* that the next location has an *even* address. One solution to this problem would be to carefully count the number of bytes you have generated and then add an extra byte if necessary to make the number come out even. An easier method is to have the assembler do the counting by using the .EVEN directive. The following example shows how .EVEN is used:

```
ALPH:   .BYTE   101,102,103
        .EVEN
NUMB:   .WORD   17743
```

NUMB is guaranteed to appear at an even address because the .EVEN directive will cause the generation of an extra byte of data if necessary.

Note that the .EVEN directive must be used whenever there is uncertainty as to whether the assembler is at an odd or an even location, and when the next entry is to be treated as a full word. This could happen even though the next item is being generated with the .BYTE directive, because often pairs of bytes are treated as words. Consider the following example:

```
              MOV      CRLF,TERM
              .
              .
              .
              .BYTE    1,2,3
              .EVEN
    CRLF:     .BYTE    15,12
```

CRLF must be at an even location because it is referenced by a MOV instruction, which *must* refer to an *even* address.

It should be noted, however, that when using .BYTE for placing character strings in a program, the programmer must convert all the characters into ASCII codes by looking them up in Table 8.1, or a similar table. Here again, the computer is quite capable of looking up codes in a table, and the assembler allows for this with the .ASCII directive. The format of .ASCII is .ASCII followed by a string of characters enclosed in slashes. Those characters are translated to ASCII codes and placed in successive byte locations. As an example, the string of bytes forming the message **HELLO!** used before could be formed with the ASCII directive as follows:

```
    MESG:    .ASCII   /HELLO!/
```

Since .ASCII generates bytes, it may use an odd number of byte locations. Thus the .EVEN directive should be used with .ASCII for the same reason it is used with the .BYTE directive.

Since slashes are used as delimiters, the messages cannot contain slashes. This can be circumvented by using other delimiters. There are also means for handling control characters and non-ASCII codes. For information on this, it is best to refer to the manual for the particular version of the assembler you are using.

Indexing with Byte Instructions

Because it is so common to use bytes in the form of arrays, it is important to note that byte instructions can be indexed in the same ways that word instructions can. The only essential difference is that since bytes can be located at odd addresses, it is legal for the effective address of a byte instruction to be odd. This should cause no special alarm because, in fact, byte instructions work essentially the way one would expect them to work.

Recall that in most of the examples in the previous chapter, an index register was modified in a loop by adding 2 each time through the loop.

Sec. 8.2   *Manipulating Characters*   177

Therefore, the examples contained an instruction such as ADD #2,R1. If these programs were rewritten to use a byte instruction, that instruction would probably appear as ADD #1,R1, or simply INC R1. For example, Figure 8.3 shows a simple program for zeroing out an array of twenty bytes. The directive .BLKB is like .BLKW except that it reserves a block of bytes.

The more interesting features of byte instructions come when auto-increment and auto-decrement modes are used. Because bytes can be at odd locations, the auto-increment/decrement modes cause incrementing or decrementing by 1 instead of 2.*

Figure 8.3   Program for Zeroing Bytes

```
            CLR     R0              ;R0 IS INDEX REGISTER
    LOOP:   CLRB    STRING(R0)      ;CLEAR BYTE
            INC     R0              ;INCREMENT INDEX
            CMP     R0,#24          ;LOOP TO END OF ARRAY
            BLT     LOOP
              .
              .
              .
    STRING: .BLKB   24
```

As a simple example of how auto-incrementing can be used with byte instructions, Figure 8.4 shows a simple program for printing out a message. For the purpose of this program, it is assumed that PCHAR is the name of a subroutine that prints the character contained in R0.

Note that the program in Figure 8.4 uses a different technique for looping than was used for previous examples. Rather than counting how many times the program goes through the loop, it loops until the data equals a predetermined number sometimes called a **sentinel** value. In this case, zero is used, because zero is not a legal ASCII code for a printing character. In fact, this technique is

Figure 8.4   A Program for Printing a Message

```
            MOV     #MESG,R1        ;INITIALIZE R1
    LOOP:   MOVB    (R1)+,R0        ;GET BYTE
            BEQ     OUT             ;STOP LOOPING WHEN A ZERO IS REACHED
            JSR     PC,PCHAR        ;PRINT CHARACTER
            BR      LOOP            ;AND LOOP UNTIL END
    OUT:      .
              .
              .
    MESG:   .ASCII  /THIS IS A MESSAGE./
            .BYTE 0                 ;ZERO BYTE TO STOP THE PROGRAM
```

*There are two exceptions to this rule that involve the stack pointer and the program counter. These exceptions occur because the stack pointer and the program counter must always point to a word location or an even address. Therefore, these registers are always incremented or decremented by 2, even with byte instructions.

so useful for dealing with messages that there is a special assembly directive just for the purpose. It is .ASCIZ, which is just like .ASCII except that a byte of 0 is added onto the end of the string. Therefore, in the example of Figure 8.4, the line

```
MESG:   .ASCIZ  /THIS IS A MESSAGE./
```

could be used. Then the .BYTE 0 would not be necessary.

EXERCISE SET 1

1. With a teletypewriter or CRT connected in LOCAL mode (that is, not connected to a computer, but talking to itself), explore the effects of all of the keys. Also, use the shift and/or control key with all of the other keys, and describe the effects. In particular:

    (a) Does your machine have upper- and lowercase? If not, what is the effect of shifting a letter? Is it possible to type all letters with shift held down? If there is lowercase, is there a shift lock key? An all caps key? What is the difference?

    (b) What is the effect of the control key? Which control characters do anything? What do they do? Do you always notice the effect?

2. Perform the steps outlined in exercise 1 with the PDP-11 console typewriter connected to the RT-11 operating system. How do you explain the different results obtained between exercises 1 and 2?

3. Do the same as exercise 2, but type R TECO before you start doing the experiment. Again, compare with previous results and try to explain the difference. (See Appendix E for a partial explanation of TECO).

4. Separate the following words into pairs of bytes, indicating which is the low-order byte and which is the high-order byte:

    (a) 006003   (b) 177777
    (c) 123456   (d) 111111
    (e) 022222   (f) 000400

5. Combine the following pairs of bytes into words expressed in octal (note orders):

	Low Order	High Order		Low Order	High Order
(a)	001	001	(b)	200	200
(c)	101	102	(d)	377	377
(e)	123	342	(f)	063	065

6 Assume that the contents of byte locations P, Q, and R are:

$$\begin{array}{ll} P & 177 \\ Q & 377 \\ R & 001 \end{array}$$

and that the condition codes are $N = 1$, $C = 1$, $V = 0$, and $Z = 1$. What will be the new values of P, Q, R and the condition codes after each of the following instructions is executed with the above contents?

(a)	CLRB	P		(b)	INCB	R
(c)	DECB	R		(d)	INCB	P
(e)	INCB	Q		(f)	ROLB	P
(g)	ROLB	Q		(h)	ASLB	P
(i)	ASLB	Q		(j)	ASRB	R

8.3 SIMPLIFIED INPUT AND OUTPUT

Input and Output of Characters in the RT-11 System
(Optional Section Intended for Persons Using RT-11)

Being able to store character codes in a computer serves little purpose unless there is some way of reading in or printing out characters. The processes of reading and printing data are extremely complex, and are handled in some depth in Chapter 11, and in great depth in the *PDP-11 Peripherals Handbook*. However, if you are using the RT-11 operating system, there are some built-in system functions that allow input and output of characters. In fact, these functions are clever enough so that if you are operating from the console teletypewriter, input and output appear there; and if you are operating from a batch stream, input comes from the batch stream, and output appears on the batch log.

These functions are made available through two system macros called .TTYIN and TTYOUT. Macros are simply packages of code that may be inserted at various places in your program. (The macros .REGDEF and .EXIT were introduced in Chapter 5.) In order to obtain the packages called .TTYIN and .TTYOUT from the *System Macro Library*, the following .MCALL assembly directive should be inserted in your program:

.MCALL .TTYIN,.TTYOUT

After the .MCALL directive appears, you may read a character by inserting .TTYIN at the appropriate point in the execution of your program. Each occurrence of .TTYIN is replaced by a set of instructions that asks the RT-11 operating system to read a character. When these instructions are executed, control is transferred to the RT-11 operating system which waits until someone types a message at the teletypewriter, terminated by a carriage return. The RT-11 operating system then places the first character of the message into R0 and returns control to your program. If you are operating under the batch stream, R0 gets the first character following the $DATA card (line).

Subsequent uses of .TTYIN will place successive characters of the message in R0. After all characters of the message have been read, including the carriage return and the line feed that end the message, the next use of .TTYIN will cause the system to wait for someone to type a second message.

Note that .TTYIN does not give you the first character of the message until the entire message, including the carriage return, has been typed. This allows the operating system to process certain control characters such as rubout, which causes the most recently typed character to be erased, and control U, which causes the entire line to be erased. (Appendix D describes these control functions for the RT-11 operating system.) Note that the operating system automatically inserts a line feed character after a carriage return is typed. As an example, the program in Figure 8.5 will read in a one-line message.

Figure 8.5 Sample Program, One-Line Message

```
        .MCALL   .TTYIN,.TTYOUT
        .
        .
        .
        MOV      #LOC,R1              ;GET BUFFER ADDRESS
LOOP:   .TTYIN                        ;GET CHARACTER
        MOVB     R0,(R1)+             ;STORE IT IN BUFFER
        CMPB     R0,#12               ;WAS IT LINE FEED?
        BNE      LOOP                 ;IF NOT, KEEP LOOPING
        .
        .
        .
LOC:    .BLKB    40                   ;ROOM FOR 32 CHARACTERS
```

The macro .TTYOUT will print out a single character from R0 on the console teletypewriter (or log file, if you are operating in batch mode). Figure 8.6 shows how the message ABC could be printed, followed by carriage return and line feed. It is also possible to use .TTYOUT to print a fixed character code by using a line such as .TTYOUT #15 which would print a carriage return. Note, however, that the contents of R0 will still be changed. For other uses of .TTYIN and .TTYOUT, consult the *RT-11 Advanced Programmer's Guide*.

Sec. 8.3 Simplified Input and Output

Figure 8.6 Program for Printing ABC Message

```
        .MCALL  .TTYIN,.TTYOUT
        .
        .
        .
        MOV     #MSG,R1         ;GET MESSAGE ADDRESS
LOOP:   MOVB    (R1)+,R0        ;GET CHARACTER
        BEQ     OUT             ;DONE IF ZERO BYTE
        .TTYOUT                 ;PRINT CHARACTER
        BR      LOOP            ;LOOP UNTIL DONE
OUT:    .
        .
        .
MESG:   .ASCII  /ABC/
        .BYTE   15,12,0
```

Input and Output of Characters at the Hardware Level *(Optional Section Intended for Persons Not Using a Resident System)*

As mentioned in the previous section, the processes of reading and printing data are complex operations. However, it is possible to read and print characters at the operator's teletypewriter with only a few instructions. This section shows how to do these operations. The explanations given here are oversimplified, and are intended to allow users to do their own input and output. For more detail see Chapter 11.

In order to print a character, it is merely necessary to move the ASCII code for the characters into a special byte address called the **printer buffer.** We can use the symbolic name PRB. Thus, we could cause an A to be printed by executing the instruction MOVB #101,PRB. There is a catch, however: once you have executed such an instruction, you must wait a certain amount of time until you can do it again. This is because the printers are slow. In the time it takes to print one character, the PDP-11 can execute thousands of MOVB instructions.

In order to tell if the printer is ready to receive a character for output, there is another special byte address called PRS for **printer status.** This byte goes negative when the printer is ready, and you should never move a byte into the PRB unless the PRS is negative. Consequently, the following subroutine can be used to print the ASCII character in R0:

```
PCHAR:  TSTB    PRS             ;TEST PRINTER STATUS
        BPL     PCHAR           ;LOOP UNTIL READY
        MOVB    R0,PRB          ;OUTPUT CHAR
        RTS     PC              ;RETURN
```

Input from the operator's keyboard operates in a manner very similar to printing. There are two special byte locations KBS (**keyboard status**) and KBB (**keyboard buffer**). Whenever someone types a character at the keyboard, the KBS becomes negative. The ASCII code for the character just typed will be available in the KBB. As soon as you examine the KBB, the KBS becomes positive again so that you can now wait for the next character. Thus, in theory at least, the following instructions could read one character from the keyboard and move it into register 0:

```
RCHAR:  TSTB    KBS             ;TEST KEYBOARD STATUS
        BPL     RCHAR           ;LOOP UNTIL SOMETHING IS TYPED
        MOVB    KBB,R0          ;GET CHARACTER
        RTS     PC              ;RETURN
```

There are, however, two minor problems. First, recall that ASCII is a 7-bit code. Since the move byte instruction fetches 8 bits from byte KBB, there is a question about the value of the most significant bit of the byte. On the standard PDP-11 operator's keyboard, this bit will be set to 1. Because a MOVB instruction is used with a register destination, bits 8 through 15 of the register will also be set to 1. To solve this problem, a BIC instruction (for BIt Clear) can be used to set the 9 high-order bits of the register (bits 7 through 15) to 0 without altering the 7 low-order bits (bits 0 through 6). The operation of the BIC instruction will be explained in the next section.

The second problem is one of philosophy of system design. The PDP-11 operator's console operates in the **full duplex** mode. This means that the keyboard and the printer are separate devices with no relationship between them. Consequently, if the previous instructions were used by themselves for input, the operator would be typing blindly and would never see what was being typed. The solution to this is called **echoing**, which requires that whenever a program reads a character, it prints it back out. This can be achieved by calling subroutine PCHAR whenever a character is read. The following subroutine can be used to read a character into R0.

```
RCHAR:  TSTB    KBS             ;TEST KEYBOARD STATUS
        BPL     RCHAR           ;LOOP UNTIL SOMETHING IS TYPED
        MOVB    KBB,R0          ;GET CHARACTER
        BIC     #177600,R0      ;CLEAR HIGH ORDER BITS
        JSR     PC,PCHAR        ;ECHO CHARACTER
        RTS     PC              ;RETURN
```

So far, we have stated the KBS, KBB, PRS, and PRB were special byte locations, but we did not say where they were. Although the actual locations are modifiable, in most PDP-11 systems they are the four even-numbered locations starting with 177560. When you use the previous three-letter symbols in your assembly language programs, you *must* define them as specific addresses. This is done with a line that contains a label, an equal sign, and the value of the address. Therefore, any program using these symbols for input/output must contain the following lines:

```
KBS=177560
KBB=177562
PRS=177564
PRB=177566
```

As an example, the program shown in Figure 8.7 will print out ABC.

Figure 8.7 Sample Program, Print ABC

```
        PRS=177564                  ;DEFINE PRINTER ADDRESSES
        PRB=177566
            .
            .
            .
        MOV     #MSG,R3             ;GET MESSAGE ADDRESS
LOOP:   MOVB    (R3)+,R0            ;GET CHARACTER
        JSR     PC,PCHAR            ;AND PRINT IT
        TSTB    (R3)                ;CHECK FOR ZERO BYTE
        BNE     LOOP                ;LOOP UNTIL END
            .
            .
            .
MSG:    .ASCIZ  /ABC/
        .EVEN
            .
            .
            .
PCHAR:  TSTB    PRS                 ;TEST PRINTER STATUS
        BPL     PCHAR               ;LOOP UNTIL READY
        MOVB    R0,PRB              ;OUTPUT CHAR
        RTS     PC                  ;RETURN
```

8.4 BIT MANIPULATION INSTRUCTIONS

The Need to Manipulate Bits

Earlier in this chapter, it was stated that the 8-bit character codes could be extracted from a word by shifting. This is in fact true; however, it turns out to be a considerable effort to extract portions of a word in this way. We later discussed the byte instructions, and this solved the problem for the moment. However, the byte instructions only work when the information is packed into a word in 8-bit chunks.

Needless to say, it is often quite useful to pack information into words or bytes in various size parcels. Here are some examples of pieces of words or bytes that have already been discussed as having some special significance:

1. Bit 15 of a word or bit 7 of a byte gives the algebraic sign.
2. Bit 0 of a word or byte tells if the number being represented is odd or even.
3. Bits 5 and 6 of an ASCII character code tell whether the character is upper- or lowercase or a control character, or in the main block of numeric and punctuation characters.
4. Bit 7 of a byte may be used as a parity check bit on an ASCII character.

The BIS, BIC, and BIT Instructions

In order to create or examine little packets of information of this kind, the PDP-11 has been supplied with three instructions. Each of these instructions has a byte counterpart. They are designed to set or clear specific bits in a word or to test specific bits.

The three instructions are as follows:

```
BIS — Bit set
BIC — Bit clear
BIT — Bit test
```

They are two-operand instructions, and the first operand is a **mask** that is used to select certain bits in the destination. For example, the BIS instruction causes each bit in the destination to be set to a 1 if the corresponding bit in the mask is a 1. The bits that correspond to 0s in the mask are not changed. In effect, this is a bit-by-bit OR operation of the mask with the destination. For example, consider the following binary numbers before and after the execution of a BIS instruction:

```
X = 1 101 111 000 010 001
Y = 1 100 010 101 101 000      Before BIS
```

Execution of the BIS X,Y:

```
X   1 101 111 000 010 001
Y   1 101 111 101 111 001      After BIS
```

Note that the mask is unchanged.

The BIC instruction is similar, except that bits of the destination are cleared to 0 if the corresponding bit of the mask is a 1. This operation is like the Boolean AND operation of the one's complement of the mask with the destination (see chapter 2). The preceding example will now be reshown, using the BIC instruction:

Bit Manipulation Instructions

```
X = 1 101 111 000 010 001
Y = 1 100 010 101 101 000         Before BIC
```

Execution of BIC X,Y:

```
X   1 101 111 000 010 001
Y   0 000 000 101 101 000         After BIC
```

The BIT instruction is quite different. It is like the CMP instruction in that no computed result is stored; instead, it is used to set condition codes. A computed result is determined that has a 1 in a given bit position only if *both* operands have 1s in the corresponding position. This is the Boolean AND operation. If there are no 1s in the entire computed result, the condition code Z will be set. If the most significant bit of the computed result is 1, then N will be set. Since an overflow or carry cannot occur, these condition codes are not used. However, in order to be consistent with how most persons would want to use the branch instructions, V is always cleared and C is left unchanged. In fact, all of the bit manipulation instructions affect the condition codes in the same way.

Again using the same values of X and Y, here is an example of how the BIT instruction operates:

```
X = 1 101 111 000 010 001
Y = 1 100 010 101 101 000         Before and after BIT
```

Execution of BIT X,Y

```
Computed result = 1 100 010 000 000 000    (not stored)
```

X and Y are unchanged. Condition codes are:

```
N = 1
Z = 0
V = 0
C = Previous value before BIT instruction
```

The three instructions BIT, BIC, and BIS have byte counterparts BITB, BICB, and BISB. These all operate the same way, except that they deal with 8-bit bytes rather than 16-bit words.

The COM Instruction

The last bit manipulation instruction is COM (for COMplement) which simply reverses all of the bits in the destination. That is, 1 bits are changed to 0, and 0 bits are changed to 1. For example, the instruction COM X will have the following effect:

X = 1 101 111 000 010 001   before COM

Execution of COM X

X = 0 010 000 111 101 110   after COM

Similarly, the COMB instruction will complement the 8 bits in a byte.

Beginning programmers sometimes confuse the COM and NEG instructions. NEG is used to obtain the negative of a signed 2's complement number. The COM instruction could be used to obtain the negative of a 1's complement number as described in Chapter 2. However, the PDP-11 uses the 2's complement system for signed numbers rather than the 1's complement system. As a result, the COM instruction is usually only used for bit manipulation purposes.

Examples Using Bit Manipulation

Figures 8.8 and 8.9 show two examples of program segments that use the bit manipulation instructions. The first, in Figure 8.8, extracts the third octal digit of the number N and prints it out as a single character.

The program segment in Figure 8.9 takes a 7-bit ASCII code and determines whether there is an odd or an even number of 1s in the code. A parity bit is the added bit in position 7 to produce a byte with odd parity (see page 171). Neither of these examples is a complete program, but each is assumed to be a segment of some larger program.

Figure 8.8 Program to Print Third Octal Digit of a Word

```
            .MCALL       .TTYOUT
            .
            .
            .
            MOV          N,R0          ;PUT NUMBER IN R0
            BIC          #177077,R0    ;CLEAR ALL BUT 3RD DIGIT
            MOV          #6,R1         ;SET UP FOR 6 SHIFTS
    LOOP:   ASR          R0            ;SHIFT RIGHT
            DEC          R1            ;6 TIMES
            BNE          LOOP          ;LOOP UNTIL DONE
            BIS          #60,R0        ;MAKE TEMP AN ASCII CODE
            .TTYOUT      R0            ;PRINT CHARACTER
            .
            .
            .
    N:      .BLKW        1
```

The example in Figure 8.8 uses .TTYOUT for output. This was described in the optional section beginning on page 179. If you are not using the RT-11 system, simply delete the .MCALL and replace .TTYOUT with

Sec. 8.4   *Bit Manipulation Instructions*   187

Figure 8.9   *Subroutine to Generate a Byte with Odd Parity*

```
    ;
    ; SUBROUTINE ODDGN GENERATES A BYTE WITH ODD PARITY
    ;
ODDGN:  BICB    #200,R0         ;CLEAR PARITY BIT
        MOVB    #1,MASK         ;START WITH MASK OF 1
        MOV     #7,R1           ;7 BITS IN CODE
        CLR     TEST            ;TEST WILL INDICATE PARITY
LOOP:   BITB    MASK,R0         ;TEST FOR BIT
        BEQ     SKIP            ;SKIP IF ZERO
        INC     TEST            ;TEST COUNTS ONES
SKIP:   ASLB    MASK            ;MOVE MASK BIT
        DEC     R1              ;COUNT SEVEN BITS
        BNE     LOOP            ;LOOP UNTIL DONE
        BIT     #1,TEST         ;TEST PARITY
        BNE     DONE            ;IF PARITY ALREADY ODD WE ARE DONE
        BISB    #200,R0         ;OTHERWISE SET PARITY BIT
DONE:   RTS     PC              ;RETURN WITH RESULT IN R0
            .
            .
            .
MASK:   .BLKB   1
        .EVEN
```

JSR PC,PCHAR. (Subroutine PCHAR, which is described on page 181, would also have to be included.)

A final example uses various features of the bit manipulation and shift instructions with character strings. This program (shown in Figure 8.10) prompts the user by typing out an asterisk, and then reads in an unsigned decimal number that is terminated by a carriage return. The value of the decimal number is placed in location DATA. Because no check is made of the number of characters typed in, the result will be modulo 65536. Similarly, since no error checks are made, if the user types characters other than decimal digits, the result will be meaningless.

Note the general way that this program works. It starts out with the contents of DATA equal to 0. Then each time a digit is picked up, the number in DATA is multiplied by 10 and the value of the digit is added. For example, suppose we type in 573: the number in DATA is 0 and the first digit is 5; the number in DATA times 10 is still 0, plus 5 is 5. Now the next digit is 7. DATA times 10 is 50, plus 7 is 57. The last digit is 3. DATA times 10 is 570; add three and we get 573. The carriage return ends the process.

Note also that since carriage returns are followed by line feeds, an extra read is placed at the end of the program to eat up the line feed so that the program would work if used subsequent times.

As in Figure 8.8, the use of .TTYIN and .TTYOUT can be replaced with the direct input/output forms shown on pages 181-182.

Figure 8.10   Decimal Read Subroutine

```
            .MCALL          .TTYIN,.TTYOUT
            .
            .
            .
;
; READS A DECIMAL NUMBER AND LEAVES IT IN R0
;
READ:       MOVB            #52,R0
            .TTYOUT                         ;PRINT * TO PROMPT USER
            CLR             DATA            ;INITIALLY ANSWER IS ZERO
LOOP:       .TTYIN                          ;GET CHARACTER
            CMPB            R0,#15          ;WAS IT A CARRIAGE RETURN?
            BEQ             DONE            ;IF SO WE ARE DONE
            BIC             #177760,R0      ;OTHERWISE STRIP EXTRA BITS
            ASL             DATA            ;DATA=DATA*2
            MOV             DATA,R1         ;SAVE DATA*2
            ASL             DATA            ;DATA IS NOW 4
            ASL             DATA            ;AND 8 TIMES ORIGINAL
            ADD             R1,DATA         ;AND NOW 10 TIMES
            ADD             R0,DATA         ;ADD IN DIGIT
            BR              LOOP            ;GET NEXT DIGITS (IF ANY)
DONE:       .TTYIN                          ;DO ONE LAST READ FOR LINE FEED
            MOV             DATA,R0         ;GET RESULT
            RTS             PC              ;AND RETURN
DATA:       .BLKW           1
```

Single and Double Operand Families of Instructions

Now that the bit manipulation instructions have been described, we can complete the description of the single and double operand families of instructions that are available on all PDP-11's. The double operand family is shown in Figure 8.11. In order to explain the notation used in the figure, the move instruction in the first row will be considered in more detail.

In the figure, the mnemonic for the move instruction is MOV(B). This indicates that the mnemonic for a 16-bit move is MOV and that the mnemonic for an 8-bit move is MOVB. In the second column the op code for move is listed as ■ 1SSDD. The symbol ■ should be replaced by 0 to obtain the operation code for the word instruction (01SSDD), and it should be replaced by 1 to obtain the operation code for the byte instruction (11SSDD). The third column specifies the name of the instruction (move). The fourth column describes the operation. In this case, d←s indicates that the contents of the destination is set equal to the contents of the source. The last column specifies the effect of the instruction on the condition code bits. The asterisks under the N and Z bits indicate that these bits reflect the number that is moved to the destination. That is, a negative

Sec. 8.4 Bit Manipulation Instructions

number would cause the N bit to be set to 1, and a zero would cause the Z bit to be set to 1. The 0 under the V bit indicates that a move instruction always sets the V bit to zero, while the dash under the C bit indicates that a move instruction does not affect the C bit.

Figure 8.11 The Double Operand Family of Instructions

Mnenomic	Op Code	Instruction	Operation	N Z V C
General				
MOV(B)	∎ 1SSDD	move	d ← s	* * 0 —
CMP(B)	∎ 2SSDD	compare	s − d	* * * *
ADD	06SSDD	add	d ← s + d	* * * *
SUB	16SSDD	subtract	d ← d − s	* * * *
Logical				
BIT(B)	∎ 3SSDD	bit test (AND)	s ∧ d	* * 0 —
BIC(B)	∎ 4SSDD	bit clear	d ← (∼s) ∧ d	* * 0 —
BIS(B)	∎ 5SSDD	bit set (OR)	d ← s ∨ d	* * 0 —

Figure 8.12* shows the single operand family of instructions. Note that the destination result of the complement instruction is described as ∼ d to indicate a 1's complement negative. In contrast, the destination result for the negate instructon is − d to indicate a 2's complement negative. The only new instruction is SWAB (for SWAp Byte) which swaps the two bytes in a word. For example, the instruction SWAB R2 will cause the low-order bits in register 2 (bits 0 through 7) to be moved to the high-order bit positions (bits 8 through 15). Similarly, the high-order bits will be moved to the lower bit positions. Note that SWAB is a word instruction that does not have a byte counterpart.

Figure 8.12 The Single Operand Family of Instructions

Mnemonic	Op Code	Instruction	dst Result	N Z V C
General				
CLR(B)	∎ 050DD	clear	0	0 1 0 0
COM(B)	∎ 051DD	complement (1's)	∼ d	* * 0 1
INC(B)	∎ 052DD	increment	d + 1	* * * __
DEC(B)	∎ 053DD	decrement	d − 1	* * * __
NEG(B)	∎ 054DD	negate (2's compl)	− d	* * * *
TST(B)	∎ 057DD	test	d	* * 0 0

*Figures 8.11 and 8.12 are part of the PDP-11 programming card that is reproduced inside the front cover of the book.

Figure 8.12 *(continued)*

Mnemonic	Op Code	Instruction	dst Result	N Z V C
Rotate & Shift				
ROR(B)	∎ 060DD	rotate right	→ C, d	* * * *
ROL(B)	∎ 061DD	rotate left	C, d ←	* * * *
ASR(B)	∎ 062DD	arith shift right	d/2	* * * *
ASL(B)	∎ 063DD	arith shift left	2d	* * * *
SWAB	0003DD	swap bytes		* * * 0
Multiple Precision				
ADC(B)	∎ 055DD	add carry	d + C	* * * *
SBC(B)	∎ 056DD	subtract carry	d − C	* * * *

8.5 OTHER CHARACTER REPRESENTATIONS
(Optional Section)

Hollerith Code

Although ASCII is the most popular character encoding for use with small computers, other encodings are worthy of note. Of special importance is the encoding used on punched-card equipment. This is also known as **Hollerith** code because of its developer, Herman Hollerith, who introduced the use of punched cards for tabulating the 1890 U.S. Census.

The basis of Hollerith code is a paper card that is the same height and width as the dollar bill in use at that time. Rectangular holes can be punched in the card in any of 80 column positions horizontally, and any of 12 row positions vertically (see Figure 8.13).

Each column is used for a single character; therefore, a card can contain 80 encoded characters. Since there are 12 rows, and since, conceivably, any possible combination of 12 punches is possible, the punch-card code could accommodate an alphabet with as many as $2^{12} = 4096$ different characters. In practice, however, if you punch too many holes in a card, it starts looking like, and having the physical strength of, a piece of cheesecloth. Consequently, the codes are restricted so that normally no column has more than three punches in it.*

---

*There are some exceptions to this rule, notably special-purpose cards such as end-of-file cards, binary cards, and some extended alphabet codes that may include lowercase letters and control characters.

Sec. 8.5   Other Character Representations   191

Figure 8.13   Hollerith Card

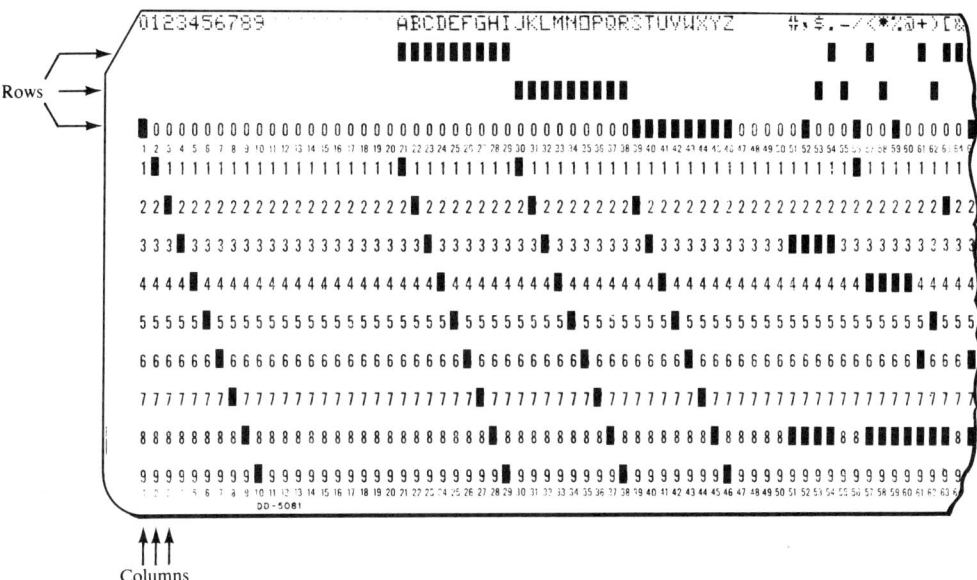

The rows on the card are numbered (from top to bottom) 12, 11, 0, 1, 2, 3, 4, 5, 6, 7, 8, and 9, respectively. The codes for the numerals 0 through 9 are punched with a single punch in the corresponding row (that is, the code for 5 is a punch in the 5 row, or a **five punch**). Letters are formed by combining one punch in rows 1-9 (a **numeric punch**) with a second punch in rows 12, 11, or 0 (a **zone punch**). This gives $9 \times 3 = 27$ possibilities, of which 26 are used. Figure 8.14 gives a table of codes for the alphabet. Note that the one code left out is 0-1, a code in the middle of the table. Hollerith left this code out because he feared that his machinery might tear a card with two adjacent rows being punched. In addition, the single punches 12, 11, and no punch at all are used for &, −, and blank space.

Figure 8.14   Hollerith Code for the Alphabet

A	1-12	J	1-11	Unused	1-0
B	2-12	K	2-11	S	2-0
C	3-12	L	3-11	T	3-0
D	4-12	M	4-11	U	4-0
E	5-12	N	5-11	V	5-0
F	6-12	O	6-11	W	6-0
G	7-12	P	7-11	X	7-0
H	8-12	Q	8-11	Y	8-0
I	9-12	R	9-11	Z	9-0

Modern Card Codes

Later, as data processing became more sophisticated, a need for more punctuation arose. This need was met by extending the numeric range from 9 to 15 by using an 8 punch in combination with a punch from 2 through 7. For example, an 8-5 punch has a decimal value of 13. In addition, the gentler modern equipment allows the 0-1 punch to be used. This gives a total possibility of 64 characters.

Assignment of punctuation to punch configurations is pretty much arbitrary, and there are, in fact, several different assignments. Figure 8.15 shows

Figure 8.15   *IBM 029-EH Keypunch Code*

Space	No punch	&	12	-	11	0	0
1	1	A	12-1	J	11-1	/	0-1
2	2	B	12-2	K	11-2	S	0-2
3	3	C	12-3	L	11-3	T	0-3
4	4	D	12-4	M	11-4	U	0-4
5	5	E	12-5	N	11-5	V	0-5
6	6	F	12-6	O	11-6	W	0-6
7	7	G	12-7	P	11-7	X	0-7
8	8	H	12-8	Q	11-8	Y	0-8
9	9	I	12-9	R	11-9	Z	0-9
:	8-2	¢	12-8-2	!	11-8-2	unused	0-8-2
#	8-3	.	12-8-3	$	11-8-3	,	0-8-3
@	8-4	<	12-8-4	*	11-8-4	%	0-8-4
|	8-5	(	12-8-5	)	11-8-5	_	0-8-5
=	8-6	+	12-8-6	;	11-8-6	>	0-8-6
"	8-7	|	12-8-7	—	11-8-7	?	0-8-7

the most popular card code. This code is often called **029 code** because it was first introduced on the IBM model 29 keypunch. In some ways, however, the name 029 code is a misnomer, because IBM makes model 29 keypunches with a variety of different code assignments. In particular, this code assignment is found in the very popular IBM model 029-EH keyboard. However, note that the assignment of numerals and alphabetic characters is standard; only punctuation changes.

The 64-character 29 code is a subset of an 8-bit code called EBCDIC (pronounced ebb-sa-dick, which is an acronym for Extended Binary Coded Decimal Interchange Code). The 8 bits provide for a possible 2^8 or 256 combinations. In addition to the 64 characters of the 29 code, EBCDIC includes lowercase letters as well as a variety of control characters. The EBCDIC code is shown in Figure 8.16 as a table with 32 rows and 8 columns. The row specifies the rightmost five bits while the column specifies the leftmost three bits. For example, the capital letter A occupies the second position in the seventh column. Thus the binary code for an A consists of the bits 110 (from the column) followed by 00001

Figure 8.16 EBCDIC Code

Rightmost Five Bits	Leftmost Three Bits							
	000	001	010	011	100	101	110	111
00000	NUL	DS	Sp	—				
00001	SOH	SOS		/	a		A	
00010	STX	FS			b	s	B	S
00011	ETX				c	t	C	T
00100	PF	BYP			d	u	D	U
00101	HT	LF			e	v	E	V
00110	LC	ETB			f	w	F	W
00111	DEL	ESC			g	x	G	X
01000					h	y	H	Y
01001					i	z	I	Z
01010	SMM	SM	¢					
01011	VT	CU2	.	,				
01100	FF		<	%				
01101	CR	ENQ	(	—				
01110	SO	ACK	+	>				
01111	SI	BEL	|	?				
10000	DLE		&					0
10001	DC1				j		J	1
10010	DC2	SYN			k		K	2
10011	TM				l		L	3
10100	RES	PN			m		M	4
10101	NL	RS			n		N	5
10110	BS	UC			o		O	6
10111	IL	EOT			p		P	7
11000	CAN				q		Q	8
11001	EM				r		R	9
11010	CC		!	:				
11011	CU1	CU3	$	#				
11100	IFS	DC4	*	@				
11101	IGS	NAK	)	'				
11110	IRS		;	=				
11111	IUS	SUB	¬	,,				

(from the row) or 11000001. Notice that many combinations are not assigned to any symbol or control character. EBCDIC is used by most IBM computers as well as computers made by other manufacturers.

RAD50 Code

Finally, there is another character code that is of special interest to PDP-11 users, called **RAD50 code.** As seen earlier, ASCII code can only be packed two characters per word. As a consequence, character strings can require a lot of memory. Therefore, the DEC software engineers devised a special code for use in assembly symbol tables and similar places where three characters can be packed into a word. In order for this code to work, there must be a restricted alphabet. This consists of the letters A through Z, the numerals 0 through 9, blank space, ., and $. This comes to 39 characters. To even things out, an unused code was added to get 40.

Now, if we compute how many combinations of three characters are possible with a 40-character alphabet, we get 40 × 40 × 40 = 64,000. Note that since this is somewhat less than 65,536, each possibility can be accounted for in a 16-bit word.

The way RAD50 code works is that each character of the alphabet is treated as a digit in the base 40 number system (see Chapter 2). Figure 8.17 shows the assignment of values to the digits in this system. Thus, for example, if you had the character string GHI to translate to RAD50 code, you would find the values of G, H, and I in Figure 8.17, that is, G = 7, H = 8, and I = 9. Then you would multiply them by the appropriate powers of 40:

$$7 \times 40^2 + 8 \times 40 + 9$$

or

$$\begin{aligned} 7 \times 1600 &= 11200 \\ 8 \times 40 &= 320 \\ 9 \times 1 &= 9 \\ \hline &11529 \end{aligned}$$

Therefore 11529_{10} is the code, except that we have computed in decimal, therefore we should convert to octal:

$$11529_{10} = 26411_8$$

Consequently, in the form we would probably see, the radix 40 code for GHI is 026411. In fact, the DEC people are so used to octal that they called the code RAD50 instead of RAD40. (Notice that $40_{10} = 50_8$.)

In assembly language, RAD50 code can be generated with the .RAD50 directive. This works a lot like .ASCII except that it outputs words instead of bytes. Therefore the line .RAD50 /GHI/ would generate the word 026411. If more than three characters are given, multiple words are filled. If the string is not a multiple of three characters, trailing blanks are added. For more information on RAD50 code, the various PDP-11 systems handbooks should be consulted.

Figure 8.17   *The RAD50 Code*

Blank	0	E	5	J	10	O	15
A	1	F	6	K	11	P	16
B	2	G	7	L	12	Q	17
C	3	H	8	M	13	R	18
D	4	I	9	N	14	S	19

Figure 8.17 (continued)

T	20	Y	25	0	30	5	35
U	21	Z	26	1	31	6	36
V	22	$	27	2	32	7	37
W	23	.	28	3	33	8	38
X	24	Unused	29	4	34	9	39

EXERCISE SET 2

1 Given that the contents of A, B, C, and D, are:

$$A—070707$$
$$B—107070$$
$$C—123456$$
$$D—054321$$

what would be the effect on A, B, C, and D and the condition codes N Z C and V after executing each of the following instructions on the original contents?

(a) BIS   A,B   (b) BIC   A,C
(c) BIC   C,A   (d) BIS   B,C
(e) BIT   C,D   (f) BIT   C,C

2 Write and run a program that reads characters typed in and prints each character out seven times followed by carriage return/line feed. The program terminates when it reads control-Z

3 Write a program which reads an entire typed line that is followed by carriage return/line feed. The program then prints out the line alternately forward and backward seven times. The line length may vary, but would not be longer than 80 characters.

4 Write a program to run in the batch stream which reads characters from data cards. It types the characters back out replacing *all* control characters (including carriage return and fine feed) with an asterisk and the letter that would be typed with "control" to get the control character. Follow each control-J or *J with a carriage return and line feed. What control characters does the batch stream insert into your data? Can control characters be punched onto cards? If so, how?

5 Write a subroutine that reads 16-bit binary numbers as a sequence of 16 ASCII 1s and 0s followed by carriage return/line feed. The subroutine returns with the binary value in R0.

6 Write a subroutine that takes the value of R0 and prints it out as a 16-bit binary number. Print one number per line as the subroutine is called successively.

7 Combine the subroutines of exercises 5 and 6 with a main program that tests the subroutines by calling them several times.

8 Write a subroutine that prints out signed decimal numbers. Modify the subroutine in Figure 8.10 to read signed decimal numbers. Write a main program that tests these subroutines by calling them a number of times. The printout routine should not print leading zeros.

*9 Write a program that reads a body of text. The program then prints out the number of times each printable character occurred in the text. Your answers should be printed in decimal using a routine such as written for exercise 8. Your printout should resemble:

```
        A       APPEARED        129     TIMES
        B       APPEARED         17     TIMES
        C       APPEARED         18     TIMES
```

CHAPTER 9

SUBROUTINES

9.1 INTRODUCTION

In previous chapters, we have seen the use of simple subroutines for performing often repeated operations such as reading or printing numbers. Subroutines are very important in the structure of computer programs.

In this chapter, we will examine the details of how the calling and returning processes function. We will also see how subroutines access data from the main program, and how complex subroutine structures can be tied together and joined with programs written in a higher-level language. The latter item is, perhaps, the most important. One of the most significant uses of assembly language for the minicomputer user is to augment such languages as FORTRAN to allow operations that would be difficult or impossible in the high-level language alone.

9.2 CALLING A SUBROUTINE

Review of the JSR Instruction

In earlier examples, it was stated that a subroutine could be called by using the instruction:

        JSR   PC,ADDR

Furthermore, the subroutine returned to the main program with the instruction:

```
         RTS      PC
```

The explanation given in Chapter 5 was that the JSR instruction used the stack pointer (register 6) to save the program counter (register 7) in an area of memory called the stack.

This explanation is true, but incomplete. For example, we have already seen programs in which subroutines called other subroutines. When subroutines are nested in this manner, several return addresses will be saved on the stack. This raises the question of how each RTS instruction gets the correct return address from the stack.

Using the Stack

In order to use an array to store return addresses, there must be an index register or pointer that indicates where the data are being stored. General register number 6, or the SP (for Stack Pointer), is always used for this purpose. The reader can now see why there were cautions against using register 6. Random use of register 6 would cause very strange things to happen the next time a subroutine were called. (This problem would exist even if the program used no subroutines. The operating system uses register 6 for its own subroutines and program interruptions that may occur without the user's awareness.)

An array that is accessed by sequentially adding and removing data in this fashion is called a **stack**. The operation of a stack is analogous to a stack of plates in a cafeteria. In order to save an item of information, a new plate is obtained from somewhere, a 16-bit binary number is printed on the plate, and the plate is placed on top of the stack of plates. To retrieve an item from the stack, the plate on the top of the stack is removed and the number on the plate is examined. Notice that plates are always added and removed from the *top* of the stack. As a result, the plate that is removed is always the plate that was most recently added. For example, in the following figure, three quantities labeled A, B, and C are first saved on the stack and then removed from the stack:

```
                            C
                    B       B       B
            A       A       A       A           A
-------  ---------  ---------  ---------  ---------------  ---------------  ---------------
Empty    Add item   Add item   Add item   Remove top       Remove top       Remove top
Stack       A          B          C        item (C)         item (B)         item (A)
```

Although C was the last item to be placed on the stack, it is the first item to be removed. This Last In–First Out sequence is often abbreviated as LIFO.

Register 6 is called the **stack pointer** because it contains the address of the item that is currently on the top of the stack. For example, assume that the stack consists of memory cells 000400 through 000776. A special case occurs if the stack is empty. In this case, register 6 contains the address of the memory cell that immediately follows the end of the stack. Since memory cell 000776 is the end of the stack, register 6 contains 001000 when the stack is empty:

	Address	Contents
	000376	??????
	000400	??????
	...	...
	000772	??????
	000774	??????
	000776	??????
register 6 001000 ⟶	001000	??????

In order to save an item on the stack, subtract 000002 from register 6 and store the item in the resulting address. If item A is saved on the stack, the result will be:

	000772	??????
	000774	??????
register 6 000776 ⟶	000776	item A
	001000	??????

To save item B on the stack, subtract 000002 from register 6 and place item B in the resulting address:

	000772	??????
register 6 000774 ⟶	000774	item B
	000776	item A
	001000	??????

Retrieving an item from the stack is just the reverse of saving an item. Fetch the contents of the memory cell whose address is contained in register 6 and then add 2 to register 6. After item B is fetched, the stack will appear as follows:

	Address	Contents
	000772	??????
	000774	??????
register 6 000776 ⟶	000776	item A
	001000	??????

Notice that memory cell 000774, which used to contain item B, now contains ??????. Memory cells that used to contain an item on the stack may contain meaningless information after the item is removed from the stack. The reason for this is that system program interruptions may use the stack and overwrite the old data. Removing another item from the stack retrieves item A, and leaves the stack empty:

		000772	?????
		000774	?????
		000776	?????
register 6 001000	⟶	001000	?????

Because return addresses are saved on the stack, subroutines can be nested without difficulty. For example, a main program called ALPHA might JSR to a subroutine called BETA. BETA in turn might JSR to a subroutine GAMMA, and GAMMA might then JSR to subroutine ETA. By the time subroutine ETA is executing, three return addresses have been saved on the stack—the return addresses to ALPHA, BETA, and GAMMA. Because of the last in–first out property of the stack, the return address that is removed from the stack when ETA is completed will be the return address to GAMMA. Similarly, GAMMA will return to BETA, and BETA will return to ALPHA. As we shall see later in the chapter, the use of the stack for storing return addresses even allows a subroutine to call itself. Such subroutines are called **recursive.**

Storing an item on the stack is much like executing the instruction

        MOV   X,-(SP)

Similarly, removal of a number from the stack is equivalent to

        MOV   (SP)+,X

Actually, users can employ these two instructions for placing their own data on the stack, and thereby use the stack for storing temporary data. As an example of this, imagine a subroutine that uses R0, R1, and R2 for internal computation. However, also assume that the main program is using these registers and does not want the subroutine to change them. The subroutine must then save the values of R0, R1, and R2, and restore them when returning. This is a very common use for the stack. (Although almost any free location could be used to save a register, the stack is very convenient and saves the programmer having to think up labels and insert .BLKW's in the program. Memory and time are also conserved because MOV R0,-(SP) is a one-word instruction, but MOV R0,SAVE is a two-word instruction.) The subroutine would have the appearance shown in Figure 9.1. Note the label RETN. In order to return, you must either do BR RETN or execute the same instructions or their equivalent. It would be catastrophic to execute RTS PC *without* restoring the contents of the registers. The RTS PC instruction takes the top of the stack to be the return address. If the registers had not been restored, the top of the stack would contain the saved value of R2, *not* the return address. The general rule is that any process may use the stack for storing data, *but* whatever a process adds to the stack, it must remove: nothing more—nothing less.

Sec. 9.2   Calling a Subroutine

Figure 9.1   *Using the Stack to Save Registers*

```
START:  MOV   R0,-(SP)      ;SAVE REGISTERS
        MOV   R1,-(SP)      ;R0, R1, AND R2
        MOV   R2,-(SP)      ;ON STACK
         .
         .
         .
RETN:   MOV   (SP)+,R2      ;RESTORE REGISTERS
        MOV   (SP)+,R1      ;NOTE REVERSE ORDER
        MOV   (SP)+,R0      ;LAST ON STACK IS FIRST OFF
        RTS   PC            ;SUBROUTINE RETURN
```

As we pointed out, the stack is just an array in memory. The question arises as to where the array is. This depends on the operating system. In the RT-11 system, programs are normally loaded starting at address 1000. The stack goes backward from there, using locations 776, 774, and so on. The hardware on some PDP-11 computers prevents the stack pointer from going lower than 400, thus giving a limited but reasonable amount of space for the stack. If more space is needed, there are provisions that allow programs to be loaded starting at higher locations. If you are running with no operating system, it would probably be necessary to set up your own stack area. An array of reasonable size just about anywhere would do.

Note that, because most stack operations involve words, the stack pointer must *always* be an even number. This is taken care of automatically once the stack pointer is properly initialized and used correctly. Even byte operations take this into account. For example, MOVB X,-(SP) causes the SP to be decremented by 2 instead of 1. In a sense, the machine is "nice" and does what is needed without the programmer having to worry about it.

Alternative Calling Methods *(Optional Section)*

It may seem strange that the JSR and RTS instructions specifically refer to the program counter. One might suppose that the program counter would always have to be saved and restored when subroutines are called. This is in fact true, but there are different places one could store the program counter. In the PDP-11, it is allowable to save the program counter in any of the general registers. For example, the instruction JSR R5,SUBR would cause the program counter to be saved in R5 and the subroutine would then return by the instruction RTS R5. This would be an alternative method for calling and returning from subroutines. However, this seems to have a disadvantage over the calling method described in the previous section because there does not appear to be a provision for subroutines that call other subroutines. This, however, has been taken care of because JSR R5,SUBR causes R5 to be saved on the stack before the program counter is saved in R5. The RTS R5 instruction undoes this by first restoring the program counter from R5 and then restoring R5 from the stack. Figure 9.2 shows how this process operates.

From Figure 9.2, we can see that the JSR R5,SUBR instruction accomplishes what JSR PC,SUBR would, but has the added advantage that the return location in the main program is more accessible to the programmer. (It is easier to use R5 than to find a location on the stack.) This is often very useful

Figure 9.2 Effect of JSR R5,SUBR Instruction

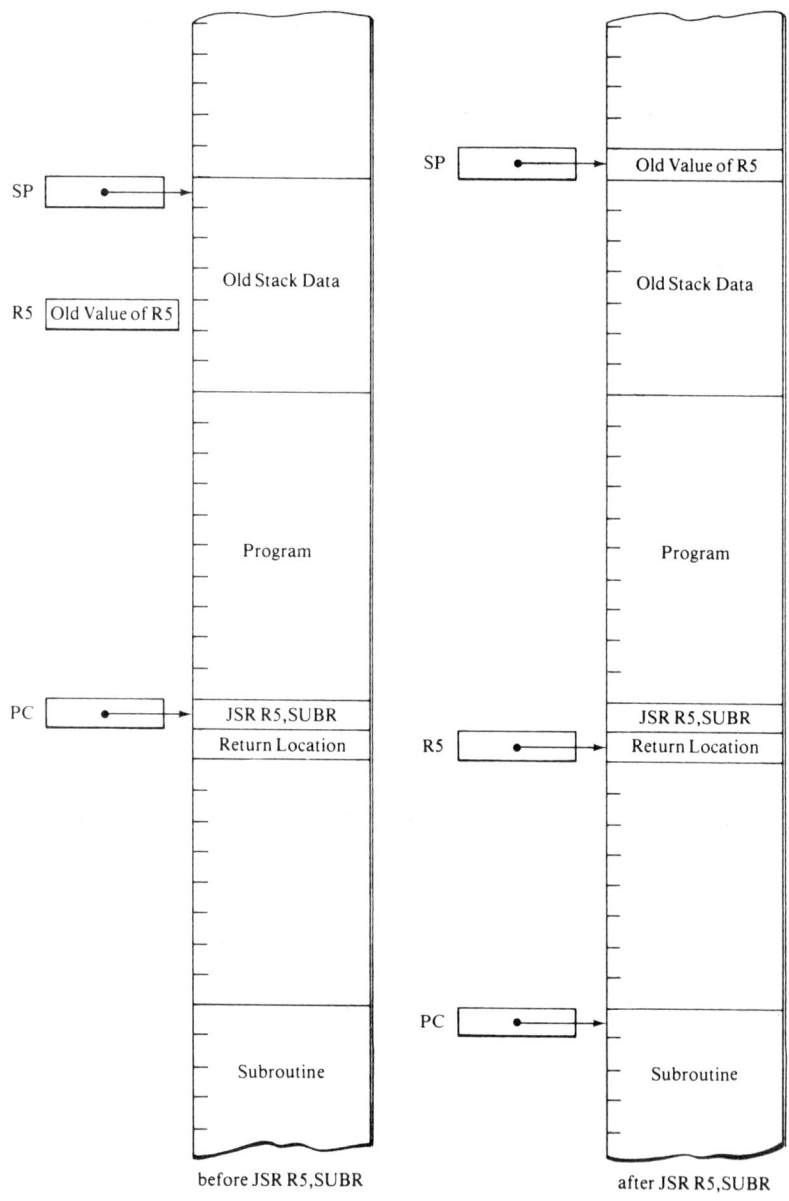

for passing information back and forth between the main program and a subroutine. This whole problem is discussed in the following sections.

Naturally any of the general registers R0 through R5 could be used with the JSR or RTS instructions. You must remember, however, that the same register must be used with both the JSR and RTS. You could not save the program counter in R5 and then expect to find it in R3.

On the other hand, it would not make sense to try to use the stack pointer (SP) to save the program counter. The value of the stack pointer would be lost, and this would disrupt communications in the system. One might almost conclude that use of the program counter (PC) would be similarly absurd. How then do all the examples of previous chapters work? Figures 9.3 and 9.4 show the effects of JSR and RTS instructions using both R5 and the program counter. The essential point is that while storing the program counter in the program counter does nothing, it does not hurt anything either. The net effect is that the program counter is directly saved on the stack.

Figure 9.3 Operation of JSR Instruction

R5 ⟶ STACK	PC ⟶ STACK	PC ⟶ STACK
PC ⟶ R5	PC ⟶ PC	Address (SUBR) ⟶ PC
Address (SUBR) ⟶ PC	Address (SUBR) ⟶ PC	
Effect of JSR R5, SUBR	Effect of JSR PC,SUBR	Net effect of JSR PC,SUBR

Figure 9.4 Operation of RTS Instruction

R5 ⟶ PC	PC ⟶ PC	STACK ⟶ PC
STACK ⟶ R5	STACK ⟶ PC	
Effect of RTS R5	Effect of RTS PC	Net effect of RTS PC

Passing Information between a Main Program and Subroutines

In most cases, the function of a subroutine is to perform some computation based on one or more numbers or pieces of information. The results of this computation may also be in the form of one or more pieces of information. These pieces of information must be communicated from the main program to the subroutine and vice versa.

In Chapter 5, a very simple method of communication was used for the RNUM and PNUM subroutines. The number being passed to or from the subroutine was placed in R0. This method is usable whenever there are only a few (no more than six) words of information being passed back and forth. The first word is placed in R0, the second in R1, and so on up through R5 (if necessary). The subroutine would be programmed to look for the information in the appropriate register. As many as six results could be transmitted back in the same way.

Obviously, this method of passing information has serious limitations when dealing with large amounts of data or arrays. The limitation of six registers for storage can be overcome by using specially set aside areas of memory that serve as communications areas. However, this does not really work well for large amounts of data because it requires loading and storing all of the locations at each subroutine call. This could require an excessive amount of computing.

One possible solution to this problem is especially useful when dealing with arrays. Here, instead of passing the values in the array, the main program passes the address of the array. The subroutine then uses this address in order to access the data in the array. As an example of how this works, Figure 9.5 shows a subroutine that adds up an array of 100 numbers. The main program passes the *address* of the array to the subroutine via R0. The *value* of the result is passed back, also using R0. Thus, we are using a combination of both methods. The calling sequence for this program would be:

```
        MOV     #ARRAY,R0
        JSR     PC,SUMUP
        MOV     R0,ANS
```

where ARRAY is the label of the array of the numbers to be added together, and ANS is the location that ultimately receives the result.

Of special note here is the fact that, in addition to the advantages just discussed, passing addresses rather than data is a much more general method of communication. For one thing, addresses can be used bidirectionally. In other words, if the subroutine has an address of a main program location, it can use that address both for accessing data and for sending results back to the main program.

In summary, we can say that transmitting values is a quick and simple technique that is very useful for subroutines that deal with only a few pieces of data. Transmitting addresses is needed for subroutines using many pieces of data.

Figure 9.5 Subroutine for Summing an Array

```
SUMUP:  MOV     R1,-(SP)        ;SAVE R1 AND R2
        MOV     R2,-(SP)        ;ON STACK
        MOV     R0,R1           ;SHIFT DATA ADDRESS TO R1
        MOV     #144,R2         ;R2 GETS ITEM COUNT
        CLR     R0              ;CLEAR SUM
SUMLP:  ADD     (R1)+,R0        ;ADD ITEM TO SUM
        DEC     R2              ;DECREMENT COUNT
        BNE     SUMLP           ;LOOP UNTIL DONE
        MOV     (SP)+,R2        ;RESTORE R1 AND R2
        MOV     (SP)+,R1        ;FROM STACK
        RTS     PC              ;RETURN
```

EXERCISE SET 1

For exercises 1-3, assume that R0 contains 000056, R1 contains 177514, R2 contains 177776, and the following memory locations contain:

Address	Contents
000770	123456
000772	001076
000774	000005
000776	004212
001000	013737

Also assume that the SP contains 000772 and that the original value of the SP was 1000. The value of the PC is 001206. The address of SUB is 001472.

1. What values are contained on the stack?

2. What locations would change, and what would be the new contents after execution of each of the following instructions (use the given contents for each instruction):

   (a) MOV   R0,-(SP)
   (b) MOV   (SP)+,R1
   (c) CMP   (SP)+,(SP)+
   (d) JSR   PC,SUB
   (e) JSR   R2,SUB
   (f) RTS   PC
   (g) ADD   R2,SP
   (h) MOV   (SP),-(SP)

*3. Which of the following instructions represent normal use of the stack? Which are abnormal and may produce unpredictable results owing to the fact that the operating system may periodically interrupt your program and modify locations *below* the stack pointer? Which instructions are catastrophies and will most likely result in program failure? Explain your answers. Use the given contents for each instruction and show the resulting changes in contents.

   (a) MOV   R0,(SP)+
   (b) CMP   -(SP),-(SP)
   (c) JSR   PC,(SP)+
   (d) JSR   PC,@(SP)+
   (e) JSR   SP,SUB
   (f) INC   SP
   (g) DEC   SP
   (h) MOV   4(SP),R0
   (i) RTS   SP

4 Write a subroutine similar to SUMUP, shown in Figure 9.5 on page 204. However, your program will have a second input argument giving the size of the array to be summed. Then write a main program that reads 10 numbers, prints them, and calls your subroutine to sum them up, and then does the same with 20 numbers.

5 Write a program that reads in a variable number of numbers (up to 100), sorts them, and prints out the sorted array. This program should be split into various subroutines, one for each of the major functions. Array addresses, sizes, and all other data should be passed in the general registers at each subroutine call.

*6 Write a pair of subroutines SREG and RREG. SREG saves the values of R0 through R5 on the stack and returns. (Note a problem due to the fact that the return address may no longer be at the top of the stack.) SREG must not modify R0 through R5.

RREG restores the values of R0 through R5 as last saved by SREG. It must return with the stack cleared to the original value (before SREG was called).

The pair of subroutines must be recallable so that a succession of subroutines calling each other could all call these subroutines.

*7 Write a main program and some subroutines to test out SREG and RREG from exercise 6.

9.3 INDEPENDENT ASSEMBLY—GLOBAL SYMBOLS

The Need for Independent Assembly

When writing a program of any appreciable size, it is most important to break the program down into a number of pieces of manageable size which are called **modules**. The more independent these modules are, the easier it is to write, test, and debug each one. When every module is debugged, it is reasonable to deal with debugging the total program.

In order to deal with programming in this fashion, it is important to be able to treat each module as a separate program. This means that each of the smaller programs must be able to be assembled by itself. Consequently, it must have all its own locations completely defined within the module as does any program. In other words, there must not be any undefined symbols.

On the other hand, these program modules are intended to be combined to form one big program. This means that although the modules may be *highly* independent, they cannot be completely independent. There must be some form of communication between the programs. This is accomplished by means of **global symbols**.

Global Symbols

A global symbol is a symbolic address that is defined in one program but accessible to other independently assembled programs. Although global symbols can be used for almost anything that ordinary symbols are used for, they are normally used for subroutine names.

For example, a program module may contain a subroutine named READ. If this subroutine is to be called from one of the other program modules, the symbol READ must be global. The definition of global symbols is accomplished by means of a directive called .GLOBL (note spelling). The .GLOBL directive is always followed by a symbol, for example, .GLOBL READ. The effect of such usage depends on the context of the remainder of the program so that .GLOBL has two possible meanings:

1. If the symbol following .GLOBL (such as READ) is defined in the program module (either with : or =), then the symbol is defined as a global symbol that is accessible to other modules.

2. If the symbol following .GLOBL is *not* defined in the module, then it is designated *undefined global*. This prevents the assembler from generating an error message for an undefined symbol. Instead, a special code is generated in the object file which indicates that certain undefined addresses must be defined when all of the modules are combined to form a single program.

Linking with Global Symbols

The process of combining all of the program modules together and resolving global symbols is performed by a system program called the **linker**.* The linker does two things. First it relocates each program module to a successive block of memory. Note that the relocation address will be different for each module, and will depend on how much memory was required by the preceding modules.

Second, the linker resolves the global references. Here the linker is finishing a process that the assembler could not do because of undefined global symbols. As in assembling, two passes are required through the object files. In the first pass, a symbol table is constructed for all defined global symbols. In the second pass, the missing addresses corresponding to undefined global symbols are supplied by looking them up in the symbol table generated during the

---

*This linker is the same linker discussed in the section on relocation in Chapter 4 (pages 79 ff). The reader is referred to this section to review the relocation concept.

first pass. If undefined global symbols still remain, it means that a .GLOBL definition is missing. An error message will result.

In addition, most systems have a provision for subroutine libraries. This is a file of object modules that the linker will search to try to resolve undefined global symbols. A module will not be loaded from the library unless it is needed to satisfy an undefined global symbol.

Figures 9.6 and 9.7 illustrate the use of global symbols. In the main program (Figure 9.6), READ is declared to be a global symbol to indicate that the linker will substitute a numerical address for READ in the instruction JSR PC,READ. (If the .GLOBL directive were omitted, the assembler would flag READ as an undefined symbol.) In the subroutine (Figure 9.7), READ is declared to be a global symbol to indicate that some other module (in this case the main program) references the address READ. If the .GLOBL directive were omitted from the subroutine, no assembly error would occur. However, in trying to resolve the reference to READ in the main program, the linker may search the subroutine library looking for an object module called READ. If the library contains a READ routine, the results during execution are unpredictable and the programmer may have great difficulty locating the error. If no READ subroutine is found, the linker prints an error message.

The difference between the .END statements in Figures 9.6 and 9.7 is significant. The main program module must have a transfer or starting address

Figure 9.6 A Main Program Module

```
        .TITLE  MAIN PROGRAM MODULE
        .GLOBL  READ            ;READ IS USED BUT NOT DEFINED
START:  .
        .
        .
        JSR     PC,READ         ;THIS LINE USES READ
        .
        .
        .
        .END    START           ;NOTE TRANSFER ADDRESS
```

Figure 9.7 A Subroutine Module

```
        .TITLE  SUB1 A SUBROUTINE MODULE
        .GLOBL  READ            ;READ IS DEFINED IN THIS MODULE
READ:   MOV     R0,-(SP)        ;BEGINNING OF READ SUBROUTINE
        .
        .
        .
        RTS     PC
        .
        .
        .
        .END                    ;NOTE NO TRANSFER ADDRESS
```

on the .END statement, but none of the other modules should have anything following the .END statement. This is because there cannot be more than one starting place for an entire program.

9.4 INTERFACING ASSEMBLY LANGUAGE WITH FORTRAN *(RT-11 Operating System)*

The Need for Combining FORTRAN and Assembly Language

In FORTRAN there are three types of program modules. These are the main program, subroutine subprograms, and function subprograms. All these program modules are independently compiled or translated into object modules. Communication between object modules is accomplished by means of global names for the subroutines and functions. Since the object modules produced by the FORTRAN compiler have exactly the same format as those produced by the assembler, it is possible to replace FORTRAN subroutines and functions with modules written in assembly language, as long as certain programming conventions are followed. Although it would also be possible to replace a FORTRAN main program with an assembly language main program, it is not usually recommended, because FORTRAN main programs perform certain initialization operations that FORTRAN subroutines and functions require.

There are various reasons why one would want to write an assembly language subroutine to be called by a FORTRAN main program or subroutine. First, there are certain operations that are not particularly easy in FORTRAN. These include character manipulation, bit operations on words (masking, packing, and so on), and multiple-precision arithmetic other than that which is provided in FORTRAN. Second, some operations are excluded from FORTRAN. These include nonstandard input/output, interfacing to nonstandard devices, and access to absolute memory locations.

The second of these categories is especially important for minicomputer users because of the specialized applications of many minicomputers. The reader should note that these routes are well traveled and libraries of FORTRAN-callable subroutines exist for facilitating use of such devices as graphics display units, the laboratory peripheral system (LPS-11), and so on.

FORTRAN Calling Conventions

When writing an assembly language subroutine that is to interface with FORTRAN programs, it is necessary to use the calling and returning instructions that FORTRAN uses. It is also necessary to use the same methods for passing data back and forth.

The simplest case is a subroutine that has no arguments in the call. Such a subroutine would be called in FORTRAN using a statement such as:

```
        CALL    XSUB
```

The object code generated by the FORTRAN compiler is exactly that which the assembler would generate for:

```
        .GLOBL  XSUB
        JSR     PC,XSUB
```

This means that the subroutine should have the simple structure shown in Figure 9.8.

Figure 9.8 *Simple Structure for a FORTRAN Callable Subroutine*

```
        .TITLE  XSUB    SAMPLE SUBROUTINE
        .GLOBL  XSUB
XSUB:   .
        .
        .
        RTS     PC
        .END
```

The next topic to deal with is the communication of data between FORTRAN programs. There are two ways that a FORTRAN main program can communicate with a subroutine. The first is by means of an argument list; the second is through common blocks.

Argument lists are transferred by passing addresses, as described earlier in this chapter. However, since there are at most six available general registers, and since FORTRAN allows a large number of subroutine arguments, the general registers alone are not usable for passing arguments. Instead, FORTRAN stores the addresses of the arguments in an array. Since the subroutine needs access to the array, the address of the array is placed in R5 prior to calling the subroutine. This means that accessing FORTRAN arguments must be done through double-deferred addressing.

As an example, a FORTRAN program having the statement CALL YSUB(A,B,C) will set aside an array of four locations. There is one location for each of three addresses, and one location at the beginning of the array that gives the number of arguments. Figure 9.9 gives the equivalent assembly language for the FORTRAN statement CALL YSUB(A,B,C). The number of arguments is given in the argument list so that an assembly language subroutine could deal with a variable number of arguments. (Other computer systems use different conventions for detecting the number of arguments such as using a special value to mark the end of the argument list.)

Figure 9.10 illustrates a subroutine that adds the elements of an array A and places the sum in S. Note that the program changes both R0 and R1;

Sec. 9.4 Interfacing Assembly Language with FORTRAN

Figure 9.9 Assembly Language Equivalent for CALL YSUB(A,B,C)

```
            .GLOBL  YSUB            ;ALL SUBROUTINES ARE GLOBAL
            .
            .
            .
            MOV     #ARGS,R5        ;R5 GETS ADDRESS OF ARGUMENT LIST
            JSR     PC,YSUB         ;CALL SUBROUTINE
            .
            .
            .
ARGS:       .WORD   3               ;NUMBER OF ARGUMENTS
            .WORD   A               ;ADDRESS OF A
            .WORD   B               ;ADDRESS OF B
            .WORD   C               ;ADDRESS OF C
            .
            .
            .
A:          .BLKW   1               ;LOCATION OF A
B:          .BLKW   1               ;LOCATION OF B
C:          .BLKW   1               ;LOCATION OF C
```

Figure 9.10 Relation of FORTRAN to Assembly Language

```
            SUBROUTINE SUM(S,A)
            INTEGER S,A(10),I
            S=0
            DO 10 I=1,10
                S=S+A(I)
         10 CONTINUE
            RETURN
            END
```

FORTRAN Subroutine

```
            .TITLE  SUM
            .GLOBL  SUM
            .MCALL  .REGDEF
            .REGDEF
SUM:        MOV     4(R5),R0        ;R0 GETS ADDRESS OF A
            CLR     @2(R5)          ;CLEAR S
            MOV     #12,R1          ;SET COUNTER TO TEN
LOOP:       ADD     (R0)+,@2(R5)    ;S=S+A(I)
            DEC     R2              ;DECREMENT COUNTER
            BNE     LOOP            ;LOOP UNTIL DONE
            RTS     PC              ;RETURN
            .END
```

Equivalent Assembly Language Subroutine

however, this is all right because FORTRAN conventions allow it. Register R5 is used to point to the argument list. Therefore 2(R5) and 4(R5) refer to the second and third locations of the list. These locations contain the **addresses** of the arguments (S and A in the FORTRAN program). Since 2(R5) refers to the address of S, @2(R5) refers to the contents of S. Therefore, when the instruction CLR @2(R5) is executed, the contents of S is cleared.

Common Blocks

The other method that FORTRAN programs can use to communicate is by means of common blocks. If a main program and subroutine both contain the statement

```
COMMON /WBLK/X,Y,Z
```

the X, Y, and Z refer to the same locations in the two programs,* and thus communication can take place without argument lists or arrays of addresses being passed. The method operates by declaring the common block name as a global name, and a special array is set aside that is large enough for the variables in the common block. This space is set aside in each program, but the linker is designed to *overlay* blocks with the same global name. (That is, the common blocks in the various programs are assigned to the same area of memory.) This ensures that the programs all refer to the same locations.

Figure 9.11 shows the assembly language equivalent of the FORTRAN COMMON statement. The .PSECT directive establishes that what follows is to go in a particular *program section*. The name WBLK identifies the particular section. The remaining five parameters indicate that the section (or block) is:

a. *Read-write.* The alternative is read-only, and has meaning only in systems that have memory protection.

b. *Data type as opposed to instruction type.* Again this is meaningful only in protected systems.

c. *Relocatable as opposed to absolute.* In assembly language, it is possible to have absolute program sections, but in FORTRAN everything is relocatable.

d. *Global as opposed to local.* If this section is to be accessible to other program modules, the name WBLK must be global.

e. *Overlaid as opposed to concatenated.* The X, Y, and Z in this block are to occupy the same locations as the X, Y, and Z in blocks with the same name in other programs. Concatenated sections would be placed one after another and would use separate space.

*It is assumed that X, Y, and Z are declared consistently in both programs.

Sec. 9.4 *Interfacing Assembly Language with FORTRAN* 213

Figure 9.11 The Assembly Language Equivalent of a Common Block

```
INTEGER X,Y(25),Z                .PSECT  WBLK,RW,DAT,REL,GBL,OVR
COMMON  /WBLK/X,Y,Z       X:     .BLKW   1
                          Y:     .BLKW   31        ;25 DECIMAL IS 31 OCTAL
                          Z:     .BLKW   1
                                 .PSECT
         FORTRAN                      Equivalent Assembly Language
```

Although some of these options may be meaningless in your system (such as a and b), they all must be specified. Error messages will result if the linker finds conflicting attributes for program sections with the same name.

After the .PSECT line, a sequence of labeled .BLKW's is given for the variables in the block. It is possible to use data generating lines (such as .WORD). This would have the same effect as a FORTRAN BLOCK DATA module. Locations in the block would have data loaded in them, but care would have to be taken to avoid overwriting data specified in a different module. In order to avoid this problem, FORTRAN prohibits the use of DATA statements for variables in common blocks, except in the BLOCK DATA module.

A block ends either when another .PSECT is encountered, or at the .END at the end of the program. If a .PSECT has no argument, it indicates that assembly is to go back to the regular program section. On the other hand, a subsequent .PSECT could have arguments, indicating the definition of another common block.

FORTRAN Functions

The final subject in this section is FORTRAN **function subprograms.** From the descriptions found in most FORTRAN handbooks, one could imagine that function subprograms are entirely different from subroutine subprograms. In fact, there is only one real difference. Functions return a single value that is available for use in an expression. This value may occupy one word as for integers, or it may occupy as many as four words for double-precision or complex data types. These words are always returned in the general registers R0–R3. Argument lists and common blocks for functions are implemented exactly the same as for subroutines. Thus, we can see that the subroutine SUM of Figure 9.10 could be rewritten as a function as shown in Figure 9.12. Note that since the function is of integer type and thus returns a 16-bit binary number, only R0 is needed for the result to be available to FORTRAN. The difference in the FORTRAN main program would be that, instead of the statement CALL SUM(S,A), there would be a statement such as S = ISUM(A).

Figure 9.12

```
            INTEGER FUNCTION ISUM(A)
            INTEGER A(10),J
            ISUM=0
            DO 10 J=1,10
               ISUM=ISUM+A(J)
         10 CONTINUE
            RETURN
            END
```
       FORTRAN Function

```
        .TITLE  ISUM
        .GLOBL  ISUM
        .MCALL  .REGDEF
        .REGDEF
ISUM:   MOV     2(R5),R1        ;R1 GETS ADDRESS OF A
        MOV     #12,R2          ;R2 GETS COUNT
        CLR     R0              ;CLEAR SUM
LOOP:   ADD     (R1)+,R0        ;ADD A(J) TO SUM
        DEC     R2              ;DECREMENT COUNT
        BNE     LOOP            ;LOOP UNTIL DONE
        RTS     PC              ;RETURN
        .END
```
    Equivalent Assembly Language Subroutine

9.5 RECURSIVE SUBROUTINES

In certain subdisciplines of computer science, such as language processing and artificial intelligence, **recursive subroutines** are important. In brief, a recursive subroutine is a subroutine that calls itself. Recursive subroutines developed from recursive definitions used in mathematics.

As an example of a recursive definition, consider the factorial function. An engineer might be content to define n factorial (or $n!$) as the product of the integers from 1 through n. ($0! = 1$ would be considered a special case.) However, while this definition is sufficient for computation, it is not in a very usable form for mathematical proofs. A mathematician would prefer the following definition:

$$0! = 1$$
$$n! = n \times (n-1)! \text{ if } n > 0$$

Definitions of this sort are amenable to use in a form of proof called **mathematical induction.** Inductive proofs are gaining importance in computer science for proving program correctness.

Sec. 9.5   Recursive Subroutines

While FORTRAN and BASIC have no provision for recursive subroutines, most of the newer higher-level languages allow them. For example ALGOL, APL, and PASCAL are among the languages that allow subroutine subprograms or function subprograms to call themselves. Since none of these languages, to date, have the popularity of FORTRAN, we have chosen to give an artificial example in FORTRAN. Figure 9.13 shows what a recursive FORTRAN program would look like for computing factorials. Note that this program would be illegal in most FORTRAN systems.

Figure 9.13   Factorial Program

```
      INTEGER FUNCTION FAC(N)           INTEGER FUNCTION FAC(N)
      INTEGER N                         INTEGER N,J
      FAC=1                             FAC=1
      IF (N.EQ.0) RETURN                IF (N.EQ.0) RETURN
      FAC=N*FAC(N-1)                    DO 10 J=1,N
      RETURN                                FAC=FAC*J
      END                            10 CONTINUE
                                        RETURN
                                        END
```

      Imagined Recursive Program   Equivalent Conventional FORTRAN

The reason the recursive program in Figure 9.13 will not work in most FORTRAN systems is that the system will fail to save all the necessary data when the program calls itself. As a result, the subroutine will not be able to pick up properly when it returns to itself. (Note that if a recursive program calls itself, it must be able to return to itself. Note also that there must be an eventual path through the subroutine to the original calling program. Otherwise, an endless loop will result.)

Although FORTRAN may not allow recursive subroutines, the PDP-11 stack provides assembly language users with the most important tool for recursive programming. In order for recursive subroutines to work, required data must be saved on a stack every time the routine calls itself. The data are then removed from the stack when the routine returns to itself. Figure 9.14 shows how a FORTRAN-callable factorial function could be written recursively in

Figure 9.14   Recursive Factorial Routine

```
           .TITLE   FACTORIAL ROUTINE
           .GLOBL   FAC
           .GLOBL   MUL
           .MCALL   .REGDEF
           .REGDEF
    FAC:   MOV      @2(R5),R0       ;GET VALUE OF N
           BNE      RECUR           ;SKIP ON UNLESS ZERO
           MOV      #1,R0           ;ZERO FACTORIAL IS 1
           RTS      PC
```

Figure 9.14 (continued)

```
RECUR:  MOV   R0,-(SP)     ;SAVE N ON STACK
        DEC   R0           ;COMPUTE N-1
        MOV   R0,N         ;SAVE IN N
        MOV   #LIST1,R5    ;GET PARAMETER LIST
        JSR   PC,FAC       ;COMPUTE N-1 FACTORIAL
        MOV   R0,K         ;K=N-1 FACTORIAL
        MOV   (SP)+,J      ;J=N
        MOV   #LIST2,R5    ;GET PARAMETER LIST
        JSR   PC,MUL       ;COMPUTE N*(N-1)FACTORIAL
        RTS   PC           ;RETURN WITH RESULT IN R0
LIST1:  .WORD 1            ;ARGUMENT ARRAY FOR FAC
        .WORD N
LIST2:  .WORD 2            ;ARGUMENT ARRAY FOR MUL
        .WORD K
        .WORD J
K:      .BLKW 1
J:      .BLKW 1
N:      .BLKW 1
        .END
```

assembly language. Note that this program has two pieces of necessary information that must be saved on the stack. One item is the argument value N, and the other is the return address, which is, of course, automatically saved on the stack. In order to avoid the problem of multiplication, this subroutine calls a FORTRAN function MUL(K,J), which multiplies K and J and returns the 16-bit product in register 0.

EXERCISE SET 2

1. Write a subroutine similar to SUMUP, shown in Figure 9.5 on page 204. However, your program will have a second input argument giving the size of the array to be summed. Then write a main program that reads 10 numbers, prints them, and calls your subroutine to sum them up, and then does the same with 20 numbers. Each subroutine including RNUM and PNUM (if used) must be independently assembled as separate modules that are linked together with global symbols. See exercise 4, page 206.

2. Write a program that reads in a variable number of numbers (up to 100), sorts them, and prints out the sorted array. This program should be split into various, independently assembled subroutines for each of the major functions. The separate subroutine modules should be linked using global symbols. Array addresses, sizes, and so on, should be passed in the general registers at each subroutine call. See exercise 5, page 206.

Exercise Set 2

3 The following is a proposed method for generating positive random numbers in the range 1–32767:

(a) Start with any positive integer in the range.

(b) For each generated number: (i) Shift the original number left once. (ii) If the two high-order bits are both 1 or both 0, set the low-order bit to 0. If one of the bits is 1 and the other is 0, set the low-order bit to 1. In other words, the low-order bit becomes the exclusive OR of the sign bit and bit 14 of the shifted number. (iii) Then clear the sign bit to 0.

Write a FORTRAN-callable subroutine or function for generating such pseudo-numbers. Test your subroutine by calling it several hundred times and printing the results with a 12I6 format. Can you think of any other means of testing the randomness of these numbers? If so, incorporate them into your program.

4 Write a FORTRAN-callable subroutine that is called by the FORTRAN statement:

$$\text{CALL} \quad \text{LOCS(A)}$$

where A is a three-location INTEGER*2 array. Your subroutine fills in A with the following:

A(1) The memory address of the JSR instruction that called LOCS

A(2) The location of the parameter list

A(3) The location of A itself

Write a FORTRAN main program that tests this subroutine. Verify its results from loading maps, symbol tables, and so on, as best as you can.

5 A recursive function known as Ackermann's function is defined over the nonnegative integer as follows:

$A(0,n) = n + 1$ for $n > 0$

$A(m,0) = A(m - 1,1)$ for $m > 0$

$A(m,n) = A[m - 1, A(m,n - 1)]$ for m and $n > 0$

Write a recursive subroutine in assembly language for computing Ackermann's function.

6 Write a FORTRAN-callable function that calls the recursive Ackermann's function of exercise 5 above, and test it with a main program that calls the function for various values. (*Warning:* Do not use numbers larger than 3 for the arguments.)

7 Write a sorting program such as described in exercise 2, above, except that:
   (a) The input and output subroutines and main program should be written in FORTAN.
   (b) The sorting program should be in assembly language.
   (c) All arguments should be passed by placing them in common blocks.

CHAPTER 10

MACROS AND CONDITIONAL ASSEMBLY

10.1 REPETITIVE BLOCKS OF CODE

The Need for Assembly Time Repetition

Quite often while solving a problem employing assembly language, one finds that large areas of a program are highly repetitive. Now the first reaction that should come to mind is that loops and subroutines are used for avoiding repetition. Although this is true, there are occasions when neither loops nor subroutines are the best method. Following is a list of some possible reasons why loops or subroutines may be undesirable on occasion:

1. Programs with loops and subroutines will run slower than programs with equivalent repeated code. This is because loops needs extra instructions for counting, indexing, testing exit conditions, and branching back. Similarly, subroutines have to be called and returned from; arguments have to be passed; and registers must be saved. On those *few* occasions when speed is critical, subroutines and loops may need to be avoided (especially at the innermost nested levels of the program).

2. Although there may be repetition in form, there may not be exact repetition. Although this could be handled by a subroutine with a complex argument structure, it often is not desirable. If the underlying process is very simple, the overhead of passing arguments and calling a subroutine may involve more overall code than if the desired code were simply repeated.

3. Finally, the code that is repeated may be data rather than instructions. Assume, for example, that an array is to be filled entirely with 5s. One way to handle this would be with an initialization routine that stores 5s over the array. Sometimes, however, initialization routines are inconvenient and it is preferable just to assemble the array with the elements initialized to 5 by repeating the directive .WORD 5 several times.

The preceding reasons are not intended to be exhaustive, but to give several ideas why one would have repetitive parts of a program. It was this motivation that led to the development of **macro assemblers.** As we shall see in this chapter, the implementation of macros is so sophisticated that other uses will also become apparent.

Repeat Blocks

The simplest form of repetition that assembly language deals with is the **repeat block.** A repeat block is a block of code that is repeated verbatim over and over again some number of times. An example of the need for this is the case given before of an array filled with 5s. This could be assembled by placing a number of .WORD 5 lines one after the other.

As a convenience to the user, the PDP-11 assembly language has a special assembly directive for indicating repeats. The .REPT directive is used in the following context:

```
        .REPT   Expression
          .
          .     Block of code
          .
        .ENDR
```

The block of code is repeated over and over, the number of times being given by the value of the expression following the .REPT directive. Figure 10.1a shows how a block of seven words containing the number 5 could be assembled using the .REPT directive. Figure 10.1b shows the equivalent code. Note that

Figure 10.1 Use of Repeat Block

```
        .REPT   7              .WORD   5
        .WORD   5              .WORD   5
        .ENDR                  .WORD   5
                               .WORD   5
                               .WORD   5
                               .WORD   5
                               .WORD   5

      (a) Repeat Block       (b) Equivalent Code
```

Sec. 10.1   *Repetitive Blocks of Code*

although this example has only one line between .REPT and .ENDR, there is no definite limit* and any needed amount of code is acceptable.

Also note the fact that the lines in the repeat block are repeated without change. There is no variability in the lines of text. That does *not* mean, however, that there is no room for variability in the generated machine language. Expressions and definitions can be used to produce variable results as is shown in the following examples.

Repeat Blocks Using the Location Counter

Suppose that a programmer wished to create an array of 100 pairs of words. The first word in each pair contains zero, while the second word contains the address of the next pair of words. This arrangement of data is known as a singly linked list and is often used for data that must be rearranged. To rearrange data, one need only move several pointers or addresses. The data words themselves are not moved.

Looking again at this structure, it appears as:

```
        0
     Address
        0
     Address
        0
     Address
        .
        .
        .
```

Clearly, there is a repetitive structure, but not exact repetition because each of the addresses is different. In order to accomplish the preceding with repeat blocks, we will use the special symbol . which is called the **location counter.** This symbol is used in the PDP-11 assembly language to represent the location of the line being assembled. Since this location keeps changing, the value of . keeps changing. To use this, we note that the address of the next word in memory can be designated by the expression . + 2. Using this, the linked list structure can be generated as shown in Figure 10.2.

Figure 10.2   Linked List Structure

```
        .REPT   144
        .WORD   0
        .WORD   .+2
        .ENDR
```

*The only limit would be that the assembler's storage capability would eventually fill up.

Repeat Blocks with Other Symbols

Although it is often possible to represent variable data in terms of complex expressions involving the . symbol, it is sometimes quite difficult or impossible. In such cases, another method of defining variable data may prove useful. This method involves definition of symbols using the = symbol. We have already used = to define register symbols in the form R0 = %0. However, as was shown in the optional section on page 182, addresses can be assigned with = as PRS = 177564. For the most part defining symbols with = and : are synonymous. There is, however, one important difference. If a symbol is defined more than once using :, it is the multiple-definition error and the program will be flagged with error messages. On the other hand, symbols defined with = may be redefined with a subsequent =. These definitions are repeated on both passes of assembly, and the symbol will take on a new value after its redefinition for the remaining lines of program.

Figure 10.3 shows how the list structure of Figure 10.2 could be implemented by redefining symbols with = rather than using the . symbol. While this particular example may seem somewhat more complex, it has the advantage of more generality. Consider, for example, the problem of filling an array of eight locations with the values of the factorials of 1 through 8. Redefinition in a repeat block gives a simple, straightforward method for generating such an array (see Figure 10.4).

Figure 10.3 *Linked List with Redefined Symbols*

```
K=0                     K=0                             A:      .WORD   0
A:      .REPT   144     A:      .WORD   0                       .WORD   A+4
        .WORD   0       K=K+4                                   .WORD   0
K=K+4                           .WORD   A+K                     .WORD   A+10
        .WORD   A+K             .WORD   0                       .WORD   0
        .ENDR           K=K+4                                   .WORD   A+14
                                .WORD   A+K                     .
                                .WORD   0                       .
                        K=K+4                                   .
                                .WORD   A+K
                                .
                                .

    Repeat Block         Equivalent of Repeat Block       Equivalent With K Evaluated
```

Figure 10.4 *An Array of Factorials*

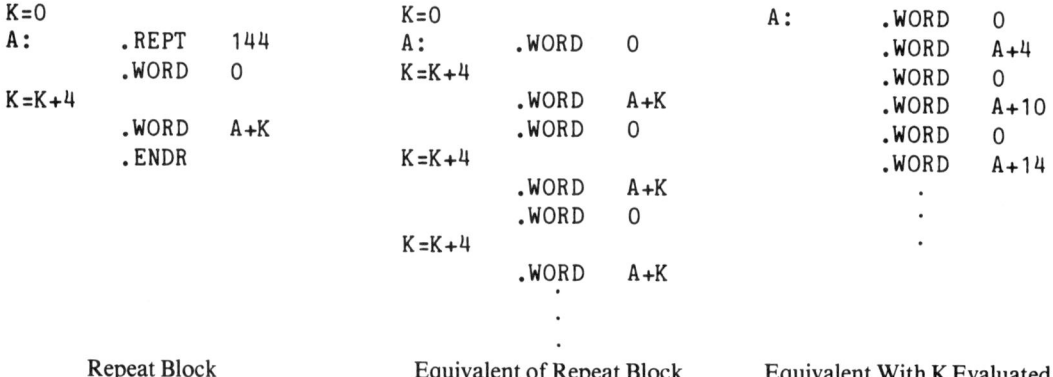

Sec. 10.2 *Symbolic Expressions*   223

Note the fact that neither K nor F is a location or even the name of a location. They are simply symbols that are assigned numeric values in the symbol table. They are not used as the address of an instruction or piece of data.

10.2 SYMBOLIC EXPRESSIONS

Review of Expressions

In previous chapters, symbolic expressions have been used in a simple form. Usually these expressions have been limited to something of the form A − 6 or A + 6, meaning the address six locations before or after A. When dealing with repeat blocks, macros, and conditional assembly, much more complexity is needed to give more power in expressions. For one thing, we should note that symbols need not be used exclusively for addresses. Symbolic names can be used for numbers that can be used for any purpose.

The assembly language programmer must be extremely careful to understand the relationships between the assembly process itself and program execution. For example, the line of assembly code K = K + 1 does not cause the register K to be incremented at execution time. In fact, it does not even cause the generation of any executable machine language code. What it does do is to cause the entry for K in the assembler's symbol table to be incremented. Do not confuse K = K + 1 with INC K. They are entirely different statements.

It is also important to note that there is a difference between symbols used for addresses in a program and symbols used for numbers. The symbols used for addresses in a program have values that must be changed when the program is relocated to an execution area. The values of symbols used for numbers do not change during relocation. Likewise, symbols used for absolute addresses do not change when the program is moved. Symbols in the symbol table are distinguished as being relocatable or absolute. (A third kind of symbol is the global symbol, but since global symbols are usually used in simple expressions where a number is, in effect, added or subtracted, they will not be considered further in this section.)

Rules for Forming Expressions

Expressions can be used in assembly language almost anywhere that a number or value is required. Expressions are formed by combining symbols and numbers with the operators +, −, *, and / almost as in FORTRAN or BASIC. Parentheses can be used except that < and > are used for left and right parentheses. It is extremely important to note that there is no operator precedence. Expressions are evaluated from left to right, with parentheses having their usual effect. For example, X + Y* < A + <5*B/K> > would be an acceptable expression. Because of the left-to-right evaluation, the expression 1 + 2*3 will be equal to 9, not 7. (The assemblers for some computers do not follow this rule.)

Just as symbols have types, expressions will have those same types. Rather than enumerate an exhaustive set of rules for determining the types of expressions, the following is a set of commonsense guidelines that will handle all but the most unusual cases:†

1. The expression must evaluate to something that could be entered in the symbol table. Thus, it should be one of the following:

   a. A number, or an absolute address.

   b. An address of a location within the program, or a location that is displaced a fixed amount from a location in the program, for example, the location 100 bytes beyond the end of your program.

   c. A global address plus or minus a fixed number.

2. An expression composed entirely of numbers and absolute symbols will be absolute.

3. A relocatable symbol plus or minus an absolute value will be a relocatable expression. The reason is because a location that is a fixed amount from some location in a program will move (and therefore have to be relocated) as the program is moved.

4. The difference between two relocatable symbols is *absolute*. The reason is because the difference between two addresses is the number of locations between those two addresses. If both are relocatable, then both will move the same amount as the program is moved. Therefore, the number of locations between them will remain *fixed*.

5. The preceding rules can, of course, apply to the subexpressions of a complex expression. In addition, there are two rules that apply to the use of multiplication and division:

6. With multiplication, at least one operand should be absolute. Then the multiplication can be thought of as repeated addition. For example, if A, B, and C are relocatable, consider the following expression: <3*A> - <2*B> - C. This could be rewritten as: A + A + A - B - B - C, which is equivalent to A - B + A - B + A - C. Note that each subexpression is the difference between two relocatables and is therefore absolute. Therefore, the entire expression is absolute.

7. With division, both operands should be absolute. It is hard to imagine anything else making sense. However, this does not preclude the use of division in complex expressions that involve relocatable parts. For example, if the difference between two addresses were desired in words rather than bytes, the following expression would work: <A - B>/2. Note that this is really the quotient of two absolute subexpressions (assuming that A

---

† Some versions of the assembler issue error messages for complex expressions. Other versions pass the expression to the linker for evaluation.

and B are relocatable). Also note that the preceding expression is preferable to the seemingly equivalent $<A/2> - <B/2>$. Although this expression may work on the PDP-11 with its propensity for even addresses, it may give problems with divisors other than 2.

An Example Using Expressions

The use of expressions and symbols that are numbers is important for ordinary assembly language programming because it gives the programmer the ability to modify the program easily. For example, consider a program that prints out a message and surrounds the message with three layers of asterisks such as:

Obviously, this must be a very important message. Figure 10.5 illustrates a subroutine for printing this message.

By using symbols and expressions, modifications can be made to the program quite easily. For example, if the message were to be surrounded by five layers of boxes instead of three, all that would need to change is the sixth line of the program, which would now state BOXES = 5. If the asterisks were to be changed to *at* signs, the fifth line of the program could be changed to read MARK = 100. (Octal 100 is the ASCII code for @.)

The Effect of Two Assembly Passes

A final consideration involved with expressions and the use of expressions concerns the order in which symbols are defined and used. Recall that two passes are needed in the assembly process because an instruction may refer to a symbolic address that is defined later on in the program. There are, however, cases where a value must be known on the first pass. In such cases, the symbols used in expressions for such a value must have been previously defined.

Essentially, since the symbol table is generated in the first pass, any symbols that affect the values in the symbol table must have been defined before being used. A simple example of such a case is the direct definition case, which will usually result in an error. For example:

```
A=B
B=5
```

will leave A undefined at the end of the first pass, and during much of the second pass. Clearly, this problem could easily be fixed by exchanging the two lines.

Figure 10.5 *Message-Printing Subroutine*

```
;
; SUBROUTINE MPRINT TO PRINT A MESSAGE SURROUNDED BY BOXES
;
        .TITLE   MESSAGE PRINT
        .MCALL   .REGDEF,.TTYOUT
        .REGDEF
        .GLOBL   MPRINT
MARK=52
BOXES=3
CR=15
LF=12
MPRINT: JSR      PC,HORIZ          ;PRINT HORIZONTAL STRIPES
        MOV      #BOXES,R1         ;PRINT MARKS AT
HLOOP:  .TTYOUT  #MARK             ;THE BEGINNING OF THE
        DEC      R1                ;MESSAGE
        BNE      HLOOP
        MOV      #MSG,R1           ;PRINT THE MESSAGE
MLOOP:  MOVB     (R1)+,R0          ;ZERO BYTE INDICATES
        BEQ      TPNT              ;THE END
        .TTYOUT
        BR       MLOOP
TPNT:   MOV      #BOXES,R1         ;PRINT MARKS AT
TLOOP:  .TTYOUT  #MARK             ;THE END OF THE MESSAGE
        DEC      R1
        BNE      TLOOP
        .TTYOUT  #CR               ;PRINT CARRIAGE RETURN
        .TTYOUT  #LF               ;LINE FEED
        JSR      PC,HORIZ          ;PRINT HORIZONTAL STRIPES
        RTS      PC                ;RETURN
HORIZ:  MOV      #BOXES,R1         ;GET NUMBER OF LINES
HLOOP1: MOV      #EMSG-MSG-1+<2*BOXES>,R2  ;GET LENGTH OF LINES
HLOOP2: .TTYOUT  #MARK             ;PRINT MARK
        DEC      R2                ;LOOP OVER LENGTH
        BNE      HLOOP2
        .TTYOUT  #CR               ;PRINT CARRIAGE RETURN
        .TTYOUT  #LF               ;LINE FEED
        DEC      R1                ;LOOP OVER NUMBER
        BNE      HLOOP1            ;OF LINE
        RTS      PC                ;RETURN
MSG:    .ASCIZ   /THIS IS A MESSAGE!/
EMSG:                              ;THIS LINE JUST DEFINES EMSG
        .END
```

A more complex problem arises when an expression is used in a way that affects the size of the program. If such an expression contains undefined symbols, it will adversely affect all subsequent addresses for the remainder of the program. For example:

```
X:      .BLKW   A
Y:      .BLKW   1
A=5
```

Since A is undefined on the first pass, the assembler will not know how many words to set aside for the array X. For lack of anything better to do, the assembler uses 0 for undefined symbols. Therefore, the address Y will be the same as the address X. However, on the second pass, A is defined as 5 so the address Y will come out to be 12 (octal) greater than the address X. This discrepancy will be flagged with a P for a *phase* error.

Sometimes these errors can be rather subtle. For example, R1 is not normally defined until the macro .REGDEF is called.* This call must be done early in the program text. Otherwise, consider a simple instruction such as CLR R1. If .REGDEF had not been called until later in the program, R1 would be assumed to be an address and CLR R1 would be assembled as a two-word instruction in pass 1. All subsequent labels in the symbol table would be defined on this basis. Later, however, when we come back to the CLR R1 on pass 2, R1 has been defined as register 1 or %1. The assembler thus assembles a one-word instruction and all the following label definitions will be wrong by one word, resulting in numerous phase errors. Note, however, that neither the CLR R1 nor the .REGDEF line is flagged with errors. The phase errors are flagged on the "innocent" label definitions that follow. This is because the assembler does not know that anything bad has happened until it sees a label definition that is different on the two passes.

EXERCISE SET 1

1 Show how the following repeat blocks would assemble in machine language. Assume that they are loaded at location 1200.

   (a) .REPT   5   (b) .REPT   7
        .WORD   .+5   .WORD   5
        .ENDR   .WORD   .-2
                                          .ENDR

---

*Some of the newer assemblers automatically define the eight register names, but we could turn the automatic definition off for the example with the directive .DSABL REG.

(c)
```
        K=0
        .REPT   4
        K=K+2
        .WORD   .+K
        .ENDR
```

(d)
```
        K=0
        .REPT   5
        K=K+1
        .REPT   K
        .WORD   K*3
        .ENDR
        .ENDR
```

2 Write a repeat block that generates an array of 100 words labeled NUMBS. This array should be set to contain the numbers 1 through 100.

  (a) Do the problem using . expressions.

  (b) Do the problem using symbol redefinition with =.

3 Assume that $I=2$, $J=3$, and $K=5$ are defined values for the assembly language symbols, I, J, and K. What are the values of the following expressions in octal?

  (a) I*J+K
  (b) I+J*K
  (c) J/I+2
  (d) I+J/K
  (e) I+<J*K>/K
  (f) I+<J*K>+K>
  (g) I+J*<I+J>
  (h) <I+J>*I+J

4 Assume that A, B, and C are relocatable symbols (that is, labels that refer to locations in the program). Also, I, J, and K are absolute symbols (that is, symbols that refer to fixed numbers). Which of the following expressions are absolute, relocatable, or neither?

  (a) A+I
  (b) B-K
  (c) A-B
  (d) A+B
  (e) A+K-B
  (f) <A-B>+<A-C>
  (g) <A-K>+<A-J>
  (h) <A+K>+<<B-C>*4>

5 The following program produces a number of phase errors due to improper order of definitions. Indicate which statements are misplaced, and which statements would be flagged with phase errors. (*Note:* Even though this is not a program in that there are no executable lines, reordering the statements could cause it to assemble without error.)

```
        I=3
    A:  .BLKW   K
    B:  .BLKW   D-C
    C:  .BLKW   I
    D:  .BLKW   K+I
        K=J
        J=I+5
        .END
```

6 Reorder the statements in the program in exercise 5, so that there are no assembly errors.

10.3 MACROS

A Simple Macro

Macros are complex blocks of assembly language that can be repeated a number of times in a program. Unlike repeat blocks, the repeated code generated by a macro need not all be in one place but may be placed at various points in the program. Also unlike repeat blocks, macros allow considerable variability to the repeated blocks. It must be noted that macros are also useful in other contexts.

Essentially, macros are named blocks of code. Anywhere the name is used in the operation field, the block of code will be inserted in (copied in) the program. In addition, there may be *parameters,* or symbols, that are modified or substituted for each time the macro is invoked, or *called.* As an example, let us consider a program that very frequently adds two numbers together and stores the result somewhere, as would happen in FORTRAN or BASIC with the statement A = B + C or LET A = B + C.

In PDP-11 assembly language, this simply requires two lines of code:

```
        MOV     B,A
        ADD     C,A
```

In order to use this as a macro, we must first create a macro name and names for the parameters (substitutable symbols). Let us use the name SUM for the macro and A, B, and C for the parameter names. Any symbol names are usable so long as they are not confused with any other symbols in the program. For example, it would not usually be a good idea to name a macro MOV or ADD.

After the names are chosen, we must then define the macro. This starts out with the directive .MACRO SUM,A,B,C and is followed by the lines of code to be generated each time the macro is called. Finally, the directive .ENDM is used to signal the end of the macro definition. Figure 10.6 shows the full macro definition.

Figure 10.6 Simple Macro Definition

```
        .MACRO  SUM,A,B,C
        MOV     B,A
        ADD     C,A
        .ENDM
```

Macro Definition versus Macro Expansion

Note that the macro definition itself does not cause any code to be placed in the program. It is when the macro is *called* that code is generated. The macro call consists of the name of the macro used as if it were an op code followed by the arguments to be substituted for the parameters. Figure 10.7 shows a number of

Figure 10.7 Simple Macro Calls and Expansion

(a) SUM	X,Y,Z		MOV	Y,X
			ADD	Z,X
(b) SUM	A,B,C		MOV	B,A
			ADD	C,A
(c) SUM	PRICE,COST,PROFIT		MOV	COST,PRICE
			ADD	PROFIT,PRICE
(d) SUM	X+6,R0,#10		MOV	R0,X+6
			ADD	#10,X+6
	Macro Call			Generated Code

examples of macro calls along with the effective generated code. Example (a) in Figure 10.7 shows a simple straightforward macro call, where the symbols X, Y, and Z are to be substituted for A, B, and C. In example (b), A, B, and C are substituted for themselves, which causes no confusion.

In example (c), PRICE, COST, and PROFIT are substituted for A, B, and C, showing that the number of characters substituted need not be the same as in the parameter name. A key point here is that character strings are substituted, not addresses. It would be improper to say that the address of PRICE is substituted for the address of A. In fact, the symbol A may never even be used as an address. What happens is that the macro processor replaces all of the substitutable parameters with the argument *character strings*. The resulting code is then processed by the assembler as normal assembly language.

Example (d) shows how this operates. Here, the character strings X+6, R0, and #10 are substituted for A, B, and C. Note here that R0 and #10 are not addresses. However, the generated code is correct assembly language and would be translated correctly into machine language.

Macro Parameters in Other Fields

It is important to understand that when macros are called, they are *expanded* by replacing the parameter occurrences with the argument character strings. It should be noted that parameters can occur anywhere within the macro definition and are identified by the use of the name surrounded by punctuation of some sort. Figure 10.8 shows a macro definition and expansion that illustrates how various fields can be substituted.

First, note that the lines of code in the macro definition do not constitute correct assembly code by themselves. The first line contains DEF in the op code field, which is not a legal PDP-11 instruction. However, DEF is a substitutable parameter, and in the macro expansion, DEF does not occur but is replaced with CLR, which is a legal PDP-11 op code.

Sec. 10.3 Macros

Figure 10.8 A Macro with Various Substitutable Parts

```
          .MACRO   TEST,ABC,DEF,HIJ
ABC:      DEF      HIJ
          INC      HIJ
          .ENDM
```
(a) Definition

```
          TEST     LOOP1,CLR,COUNT
```
(b) Macro Call

```
LOOP1:    CLR      COUNT
          INC      COUNT
```
(c) Macro Expansion

Another point this example shows is that labels can be substitutable. In fact, it is almost always necessary for a label that appears in a macro definition to be a substitutable parameter. Suppose that ABC were not substitutable; then if the macro were called two or more times, ABC would appear as a label more than once, and would result in a multiple-definition error. There are features for dealing with labels that help solve some of these problems; however, their discussion is beyond the scope of this chapter.

The basic purpose of macros in assembly language is to allow the programmer to extend the language and to create new languages. A simple example of this would be the problem created by a programmer who forgot that there is no *add byte* instruction in the PDP-11. Imagine that this programmer wrote a large program with many add byte instructions. One solution would be to write an add byte macro as shown in Figure 10.9. This instruction could then be used almost as if it were an instruction in the machine. One slight problem is that TEMP1 and TEMP2 must be set aside somewhere as locations in the program. Also, this "instruction" does have a large number of words. It should be clear that there is room for improvement in this macro example. This is left as an exercise for the reader.

Figure 10.9 The ADDB Macro

```
          .MACRO   ADDB,X,Y
          MOVB     X,TEMP2
          MOVB     Y,TEMP1
          ADD      TEMP2,TEMP1
          MOVB     TEMP1,Y
          .ENDM
```

When you write a macro such as ADDB, in effect you are creating a new and more powerful machine, one that has an ADDB instruction. In fact, sometimes programmers use macros to generate an assembly language for an entirely different machine. Each instruction on the other machine is transformed into a macro that either creates machine language for the other machine, or creates PDP-11 code that simulates the other machine. This could help solve the problem of assembling the first assembly language translator for a newly designed computer.

10.4 CONDITIONAL ASSEMBLY

Definition of Conditional Assembly

Often, especially in large programs, there may be portions of code that are sometimes needed and sometimes not needed. Examples include:

a. Portions of a program needed for debugging and not needed when the program is running.
b. Macros and subroutines for multiplication, division, and so on which are not needed with PDP-11's that have an extended instruction set.
c. Code that is needed to support optional computer features.

Code that is not needed can be removed from the program to save memory. However, it is not necessarily an easy task to remove code from a program. Editing out areas of a large program or pulling cards from a deck are risky propositions at best. There is always the chance of removing too much, or of removing the wrong things. It is also difficult to go back to the original code if you change your mind. **Conditional assembly** is a method for dealing with these problems.

Conditional assembly allows a certain identified block of code in a program to be included or to be ignored by the assembler. The block of code is called a **conditional block,** and is delimited by two assembly directives. The beginning of the block is marked by .IF and the end by .ENDC . The .IF directive includes a description of a logical condition. If the condition is true, the code in the conditional block is assembled into the program. Otherwise, the entire block is skipped over as if it did not exist.

Example of Conditional Assembly

Figure 10.10 shows a simple example of a conditional block. The value of the symbol TEST determines whether or not the block of code is assembled. If TEST is *not equal* to 0, then the code is assembled. Otherwise it is skipped over.

Of special note is the fact that the block of code contains the definition of the label XCODE. Consequently, if this block of code is skipped over, references to the symbol XCODE would result in an error flag for an undefined symbol. To prevent this, it would be necessary either to:

Figure 10.10 Conditional Block

```
              .IF    NE,TEST
              MOV    X,Y
      XCODE:  INC    R0
              ADD    W,R1
              .ENDC
```

1. include all references to XCODE in conditional blocks that are *skipped* when TEST equals 0, or
2. include an alternative definition for XCODE that is *included* when TEST equals 0.

Also note that this conditional block generates machine instructions and therefore affects the location counter. Therefore, the symbol TEST must be defined earlier in the program. Usually symbols that control conditional blocks are defined with = early in the program where they can be easily accessed for modification.

Figure 10.10 uses the relational operator NE for *not equal*. As would be expected, the six arithmetic relations EQ, NE, LE, LT, GE, and GT (for equal, not equal, less than or equal, less than, greater than or equal, and greater than) are all usable. They all compare their argument expression with zero. The syntax is .IF relation,expression. For example, .IF GE,X-5 will skip over code unless the value of the expression X-5 is greater than or equal to zero.

Other Conditional Assembly Codes

In addition to the preceding arithmetic conditions, there are six symbolic conditions. These are as follows:

1. DF—defined. The condition is true, if the argument is a defined symbol. For example, .IF DF,XYZW will generate code if XYZW is a defined symbol in the symbol table. Note a danger here—if XYZW is later defined in pass 1, it will be defined for all of pass 2.
2. NDF—not defined. This is the opposite of DF.
3. B—blank. The condition is true if the following macro parameter is substituted with blanks. For example, consider the following macro:

```
      .MACRO   BLANK,X,Y,Z
      .IF      B,Y
      .WORD    X,Z
      .ENDC
      .ENDM
```

The macro call BLANK 5,ABC,6 will generate no code, whereas BLANK 5,,6 will generate two words of code.

4. NB—not blank. This is the opposite of B.
5. IDN—identical. This condition code is true if the following two macro type arguments are identical character strings after macro parameter substitution.
6. DIF—different. This is the opposite of IDN.

Clearly, the last four conditional assembly codes are only usable within a macro definition. In fact, one of the main uses of conditional assembly is within macros. Conditional assembly can be used to control the lines of code that are assembled depending upon argument values, or even upon the number of times the macro is called. As an example, consider a macro that prints out messages. The first time that the macro is called, a subroutine for printing the message must be generated. The subsequent uses of the macro simply generate subroutine calls. Figure 10.11 shows a macro that will generate code to accomplish this. The macro is called by MESG #STRING where STRING is the label of .ASCIZ message string.

10.5 NESTING AND RECURSION

Without exploring the subject in depth, we can note that conditional blocks can be nested within other conditional blocks, and macro definitions can appear within macros. The .IF—.ENDC and .MACRO—.ENDM directives must occur in pairs like parentheses. This allows complex structures for multiple decisions and for macros that define other macros when called.

Also note that macro expansions can call other macros. For example, the macro of Figure 10.11 uses the macro .TTYOUT. This causes no problem because after expansion, control is returned to the assembler proper which may encounter additional macro calls. This produces additional generated code that is simply added to whatever is already there.

An interesting point here is that a macro may call itself. This forms a kind of loop where the macro is expanded repeatedly. However, as in normal programming loops, there must be a way to end the loop. Thus, if a macro does call itself, that call must be within a conditional block which eventually is skipped over. Macros of this sort are called **recursive macros,** since they behave in much the same way as recursive subroutines which were described in Chapter 9. Figure 10.12 shows a recursive macro for generating a table of numbers from 1 through N by calling the macro TABLE N. Note that TABLE calls the macro TAB, which is the recursive macro. In the .IF line, N is enclosed by parentheses because it might be replaced by an expression. Because of limitations on nesting depth, this macro may not work if N is very large. The current RT-11 assembler will not allow N to be greater than 17 octal.

Sec. 10.5 Nesting and Recursion

Figure 10.11 *A Macro Employing Conditional Assembly*

```
;
; MACRO TO PRINT A MESSAGE
;
MESGI=0
        .MACRO  MESG,X
        MOV     R0,-(SP)        ;SAVE R0
        MOV     R1,-(SP)        ;AND R1
        MOV     X,R1            ;GET ADDRESS OF MESSAGE
        JSR     PC,MESGS        ;PRINT MESSAGE
        MOV     (SP)+,R1        ;RESTORE R1
        MOV     (SP)+,R0        ;AND R0
        .IF     EQ,MESGI        ;FIRST USE?
MESGI=1                         ;YES BUT DON'T USE AGAIN
        .MCALL  .TTYOUT         ;GET .TTYOUT MACRO
        BR      MESGE           ;SKIP OVER SUBROUTINE
MESGS:  MOVB    (R1)+,R0        ;GET CHARACTER
        BEQ     MESGD           ;DONE?
        .TTYOUT                 ;NO PRINT R0
        BR      MESGS           ;AND LOOP
MESGD:  .TTYOUT #15             ;OUTPUT CR
        .TTYOUT #12             ;AND LF
        RTS     PC              ;AND RETURN
MESGE:                          ;SKIP AROUND ADDRESS
        .ENDC                   ;END OF CONDITIONAL BLOCK
        .ENDM                   ;END OF MACRO
```

Figure 10.12 *A Recursive Macro*

```
;
; MACRO FOR GENERATING A TABLE OF CONSECUTIVE NUMBERS
;
        .MACRO  TABLE,N
TABK=1                          ;INITIALIZE TABK
        TAB     N               ;START PROCESS
        .ENDM
;
; RECURSIVE MACRO TO BE USED BY TABLE
;
        .MACRO  TAB,N
        .IF     LE,TABK-<N>     ;HAVE WE GENERATED ENOUGH
        .WORD   TABK            ;NO, PRODUCE WORD
TABK=TABK+1                     ;INCREMENT TABK
        TAB     N               ;GENERATE MORE
        .ENDC
        .ENDM
```

EXERCISE SET 2

1. Given the following macro definitions:

   ```
   .MACRO  ORD   A,B
   MOV     A,B
   CLR     A
   SUB     B,A
   .ENDM
   .MACRO  SPEC  A,B,C
   MOV     #A,AA
   B       A,C
   CLRB    C+6
   .ENDM
   ```

   show the assembly language expansions resulting from the following macro calls:

   (a) ORD   SUM,TOTAL   (b) ORD   R0,(R1)+
   (c) ORD   A(R0),B   (d) ORD   B,A
   (e) SPEC   XMAX,MOV,W   (f) SPEC   1000,ADD,C+6
   (g) SPEC   X,ORD,1000   (h) SPEC   B,ORD,A

2. Assuming that the symbols A and B are defined as A = 5 and B = 7, what code, if any, is assembled by the following conditional assemblies?

   (a) IF   EQ,A-3   (b) .IF   NE,A-3
       MOV   X,Y   MOV   #3,W
       .ENDC   .ENDC

   (c) .IF   GT,B   (d) C=0
       MOV   R,R0   .IF   LT,B-4
       .ENDC   C=1
                                   .ENDC
                                   .IF   EQ,C
                                   MOV   H,Q
                                   .ENDC

   (e) C=0   (f) C=0
           .IF   EQ,B   .IF   NE,B
       C=1   C=1
           .IF   EQ,C   .IF   EQ,C-1
           MOV   U,V   MOV   I,J
           .ENDC   .ENDC
           MOV   L,M   MOV   G,F
           .ENDC   .ENDC

3. Write a macro that saves the contents of general registers R0 through R5 on the stack.

Exercise Set 2

4 Write a macro called SAVER that saves the contents of registers R0 through R*n* on the stack, where *n* is determined from a macro parameter. For example, SAVER 3 would save registers R0 through R3. *Hint:* Use a repeat block in the macro. Also, note that registers can be designated by a percent sign followed by an expression, for example, %5-3 means R2.

5 Rewrite the macro SUM A,B,C shown in Figure 10.6 on page 229. The modified macro should use conditional assembly to take advantage of the fact that a simpler expansion can result if the computation is:

   (a)   SUM A,A,C   (MOV is not necessary)

   (b)   SUM A,B,#1   (INC can be used instead of ADD)

*6 Rewrite the ADDB macro in Figure 10.9 on page 231 so that it is more efficient or improved in each or a combination of the following ways. If no improvement can be made, say so. Which criteria contradict each other?

   (a)   The macro expansion should have as few words as possible in line in the code.

   (b)   Overall memory use should be reduced assuming many calls.

   (c)   The execution of the macro should be as fast as possible.

   (d)   The condition codes should have the values that a real ADDB instruction would have when finished.

   (e)   The program should not destroy the contents of general registers, but should work right when the arguments are general registers.

*7 Imagine that there is a simple computer with an architecture similar to the PDP-11 in that it has a memory of 16-bit two's complement words. However, it only has one general register called "the accumulator." All operations must operate through the accumulator and there are 10 instructions, as follows:

LDA	M	Load memory location M into the accumulator.
STA	M	Store the accumulator into location M.
ADDA	M	Add the contents of M to the accumulator.
SUBA	M	Subtract the contents of M from the accumulator.
JUMP	M	Jump to location M.
JMI	M	Jump to location M if the accumulator is negative.
JZ	M	Jump to location M if the accumulator is 0.
READ		Read a number into the accumulator.
PRINT		Print out the value of the accumulator.
STOP		Stop execution.

The following program prints out the first 10 powers of two by computing 2X as X+X:

```
                .TITLE   HYPOTHETICAL COMPUTER PROGRAM
        START:  LDA      MTEN        ;INITIALIZE COUNT TO
                STA      COUNT       ;NEGATIVE 10
                LDA      ONE         ;INITIALIZE POWER
                STA      POWER
        LOOP:   LDA      POWER       ;MULTIPLY POWER BY TWO
                ADDA     POWER
                STA      POWER
                PRINT                ;PRINT POWER
                LDA      COUNT       ;INDEX COUNT
                ADDA     ONE
                STA      COUNT
                JMI      LOOP        ;LOOP WHILE NEGATIVE
                STOP                 ;AND THEN STOP
        MTEN:   .WORD    -12         ;INITIAL VALUE OF COUNT
        ONE:    .WORD    1           ;THE CONSTANT ONE
        COUNT:  .BLKW    1           ;VARIABLE DATA AREA
        POWER:  .BLKW    1
                .END     START
```

Write a set of macros that simulates this hypothetical machine by replacing each instruction with PDP-11 instructions that have an equivalent effect. Test your macros with the sample program.

*8 Write a hypothetical machine program as described in exercise 7 that reads two signed numbers and multiplies them together producing a signed result. Is it possible to make your program efficient even though there is no shift instruction? Test your program with the macros you wrote for exercise 7.

CHAPTER 11

INPUT AND OUTPUT

11.1 INTRODUCTION

Chapter 8 described simple methods for reading and for printing alphabetic information. This chapter explains the input and output operations in greater detail. There are great differences in speed between the processor and memory on one hand and the input and output devices on the other. The processor and memory are all-electronic devices that can perform hundreds of thousands or millions of operations per second. In contrast, most input and output operations involve mechanical motion of some kind. As a result, input/output devices typically perform only tens or hundreds of operations per second. The problem is to find a satisfactory way of connecting the very fast processor to the comparatively slow input/output devices.

11.2 DEVICE POLLING

Definitions

The simplest method of communicating with an input or output device is called **device polling.** The processor directs the input/output device to perform a simple operation, such as printing a single ASCII character. The processor then repeatedly asks the device, "Have you finished printing the character?" On some devices, printing a single ASCII character will require one-thirtieth of a second. As a result, the processor may ask "Have you finished?" thousands of times before the device finally responds "Yes." At this point, the processor can ask the device to print a second ASCII character. The following sections describe device polling in greater detail.

Address Assignments

In order to perform input or output, the processor needs some method of transferring information between itself and the input/output devices. On the PDP-11 computer, this is accomplished by assigning each input/output device one or more addresses, as if they were memory cells. This is called **memory mapped input/output.**

Consider the computer system shown in Figure 11.1. This system consists of a processor, 20,000 (octal) bytes of memory, and a teletypewriter terminal. Notice that an ASCII terminal is really two different devices. The keyboard is an input device while the printing mechanism is an output device. Unlike a typewriter, there is no direct connection between the keyboard and the printing mechanism. It is quite possible to type at the keyboard and have nothing printed.

As Figure 11.1 indicates, addressable memory locations 177560 and 177562 are registers that control the use of the keyboard while addressable memory locations 177564 and 177566 control the printer. The processor does not distinguish between normal memory cells and the special memory cells controlled by the input/output devices. In performing a fetch, for example, the processor in Figure 11.1 sends out an address and waits for something to respond with the contents of the addressed location. If the (word) address is between 000000 and 017776, memory sends back the contents. If the address is 177560 or 177562, the keyboard controller responds, while if the address is

Figure 11.1   A Small Computer System

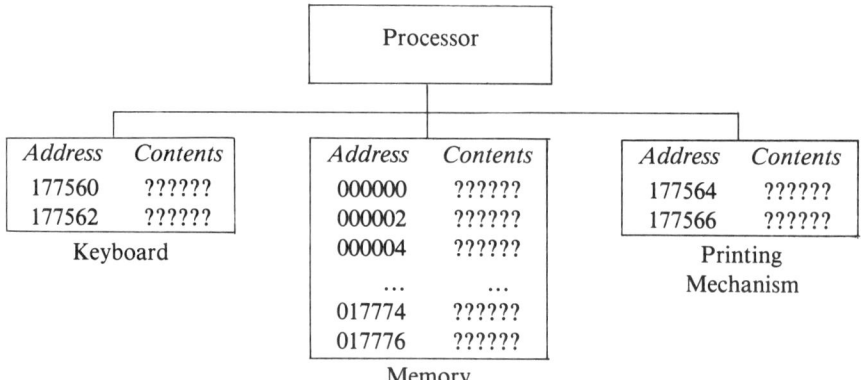

Sec. 11.2   Device Polling   241

177564 or 177566, the printing mechanism controller responds. (In our example, any other address would result in an addressing error.)

Each input or output device has its own standard addresses. On virtually any PDP-11, for example, the operator's keyboard is controlled through addresses 177560 and 177562. The assignment of addresses to a particular input/output device is a fairly arbitrary decision that was made by the people who designed the PDP-11 and in fact can be changed by the user. However, the following convention was observed: Word addresses between 000000 and 157776 (167776 for the LSI-11) are normal memory addresses, while word addresses from 160000 (170000) to 177776 are used for input/output devices and other special purposes.*

The Keyboard Buffer

As previously noted, the console keyboard controls memory cells 177560 and 177562. Memory cell 177562 is called the **keyboard buffer.** The low-order seven bits in the keyboard buffer contain the ASCII code for the key that was most recently struck on the keyboard. For example, if the C key were pressed most recently, the keyboard buffer would contain the following:

```
Address                    Binary Contents
177562     | ? ? ? ? ? ? ? ? ? 1 0 0 0 0 1 1 |
            15 14 13 12 11 10 9 8 7 6 5 4 3 2 1 0  Bit number
```

Note that the ASCII code for the capital letter C, which is 103 in octal or 1000011 in binary, occupies bit positions 0 through 6. Bits 7 through 15 are labeled with question marks to indicate that their settings are unpredictable. On most PDP-11 systems, bit 7 will be set to a 1, while bits 8 through 15 will be set to 0. However, it is better programming practice and safer to make no assumptions about the setting of these bits.

Reading characters from the keyboard buffer is quite simple. For example, the following statements will branch to statement CAPZ if the most recently struck key was uppercase Z.

```
            MOV     177562,R4
            BIC     #177600,R4
            CMP     R4,#132
            BEQ     CAPZ
```

After the character is moved to register 4, the bit clear instruction is used to set the 9 high-order (garbage) bits to 0:

---

*Larger PDP-11 computers can have an option called memory management. This allows a much larger memory address space for the machine. As a result, much of the literature uses 18-bit addresses to specify the device addresses, and shows them as 777560, 777562, and so on. For smaller machines, the upper two bits can be ignored.

	ASCII character
Contents of R4 before BIC	? ? ? ? ? ? ? ? ? a a a a a a a
Mask 177600 in binary	1 1 1 1 1 1 1 1 1 0 0 0 0 0 0 0
Contents of R4 after BIC	0 0 0 0 0 0 0 0 0 a a a a a a a

While it is legal assembly language to use numeric addresses in an instruction such as MOV 177562,R4 it is poor programming style. It is preferable to define symbols for addresses and more complicated constants as shown in the previous chapter. Accordingly, the preceding example can be rewritten as follows:

```
MASK=177600
KBB=177562
        MOV     KBB,R4
        BIC     #MASK,R4
        CMP     R4,#132
        BEQ     CAPZ
```

Using symbols significantly reduces errors. In addition, although device addresses are fixed for a given computer, they may vary from one machine to another. If your program is to be run on another PDP-11, modification is much easier, since only the line KBB = 177562 would need to be changed, whereas there might be many references to the keyboard buffer.

The keyboard buffer is quite different from normal memory cells. First, the contents of the buffer changes when the key is pressed. Secondly, the buffer is a *read-only* memory cell that ignores store requests. That is, an instruction such as CLR 177562 has *no effect* on the contents of the buffer. As a result, the following instructions will not achieve the desired result because the BIC instruction will not set the high-order bits to 0:

```
MASK=177600
KBB=177562
        BIC     #MASK,KBB
        CMP     KBB,#132
        BEQ     CAPZ
```

A MOVB instruction can be used to move a character from the buffer to a byte in memory. Byte 177562 contains the 7-bit ASCII character plus one high-order bit. This bit should be set to 0 as follows:

```
KBB=177562
        MOVB    KBB,CHAR
        BICB    #200,CHAR
            .
            .
            .
CHAR:   .BLKB   1
```

Sec. 11.2 Device Polling 243

The Keyboard Status Register

In addition to memory location 177562 (the keyboard buffer), the keyboard also controls memory location 177560, which is called the **keyboard status register**. One of the functions of this register is to indicate that a new character has been typed. The keyboard status register is as follows:

```
                              Ready bit
                                ↓  ┌── Interrupt bit
177560   | 0 0 0 0 0 0 0 0 ? ? 0 0 0 0 0 0 |
          15 14 13 12 11 10 9 8 7 6 5 4 3 2 1 0   Bit Number
```

All bits in the register are always 0, except for two bits, 6 and 7. Bit 7 in the status register is called the **ready bit**.* The ready bit is a read-only bit that indicates that the keyboard is *ready* to be read, according to the following rules:

1. When a key is pressed, the ready bit is set to 1 to indicate that a new character has been typed.

2. When a program fetches a character from the keyboard buffer (memory cell 177562), the ready bit is set back to 0 to indicate that the buffer now contains an old character.

In order to read a character, the program tests the setting of the ready bit. If it is equal to 1, the program can fetch the new character from the buffer. If the ready bit is 0, the keyboard is not ready, and the program should keep on testing the ready bit until the operator types a new character, thereby setting the ready bit to 1. This continual testing of the ready bit is called device polling.

The ready bit can be tested with the following bit test instruction:

```
        KBS=177560
                BIT     #200,KBS
```

However, a test byte instruction can be used instead. Recall that word 177560 consists of two 8-bit bytes:

```
| 0 0 0 0 0 0 0 0 | ? ? 0 0 0 0 0 0 |
 15 14 13 12 11 10 9 8  7 6 5 4 3 2 1 0
    Byte 177561          Byte 177560
```

The ready bit happens to be the sign bit for byte 177560. If the ready bit is 0, the byte contains a positive number, whereas if the ready bit is 1, the byte contains a negative number. The following two instructions are used to make the processor wait until the operator strikes a key:

*Documentation from Digital Equipment Corporation may refer to bit 7 as the **done** bit.

```
            KBS=177560
    LOOP:   TSTB    KBS
            BPL     LOOP
```

As long as the ready bit is 0, the program will continually branch back to statement LOOP. When the operator strikes a key, the ready bit will be set to 1, byte 177560 will become negative, and the program will fall out of the loop. This **polling loop** is generally followed by instructions that empty the buffer, such as:

```
    MASK=177600
    KBB=177562
            MOV     KBB,R0
            BIC     #MASK,R0
```

Figure 11.2 contains a subroutine called RCHAR that reads a character from the keyboard and places it in R0. Note that KBB is defined as KBS+2. The reason for this is that, while the addresses may change, the relative distance between them is almost always 2.

In addition to the ready bit, the keyboard status register contains an interrupt bit (bit 6) that will be described later. However, in order to use device polling, the interrupt must be set to 0 before any characters are typed. As a result, programs that use device polling to read a character from the keyboard should usually contain a statement such as CLR KBS near the beginning of the program.

Figure 11.2 A Subroutine to Read a Character

```
;THE FOLLOWING SUBROUTINE READS A CHARACTER FROM THE KEYBOARD
;AND LEAVES THE CHARACTER IN REGISTER 0
KBS=177560
KBB=KBS+2
MASK=177600
R0=%0
PC=%7
            .GLOBL  RCHAR
    RCHAR:  TSTB    KBS             ;WAIT UNTIL CHARACTER TYPED
            BPL     RCHAR
            MOV     KBB,R0          ;GET THE CHARACTER
            BIC     #MASK,R0        ;AND CLEAR GARBAGE BITS
            RTS     PC
            .END
```

The Console Printer

The output device associated with the operator's console may be a printing mechanism similar to that of a typewriter or it may be a cathode-ray-tube

Sec. 11.2 Device Polling 245

display (CRT) that resembles a television set. Although the two output devices are physically very different, they are controlled or programmed in the same manner. For simplicity, the output device will be called the **console printer** or simply the printer.

Like the keyboard, the printer controls two 16-bit addressable memory locations. Memory location 177564 is the printer status register, and location 177566 is the printer buffer. The following illustrates these registers:

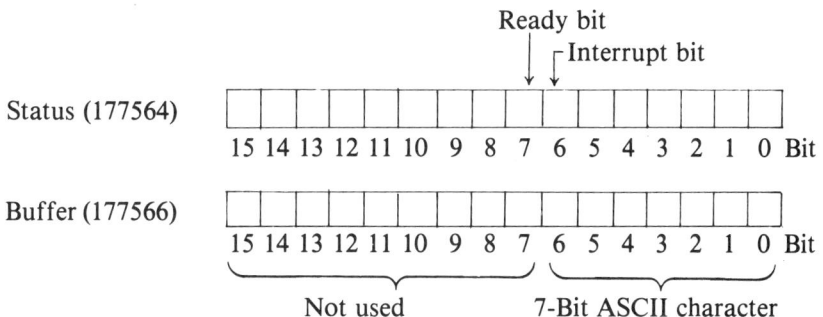

A character is printed by moving the ASCII code for the character to the buffer. For example, the instruction:

```
        PRB=177566
              MOV      #101,PRB
```

will cause the letter A to be printed because 101 octal is the ASCII code for A. The move instruction sends a full 16-bit word to the buffer. The buffer ignores the nine high-order bits and interprets the seven low-order bits (bits 0 through 6) as an ASCII character.

Neophyte programmers, who may forget that the printer is an ASCII device, sometimes write instructions such as:

```
        PRB=177566
              MOV      #123456,PRB
```

hoping to have the character string 123456 printed. This, of course, will not achieve the desired result. However, it is instructive to see what the instruction will do. The octal number 123456 is represented in binary as follows:

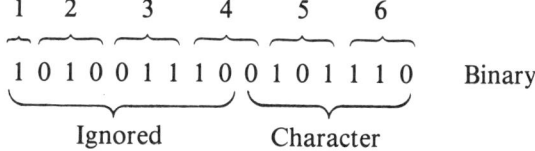

The nine high-order bits are ignored. The seven low-order bits, 0101110 in binary or 056 in octal, are interpreted as an ASCII character. The ASCII code for a dot or period is 056 octal, so the instruction will cause a . to be printed.

The ready bit (bit 7) in the printer status register indicates when the printer is ready to print another character. Recall that the processor and memory are generally much faster than the input/output devices. As a result, instructions such as the following will not produce the desired result:

```
PRB=177566
        MOV     #101,PRB
        MOV     #102,PRB
```

The first instruction sends the character A to the printer. The second instruction intends to print the character B (octal 102). However, the B is sent before the A has been printed. In such cases, the printed results are unpredictable. A single garbage character may be printed.

When the printer is ready to print a new character, the ready bit is set to 1. When a character is moved to the buffer, the ready bit is immediately set to 0 to indicate that the printer is busy printing a character. After the character is printed, the ready bit is returned to 1 to indicate that another character can be transmitted. As a result of these conventions, the format of the polling loop for an output device is almost identical to that of an input device. The following instructions would be used to print the character A:

```
PRS=177564
PRB=PRS+2
LOOP:   TSTB    PRS             ;IS THE READY BIT 1
        BPL     LOOP            ;IF NOT, WAIT
        MOV     #101,PRB        ;IF YES, PRINT THE CHARACTER
```

The printer status register, like the keyboard status register, contains an **interrupt bit.** This bit should be set to 0 at the start of the program with an instruction such as CLR PRS.

Figure 11.3 contains a subroutine called PCHAR that is designed to print the character contained in register 0. The symbol PRS refers to the Printer Status register and PRB refers to the keyboard Printer Buffer. Notice the similarity between the RCHAR subroutine (Figure 11.2) and the PCHAR subroutine.

Figure 11.3 *Subroutine to Print a Character*

```
        ;THE FOLLOWING SUBROUTINE PRINTS THE CHARACTER IN R0
PRS=177564                      ;PRINTER STATUS REGISTER
PRB=PRS+2                       ;PRINTER BUFFER
R0=%0
PC=%7
        .GLOBL  PCHAR
PCHAR:  TSTB    PRS             ;WAIT UNTIL THE PRINTER IS READY
        BPL     PCHAR
        MOVB    R0,PRB          ;THEN PRINT THE CHARACTER
        RTS     PC
        .END
```

11.3 OTHER INPUT/OUTPUT DEVICES

General Input/Output Devices

The strategy used for input and output with the keyboard and printer is used for many other input or output devices. These devices will have two registers that are assigned addresses in the addressable space of the machine. The two registers are a status register and a buffer register. On almost all devices, the status register uses bit 7 for the ready bit and bit 6 for the interrupt bit. The buffer register is used to transmit data in or out in much the same way as with the keyboard or printer buffer. For example, Figure 11.4 is a subroutine for printing a character on the line printer.

Figure 11.4 A Subroutine to Print a Character on the Line Printer

```
;THE FOLLOWING SUBROUTINE PRINTS THE CHARACTER IN R0
;ON THE LINE PRINTER
LPS=177514                      ;STATUS REGISTER
LPB=LPS+2                       ;BUFFER REGISTER
R0=%0
PC=%7
        .GLOBL  PLP
PLP:    TSTB    LPS             ;WAIT UNTIL THE PRINTER IS READY
        BPL     PLP
        MOVB    R0,LPB          ;THEN PRINT THE CHARACTER
        RTS     PC
        .END
```

It should be noted that this program is virtually identical to the program in Figure 11.3. The only difference (other than symbolic names) is that the status and buffer registers are located at 177514 and 177516 instead of 177564 and 177566. These addresses are the standard addresses for the line printer.

There are, however, some differences between the line printer and the console printer. The main one is that the line printer has an extra bit in the status register (bit 15), which is the error bit. The error bit is set to 1 if the printer is incapable of printing. This may mean that the printer is manually turned off, that it is out of paper, or various other possible conditions that make it nonfunctional. Since the error bit is in bit 15, it is in the word sign position of the status register, and may be tested with a TST instruction, just as the ready bit is tested with a TSTB instruction.

Some devices have more than one error bit because different kinds of errors can occur. For example, the card reader can fail to work because of an empty hopper, a full stacker, a bad read, and so on. Each of these errors requires different remedial action both from the program and from the operator. Thus more than one error bit is needed.

The buffer registers on different devices tend to be similar; however, the number of bits changes. While an ASCII device has 7 bits, a byte-oriented device like the paper tape reader or punch will have 8 bits and the card reader has 12 bits for the 12 rows on a punched card. (Actually there are two buffer registers for the card reader. The first contains the 12-bit column image; the second contains an 8-bit compressed, alphanumeric code.)

The Paper Tape Reader/Punch

The paper tape reader/punch operates in much the same way as the console keyboard and printer. There are, however, several differences. First, both the reader and punch have an error bit in the status register to indicate that they are out of tape. This works much like the error bit on the line printer, and is at bit 15 of the punch status register and the reader status register. A second difference is that eight data bits are input and output through the buffer register. Otherwise, the punch is essentially the same as the console printer or the line printer. When a bit pattern is moved to the punch buffer register, that bit pattern is punched on paper tape. Bit 7 of the punch status register is the ready bit which tells when the punch is ready for more data.

There is, however, a significant difference in how the paper tape reader operates. The reader becomes ready as soon as someone loads tape into the mechanism. However, one does not want the reader to start reading the tape as soon as it is ready, because the computer may not be ready to use the data. The effect would be for the reader to snatch the tape out of the operator's hands as soon as it was loaded into the machine.

In order to prevent this, there is another bit (the **go bit**) in the status register. The go bit, which occupies bit position 0, is normally set to 0. Nothing will happen until the go bit is set to 1; then the reader will read one character (or **frame**) from the tape. The go bit is immediately reset to 0 so that an examination of the register will never show it to be a 1. (This kind of bit is sometimes called a **write-only** bit, because you can write a 1 into it, but you can never read it back.)

Figure 11.5 shows the four registers for the punched paper tape reader and punch. Figure 11.6 shows a subroutine that reads a single tape frame into R0. If there is an error, a whole word of -1 is returned.

Paper Tape

Figure 11.7 shows a section of paper tape in which the absence of a hole in a particular position corresponds to a binary 0 and the presence of a hole corresponds to a binary 1. The tape consists of a number of columns across the tape called **frames.** In this example, each frame or column contains a single ASCII character. The tape begins on the left-hand side with a **leader** that consists of blank tape. More accurately, the leader consists of several ASCII **null characters** (octal 000). The small holes in this area of the tape are **feed holes** or **sprocket holes** that are used to move the tape. They perform the same function

Sec. 11.3   Other Input/Output Devices

Figure 11.5 Paper Tape Device Registers

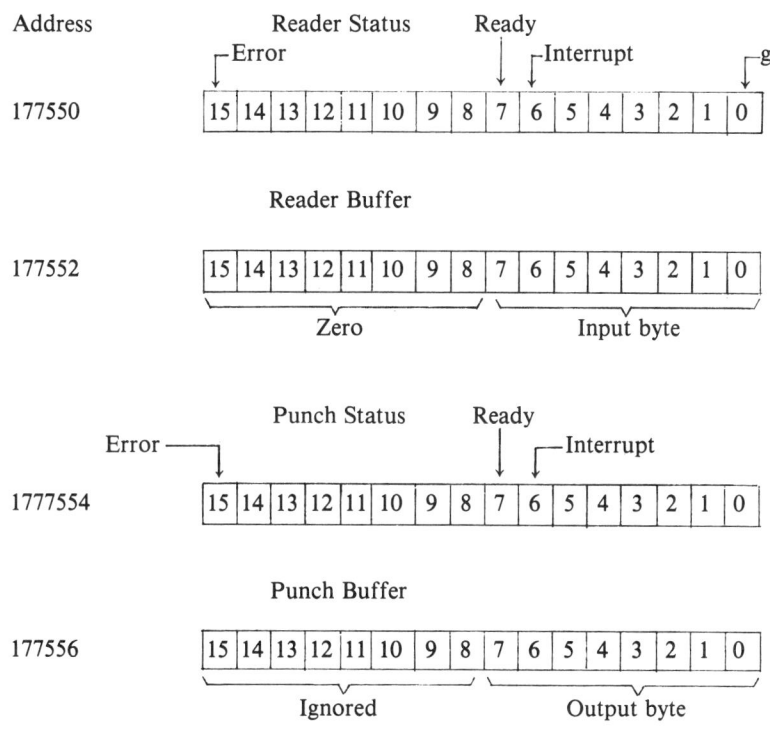

Figure 11.6 Subroutine for Reading a Paper Tape Byte

```
;THE FOLLOWING SUBROUTINE READS A PAPER TAPE
;BYTE INTO R0.  ERRORS SHOW AS -1.
MASKA=177400
PRS=177550                      ;STATUS REGISTER
PRB=PRS+2                       ;BUFFER REGISTER
R0=%0
PC=%7
        .GLOBL  PTREAD
PTREAD: INC     PRS             ;SET GO BIT
LOOP:   TST     PRS             ;TEST FOR ERROR
        BMI     ERROR
        TSTB    PRS             ;TEST FOR READY
        BPL     LOOP
        MOVB    PRB,R0          ;FETCH BYTE
        BIC     #MASKA,R0       ;CLEAR 8 HIGH ORDER BITS
        RTS     PC
ERROR:  MOV     #-1,R0          ;RETURN -1
        RTS     PC
        .END
```

Figure 11.7 *A Short Section of Paper Tape*

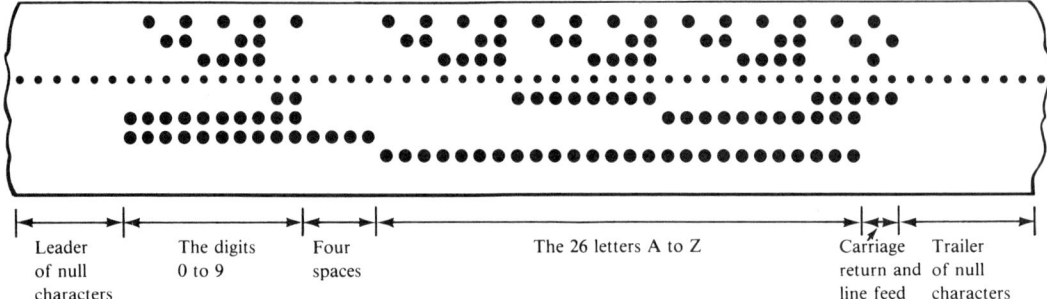

as the feed holes on both edges of computer paper.

The 10 frames after the leader contain the ASCII code for the digits 0 through 9 (octal 060 through 071). The next four frames contain spaces or blanks (octal 040). The spaces are followed by the capital letters A through Z (octal 101 to octal 132), which are followed by a carriage return and line feed (octal 015 and 012). A trailer composed of null characters is at the end of the tape. Most tapes are much longer than the one shown in Figure 11.7. The leaders and trailers are typically more than one foot long and the tape might contain several thousand characters.

Following is a single frame of a paper tape:

  ○ Bit 0
  ○ Bit 1
  ○ Bit 2
  ● Feed hole
  ○ Bit 3
  ○ Bit 4
  ● Bit 5
  ○ Bit 6
  ○ Bit 7

A ○ represents an unpunched area of the tape while ● represents a hole. The symbol ● represents the feed hole. Each frame contains 8 bits or one byte of information. In the frame shown, only bit 5 is punched (in addition to the feed hole, which must be punched). This frame contains 00100000 in binary or 040 in octal. When 7-bit ASCII characters are punched on paper tape, only bits 0 through 6 are used. This is why there are no punches in the bottom row of the tape in Figure 11.7.

It is important to distinguish between null characters (octal 000) and blank characters (octal 040). The null character is represented by a frame without any punches (000). However, printing devices ignore null characters. In particular, a null character will *not* cause a printer to leave a blank space.

The Line Clock

The **line clock** is a simple but useful device that can be used for various timing purposes.* The line clock receives timing information from the 60-hertz (60 cycles/second standard) alternating-current power line. This is somewhat different from the other devices because, while there is a status register, there is no buffer register. As the following illustrates, the status register contains a ready bit and an interrupt bit:

The device simply sets the ready bit to one every sixtieth of a second. (In countries that use 50-cycle electrical power, which includes most of the world outside North America, the ready bit would be set to 1 every fiftieth of a second.) Since there is no buffer associated with the device, the program must reset the ready bit to 0 each time it becomes set.

Controlling the device is quite simple. For example, the following section of code will delay the program for one second:

```
LCS=177546                  ;LINE CLOCK STATUS REGISTER
        MOV     #74,R1      ;INITIALIZE COUNTER TO 60 DECIMAL
RLOOP:  CLR     LCS         ;CLEAR DONE AND INTERRUPT BITS
LOOP:   TSTB    LCS         ;HAS 1/60TH SECOND PASSED
        BPL     LOOP        ;IF NOT, GO BACK
        DEC     R1          ;DECREMENT COUNTER
        BNE     RLOOP       ;AND GO BACK UNTIL 1 SECOND HAS ELAPSED
```

This code is not as useless as it may appear. For example, most printing devices ring a bell or a buzzer when the ASCII bell character (octal 007) is received. If a device error occurs on the line printer or the paper punch, the code shown could be used as a timer so that the bell on the console printer could be rung once per second until the operator corrected the error.

EXERCISE SET 1

1   Write a program that prints the 95 printable ASCII characters (octal 040 to 176) on a single line. If your printer does not have room for 95 characters, print the characters on three lines. If your printer does not print

*This kind of line clock is not used on the LSI-11.

lowercase characters, what does it do when your program places the codes for lowercase characters in the buffer?

2. Some printing devices do not respond to some of the ASCII control characters such as the horizontal tab (octal 011). Write a test program to determine which control characters (octal 000 to 037 and 177) your printer responds to.

3. Write a program that allows you to use the keyboard and the printer as a typewriter. Your program should do more than simply echo each character that is typed. For example, when a carriage return is typed, your program should send a carriage return and a line feed to the printer. If your printer does not respond to horizontal tab characters, your program should simulate the tab by sending an appropriate number of blanks to the printer. Finally, your program should send a bell character (octal 007) to the printer when the printer is within five positions of the end of the line.

4. Write a program that rings the bell on the printer once per second.

5. Write a program to duplicate a paper tape. Your program should ignore any null characters that are read. However, the duplicate tape should begin and end with one foot of blank tape.

11.4 INTERRUPTS

Introduction

There are several problems with device polling. First, the polling loop completely ties up the central processor. The processor may have to ask the device "Are you done yet?" several thousand times before the device completes the input/output operation. This wastes the computational power of the processor and does not allow other tasks to be accomplished. The programmer could attempt to avoid this waste by leaving the polling loop for a short period of time in order to perform other computations. However, there is a danger that information will be lost. A fast operator might be able to type two characters on the keyboard before the program returned to poll the status register of the keyboard. The second character would overwrite the first character in the buffer, and the first character would be lost. In addition, attempting to poll a device periodically generally results in complicated logic that is difficult to debug, particularly when several devices with differing speeds are active at the same time.

The solution to many of these problems is to use **interrupts** rather than device polling. Instead of repeatedly asking the device "Are you done yet?", the processor allows the device to "Interrupt me when you are done." The use of interrupts is controlled by the interrupt bit (bit 6) in the status register of the device. If bit 6 is equal to 0, the interrupt system is turned off and device polling must be used. If the interrupt bit for the device is set to 1, the device will interrupt the processor whenever an input/output operation has been completed. An input device will interrupt whenever a new character is received. An output device will interrupt whenever the device finishes printing or punching a character and is therefore ready to print or punch the next character.

When using interrupts, there must be a separate program called an **interrupt servicing routine** for each input/output device that has its interrupt bit turned on. As long as no interrupt occurs, the processor continues to execute a main program of some kind. When a device interrupts the processor, the processor temporarily stops executing the main program and transfers control to the interrupt servicing routine associated with the device. Once the interrupt servicing routine has provided whatever service the device needs, the processor resumes execution of the main program.

In order to implement interrupts, two problems must be solved. First, when a device interrupts, how does the processor find the starting address of the interrupt servicing routine? Second, how does the processor save enough information to return to the main program after the interrupt servicing routine has been completed? It is obvious that the processor must save the program counter in order to later return to the appropriate return address. However, other information must be saved as well. An interrupt may occur at any time. In particular, an interrupt might occur between the time that the main program executed the two following instructions:

```
        CMP    A,B
                        ←――― Interrupt occurs here
        BLT    ALOW
```

The interrupt servicing routine is almost certain to change the N, Z, V, and C bits that determine whether to branch or not. (N, Z, V, and C refer to the Negative, Zero, oVerflow, and Carry bits that were described in Chapter 5.) As a result, the current setting of these bits must also be saved when an interrupt occurs.

The Processor Status Register

In order to facilitate interrupts, the various bits that must be saved when an interrupt occurs are stored in a special register called the **processor status register**. The processor status register contains 16 bits of information called the **processor status word** (PSW). However, as the following illustrates, smaller PDP-11 processors may only use 8 of the 16 bits:

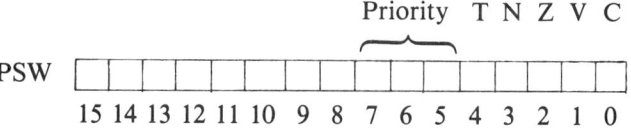

Bit positions 0 through 3 contain the four condition code bits. These bits are modified by arithmetic instructions such as ADD and are tested by the various branch instructions. The T (for Trap) bit in position 4 will be explained later.

The priority bits in positions 5, 6, and 7 allow a program to prevent interrupts. When a main program is running, these bits are typically set to 0. This allows any device to interrupt the main program. However, when an interrupt routine is running, these bits may be set to 1s to prevent the interrupt routine from being interrupted by another interrupt routine. For example, when the clock interrupt routine is being executed, these bits might be set to 1s to prevent the paper punch from interrupting the clock interrupt routine. The servicing of interrupts is delayed by this process rather than lost. The paper punch will continue to request the interrupt. Later, the paper punch will be allowed to acquire interrupt servicing if the priority bits eventually are set to 0.

Three bits are used for the following reason: On larger PDP-11 processors, the priority bits can be set to intermediate values between 000 and 111 binary. These intermediate values allow more important devices to interrupt while less important devices cannot. For example, if the priority bits are set to 5 octal (101 binary), the line clock can interrupt but the paper tape reader/punch cannot. For compatibility with smaller PDP-11 systems, only priorities of 000 and 111 (binary) will be used here. On any PDP-11 system, a priority of 000 will allow any device to interrupt and a priority of 111 will prevent all devices from interrupting.

The Interrupt Process

Assume that a main program is running and that the current processor priority is 000 (binary). When an interrupt from a device is received, the processor first finishes the execution of the instruction that it is currently executing. (This, of course, leaves the program counter pointing to the next instruction in the main program.) The processor then saves the current contents of the processor status register on the stack. Then the processor places the current value of the program counter on the stack. For example, if the stack pointer (register 6) contains 001000 before the interrupt, then the PSW will be saved in memory location 000776 and the PC will be saved in 000774. This is all the information that the processor needs to resume executing the main program when the interrupt routine has been completed.

To complete the interrupt process, the processor must now branch to the starting address of the appropriate interrupt servicing routine in memory. To accomplish this, each device is allocated two consecutive words in memory. The first word contains the starting address of the interrupt routine (the new PC), and the second word contains the new processor status word that is to be loaded into the processor status register. These two words are called the **interrupt vector** for the device. The interrupt vectors for the various devices are located between addresses 000000 and 000374.

For example, the interrupt vector for the line clock begins at address

000100. After the processor has saved the old PSW and the old PC on the stack, the processor asks the interrupting device to supply the address of its interrupt vector. (At this point, the processor does not know which device has caused the interrupt.) In this case, the clock responds by sending the address 000100 to the processor. The processor loads the contents of memory cell 000100 (the new PC) into the program counter and loads the contents of memory cell 000102 (the new PSW) into the program status register. This completes the interrupt. If the contents of memory cells 000100 and 000102 are as the following shows, the processor will begin executing the interrupt servicing routine that begins at memory cell 004000:

Address	Contents	
000076	??????	
000100	004000	New PC
000102	000340	New PSW
000104	??????	

Because the contents of 000102 is 000340, the interrupt servicing routine will run with the three priority bits in the PSW set to 111 (binary). As a result, the interrupt routine itself cannot be interrupted.

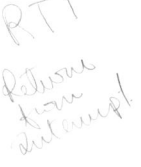

At the end of the interrupt servicing routine, the RTI instruction (ReTurn from Interrupt) is used to return to the main program. Conceptually, the RTI instruction is similar to the RTS (ReTurn from Subroutine) instruction. However, the RTI instruction, with operation code 000002, does not have any arguments. In addition, the RTI instruction removes two words from the stack since it must restore both the PC and the PSW to their old values. This will resume the execution of the main program. In this example, the process of restoring the processor status register to its original value will cause the three priority bits to be set to 000, which will allow future interrupts to be serviced.

In writing an interrupt servicing routine, the programmer must be cautious about modifying processor registers R0, R1, and so on. Unlike a subroutine call, an interrupt can occur at virtually any time. If the interrupt servicing routine modifies the contents of a register, the results may be catastrophic since the routine being interrupted may be using that register. There are two standard ways to solve this problem. First, the interrupt servicing routine can be written in such a way that registers R0 through R5 are not used. Second, the interrupt servicing routine can simply save the current contents of any registers that it modifies and restore the registers to their original values at the end of the interrupt servicing routine.

A Clock Interrupt Servicing Routine

A clock interrupt servicing routine can be used to keep track of time. As shown in Figure 11.8, the interrupt servicing routine simply adds 1 to a counter and then returns. (When using interrupts with the clock, it is not necessary to reset

Figure 11.8 Clock Interrupt Servicing Routine

```
;
;AN INTERRUPT ROUTINE FOR THE LINE CLOCK
;
CLKINT: INC     COUNT
        RTI
COUNT:  .BLKW   1
```

the ready bit to 0). Sixty times each second, the main program will be interrupted by the clock and the clock interrupt servicing routine will be executed. The counter can count with unsigned numbers up to $2^{16} - 1$ or 65,535/60 or 1092 seconds, which is approximately 18 minutes. If longer intervals of time must be measured, a double-precision counter would have to be used.

As shown in Figure 11.9, the main program must set the counter to 0 and initialize the clock interrupt vector. Before initializing the interrupt vector, the status register is cleared to make sure that the interrupt bit is off.* This prevents any premature interrupts. The interrupt vector for the clock is located at addresses 000100 and 000102. The starting address of the interrupt servicing routine, CLKINT, is loaded into memory cell 000100. Memory cell 000102 is initialized to 000340 to prevent the clock interrupt servicing routine from being interrupted by another interrupt. (The clock interrupt servicing routine is so short that there is no real advantage to allowing interrupts within it.)

The last step of the initialization process is setting the interrupt bit (bit 6) in the clock status register to 1.* The first interrupt may occur at anytime in the

Figure 11.9

```
;THIS IS THE MAIN PROGRAM THAT PERFORMS
;INITIALIZATION FOR THE CLOCK INTERRUPT ROUTINE
CLKST=177546                    ;ADDRESS OF CLOCK STATUS REGISTER
CLVEC=100                       ;ADDRESS OF CLOCK INTERRUPT VECTOR
START:  CLR     CLKST           ;TEMPORARILY PREVENT INTERRUPTS
        CLR     COUNT           ;SET TIME TO ZERO
        MOV     #CLKINT,CLVEC   ;SET UP INTERRUPT VECTOR
        MOV     #340,CLVEC+2
        BIS     #100,CLKST      ;ALLOW INTERRUPTS
COMPUT: .
        .                       Rest of the Main Program
        .
;THIS IS THE CLOCK INTERRUPT ROUTINE
CLKINT: INC     COUNT
        RTI
COUNT:  .BLKW   1
        .END    START
```

*On the LSI-11, clock interrupts cannot be enabled or disabled with software, because there is no status register. Instead, there is a switch on the front panel which turns off the clock.

Sec. 11.4   Interrupts   257

next one-sixtieth of a second. The interrupt might occur before the statement labeled COMPUT in the main program is executed. Alternatively, several hundred statements in the main program might be executed before the first interrupt. This unpredictability can make debugging difficult. It is not at all unusual to have a program that runs correctly on one occasion and fails on others.

The main program in Figure 11.9 could use the value of COUNT in a variety of ways. It could be used to compute the time required to execute certain sections of the main program. If the main program can obtain the current time of the day from the computer operator, the program can use COUNT to keep track of time for the operator. (For this application, a double-precision counter should be used because there are more than 65,535 sixtieths of seconds in a day.)

Printing a Message with Interrupts

Figure 11.10 contains a main program and an interrupt servicing routine that will print a message on the operator's printer. When bit 6 in the printer status register is 1, the printer will interrupt whenever it finishes printing a character. In other words, if the interrupt bit is 1, the printer interrupts when the done bit makes a transition from 0 to 1. The printer interrupt servicing routine simply sends the next character of the message to the printer buffer and then returns. When the printer finishes printing the new character, another interrupt will occur.

The interrupt servicing routine that begins at PRINT saves the value of R0 on the stack at the beginning of the routine and then restores R0 to its original value just before the RTI instruction. As a result, the main program is free to use R0 for its own purposes. The rest of the interrupt servicing routine is straightforward. The variable POINTR contains the address of the next character. If the character is not a null, the interrupt servicing routine sends the character to the printer buffer and returns. Because a character has been sent to the buffer, another interrupt will occur sometime in the future when the character is printed. However, if the character is a null, the interrupt servicing routine sets the flag FINISH equal to 1 and returns without sending anything to the buffer. As a result, no more interrupts will occur (which is, of course, appropriate since the message has been printed).

The main program begins with the standard initialization sequence for an interrupt servicing routine. After setting the interrupt bit to 0 to prevent any possibility of premature interrupts, the interrupt vector is initialized. The interrupt vector for the console printer occupies memory cells 000064 and 000066. After initializing the pointer and the finish flag, the program turns the interrupt bit on. Normally, a device interrupts when the interrupt bit is 1 and the ready bit makes a transition from 0 to 1. However, devices also interrupt when the ready

Figure 11.10 Printing a Message Using Interrupts

```
            .TITLE  PRINT ROUTINE WITH INTERRUPTS
;THIS IS THE MAIN PROGRAM THAT PERFORMS INITIALIZATION FOR THE
;PRINTER INTERRUPT ROUTINE AND THEN PERFORMS SOME OTHER CALCULATIONS
;WHILE THE PRINTER INTERRUPT ROUTINE DOES THE PRINTING
;
PRS=177564                      ;PRINTER STATUS REGISTER
PRB=PRS+2                       ;PRINTER BUFFER
PRVEC=64                        ;ADDRESS OF THE PRINTER INTERRUPT VECTOR
R0=%0
R1=%1
SP=%6
PC=%7
START:  CLR     PRS             ;TEMPORARILY PREVENT INTERRUPTS
        MOV     #PRINT,PRVEC    ;SET UP THE INTERRUPT VECTOR
        MOV     #340,PRVEC+2    ;SET UP THE INTERRUPT VECTOR
        CLR     FINISH          ;SET TO ONE WHEN PRINTING COMPLETE
        MOV     #MESS,POINTR    ;ADDRESS OF THE NEXT CHARACTER
        BIS     #100,PRS        ;ALLOW THE PRINTER TO INTERRUPT
;THE FIRST INTERRUPT WILL OCCUR IMMEDIATELY
         .
         .            Part of the main program
         .
LOOP:   TST     FINISH          ;WAIT UNTIL PRINTING IS COMPLETED
        BEQ     LOOP
         .
         .            More of the main program
         .
MESS:   .ASCII  /THIS IS A SAMPLE MESSAGE/
        .BYTE   15,12,0
        .EVEN
POINTR: .BLKW   1               ;POINTS TO THE CURRENT CHARACTER
FINISH: .BLKW   1               ;SET TO ONE WHEN PRINTING COMPLETE
;
;THIS IS THE INTERRUPT ROUTINE THAT PRINTS THE MESSAGE
;
PRINT:  MOV     R0,-(SP)        ;SAVE R0 ON THE STACK
        MOV     POINTR,R0       ;AND GET THE POINTER
        TSTB    (R0)            ;IF THE CHARACTER IS NOT A NULL
        BNE     PRNTIT          ;GO PRINT IT
        INC     FINISH          ;ELSE SET THE FINISH FLAG
        BR      OUT             ;AND RETURN
PRNTIT: MOVB    (R0)+,PRB       ;PRINT THE CHARACTER
        MOV     R0,POINTR       ;UPDATE THE POINTER
OUT:    MOV     (SP)+,R0        ;RESTORE R0
        RTI                     ;RETURN FROM INTERRUPT
        .END    START
```

bit is 1 and the program changes the interrupt bit from 0 to 1. As a result, the first interrupt occurs immediately after the bit set instruction.

The main program proceeds to execute the section of code labeled "part of the main program." After each character is printed, an interrupt occurs and the interrupt servicing routine sends the next character to the printer. However, the interrupt servicing routine only requires a small fraction of the processor's time, and the processor spends most of its time in the main program. By using statements such as those at LOOP, the main program can determine if the message has been printed. This would be necessary if the main program wished to print a second message. To print a second message, the main program would simply turn the interrupt bit off, place the starting address of the new message in POINTR, clear FINISH, and then turn the interrupt bit back on.

When using interrupts with other input or output devices, the programmer must allow for obvious differences between devices. If the status register of a device contains error bits, the interrupt routine should check the setting of these bits. The address of the interrupt vector is different for each device. In addition, care is sometimes required to ensure that the first interrupt and the last interrupt are processed correctly. Other than this, the assembly language statements required to use interrupts with other devices are very similar to those illustrated in Figure 11.10.

Traps

When the processor detects an error of some kind, it initiates an interrupt. For example, if the processor detects an illegal operation code, it initiates an interrupt using the interrupt vector in memory cells 000010 and 000012. The interrupt servicing routine whose starting address is contained in memory cell 000010 can then print a message to the computer operator about the illegal operation code.

To distinguish interrupts initiated by the processor from those that are initiated by input or output devices, the processor initiated interrupts are called **traps** (because they "catch" errors). Traps are identical to normal interrupts except in two ways: (1) There is no status register or buffer associated with a trap. (2) The priority bits in the processor status register have no effect on a trap. When the error occurs, the old program counter and the old processor status word are saved on the stack and a new program counter and processor status word are obtained from the interrupt or trap vector.

There are a variety of traps in addition to the illegal instruction trap. For example, an illegal memory reference will cause a trap to occur using the trap vector in addresses 000004 and 000006. A power failure will cause a trap to occur using the trap vector in addresses 000024 and 000026. (The processor can execute at least several instructions before the power fails completely.)

Traps can also be caused by special instructions. For example, the EMT (EMulate Trap) instruction causes a trap to occur using the trap vector in

000030 and 000032. This particular instruction is used to request services from the operating system. For example, with the RT-11 operating system, EMT 340 asks the operating system to read a character from the input device, EMT 341 prints a character, and EMT 350 causes a program to terminate. These instructions are contained in the expansion of the .TTYIN, .TTYOUT, and .EXIT macros. The operation codes for the EMT instruction range 104000 to 104377. (The first eight bits are really the operation code and the last eight indicate the particular service that is desired.) One advantage of this approach is that your program does not have to know the starting address of each service routine. The EMT processor whose starting address is contained in memory cell 000030 can examine your request and then branch to the appropriate service routine. The EMT concept is sometimes called a software interrupt and is the basis of most modern operating systems.

The TRAP instruction is another such instruction, and is identical to the EMT instruction except that the operation codes range from 104400 to 104777 and the trap vector begins at 000034. By convention, the EMT instruction is reserved for communication with the operating system. The TRAP instruction is provided for general use by users.

In addition to the TRAP instruction, there is a trap bit (bit 4) in the processor status register. When the trap bit is set to 1, a trap to the vector at address 000014 will occur after each instruction is executed. This makes it possible to trace or "single step" through the main program one instruction at a time.

11.5 OTHER CONSIDERATIONS

Using Interrupt Routines with an Operating System

Special care must be used when writing interrupt routines that are to run under an operating system such as RT-11. This care is required because the operating system itself uses interrupts, so the user should be sure not to conflict with system use. For example, RT-11 performs all of its input and output using interrupts. The clock interrupt is always enabled and the console keyboard interrupt is always enabled. Other device interrupts may be enabled, and all of these and some other devices are supposed to have their interrupt vectors loaded with addresses and priorities determined by the RT-11 system.

If the casual user changes the contents of interrupt vectors, or enables various device interrupts, it is likely to cause the operating system to fail. In order to be in full compliance with all of the conventions used by the RT-11 system, the reader should consult the *RT-11 Advanced Programmer's Guide*, published by the Digital Equipment Corporation. However, sometimes it may be possible to avoid all of the burdensome conventions of RT-11 by exercising care.

First, the programmer should save every interrupt vector before reloading it with new data. Then, before exiting, all the vectors should be restored to their original values. If there is any doubt as to whether your program executed enough instructions to do this, you should re-boot the system. This is really a courtesy to subsequent users, because these kinds of errors may not show up immediately and may eventually cause some other user's program to fail.

Direct Memory Access Devices

Interrupts and single-byte or word transfers work well for slow or medium-speed input/output devices. However, a different approach is needed for high-speed devices such as magnetic tape or disk. These devices are capable of transferring hundreds of thousands of bytes of information per second, which is faster than the maximum interrupt rate on many PDP-11 computers.

This problem is solved by using direct memory access devices. Such devices can transfer information to and from memory without using the processor. For example, assume that a block of 1000 (octal) characters is to be read from magnetic tape and placed in memory cells 040000 through 040777. The processor initiates the data transfer by moving the byte count (001000) and the starting address (040000) to special registers associated with the tape unit. While the processor executes a program, the tape unit proceeds to transfer all 1000 (octal) bytes into memory. The transfer is achieved in the following way: When the tape unit has another character to transfer to memory, the tape controller asks for permission to use wires which connect the processor to the addressable locations. These wires are called the **bus**.* If the processor is currently performing a fetch or store operation, the processor completes the operation and then grants permission to use the bus. The tape controller then uses the bus for perhaps a millionth of a second to transfer the byte to memory. The tape controller then returns control of the bus to the processor, which continues to execute the program until the tape again requests to use the bus. Once all 1000 bytes of information have been transferred to memory, the tape unit interrupts the processor (using the interrupt vector beginning at address 000224) to indicate that the input operation has been completed. Additional information on direct memory access devices can be found in the *PDP-11 Peripherals Handbook*.

Other Input/Output Strategies

Even more complicated input/output strategies are used on some computers. For example, many large computers use special devices called **channels** to perform input and output. A channel is simply a special-purpose processor de-

---

*On larger PDP-11's the bus is called the UNIBUS®. The LSI-11's use a different bus called the Q-BUS®.

signed to execute special input/output instructions. The instructions that a channel executes are called channel commands to distinguish them from the machine language instructions that are executed by the central processing unit.

Assume, for example, that a channel is designed to control magnetic tape units. The channel would have a command that instructs it to read a block of characters from a tape and place the block of characters into a designated area in memory. The channel would also have commands to allow simple branching and looping. To read a series of blocks from a tape unit, a channel program composed of these channel commands is created and the central processing unit instructs the channel to execute the program. The central processing unit could then perform computational tasks while the channel reads a series of blocks from the tape. When the channel has finished executing the channel program, the channel interrupts the central processing unit.

The more sophisticated input/output strategies tend to require less intervention by the central processing unit. With some less sophisticated strategies, such as device polling, the processor is totally dedicated to the input/output operation. With interrupts, processor intervention is required only after each character is read or written. When direct memory access is used, processor intervention is required only after an entire block of characters is transferred. With channels, a large number of blocks of information can be transferred without intervention by the central processing unit.

The strategies just discussed are not exhaustive, but they do illustrate the complexity of input/output operations on modern computer systems. Even more complex strategies are used on some computer systems. However, a discussion of these is beyond the scope of this text.

EXERCISE SET 2

1. Using interrupts, write a program that rings the bell on the console printer once per second.

2. Using interrupts, write a program that allows you to use the keyboard and the printer as a typewriter. As in exercise 3, page 252, your program should process carriage returns and horizontal tabs in the obvious manner. In addition, your program should ring the bell when the printer is within five positions from the end of the line.

3. Using interrupts, write a program that keeps two input and two output devices running simultaneously. For example, if your system has a teletypewriter and a high-speed paper tape reader and punch, your program should allow you to duplicate a paper tape at the same time that you are copying from the keyboard to the printer.

4. Write a program that determines the largest legal memory address on your computer system. In order to do this, your program should use the illegal

Exercise Set 2

address trap vector at memory addresses 000004 and 000006. Simply execute the following main program segment until the trap occurs (or until all addresses have been tested). After the illegal address trap, R0 contains the smallest illegal address.

```
        CLR    R0
LOOP:   TST    (R0)+
        TST    R0
        BEQ    ALLOK
        BR     LOOP
```

CHAPTER 12

FLOATING POINT NUMBERS AND EXTENDED INSTRUCTIONS

12.1 INTRODUCTION

In Chapter 6, numbers were discussed in terms of the basic integer operations. In this chapter, we will look at how fractional quantities are handled and how this is done in the PDP-11 in particular. We will also look at the floating point and extended instruction sets that are available on the newer PDP-11's and the more expensive, older PDP-11's. In addition to providing instructions for multiplication and division of integers, instructions are also provided for handling fractions encoded in the floating point format.

12.2 FIXED AND FLOATING POINT NUMBERS

Fractions

In order to use fixed and floating point numbers effectively, it is important to understand the principles of their operation. In order to keep the discussion simple at first, we will discuss fixed and floating point in terms of a decimal representation. We will then go into PDP-11 representation and see how some rather clever tricks are employed to make the representation efficient.

There are various ways to express fractional quantities. The most basic method is in terms of pairs of integers: 1/2, 5/12, 537/8946, and so on. This method of representing fractions could be implemented quite easily in a computer. However, it is not normally used either in computers or in real life because of an inherent awkwardness. Instead, a preferred method is to restrict fractions to a set of standard denominators such as tenths, hundredths, thousandths, and so on. Because these denominators are powers of 10, fractions using them are called **decimal fractions.** They are usually represented with a decimal point or **radix point,** such as 5.4, 7.92, 0.093, and so on. There are other fraction schemes using denominators such as 12, 14, 16, 32, 60, and so on. Although some of these are going out of use with the introduction of the metric system, others still linger. Most computers use either decimal fractions or binary fractions (which will be discussed later).

Fixed Point Numbers

In computers, two methods are commonly used for dealing with fractional quantities. These are the **fixed** and **floating point** methods. The simpler of these methods is the fixed point. This operates on the basis that often there is a smallest fraction, so there would never be a need to consider anything smaller. A good example of this is money calculation. Most normal U.S. money calculation deals with units of dollars, and the smallest unit considered is one cent, or 1/100 of one dollar.*

Because there is no need to deal with fractions of a cent, the whole problem could be reformulated in terms of integer numbers of cents. For example, $537.23 is the same as 53723 cents. However, since most people get confused when talking about large numbers of cents rather than dollars, a preferred method for talking about the same thing is to say that the number 53723 has an assumed decimal point two places from the right. This number therefore represents 537.23 dollars. This is therefore called the fixed point system because the decimal point is assumed to be at some fixed place in the number.

The fixed point system is very useful for dealing with money, and is therefore used extensively in business languages such as COBOL. Fixed point numbers can also be used for scientific calculations by *scaling* the problem into appropriate units. Consequently, scientific problems are often stated in terms of integral numbers of:

    milliamperes

    microseconds

    centimeters

    kilograms

    tonnes (a metric ton = 1000 kilograms)

*Certain tax computations and interest computations do deal with fractions of cents, such as the mil. The fixed point scheme described here would have to be modified to handle these cases.

The last two items on the list are a variation of what was described previously because the decimal point is effectively moved to the right off the end of the number. Therefore instead of counting fractions of a unit, we are counting multiples of a unit. At times this is necessary in order to prevent the numbers from becoming so large that multiple precision is required in the machine unnecessarily. For example, if the weight of a supertanker were expressed in milligrams, many digits of unnecessary precision would be required. Consequently, tonnes or even kilotonnes would be used.

The problem of scaling things to the correct units can be quite complex and was, in fact, one of the hardest parts of programming some of the early computers. The difficulty lies in the fact that many scientific problems involve both very large and very small numbers. For example, a problem involving a nuclear-powered ship might use kilotonnes for the ship, but would use milligrams for the fuel pellets, and thus the units of mass would be inconsistent from one part of the problem to another.

Floating Point Numbers

A solution to this problem is the use of floating point numbers. A floating point number actually consists of two parts. One part contains the sign and digits of the number. The other part states where the decimal point is assumed to be. A method similar to this is often used by scientists in normal writing so that their calculations can all be made in standard units. This **scientific notation** represents numbers as certain significant digits times a power of 10. For example:

$$-5.347 \times 10^{15} = -5347000000000000$$

or

$$4.912 \times 10^{-9} = 0.000000004912$$

In effect, what we have is $\pm a \times 10^{\pm b}$, where a and b are numbers in some limited range. Note that there is a sign associated with each number.

The representation of floating point numbers in a computer requires that the two signed numbers $\pm a$ and $\pm b$ be stored somewhere. There must also be an understanding of what the numbers mean. Although it is possible to store the two numbers in two separate memory locations, this is inefficient because b tends to be relatively small and it would be wasteful to use a whole word to store it. Instead, some means of packing a and b together is usually used. Let us imagine that we have a machine that has eight-digit, signed, decimal words, for example, +73214692. (Remember that we will use decimal for a while.)

A nice compromise for packaging a and b into this word would be to use two digits for b and the remaining six for a. This gives us six *significant* digits in the number and a range of values spanning a factor of 10^{99}. Thus, the computer word +51314159 would let +314159 represent a and 51 represent b.

There are two questions that should arise here. The first is "Where is the decimal point assumed to be in *a*?" Although the decision is arbitrary, most computer manufacturers place it at the far left. Therefore, $a = +0.314159$. The second question is "What happened to the sign of *b*?" The computer word only had one sign and we used it for *a*. However, if we are to represent small as well as large numbers, we must have a sign for *b* as well. The usual technique is to store in the two digits a number that is a fixed amount larger than the actual value of *b*. Using 50 as the fixed amount, the number 50 indicates that *b* is 0, the number 51 indicates that *b* is 1, the number 52 indicates that *b* is 2, and so on. Numbers smaller than 50 represent negative exponents. For example, the number 49 indicates that *b* is -1, and the number 41 indicates that *b* is -9. Since the number 51 gives a value for *b* of 1, the word $+51314159$ represents $+0.314159 \times 10^1$ or simply 3.14159. Figure 12.1 shows examples of floating point numbers along with their equivalents.

Figure 12.1 Decimal Floating Point Representations

Floating Point	Scientific Notation	Normal Decimal
-46134926	-0.134926×10^{-4}	-0.0000134926
$+50934821$	$+0.934821 \times 10^0$	0.9344821
$+50999999$	$+0.999999 \times 10^0$	0.999999
$+51100000$	$+0.100000 \times 10^1$	1.000000
-53426910	-0.426910×10^3	-426.910

As we can see from Figure 12.1, there are three explicit portions of a floating point word—the sign of *a*, the digits that represent *b*, and the digits that represent the magnitude of *a*. The latter is usually referred to as the **fraction part** because of the assumed placement of the decimal point in *a*. The digits representing *b* are usually called the **exponent** because they represent a power of 10. Figure 12.2 shows the named parts in the floating point format.

Figure 12.2 Floating Point Format

Sign	Exponent	Fraction

Normalized Floating Point Numbers

A final note about floating point representations has to do with **normalization**. From the previous discussion, it can be seen that $+51100000$ represents $0.1 \times 10^1 = 1$. Similary, $+54000100$ represents $0.0001 \times 10^4 = 1$. Consequently, $+51100000$ and $+54000100$ both represent the same number. To prevent possible confusion, most floating point systems insist that numbers be adjusted so that the leftmost digit of the fraction is *not* 0 (as in $+51100000$). This is called the **normalized** floating point representation. The primary importance beyond preventing confusion is that normalized floating point numbers preserve the maximum number of significant digits. Accuracy or precision could be lost with unnormalized numbers such as +54000100. The one exception to the normalization rule is 0, which has a normalized representation of +00000000.

We can now look at the range of numbers possible with this floating point representation. Figure 12.3 shows the range of numbers. Note that there is a gap between $\pm 10^{-51}$ and 0. This means that very small numbers should be avoided since the information content of the word may be insufficient to allow their representation.

Figure 12.3 Range of Normalized Decimal Floating Point Numbers

Smallest number	$-99999999 =$	-0.999999×10^{49}	$\approx -10^{49}$
Largest negative number	$-00100000 =$	$-0.100000 \times 10^{-50}$	$= -10^{-51}$
Zero	$+00000000 =$	0.000000×10^{0}	$= 0$
Smallest positive number	$+00100000 =$	0.100000×10^{-50}	$= +10^{-51}$
Largest number	$+99999999 =$	0.999999×10^{49}	$\approx +10^{49}$

12.3 FLOATING POINT OPERATIONS

Being able to represent numbers in the floating point form is really of no use unless there is some way of performing operations on the numbers. The usual operations available in computers are addition, subtraction, multiplication, and division. (Other mathematical operations and functions are programmed from these four.) In this section, we will see how these operations can be performed on the decimal floating point representations of the previous section.

Addition and Subtraction

First, let us consider addition and subtraction. (These operations go together, the difference being only in how the signs are treated.) Recalling a rule learned early in our schooling, the first step in adding numbers with decimal points is to line up the points. Thus:

$$\begin{array}{r} 573.426 \\ + \ 8.93425 \\ \hline \end{array} \quad \text{must be rewritten as} \quad \begin{array}{r} 573.426 \\ + \ \ \ 8.93425 \\ \hline 582.36025 \end{array}$$

Then simple digit-by-digit addition is performed. A similar kind of rule applies to either scientific notation or floating point encodings of numbers. Two numbers in this notation cannot be added unless their exponents are first made the same. Therefore, for a similar example:

$$.573426 \times 10^3$$
$$+ .893425 \times 10^1$$
must be rewritten as
$$.573426 \times 10^3$$
$$+ .00893425 \times 10^3$$
$$.58236025 \times 10^3$$

Let us now go through a step-by-step process with these same two numbers in the floating point format and see how the process could operate in a computer.

Step a: Align the two numbers one above the other:

$$+53573426$$
$$+51893425$$

Step b: Unpack the numbers to separate the fraction and exponent parts:

$$53 \quad +573426$$
$$51 \quad +893425$$

Step c: To line up the smaller number with the larger, exchange the numbers, if necessary, so that the number with the larger exponent is first:

$$53 \quad +573426$$
$$51 \quad +893425$$

Step d: Compute the difference in the exponents:

$$\begin{array}{r} 53 \\ -\ 51 \\ \hline 2 \end{array} \quad \begin{array}{l} +573426 \\ +893425 \end{array}$$

Step e: Shift the second number right by the amount of the difference, and make the exponents the same:

$$53 \quad +573426$$
$$53 \quad +008934\boxed{25}*$$

Step f: Add the fraction parts. The exponent of the result remains the same:

$$53 \quad +573426$$
$$53 \quad +008934$$
$$\overline{53 \quad +582360}$$

Step g: Repack the result into the floating point format:

$$+53582360$$

---

*These digits are lost except in double-precision operations. Alternatively, we could round the number up when the leftmost digit is 5 or greater. This truncation or rounding results in unavoidable computational error.

Sec. 12.3   Floating Point Operations   271

Complications with Addition and Subtraction

This process clearly works for the example given. However, two complications can arise that require two additional steps.

The first problem is that the sum of two numbers may require more digits than either of the original numbers. For example, suppose we add +53573426 and 53698421. Applying steps a through e, we find that no shifting was necessary and we get:

$$53 \quad +573426$$
$$53 \quad +698421$$

Now apply step f:

$$53 \quad +573426$$
$$\underline{53 \quad +698421}$$
$$+1271847$$

We now note that the resulting fraction part has more than six digits. This would prevent us from repacking the word into an eight-digit register. The solution is to shift the fraction part one place to the right and add 1 to the exponent as follows:

Step f_1: $54 \quad +127184\boxed{7}$ *

Step g: Repack the result into the floating point format.

$$+54127184$$

The second problem is in a sense the opposite. This occurs with subtraction, or adding numbers with unlike signs. Again steps a through e are the same; but when we perform the subtraction at step f, we may end up with fewer than six digits. For example, if we add +53573426 and −53573213, we would have the following at step f:

$$53 \quad +573426$$
$$\underline{53 \quad -573213}$$
$$53 \quad +000213$$

Note that if we repacked this number, the result would not be normalized. We must therefore normalize the result to get:

Step f_2: $50 \quad +213000$

Note that the trailing zeros indicate a loss of accuracy. This usually happens

---

*This digit is lost. It could be saved with double-precision arithmetic or used to round up the result to +127185. This is similar to what happens in step e and also contributes to unavoidable error.

when two nearly equal numbers are subtracted. Step f_2 must take into account that the result could be zero. In that case, the normalized form is:

$$00 \quad +000000$$

Multiplication and Division

The rules for floating point multiplication and division come straight from the rules of scientific notation. When you multiply, you add exponents; when you divide, you subtract exponents. The fraction parts are either multiplied or divided. For example:

$$(0.5 \times 10^{15}) \times (0.8 \times 10^4) = (0.5 \times 0.8) \times 10^{15+4} \quad 0.4 \times 10^{19}$$

Similarly:

$$(0.4 \times 10^{19}) \div (0.5 \times 10^{15}) = (0.4 \div 0.5) \times 10^{19-15} = 0.8 \times 10^4$$

The rules for multiplying floating point numbers are as follows:

Step a: Align the two numbers one above the other:

$$+65500000$$
$$+54800000$$

Step b: Unpack the numbers as for addition:

$$65 \quad +500000$$
$$54 \quad +800000$$

Step c: The fractions are then multiplied. No adjustments are necessary for the exponents or fraction parts (note where the decimal point occurs in the result, that is, 0.50×0.80 equals 0.4000):

$$\begin{array}{rr} 65 & +0.500000 \\ 54 \ \times & +0.800000 \\ \hline & +0.400000 \end{array}$$

Step d: The exponents are added, but each exponent has an excess of 50, so the result would have an excess of 100. Therefore we must subtract 50:

$$\begin{array}{r} 65 \\ +\ 54 \\ \hline 119 \\ -\ 50 \\ \hline 69 \quad +400000 \end{array}$$

Step e: The result is then repacked:

$$+69400000$$

Since the fraction parts are always less than 1, the product of two fraction parts must be less than 1. Consequently, the problem that arose in the example of step f_1 in addition does not arise. However, the product could be smaller than 0.1. Therefore, normalization is sometimes necessary. This operates the same way as for step f_2 of addition. For example, if +51150000 is multiplied by +52200000, we have:

Steps c and d: 51   +150000
                 + 52   × +200000   (Note that 0.15 × 0.20
                 ―――   ―――――――   is equal to 0.0300)
                  103
                 − 50
                 ―――
                   53   +030000

Normalization is needed to get:

Step d_1:   52   +300000

producing a result of +52300000. Note that the example is, in fact, 1.5 × 20 = 30.

Division operates in much the same form as multiplication. The details of division are left as an exercise for the reader.

Discussion

This floating point representation may seem awkward. From left to right, a floating point number consists of the sign of the fraction, a two-digit exponent in excess 50 representation, and a six-digit fraction. This format was chosen to simplify the process of comparing two floating point numbers.

Assume that we wish to determine if a floating point number X is larger than a floating point number Y. This can be done by computing Y − X with floating point subtraction and testing to see if the result is negative. However, there is a faster and easier way. Treat the representations of X and Y as if they were signed 8-digit integers and compute Y − X using *integer* subtraction. If the resulting integer is negative, then X (as a floating point number) is larger than Y. For example, assume that X equals 10.0 and that Y equals 1.0. The floating point representations of X and Y are +52100000 and +51100000, respectively. Subtracting +52,100,000 from +51,100,000 as signed integers yields −01,000,000 indicating that X (10.0) is larger than Y (1.0). (In this case, X and Y are both positive and the exponent of X exceeds the exponent of Y by 1, so X is larger.)

The reader should verify that this shortcut works for any pair of floating point numbers provided that both numbers are normalized. In order for this shortcut to work, the exponent must be placed between the sign of the fraction and the fraction itself. This is also the reason that an excess representation (in this case excess 50) is used for the exponent. On computers that do not have a machine language instruction for comparing floating point numbers, variations of this shortcut are used to generate efficient software for comparing floating point numbers. On computers that have such instructions, variations of this shortcut are used to simplify hardware design.

EXERCISE SET 1

1. Convert the following numbers into the normalized, decimal, floating point representation as described in this chapter:
   (a) 5
   (b) 374
   (c) 3.14159
   (d) 0.0005
   (e) 0.8035×10^{23}
   (f) 0.4923×10^{-15}
   (g) 8.496×10^{18}
   (h) 954.2×10^{-12}

2. Convert the following decimal floating point numbers to scientific notation and to ordinary decimal notation (no exponent):
   (a) +51300000
   (b) −53742000
   (c) +50894026
   (d) +45805216
   (e) −56293465
   (f) −57100000
   (g) +38950125
   (h) −64790881

3. Perform the indicated operations on the following pairs of decimal floating point numbers. Show your steps along the way. Express your results as a normalized floating point number:
   (a) +53215904 + +53116895
   (b) +52159099 + +49889621
   (c) +50912065 − +54891126
   (d) −52998046 + −50479138
   (e) −53885304 − −53885034
   (f) +57900000 × +48800000
   (g) +51426931 × −44357926
   (h) −43250000 × −41250000
   (i) −55255000 ÷ +51500000
   (j) −41800000 ÷ −44200000

4. List all the steps for performing floating point division. What conditional steps are there? Is normalization a problem (assume that the operands are normal)? Does fraction part overflow occur as in step f_1 of addition? Assuming that the operands are normalized, how much overflow can occur?

5. A popular method for computing square roots on the computer is to use the so-called Newton-Raphson formula. To compute the square root of N, you guess a value (call it X). Then you apply the formula

$$X\text{new} = \frac{1}{2}(X\text{old} + \frac{N}{X\text{old}})$$

The new value of X will be much closer to the correct square root than the old value. The formula can be applied repeatedly to obtain an answer that is as accurate as desired. The speed of the method depends upon the number of times the formula needs to be applied, and this depends upon the accuracy of the original guess and final accuracy desired.

(a) Mathematically, what is the square root of a number expressed in scientific notation? That is, how are the exponent and fraction of the square root related to the exponent and fraction of the original number?

(b) How could the answer to part (a) provide a simple method for obtaining a good guess for the square root of a floating point number?

(c) In the worst cases, how far is your guess from the correct answer?

(d) Using the worst cases, how many iterations of the Newton-Raphson formula are needed to produce an answer that is accurate to six digits? (Use a calculator or a computer to test the worst cases.)

*6 Write a PDP-11 assembly language program that reads a character string representing a signed decimal number. The string will consist of a sign, decimal digits, and an imbedded decimal point, such as $+89.462$, -0.009461, and so on. The program will then print out the equivalent normalized, decimal, floating point representation, such as $+52894620$, -48946100, respectively. Your program should loop to work out at least 20 different examples. *Hints:*

(a) Ignore leading zeros (except as noted in hint c).

(b) Stack up the six digits in an array of six bytes.

(c) Count digits before the decimal point or leading zeros after the decimal point in order to determine the exponent.

*7 The same as exercise 6, except that your program will accept any legal FORTRAN REAL constant, including E notation.

12.4 PDP-11 FLOATING POINT NUMBERS

Binary Floating Point

PDP-11's with the FIS (Floating Point Instruction Set) option have instructions for adding, subtracting, multiplying, and dividing floating point numbers. PDP-11's without FIS use software to simulate the floating point instructions.

Floating point numbers in the PDP-11 operate in much the same way as those described in the previous section. However, since the PDP-11 is a binary computer, floating point numbers are encoded in binary rather than decimal.

This means that the fraction is expressed as a binary number, and that the exponent is a power of 2 rather than a power of 10.

Binary Fractions

Recall from Chapter 2 the binary number

$$11011 = (1 \times 2^4) + (1 \times 2^3) + (0 \times 2^2) + (1 \times 2^1) + (1 \times 2^0)$$
$$= 16 + 8 + 0 + 2 + 1 = 27$$

Binary fractions work much the same way, but with negative exponents. Therefore:

0.100011

$$= (1 \times 2^{-1}) + (0 \times 2^{-2}) + (0 \times 2^{-3}) + (0 \times 2^{-4}) + (1 \times 2^{-5}) + (1 \times 2^{-6})$$
$$= \tfrac{1}{2} + 0 + 0 + 0 + \tfrac{1}{32} + \tfrac{1}{64} = \tfrac{35}{64}$$

Binary fractions may seem strange at first, but in fact they are in quite common use—the normal division of inches in the English measuring system is into binary fractions. It would not be unusual for a machinist to have a drill with a diameter of 35/64 of an inch. Most home carpentry sets have drills measured in sixty-fourths of an inch up to 1/4 inch.

One point to note is that not all fractions can be expressed as a binary fraction exactly. We should expect this because of our familiarity with decimal fractions. We all know that 1/3 cannot be expressed in decimal. The best we can do is something like 0.333333. This is not exact. We can make it better by adding three's, but no finite number of three's will make the number exact. As we would expect, it is also impossible to express 1/3 exactly in binary. However, it may come as a surprise that the fraction 1/5 cannot be expressed exactly either. We are used to decimal where $1/5 = 0.2$; but in binary, we cannot do this. The following table shows how 1/5 can be sandwiched by binary fractions but will never be equal to any of them:

$$\tfrac{1}{4} > \tfrac{1}{5} > \tfrac{1}{8}$$

$$\tfrac{1}{4} > \tfrac{1}{5} > \tfrac{3}{16}$$

$$\tfrac{7}{32} > \tfrac{1}{5} > \tfrac{3}{16}$$

$$\tfrac{13}{64} > \tfrac{1}{5} > \tfrac{3}{16}$$

$$\tfrac{13}{64} > \tfrac{1}{5} > \tfrac{25}{128}$$

. . .

Floating Point Representation

As in decimal, binary floating point numbers have an exponent and fraction. For example, if the exponent were +9 and the fraction were +35/64, we would have the number

$$+\frac{35}{64} \times 2^9$$

Now let us look at how these are distributed in a floating point word. First we need a sign for the fraction. One bit suffices for this. Next we need an exponent. If we use a range from 2^{-128} to 2^{+127}, this is roughly equivalent to a decimal range from 10^{-38} to 10^{+38}—a range that is fairly adequate. Since the range from −128 to +127 has 256 steps, eight bits are needed for the exponent.

The PDP-11 uses a method for signs for the exponents that is similar to the excess 50 used in the previous section. It is, however, an excess 128 decimal $(10000000)_2$. Therefore, we have the following table for exponents:

Decimal Exponent	Binary Representation	Octal Representation
+127	11111111	377
+ 1	10000001	201
0	10000000	200
− 1	01111111	177
−128	00000000	000

If the sign requires 1 bit and the exponent 8, then all that would be left in a 16-bit word for the fraction is 7 bits. This gives barely two significant digits. Clearly this is not enough for any serious computation. Therefore floating point words consist of two PDP-11 words or 32 bits. This allows 23 bits for the fraction part.

However, the PDP-11 designers have found a clever way to add an extra bit, making 24 bits for the fraction part. Recall that in the normalized floating point representation, the leading digit of the fraction is never zero. Now, in the binary system, the only two possibilities are 0 and 1. Therefore, if we exclude 0, the leading digit must be 1. If the digit is always 1, we need not explicitly say so on every number. Therefore, this bit is left out and is called the **hidden bit.**

The only problem with assuming that a certain bit is always 1 is that we cannot represent 0. The PDP-11 gets around this by reserving the exponent −128 to mean that the number is 0. Now let us look at the example $+35/64 \times 2^9$:

The sign bit is 0 for + (1 for −).
The exponent is 10001001 for +9.
The fraction is 0.10001100000000000000000 for

$$\frac{35}{64} = (\frac{1}{2} + \frac{0}{4} + \frac{0}{8} + \frac{0}{16} + \frac{1}{32} + \frac{1}{64}).$$

Packed together into 32 bits, this becomes:

```
0      10001001         00011000000000000000000
Sign   Exponent                Fraction
                 (Note: The leading 1 is hidden)
```

Stored as two PDP-11 words, this is:

Binary	Octal
0100010010001100	042214
0000000000000000	000000

The FIS Option

There are several ways that floating point numbers can be handled in PDP-11's, depending upon the model. Some models have no floating point operations, and all must be done in software. Newer or more exotic processors such as the PDP-11/23, 11/34, 11/45, 11/50, and 11/70 have an extensive set of floating point instructions available. The older or more modest machines such as the PDP-11/03, 11/40, and the LSI-11 can optionally have four floating point instructions. This is known as the Floating point Instruction Set or **FIS option.** These instructions are:

FADD	Floating add
FSUB	Floating subtract
FMUL	Floating multiply
FDIV	Floating divide

These instructions operate in essentially the same fashion, where two floating operands are combined to form a floating result. The floating operands and result are in the 32-bit format described previously.

The two operands must be placed in a four-word area anywhere in memory called the **floating point operand stack.** The organization of the stack is as follows:

First location—High part of second operand

Second location—Low part of second operand

Third location—High part of first operand

Fourth location—Low part of first operand

So that the instruction can know where the stack is, a register R0-SP must be used to point to the top of the stack (the first location).

After the instruction is completed, the result will appear in the third and fourth locations of the stack, and the register will be adjusted to point to the third location of the stack. Since the use of the operand stack is consistent with the regular PDP-11 stack, the SP can easily be used for pointing to the operand stack, making it reside on top of the regular stack. Figure 12.4 shows a simple set of instructions for accomplishing the computation equivalent to the FORTRAN statement X = Y + Z.

Figure 12.4 Floating Point Sum of Two Numbers

```
            MOV     Y+2,-(SP)       ;PUT Y ON STACK
            MOV     Y,-(SP)
            MOV     Z+2,-(SP)       ;PUT Z ON STACK
            MOV     Z,-(SP)
            FADD    SP              ;Y+Z
            MOV     (SP)+,X         ;MOVE RESULT TO X
            MOV     (SP)+,X+2
              .
              .
              .
X:          .BLKW   2               ;LOCATIONS FOR X
Y:          .BLKW   2               ;LOCATIONS FOR Y
Z:          .BLKW   2               ;LOCATIONS FOR Z
```

The condition codes N and Z are used to indicate whether the floating point result is negative or zero. Errors can occur from such things as trying to divide by 0, or creating too large or too small a number. These errors cause a trap or simulated interrupt to a vector at location 244. (See Chapter 11 for an explanation of interrupts and vectors.) If you are using an operating system such as RT-11, an error message will be printed indicating the error. The four instructions are summarized in Figure 12.5. The op codes for these instructions occupy the upper 13 bits of the 16-bit word, leaving 3 bits to designate the register that points to the floating point operand stack. The symbol R is used to indicate this place in the op code.

Figure 12.5 The Floating Point Instruction Set

Mnemonic	Op Code	Instruction	N Z V C
FADD	07500R	floating add	* * 0 0
FSUB	07501R	floating subtract	* * 0 0
FMUL	07502R	floating multiply	* * 0 0
FDIV	07503R	floating divide	* * 0 0

Floating Point Constants

Floating point constants can be entered in assembly language using the .FLT2 directive. This operates like the .WORD directive, except that its argument is a FORTRAN-style REAL constant. A two-word floating point number will be placed in the next two locations to be assembled. For example:

```
            X:      .FLT2   3.579E-3
```

will cause the two-word floating point equivalent of 0.003579 to be placed in locations X and X+2, respectively. Another directive, .FLT4, allows one to enter four-word, double-precision floating point numbers into the program. However, the FIS instructions do not use double-precision operands. Therefore these numbers can only be used with software operations, or with the *Floating Point Processor* of the larger PDP-11's such as the 11/45 and 11/70.

EXERCISE SET 2

1. Show how the following numbers would appear in the PDP-11 floating point format. Show your answer both as 32-bit binary strings and as pairs of 16-bit words in octal.

   (a) 1/2
   (b) $\frac{893}{1024} \times 2^{15}$
   (c) $\frac{-977}{1024} \times 2^{-20}$
   (d) 3.125
   (e) 0.2
   (f) 0.0005

2. The following pairs of PDP-11 words shown in octal represent floating point numbers. Show them as 32-bit binary numbers and as decimal numbers:

   (a) 040200 000000
   (b) 140720 000000
   (c) 037060 000000
   (d) 042513 460000
   (e) 040052 525252
   (f) 140327 651342

3. Using the FIS instruction set, write FORTRAN callable subroutines that add, subtract, multipy, and divide floating point numbers supplied as real arguments. Write a FORTRAN main program that calls and tests your subroutines, and then execute it.

4. See exercise 5 on page 274. Write a FORTRAN-callable subroutine that computes square roots using the Newton-Raphson formula:

$$X\text{new} = \frac{1}{2}(X\text{old} + \frac{N}{X\text{old}})$$

Your subroutine should return six real (floating point) values:

(a) Your initial guess at the answer.
(b) Xnew after one application of the formula.
(c) Xnew after two applications of the formula.
(d) Xnew after three applications of the formula.
(e) Xnew after four applications of the formula.
(f) Xnew after five applications of the formula.

Write a FORTRAN main program that calls and tests your subroutine for a wide variety of values that vary by many orders of magnitude, such as 10^{20} and 10^{-20}. Compare all six of your returned values with that returned by the standard SQRT function. If you use the initial-guess strategy outlined in exercise 5 on page 274 you should converge on the correct answer in three or four applications of the formula. (Your answer may differ very slightly from the SQRT value due to round-off or truncation errors.)

*5 Write a FORTRAN-callable subroutine that adds two floating point numbers *without* using FADD or any of the floating point instructions. Write a FORTRAN main program that calls and tests your subroutine for several values.

*6 Write a program that reads decimal numbers and converts them to PDP-11 floating point format. The program can either be tested by linking to a FORTRAN main program or by comparing against a table generated by .FLT2 directives. Optionally, your program can accept the following input types which are listed in order of increasing difficulty:

(a) Unsigned whole numbers (no sign, no decimal point)

(b) Signed whole numbers

(c) Signed numbers with an imbedded decimal point, such as 53.742

(d) Full E format, such as 42.7E-15

(*Hint:* See Figure 8.10 on page 188.)

12.5 EXTENDED INSTRUCTION SET OPERATIONS

The extended instruction set (EIS) is an option available on the LSI-11 and some of the larger PDP-11's. When this option is installed, the programmer can use certain arithmetic instructions, such as multiply, divide, some shift instructions, and exclusive OR (*XOR*).* The use of these instructions eliminates the need for the slower, programmed operations (see Chapter 6). The extended instruction set consists of the following five instructions:

MUL	Multiply
DIV	Divide
ASH	Shift arithmetically
ASHC	Shift arithmetically, combined
XOR	Exclusive OR

*Some processors may accept the exclusive OR (XOR) instruction even though the rest of EIS is not present. Its inclusion here is primarily because the format of XOR is essentially the same as the other EIS instructions.

EIS Format and Exclusive OR

As with the floating point instructions, there are not enough bits in the PDP-11 word to allow these instructions to address two general mode operands. To get around this, these instructions address one general register, and one general mode operand. Thus the format for the EIS instructions is a 7-bit operation code, a 3-bit register designator, and a 6-bit general mode operand designator. To see how this works, let us look at the XOR instruction, which is the simplest of this group.

In several ways, the XOR instruction is similar to the BIS instruction. First, both are bit-by-bit operations in that each bit of the result is determined by looking at the corresponding two bits of the input operands. Second, the rules for combining the bits are similar. In the BIS instruction, the resulting destination bit is a 1 if either the source bit is a 1 or the destination bit is a 1 or both the source and destination bits are 1. In fact, the similar instruction on many machines is called the OR instruction because of its similarity to the logical OR operation. In logic the **exclusive OR** means one *or* the other *but* not both. As a result, the XOR instruction sets the destination bit to 1 if either the source bit or the destination bit (but not both) is equal to 1. If both bits were 1s (or 0s), the resulting bit would be 0. The following example illustrates the operation:

	Binary	*Octal*
Source operand	0 000 001 010 011 100	001234
Destination operand	0 000 001 001 001 001	001111
New value in destination	0 000 000 011 010 101	000325

Other than the slight difference in operation itself, there is a major difference in use. BIS can have any general form of operand for its source and destination, for example, BIS #777,(R3)+. However, the XOR instruction can only have a register for the source operand. For example:

```
        XOR     R0,X

        XOR     R1,(R3)+

        XOR     R2,R4
```

Note that the XOR instruction does not have a byte counterpart.

Multiplication

Multiplication is somewhat more complex. Recall that if two 16-bit quantities are multiplied, the result may require as many as 32 bits. The PDP-11 multiply instruction may be used to multiply together two 16-bit signed (in two's complement) numbers to yield a signed 32-bit product. The product occupies a pair of processor registers. As the following shows, the register on the left, which contains the high-order bits of the product, must be an even-numbered register. The register on the right, which contains the low-order bits of the product, must be the higher-numbered register (which must, of course, be an odd-numbered register):

High-order word		Low-order word
Even-numbered		Odd-numbered
register n		register $n+1$

In order to obtain a 32-bit product, one of the 16-bit numbers is placed in the even-numbered register with an instruction such as MOV. The MOV is then followed by the MUL instruction. The source operand of the MUL instruction is, of course, the other 16-bit number. The destination of the MUL instruction must be the even-numbered register of the register pair. For example, if 3002 is multiplied by 5000, the octal result is 17012000. Thus, the following program segment:

```
        MOV     #3002,R0
        MUL     #5000,R0
```

will cause 012000 to be left in R1, and 000074 to go into R0. Note that the result in R0 may look a bit odd unless we recall that PDP-11 words do not divide evenly into octal digits. Thus, the problem about unpacking double-precision words is similar to unpacking bytes as shown in Chapter 8 (see page 171). The result may be clearer in binary:

$$
\begin{array}{rr}
(3002)_8 = & 11000000010 \\
\times\ (5000)_8 = & 101000000000 \\
\hline
111100\ & 001010000000000 \\
(000074)_8 & (012000)_8
\end{array}
$$

In order to get a full 32-bit result, the destination register must be an even-numbered register, such as R0, R2, or R4 (but *not* R6 = SP). If you are sure that the magnitude of the result is less than 2^{15}, or if you are content with the low-order bits, an odd-numbered register can be used. The 16-bit result will then occupy that single register. In either case, the C bit is set if the result extends (or would extend) into the high-order word. The N and Z bits are used in the usual fashion. The V bit is always cleared, because the result can never overflow 32 bits.

Division

Division is essentially the opposite of multiplication. A 32-bit signed dividend is divided by a 16-bit signed divisor to produce a 16-bit signed quotient. Since division may not come out even, a 16-bit remainder is also produced. As with multiplication, the 32-bit dividend occupies an even register and the next odd one. The least significant part is in the odd register. However, since division always requires a double-precision dividend, the divide instruction must always refer to an even register.

The results appear in these same registers. The quotient is in the even register; the remainder is in the odd register. The remainder is computed so that its sign is the same as the quotient, and its magnitude is less than the divisor. The Euclidean formula applies so that:

$$\text{Dividend} = \text{Divisor} \times \text{Quotient} + \text{Remainder}$$

The divisor is a general operand, so the following instructions would divide 7005 by 100 in octal:

```
CLR   R0            ;CLEAR THE 16 HIGH ORDER BITS
MOV   #7005,R1      ;DIVIDEND IN THE 16 LOW ORDER BITS
DIV   #100,R0
```

The quotient 000070 would be in R0, and the remainder 000005 would be in R1.

The N and Z bits behave in the normal manner. The V bit may be set, because if the divisor is too small (in magnitude), the quotient might be too large (in magnitude) to fit in a 16-bit signed word. The C bit is set if you attempt to divide by 0.

Negative Numbers

In both multiplication and division, signed operations are dealt with according to the normal rules of algebra. In other words, the product of two positive, or two negative, numbers is positive. The product of a positive and a negative number is negative. Similarly, with division, the quotient and remainder will be positive if the dividend and divisor have the same sign. They will be negative if the dividend and divisor have opposite signs. (Note that a possible exception to this rule occurs when either the quotient or remainder is zero. However, the rule still applies to the nonzero member of the pair.)

A second consideration has to be kept in mind with the 32-bit numbers. These really just operate as ordinary two's complement numbers, as described in Chapter 6. Carries and borrows propagate through all 32 bits, and the leftmost bit of the low-order part is not the sign but is just another bit in the number. The sign bit will extend to the right as far as necessary, as in all two's complement numbers. Thus, for example, the 32-bit binary representations of $+5$ and -5 appear as:

$$+5 = 00000000000000000000000000000101$$
$$-5 = 11111111111111111111111111111011$$

Extended Shift Instructions

The arithmetic shift instructions shown in Chapter 6, ASL and ASR, can only shift left or right one place. This means that the programmer must use repetition or a loop for multiple shifts. The extended instructions ASH and ASHC both allow an arbitrary amount of shifting, either left or right. These instructions can only be used to shift the contents of general registers, but the amount of shift is a general operand. For example:

```
        ASH     #6,R0
```

will cause the contents of R0 to be shifted left six bit positions. Negative numbers cause a right shift so that:

```
        ASH     #-5,R3
```

will cause the contents of R3 to be shifted right five places.

In effect, the ASH instruction operates like repeated operations of ASL or ASR (see Chapter 6, page 130 ff). Therefore the effect is like multiplying or dividing by a power of 2. For example:

```
        ASH     #6,R0       Multiplies R0 by 64
        ASH     #-5,R3      Divides R3 by 32
```

Carefully review how fractions are truncated when shifting two's complement numbers (see pages 131-132).

For either a left or right shift, the last bit shifted out is left in the C bit. The N and Z bits show whether the result is negative or zero. A left shift can cause overflow, because the number is becoming larger. Note that when overflow occurs with two's complement numbers, there is an unexpected sign change. Therefore, the V bit is set if the sign changes at any time during the shifting.

Because the hardware only examines the low-order six bits of the shift count, the values must be in the range from -32 to $+31$. This is not really too much of a problem since a shift of 16 or higher shifts out the entire number.

The ASHC (Arithmetic SHift Combined) instruction is essentially the same except that it operates on two registers that form a double-precision number. As with multiplication and division, the more significant part is in the even-numbered register, and the least significant part is in the next register. For example:

```
        ASHC    #14,R0
```

would multiply the double-precision number in R0 and R1 by 4096. As with ASH, negative shift counts produce right shifts.

Because of a quirk in the way that ASHC works, it can be used with an odd register to get a right rotate. For example:

```
        ASHC    #-15,R3
```

would rotate the contents of R3 right 13 (or 15$_8$) places. Note that a right rotate of 13 is the same as a left rotate of 3. The extended instruction set is summarized in Figure 12.6.

Figure 12.6 The Extended Instruction Set

Mnemonic	Op Code	Instruction	Operation	N	Z	V	C
MUL	070RSS	multiply	r ← r x s	*	*	0	*
DIV	071RSS	divide	r ← r/s	*	*	*	*
ASH	072RSS	shift arithmetically		*	*	*	*
ASHC	073RSS	arith shift combined		*	*	*	*
XOR	074RDD	exclusive OR	d ← r ⊻ d	*	*	0	–

EXERCISE SET 3

1. What would be the result of the exclusive OR operation (XOR) on the following pairs of operands (given in octal)?

    (a) 1 0 1 0 1 0
       1 1 0 0 1 1

    (b) 1 2 3 4 5 6
       0 1 0 1 0 1

    (c) 1 2 3 4 5 6
       1 2 3 4 5 6

    (d) 1 2 3 4 5 6
       0 5 4 3 2 1

    (e) 1 7 7 7 7 7
       0 1 7 4 3 2

    (f) 0 5 0 3 0 2
       1 7 7 7 7 7

2. Do the following two program segments always store the same value in Z? If so, explain why. If not, show an example where they do not. (Assume that X, Y, Z are memory locations.)

    (a) MOV   X,R0
        MOV   Y,R1
        XOR   R0,R1
        XOR   R1,Z

    (b) MOV   X,R0
        MOV   Y,R1
        XOR   R1,Z
        XOR   R0,Z

3. (a) Assume that your computer has no XOR instruction. How could you reprogram the following line of code to work on your machine? (Be careful not to destroy the contents of any register, even R0.)

    XOR   R0,X

   (b) Write a macro for XOR that will work for any valid substitution for the parameter X, for example, (R1)+.

4. Multiply the following pairs of 16-bit numbers (shown in octal). Show the

Exercise Set 3

result as a 32-bit binary number, and as a pair of 16-bit words in octal. Compute the result as the MUL instruction would.

(a) 000024 × 000011 (b) 000024 × 100001
(c) 000024 × 177777 (d) 177777 × 177777
(e) 177776 × 177677 (f) 123456 × 010000

5 (a) Figure 8.10 on page 188 shows a program for reading decimal numbers. Simplify this program by using the MUL instruction as appropriate. Combine the program with output and control as necessary to execute and test it.

(b) Modify the program to accept input in any base from 2 through 10. Also execute and test it.

6 Write a FORTRAN-callable subroutine to raise an integer to an integer power, for example I**J. Write a FORTRAN main program that tests your subroutine. Link them and execute some tests.

7 Use the DIV instruction to construct a routine for outputting decimal numbers. Combine that with the input routine from exercise 5a above. Test your program by reading decimal numbers, adding them, and printing the results.

8 (a) Write and test a program that takes two double-precision (32-bit two's complement) integers and multiplies them producing a 64-bit result.

(b) Include multiple-precision decimal input and output routines in your program.

CHAPTER 13

ADVANCED ASSEMBLY LANGUAGE TOPICS

13.1 INTRODUCTION

One topic that becomes clear when studying assembly language is often hidden when using high-level language. This is the relationship between programs and data. We have seen in previous chapters that instructions (the program) and data utilize the same memory in the computer. In fact, this is true not only of the PDP-11, but also of most general purpose computers, both large and small.*

In effect, this means that there is little difference between programs and data. This chapter will look at the ramifications of this, and we will see how various parts of an operating system treat programs that people write as data. In fact, your program can always be thought of as data that are input to one of various processors. These processors have all been used in the material in the previous chapters, but the processes have not been fully identified. This chapter will proceed in that direction. In addition, we will look at some topics involved with program manipulation, such as writing position-independent code.

---

*Some special purpose microcomputers such as the Texas Instruments TMS-1000 have separate program and data areas. However, many of the principles described here still apply.

13.2 PROGRAM FORMAT

General Forms

An assembly language or FORTRAN program normally goes through various stages of translation before it can be executed. At each stage, the program is treated as data in a specific form. We will look at each of these forms and their structures, as well as how the various processors deal with them.

On the PDP-11, assembly language and FORTRAN programs have the following forms:

1. *Source code.* This consists of the alphabetic strings that make up the statements of the language.
2. *Object code.* This is a translated program with all operations converted to binary, PDP-11 op codes. However, although some addresses are translated into binary addresses, others are not. This is because the assembler (compiler) does not assign values to global symbols, and also because program addresses may need to be relocated. As a consequence, information must be provided to tell the linker how to complete the program translation.
3. *Core image file or absolute loader file.* The linker takes one or more object files, relocates the program areas so that they all will occupy unique, usable areas of memory. Global symbols are assigned binary values. The result is a core image or absolute loader file that contains binary codes which can be loaded into memory without further modification.
4. *A loaded program.* This is a specified area of memory in the computer which contains a program that is ready for execution. The difference between a loaded program and a core image file or an absolute loader file is where each resides. The loaded program is in memory, whereas the files reside on some input/output or mass storage media. There is a small program called the **loader** which loads a program from a core image or absolute loader file into memory.

Source Code

Source code in the PDP-11 consists of an indefinitely long string of ASCII characters. This string is broken into pieces called **statements** or **lines.** The exact format of a line of source code depends upon the language (such as assembly language or FORTRAN). However, each line is terminated by one or more control characters. In the PDP-11, this is normally a carriage return/line feed pair. Usually line lengths are limited to some fixed upper bound, such as 80 characters.

There are a number of processors that operate on source code. These are programs that, in effect, treat the source code as data, that is, a string of characters upon which to perform certain operations. Some of these programs perform relatively simple operations, such as PIP which is a program for copying a file from one place to another. PIP is used when you type a COPY command (see Appendix D). Other programs such as the editor (see Appendix E) or the assembler perform specific operations on the source text itself.

Source Editing

The editors TECO or EDIT are generally used to modify and update source code. However, neither TECO nor EDIT are keyed into any particular language; they can operate with *any* line-oriented ASCII text. The editors do recognize carriage return/line feed pairs and form feeds as special, but other characters are just treated as ordinary data. The way the editors work is that they copy the entire program into memory as one big array of characters. (Large programs may not fit and must be broken into pages, each of which is edited separately.) The various edit commands are interpreted to cause the editor to locate places in the array of characters and to insert or delete characters from the array. Insertion and deletion are often slow, because the entire tail end of the array must be recopied in order to make or take up space. However, the PDP-11 is fast enough so that the user does not usually notice any delays unless inserts or deletes are repeated. When editing is finished, memory is then copied back out to a mass storage file.

The Assembly Process

We should already be somewhat familiar with the assembly process because it has been covered in various chapters from Chapter 4 on. However, certain points come into focus if we look at the process in terms of data operations. As with most processors, the assembler reads data from input files* and writes data to output files. In its simplest operation, there is one input file that contains source code. There are *two* output files. The first receives the translated program in object format, the **object file.** The second output file receives the listing. Both files receive similar information, but there are some differences, and the format is completely different, as we shall see in the next section.

As we have stated before, assembly on the PDP-11 is a two-pass process. That is, the input file must be read all the way through by the assembler two times. This is because the assembler cannot assign addresses to locations that are defined later in the program. These are known as **forward references,** and they occur in situations such as shown in Figure 13.1. The symbol NEXT is

---

*For our purposes here, we will consider a file to be a collection or string of data that comes from or goes to some input/output device such as the card reader, the line printer, a disk, or a tape.

referred to by the BGT instruction. However, the code for this instruction cannot be assigned because the assembler has not yet read the line that defines NEXT. Although it might appear in this example that the assembler need only look ahead a little to resolve the forward reference, we must remember that forward references may often reach ahead many pages in a long program.

Figure 13.1 A Forward Reference

```
            BGT     NEXT
             .
             .
             .
    NEXT:
```

The solution used on the PDP-11 is to look ahead once through the whole program. During this first pass, the symbol table is created. The assembler then uses a second pass to substitute numbers for names to create the machine language program. The remarkable thing is that in the PDP-11 assembler, the processes for pass 1 and pass 2 are almost identical. The main difference is that during pass 1, all output is suppressed. If output were generated during pass 1, there would be an undefined symbol error message for each forward reference.

During the second pass, the same process is repeated. However, now there is already a complete symbol table left from the first pass. This symbol table will contain the resolved values of all forward references. The object file and listing can be output during the second pass, because there will not be any undefined symbols unless the programmer really left them undefined.

It should be noted that the PDP-11's use of a two-pass assembler is not the only solution to the forward reference problem. There are other solutions. One would be to insist that programmers avoid forward references. Most users would not like this. Another solution is to produce code during the first pass, making note of forward references. Then, when forward references are resolved, the object file is fixed as dictated by the noted references. This is sometimes called a **one-and-a-half pass assembler.** Still another solution is to leave the resolution of forward references to another processor such as the linker, the loader, or the processor itself through some indirect addressing scheme.

Data for the Assembler

As we stated before, the input and output files for the assembler are really data input and output for a program. Two of the three data files, namely the source and listing files, are meant to interface to human users. Therefore these files are **character files** that can be printed as characters on a page. The reader should already be familiar with the appearance of both of these files. However, a file's appearance to a person is quite different from the way that the computer must access the data. We are used to looking at words, lines, and pages as single objects. The computer is much more restricted, so that alphabetic data must be processed by a program character by character, or at best in small strings of characters (two or three at a time on the PDP-11).

As the assembler reads the source file, it must be able to distinguish the various **fields** on a line. These are the label field, op code field, operand field, and comments. There are two popular methods for identifying fields. One is to use fixed fields that start at particular character positions on a line. For example, FORTRAN statements occupy positions (columns) 7 through 72 of a line. Essentially, FORTRAN has this rule because the language was originally implemented in a punched card environment. Similarly, early IBM assemblers had fixed field locations.

The second method to identify fields is to use punctuation such as the colons, semicolons, commas, spaces, and so on as used in the PDP-11 assembly language. This method tends to be more desirable for some minicomputer applications because input is from a teletypewriter, where character positions are less easily identifiable than with cards. However, with modern data entry hardware and editing software, there is more flexibility. As a consequence, many assemblers use a combination of partially fixed fields and punctuation. For example, the CDC COMPASS assembler requires labels to start in column 1, and op codes to start later than column 1. Consequently, there is no need for a colon.

We can now roughly outline the functions of the subroutine that performs pass 1 and pass 2 in the PDP-11 assembler. At each cycle of its process, the assembler fetches a line of source code and examines it character by character. Initial spaces* are ignored. The first nonblank character is assumed to be the start of a symbol. The assembler stores successive characters until a punctuation character is found. This is usually a space, a colon or an equal sign.

If the character is a colon, it means that the accumulated symbol is a label, and an entry is made in the symbol table. The process then goes back to look for initial spaces. If the terminating character is an equal sign, the assembler expects to see an expression that is evaluated and entered in the symbol table. If the terminating character is a blank, the assembler assumes that the accumulated symbol is an op code.† Op codes and assembly directives are grouped into classes. For example, ADD, MOV, and SUB are similar, and BR, BEQ, and BNE are similar. Each class of op code has a special subprocessor that deals appropriately with the operand field and generates object code. The entire line of code is then terminated either by a carriage return/line feed or a semicolon. Comments are, in effect, ignored by the assembler.

If this is the second pass, the generated object code (if any) is output to the object file, and a listing line is generated. The listing line consists of a line

---

*Horizontal tabs and spaces are treated essentially the same.
† There is a provision for having expressions in the op code field. However, as it has not been previously used, we will not introduce the concept here.

number, the octal value of the address, and the object code (with relocation marks) followed by the source code as it appears on the input line for each line of source code. This overall cycle repeats and is eventually terminated by processing the .END directive.

Macro Expansion

The macro processor is virtually a separate entity that is, in effect, an extension to assembly language. As described in Chapter 10, there are two parts to macro processing: macro definition and macro calling or expanding. When a macro is defined, the lines following .MACRO up through the corresponding .ENDM are simply copied to a macro definition area.

When the macro is called, its name is in the op code field of an input line. This causes the macro expansion processor to be entered. The expansion processor copies the lines of alphabetic text in the definition area to an expansion area. While doing this, substitutable parameters are replaced by arguments in the calling line. In most cases, this is a character string for character string substitution with no interpretation.

After the expansion is complete, control is returned to the subroutine that processes the assembly passes. However, there is a slight difference. If there is any code in the macro expansion area, lines are fetched from there rather than the source file. Otherwise the processor proceeds as before. This continues until the expansion area is empty, and then lines will again be taken from the source file. This action is the same on both passes.

If one of the lines of the macro expansion happens to be a macro call, the same expansion process occurs, except that the expanded macro is always added to the beginning of whatever may be left in the expansion area. This allows macros to call macros, which call macros, and so on. There is no limit, except for the memory limit of the expansion area. Because the macro expansion area operates as a push down stack, macros can even be recursive and call themselves. Note that a recursive macro must have its call to itself in a conditional block so that the process can terminate.

EXERCISE SET 1

1   Write a program that prints out the contents of *all* its own locations (both instruction and data) in both octal and binary. The program should also print out the contents of the eight general registers in octal and binary as well.

   (a)   Identify which parts of your program (if any) function as instructions only, data only, or both instructions and data. Why?

Exercise Set 1

(b) Does your printout have any strange features? Why? Can anything be done about them?

2 Write a simple editor program that operates somewhat like the BASIC language system editor.

(a) Each line is preceded by a six-digit octal number.

(b) The lines can be entered in any order, but will be printed with increasing line numbers.

(c) If a line is entered with a line number that is the same as an earlier line, the earlier line will be deleted.

(d) A line number of 177777 terminates input and causes the edited data to be printed.

(e) To verify your program, input lines should be printed as well as edited lines.

For example, the input:

```
000100  FIRST LINE
000070  SECOND LINE
000120  THIRD LINE
000130  FOURTH LINE
000120  FIFTH LINE
177777
```

would cause the following printout:

```
000070  SECOND LINE
000100  FIRST LINE
000120  FIFTH LINE
000130  FOURTH LINE
```

3 The following instructions would be found in different groups because of the different operand structures they have:

```
CLR    ADD    BR    JMP

JSR    RTS    EMT   HALT
```

Describe the operands of each instruction, being as general as possible. Describe what the assembler would do in its operand processing.

4 Describe the functions of the following assembly directives. What processes would be performed during each pass?

```
.LIST   .WORD   .REPT   .ASCII
```

5 Hand assemble the following program step-by-step showing the macro definition area and macro expansion area as each line is processed.

```
                    .MACRO  FAC     A,N
                    .IF     EQ,N
        A=1
                    .IFF
                    FAC     A,N-1
        A=A*N
                    .ENDC
                    .ENDM
                    FAC     NUM,3
                    .END
```

Note: .IFF means "if false," and causes code to be assembled when the original condition is false.

13.3 OBJECT CODE

Binary Files

Since the source code and listings are meant to communicate with people, they are generated as character files in ASCII. However, the object code is not generally intended to be seen by humans, but rather to be read into the computer during linking. As a result, it is preferable to use a data format that is better for machine use than ASCII. Character files are not very compact because they usually use spaces, tabs, and other punctuation to make the data readable (by humans). For example, a 16-bit binary number could be expressed as a 6-digit octal number with one space to separate it from the next number. This would require seven ASCII characters or seven bytes of data. However, in its internal representation, a 16-bit binary number only occupies two bytes. Consequently, data items are much more compact and can be transmitted much more efficiently if they are kept in internal binary form. Files stored in this manner are called **binary files.**

Normally the large amounts (or potentially large amounts) of data that are stored in binary files need to be broken down into smaller pieces in the same way that character files are broken into lines. These identifiable strings of data are referred to as **records.** There are essentially two methods of segmenting a binary file: fixed length records and variable length records. With fixed length records, there is an understanding that all records are exactly a certain fixed size. Consequently, there is no need to provide any control information to delineate the data. For example, in RT-11. SAV files, every record is exactly 256 words (512 bytes) long, and the records are simply placed one after another.

In object files, as we shall see, there is a need for various kinds of data in differing amounts. As a consequence, variable length records are more appropriate. There are two main ways to delimit variable length records. The first is to use a **length count** which is part of the data in the record. This is similar to what is done in FORTRAN with the H notation. (H stands for Hollerith.) For example:

17HHERE'S A MESSAGE.

The initial 17H defines the length of the message that can contain any characters.

The other method to delimit records uses control characters such as the carriage control/line feed used with ASCII text. One problem with this method is that it becomes awkward to deal with text that itself contains control characters. This is especially important with binary files where any combination of bits can be valid information. One solution to this problem is to use double control characters to indicate a single control character in the text. This is used in FORTRAN when one wishes to use apostrophes to delimit a string that contains an apostrophe. The previous example can be rewritten:

'HERE''S A MESSAGE.'

Two apostrophes in a row are treated as a single apostrophe of text.

Formatted Binary Files

The standard way to handle files with variable length records in the PDP-11 is with **formatted binary files.** The PDP-11 formatted binary files use a length count for specifying the length of a record. Because these files were originally used extensively with punched paper tape, there are provisions for leader and trailer, and unused gaps in the file that are probably not needed or used much with more modern media such as disk or magnetic tape. The file is byte-organized to allow text to be any number of bytes from none at all to over 65,000.* Odd-numbered lengths are acceptable and since these are binary files, the text bytes can be any of the 256 possible combinations of eight bits. Figure 13.2 shows the general record structure.

The portions of the binary record are as follows:

Leader: To accommodate loading paper tape, a leader of blank tape is allowed at the beginning of the file, and in fact, in front of any record. Files not on paper tape do not need a leader and often start with the first byte of the header.

Header: In order to signal the end of the leader, a nonzero byte is needed. The PDP-11 uses two bytes, a 001 followed by a 000.

Byte count: The next item in the record is the byte count. This is a 16-bit word that appears as the least significant eight bits followed by the most signifi-

---

*Usually sizes range from 1 or 2 bytes to no more than around 100.

cant eight bits in the normal PDP-11 fashion. The byte count is actually four greater than the number of text bytes because the header and byte count are included in the count. Therefore, the minimum byte count would be 000004 indicating a zero length record.

Figure 13.2 Record Structure for Formatted Binary File

```
beginning of record                                                end of record
```

- Leader, bytes of all zero (blank paper tape)
- Header word (two bytes 001 followed by 000)
- Byte count word (two bytes) = text size + header size + byte count size = text size + 4
- Text, arbitrary amount of binary data
- Check sum's byte (sum of all bytes from header through check sum = 0 mod 256)
- Trailer, bytes of all zero (runs into leader of next record)

Text: The text can be virtually any length and its bytes can be any data. The byte count indicates the actual length.

Check sum: In order to verify the accuracy of the transmission of the binary data, a check sum is placed at the end of the record. If all of the bytes are added together (using byte addition*), starting with the 001 byte in the header, and including the check sum itself, the sum should end with eight bits of zero. This is the same as an 8-bit two's complement zero. Note that the check sum is an extra byte and is not included in the byte count. This means that if the text is an even number of bytes, the total record size will be an odd number.

Trailer: A string of zero bytes can follow a record and would in effect become the leader for the next record. Usually, there is no leader or trailer between records. However, the last record must often be trailed by zeros. This is because most PDP-11 devices operate with 256-word fixed length blocks. Consequently, the last record must be trailed out to use up the last block. Some systems insert a one byte trailer when necessary in order to assure that all records start on an even byte boundary. However, the present version of

---

*Because there is no ADDB instruction in the PDP-11, data must be shifted in order to use the ADD instruction to add the bytes.

MACRO-11 does not do this. Thus if the text fields of a file consist of an even number of bytes, every other record starts on an odd byte boundary. Figure 13.3 shows a formatted binary record that contains the text 123 005 377 000.

Figure 13.3 Formatted Binary Record

```
001 ⎫
000 ⎬ Header  =  00001                    There may or may not be 000 bytes
010 ⎫                                      leading or trailing the record.
000 ⎬ Byte count = 000010 = 4 + 4
123 ⎫
005 ⎪
377 ⎬ Text = 123, 005, 377, 000
000 ⎭
340 ⎬ Check sum:   001 + 000 + 010 + 000 + 123 + 005 + 377 + 000 + 340 = 000
```

The Object Module

The **object module** is a formatted binary file that is produced by the assembler during the assembly process. The object module contains all the binary machine language produced by the assembler. However, additional information is needed. Recall that assembly language programs are usually assembled so that they can be loaded at differing places in memory, and so that several modules for programs and subroutines can be linked together.

Therefore, the PDP-11 object modules normally have three areas. The first provides general information about the program and its use of global symbols. The second is the translated machine language, and the third area tells how the machine language must be modified in order to relocate the program to any memory area, and where global addresses or parameters must be provided. More specifically, these three sections are identified as the global symbol directory, the text, and the relocation directories.

Global symbol directory: The global symbol directory is one or more* formatted binary records. These records are made up of four word segments that:

1. Specify the length of the program and the lengths of all program sections (as defined with .PSECT).
2. Specify the relative locations of all defined global symbols.
3. Name all undefined global symbols referred to in the program.
4. Provide miscellaneous information such as the program name from the .TITLE directive.

*The present version of the assembler produces records no larger than 56 (base 8) bytes. Consequently, a large global symbol directory will require several records.

Text: The translated binary language is called the text and consists of a number of formatted binary records. Each record, which is called a text block, contains the relative address where the text is to be stored as well as some binary machine language.

Relocation directories: Each text block is optionally followed by a formatted binary record that contains coded directions for modifying the preceding text block. These are some examples of the kinds of directions that are found in relocation directories:

1. Modify a given address in the preceding text block by adding the actual program origin. Recall that the assembler normally assigns an origin of 000000 to programs and this is usually modified when the program is actually loaded.
2. Replace a given address in the text block with a computed displacement from the value of the program counter when the instruction is executed.
3. Replace an address with the actual location assigned to a global symbol.

There are other variations of these kinds of relocation, but they are too numerous to discuss here.

The binary records in the object module all contain codes that identify the type of record. In addition, there are codes to identify ends of sections, and the end of the module itself. This allows several modules to be concatenated (joined together) into a single file.

The Linking Process

Linking several object modules together into a single, absolute, machine language program is essentially a two-pass process. This is required for the same reason that assembly uses two passes (see notes on page 291). Global symbols may be used by one module, but not defined until a later module.

During the first pass of linking, allocating space and defining global symbols is performed. The information needed to do this is contained in the global symbol directories of the modules. As the linker reads through the global symbol directories, it can allocate space in the computer's memory based on the size information provided for each program section. Then actual addresses can be assigned, and global symbols are assigned absolute addresses. It then becomes possible to perform the modifications specified in the relocation directories.

Thus, during the second pass, the text blocks are assigned actual, rather than relative, addresses. Specific locations are modified in accordance with the relocation directories. The result is absolute machine language that can be loaded directly into a specified area of the PDP-11 memory and executed without modification.

Program Sections

Program sections are blocks of code in a program that are used for some particular purpose requiring that they have an integrity of their own. When producing hand-written code a programmer can avoid the use of program sections by writing different pieces of the program on different pieces of paper. He then arranges the sheets of paper by hand so that the code has the proper order. For example, he would put definitions on one sheet, the main program on a second, internal subroutines on another, then data blocks composed of words, and then blocks of bytes. From time to time while writing the program, the programmer might refer to one sheet or another. When done, he would enter the program from the sheets in order.

When programs are generated automatically by some processor, such as the macro expander or FORTRAN compiler, it is often useful to produce code for these different blocks, and this can be done with program sections. Code can be entered a few lines at a time into each program section using the .PSECT directive. When the program is linked, the blocks of code are rearranged so that they appear in the appropriate program sections.

Essentially, there are three major types of program section.* First, absolute sections are assigned an absolute location in memory. The addresses of absolute sections and any global symbols defined in them are predefined during assembly, and the linker does not need to process these addresses further. Second, there are concatenated sections. These are local blocks within a given program module that are not used by other program modules. They have names to distinguish them, but the names are local to the module. Finally there are overlaid sections. These are like FORTRAN common blocks and contain data or instructions that are shared by several program modules. These sections have global names so that the linker will allocate the same space for similarly named sections from other modules.

During the first pass of linking, the linker must allocate space for the program sections. Recall that the global symbol directory of a module has the size of each program section along with its type. The linker allocates the absolute sections to the specified addresses, but keeps track of the address used so that the relocatable sections can be moved out of the way. Concatenated sections are placed one after the other and space is allocated for each differently named, overlaid section. The linker now has a full memory map for this entire program, which can be printed upon request, and we are now ready for pass 2 of linking.

*Actually, in the PDP-11, there are 5 binary attributes giving 32 different types of program sections. However, for most purposes, we can simplify the number to three.

Subroutine Libraries

Most systems operate with a library of preassembled (compiled) subroutines. For example, in the RT-11 system, there is a system library that contains the following kinds of subroutines:

1. *Standard FORTRAN subroutines and functions* like SIN, SQRT, EXIT, and so on.
2. *Internal FORTRAN subroutines and functions.* These are automatically called by more complex statements such as READ and WRITE. In fact, if your PDP-11 does not have the extended instruction set, simple operations such as multiplication and division will require a subroutine. In order to avoid confusion with user subroutines, the internal FORTRAN subroutines all have odd global names containing periods or dollar signs such as MUF$MS or CIF$.
3. *Special subroutines.* These are FORTRAN or assembly language–callable subroutines for performing special PDP-11 functions. For example, there is a FORTRAN subroutine that allows the programmer to perform a function quite similar to the .TTYIN macro.

These subroutines are assembled into a special kind of object file that has features which aid in searching for global symbols. The way this is used is that at the normal end of pass 1 of linking, if there are any undefined global symbols, a library search is initiated. Recall that the global symbol directories contain lists of undefined global symbols as well as symbol definitions.

If there are any undefined global symbols, the library is searched for object modules that define these symbols. As such object modules are found, they are added to the program. Modules that do not define missing global symbols are not added because this would make the overall program larger than necessary.

Note, however, that the modules added to the program may themselves refer to undefined global symbols. These symbols have to be added to the list that is searched for. Because of this, it is usually necessary to define these additional global symbols later in the library so that it is not necessary to make multiple passes over the library. As a consequence, the order of the object modules in a subroutine library can be very important.

13.4 LOAD FILES

General Formats

The output from the linker is a file that can be directly loaded into memory by a small, simple program. These are called **load files.** There are three main formats

Sec. 13.4   *Load Files*

for load files used by the PDP-11 systems. The first two are oriented to paper tape systems, but can be used in other environments. The third format is basically intended for use with disk systems.

The first format is called the **bootstrap loader** format. This is intended to be read in by the paper tape bootstrap loader. This loader is virtually the simplest program possible, consisting of only 14 words of code. The bootstrap loader is usually loaded in by hand from the operator's console. The normal use for the bootstrap loader is to load in a more complicated loader called the absolute loader.

Bootstrap loader tapes are distinguishable by the fact that instead of a blank leader, they have 351s punched for several inches as a leader. The nature of the format can be determined by studying the code for the bootstrap loader that is given on the PDP-11 programming card. This is left as an exercise for the reader.

The second format is the **absolute loader** format. This format uses formatted binary records as described on page 297. The text of each record consists of a 16-bit address (two bytes) followed by a block of code that is to be loaded starting at the given address. For example, consider a record that has the following six bytes of text:

    300   004   123   211   012   377

The two bytes 300 and 004 combine to be the word 002300. (Note that the least significant byte is first.) Therefore the block of code will be loaded starting at the address 002300. The byte-by-byte contents will therefore be:

    002300   123
    002301   211
    002302   012
    002303   377

The end of the file is identified by a short record that has an address, but no code. The total formatted binary record will have a byte count of six. All other records must have at least one byte of code and will have byte counts greater than six. The address in the last record is called the **transfer address** and indicates where program execution is to begin. If execution is not desired, the number 000001 is used for the transfer address. This is an odd number, and therefore not a valid location to jump to. Note that if no symbol is placed on the .END card of an assembly language program, 000001 is shown on the assembly listing.

The third format is **core image** format. The core image file has a simple structure of fixed length records of 256 words or 1000 octal bytes. This is the size of a block of information on a disk. In the RT-11 .SAV files, block 0 is loaded into locations 000000-000777. Block 1 is loaded into 001000-001777, and so on. Reserved locations in block 0 give the length of the program and the transfer address. These are locations 000050 and 000040, respectively. Other locations in the range 000040 through 000057 are used for other system information as can be noted from the RT-11 handbooks.

Locations 000000–000777 are somewhat special. In particular, 000000–000377 are used for interrupt vectors, and 000400–000777 are normally used for the stack. As a consequence, block 0 of a .SAV file is treated specially. The remaining blocks, however, are simply placed into consecutive 256-word blocks of memory.

13.5 PROGRAM EXECUTION

Hardware Operation

In Chapter 3, the instruction cycle was discussed in general terms. At this point, it is intended to extend the concept in more detail. Figure 13.4 shows a general flowchart for the instruction cycle of the PDP-11, or in fact most computers.*

Figure 13.4   The Instruction Cycle

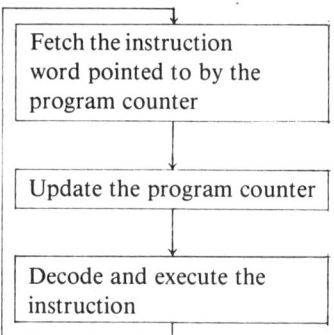

In the PDP-11 there are instructions of different numbers of words. Consequently, it may seem that updating the program counter is not a well-defined operation. However, from the point of view of this flowchart, all instructions are assumed to be one-word long, but the execution of the instruction may require fetching additional words from the program. Consequently, updating the program counter means PC ← PC + 2.

Decoding the instruction may then appear to mean choosing from the 65536 possible 16-bit words. However, this is not the case, because certain patterns form groupings of similar kinds of operations. For example, the machine language instructions 005037 and 005002 are both CLR instructions but have different operand modes. Accordingly, the instructions on the PDP-11 are

---

*Some computers update the program counter after execution, that is, before the fetch.

grouped into single operand instructions, double operand instructions, and others that fall into several classes. Some simple rules identify how the instructions fall into these classes. First, all of the double operand instructions have a second octal digit (bits 12-14) in the range from 1 through 6. If the second digit is 7, the instruction is an extended instruction set or floating point instruction. All other instructions have 0 for a second digit. The single operand instructions have a third digit of 5 or 6.

Quite often the first digit (bit 15) indicates whether the instruction is a byte or word instruction: 1 is for byte, 0 is for word. For example, 0050dd is CLR, whereas 1050dd is CLRB. However, there are some exceptions such as 16ssdd, which is SUB.

The number of bits used in distinguishing the op codes varies for the different classes of instructions. For example, double operand instructions use only 4 bits, single operand instructions use 10 bits. The remaining 12 or 6 bits are used for determining the mode and register of the operand(s). Nonetheless, each instruction must have a unique code and this can be seen from the "numerical op code list" on the PDP-11 Programming Card at the front of the book.

The different codes are decoded by a logic circuit that activates the necessary circuit for executing each instruction.

Position-Independent Code

One particular advantage of the PDP-11 architecture lies in the ability to use the program counter as an ordinary index register. This allows addressing data and instructions relative to where the program is currently executing. The advantage of being able to do this is that when programs address their own locations relative to the program counter, the relative addresses do not change if the program is relocated.

For example, assume that a program is executing an instruction with the program counter equal to 001024, and that instruction is accessing data at 001546, the relative location from the program counter is 001546-001024 = 000522. In fact, this is the same kind of addressing used with the PDP-11 mode 67. (See Chapter 7 page 158.) Now if the program is relocated 1000 locations higher, both the program counter and the data address will move to 002024 and 002546, respectively, but the difference will remain at 000522. As a result, this program could be loaded anywhere in memory without requiring this particular instruction to be modified. If the entire program is written this way, it is said to be in **position-independent code**. In order for a program to be in position-independent code, the programmer must take special care in using only those instructions that are position-independent. The following set of rules gives the most important cases:

Rule 1: Addressing a location within your program. As shown before, all addresses in your program must be accessed using mode 67 addressing.

However, since this is the normal mode (AMA *not* enabled), nothing special needs to be done. MOV A,B works all right.

Rule 2: Addressing a fixed location in memory, or a device register at a fixed address. Mode 67 no longer works, because the PC added to a fixed displacement addresses different locations when the program is moved. However, mode 37 works, because this is followed by the actual (fixed) address. Mode 37 can be forced by placing @# before the address. For example, assume that PRS and PRB are fixed locations in memory and that A is an address inside your program. Then both TSTB @#PRS and MOVB A,@#PRB are position independent.

Rule 3: Branch and jump instructions. Branch instructions are program counter relative over a short range and give no added problems. The jump instructions use general operands and therefore use either mode 67 or 37, depending on whether the jump is within the program or to a fixed place in memory.

Rule 4: Addressing arrays in the program. Arrays cause a special problem because the actual address is needed either for register-deferred access, or index register mode instructions. Essentially, to get around this, it is necessary to use a trick that relies on the fact that the location counter in the assembler has a value close to that of the program counter. Thus, if you want to load the address A into R0 you can first load A − . into R0. (Since both A and the location counter are relocatable, the difference between them is absolute.) Then add the program counter to R0. The only problem is that the result will be off by six, because the program counter will have been incremented a few times. Therefore, the following instructions are used:

```
        MOV     #A-.-6,R0
        ADD     PC,R0
```

Now the address of A is in R0, and register-deferred instructions such as MOV (R0)+,B can be used to perform array operations on A.

Position-independent code can be very useful for operating systems programs. For example, in the RT-11 system, the systems programs are capable of being loaded wherever there is free space. Many of these programs such as input/output device handlers and user service routines are dynamically brought into memory as they are needed, using available space.

EXERCISE SET 2

1 Design a variable length record binary file format that uses control characters instead of byte counts. The format should be usable from paper tape,

Exercise Set 2

meaning that it is necessary to have a leader and trailer possible. All bit patterns must be allowable for data bytes.

2 Write a program that punches out and reads binary files in the format you designed in exercise 1, above.

3 Write a program that reads formatted binary files from punched paper tape in the standard DEC format. The records should be dumped on the printer in octal, showing record boundaries. Test your program using some absolute loader files punched out by the assembler in ABS mode (use the directive .ENABL ABS).

4 Write a program that reads a program from paper tape in absolute loader format, loads it, and runs it. Generate a program to test your loader using the assembler in ABS mode.

5 The following is the code for the paper tape bootstrap loader as it would appear entered at location 077744:

Address	Contents	Address	Contents
077744	016701	077762	116162
077746	000026	077764	000002
077750	012702	077766	077400
077752	000352	077770	005267
077754	005211	077772	177756
077756	105711	077774	000765
077760	100376	077776	177550

(a) Hand disassemble the program into assembly language.
(b) Explain how it works.
(c) Is the program position-independent? Why or why not?
(d) How does the program stop?

*6 Write a program that converts a program in absolute loader format into a format that can be loaded by the bootstrap loader. What restrictions are there to the programs you can write to be loaded this way?

7 Take a program written for some previous exercise and rewrite it so that it is in position-independent code. Test it by including it as part of a program that moves the program and runs it from the moved place.

APPENDIX A
Running Machine Language Programs with On-Line Debugging Technique

It is possible to create and run machine language programs from the operator's console by using a program called ODT (On-line Debugging Technique).

ODT is a machine language computer program and, in order to use it, it is necessary to load the ODT program into memory and execute it. The procedure for doing this varies from one PDP-11 installation to another. In order to run ODT from an LSI-11, it is simply necessary to halt the machine. This may be done on some systems by pressing the break key on the console typewriter.

If you are running a standard PDP-11 using the RT-11 operating system, you must use the software version of ODT. To do this, you must first make ODT runnable by typing:

```
LINK/BOTTOM:2000 SY:ODT
```

You can then type RUN ODT and ODT will start executing.

Once it is executing, ODT will print an asterisk(*) or an at sign (@) on the console printer to indicate that it is ready to accept commands from you. If you type an octal address (such as 1000) followed by a slash (/), ODT will print out the contents of the designated memory cell. If you press the carriage return key, which is often marked CR or RETURN, ODT will print another asterisk (or at sign) indicating its willingness to accept another command. The printed output, which the following shows, indicates that memory cell 001000 currently contains 177134:

   *1000/177134 <u>cr</u> (*Note:* cr represents the carriage
   *   return key; do not type a
                  c and an r!)

(You typed the underlined characters. Characters not underlined are printed by the computer.)

If you wish to examine the contents of a series of memory cells, type a line feed key (often marked LF) instead of CR. ODT will print out the next consecutive address along with its contents instead of printing the asterisk. For example, to examine the contents of memory cells 001000, 001002, and 001004, type:

   *1000/177134 <u>lf</u> (*Note:* lf represents the line
   001002/004767 <u>lf</u>   feed key; do not
   001004/001744 <u>cr</u>   type an l and an f!)
   *

Notice that, as long as you continue to type line feeds, ODT will keep on printing the addresses and contents of consecutive memory cells. When you want to give ODT a new command, type a carriage return instead of a line feed, and ODT will respond by typing an asterisk (or an at sign). In this example, memory cells 001000 through 001004 contain 177134, 004767, and 001744, respectively. When you run ODT, of course, the results may be different.

In order to change the contents of a memory cell, simply type the new contents before you type lf or cr. For example, a trivial machine language program that moves the number 000020 to memory cell 001010 and then halts can be entered into memory beginning at address 001000 by typing the following:

   *1000/177134 <u>012737</u> <u>lf</u>
   001002/004767 <u>000020</u> <u>lf</u>
   001004/001744 <u>001010</u> <u>lf</u>
   001006/011300 <u>000000</u> <u>cr</u>
   *

The third line of output should be interpreted as follows: The address 001004, as well as the old contents, 001744, were typed by ODT. The user typed the new contents, 001010, as well as the line feed.

Care should be taken in modifying the contents of memory cells. In some systems, the ODT program itself may be using memory, and if one of these memory cells is modified, ODT could stop functioning. For the procedures described here, memory cells 001000 through 001600 should be safe.

It is possible to execute the machine language program in memory cells 001000 through 001006 by giving ODT the command:

Running Machine Language Programs with On-Line Debugging Technique

```
      Software ODT        LSI-11 ODT
         *1000;G            @1000G
```

This command tells ODT to Go execute the machine language program beginning in memory cell 001000. This command causes control to be transferred from ODT to our machine language program. The machine language instruction in memory cells 001000 through 001004 will cause the number 000020 to be moved to memory cell 001010, after which the HALT instruction in memory cell 001006 will halt the machine.

At this point, we would like to examine the contents of memory cell 001010 to see if the program has worked properly. This is done by simply typing 1010/ in response to the asterisk or at sign. The response should be:

```
          *1010/000020
```

if your program worked properly.

However, something more is needed if you are running the software version ODT. This is because the HALT instruction will literally have halted the machine and ODT commands will no longer work. To avoid this situation, the following command must be issued before you type 1000;G:

```
            *1006;B
```

Memory cell 001006 will be designated as a Breakpoint. The HALT instruction in memory cell 001006 will not be executed. Instead, control is returned to the ODT program. At this point, it is possible to issue ODT commands to examine or change the contents of a memory cell, execute the program a second time, change the location of the breakpoint, and so on. When you are finished with the ODT program, depress the CONTROL button on the terminal as though it were a SHIFT button and type the letter C. This action is called **control C** and will properly terminate the execution of ODT. Figure A.1 is a summary of ODT commands.

Figure A.1 ODT Commands

Command	Description
For all ODT systems:	
@ or *1000/123456 cr	Examine the contents (123456) of memory cell 001000.
@ or *1000/123456 3 cr	Change the contents of memory cell 001000 from 123456 to 000003.
@ or *1000/123456 3 lf	Same as above, but display the contents of memory cell 001002 next.

Figure A.1 *(continued)*

Command	Description
For software ODT systems only:	
*1020;B	Make memory cell 001020 a breakpoint. That is, when the processor is about to execute the instruction in 001020, immediately return control to ODT.
*;B	Eliminate all existing breakpoints.
*1000;G	Execute (GO) the program beginning in memory cell 001000.
*control C	Terminate the execution of ODT (hold down the control key and type the letter C)
For LSI-11 ODT:	
@1000G	Execute (GO) the program beginning in memory cell 001000.

APPENDIX B
Routines for Reading and Printing Numbers

This appendix gives two subroutines that can be used by students so that they can read and print numbers in early exercises. The subroutines are simply copied into the student's program as is. Two versions of both subroutines are given. One version is intended for RT-11 users. The other is for use with no operating system. Figure 5.12 on page 116 shows how these subroutines are placed in a program.

The subroutines are used as follows.

Reading

To read an octal number from the console typewriter, execute the instruction:

```
        JSR     PC,RNUM
```

The number will be placed in R0. The number should be typed as a 6-digit octal number (fewer digits can be used if desired). The octal digits should be followed by a carriage return. An asterisk is typed showing the user that a number is being requested.

Appendix B

If you are using a batch system, simply type the numbers on cards starting each number in column 1 of a separate card. The data cards are placed after a $DATA card, which is placed after your program. See Appendix C for the batch deck arrangement. (Note, if you are running batch, you should leave out the line that produces the prompting asterisk. See Figure B.1.)

Printing

To print an octal number, simply put the number into R0, and then execute the instruction:

JSR   PC,PNUM

The numbers will appear one per line on either the console typewriter or the batch log file. Figures B.1 and B.2 show these subroutines for use with RT-11 and without an operating system, respectively. When using the subroutines in Figure B.2, it is recommended that locations KBS and PRS be cleared at the beginning of your program. Also note that subroutine RNUM in Figure B.2 calls subroutine PCHAR which is defined at the end of subroutine PNUM.

Figure B.1 *RT-11 Input/Output Routines*

```
;
;SUBROUTINE RNUM READS AN OCTAL NUMBER, LEAVING ITS
;BINARY VALUE IN R0
;
        .MCALL  .TTYIN,.TTYOUT  ;GET THE MACRO .TTYIN AND .TTYOUT
RNUM:   MOV     R1,-(SP)        ;SAVE R1 ON THE STACK
        CLR     R1              ;CLEAR ACCUMULATED RESULT
        .TTYOUT #52             ;TYPE * AS A PROMPT †
RNUML:  .TTYIN                  ;READ CHARACTER INTO R0
        CMPB    R0,#15          ;WAS IT CARRIAGE RETURN?
        BEQ     RNUME           ;YES, EXIT
        BIC     #177760,R0      ;NO, CHANGE CHARACTER TO DIGIT
        ASL     R1              ;MULTIPLY ACCUMULATION BY 2
        ASL     R1              ;AND 2 MORE = 4
        ASL     R1              ;AND 2 MORE = 8 (DECIMAL)
        ADD     R0,R1           ;ADD NEW DIGIT TO 8 * ACCUMULATION
        BR      RNUML           ;LOOP UNTIL END OF NUMBER
RNUME:  .TTYIN                  ;DUMMY READ OF LINE FEED
        MOV     R1,R0           ;PUT RESULT IN R0
        MOV     (SP)+,R1        ;RESTORE R1
        RTS     PC              ;RETURN
```

Read Routine

† This line should be omitted if using a batch system.

Figure B.1 (continued)

```
        ;
        ;SUBROUTINE PNUM PRINTS OUT THE CONTENTS OF R0 IN OCTAL
        ;
        .MCALL  .TTYOUT         ;GET THE MACRO .TTYOUT
PNUM:   MOV     R0,-(SP)        ;SAVE R0 ON THE STACK
        MOV     R1,-(SP)        ;SAVE R1 ON THE STACK
        MOV     R2,-(SP)        ;SAVE R2 ON THE STACK
        MOV     R0,R1           ;R1 HOLDS NUMBER BEING PRINTED
        MOV     #6,R2           ;R2 COUNTS DIGITS
        MOV     #30,R0          ;R0 GETS 6 ASCII CODE BITS
        BR      PNUMM           ;FIRST DIGIT HAS ONLY ONE BIT
PNUML:  MOV     #6,R0           ;R0 GETS 4 ASCII CODE BITS
        ASL     R1              ;SHIFT R1 LEFT WITH HIGH BIT
        ROL     R0              ;  GOING TO C BIT AND THEN TO R0
        ASL     R1              ;GET THE SECOND BIT
        ROL     R0
PNUMM:  ASL     R1              ;GET THE THIRD BIT
        ROL     R0
        .TTYOUT                 ;PRINT THE OCTAL DIGIT
        DEC     R2              ;DECREMENT CHARACTER COUNT
        BNE     PNUML           ;AND LOOP SIX TIMES
        .TTYOUT #15             ;THEN OUTPUT CARRIAGE RETURN
        .TTYOUT #12             ;AND LINE FEED
        MOV     (SP)+,R2        ;RESTORE ALL THREE REGISTERS
        MOV     (SP)+,R1        ;FROM STACK
        MOV     (SP)+,R0
        RTS     PC              ;AND RETURN
```

Print Routine

Figure B.2 Nonsystem Input/Output Routines

```
        ;
        ;SUBROUTINE RNUM READS AN OCTAL NUMBER, LEAVING ITS
        ;BINARY VALUE IN R0 (CODE FOR PNUM IS ASSUMED TO BE
        ;INCLUDED)
        ;
RNUM:   MOV     R1,-(SP)        ;SAVE R1 ON THE STACK
        CLR     R1              ;CLEAR ACCUMULATED RESULT
        MOV     #52,R0          ;TYPE * AS A PROMPT
        JSR     PC,PCHAR
```

Read Routine   (continued on page 316)

(Note: The read routine uses the print routine; therefore, the print routine must always be included.)

Figure B.2 (continued)

```
RNUML:  JSR     PC,RCHAR        ;READ CHARACTER INTO R0
        CMPB    R0,#15          ;WAS IT CARRIAGE RETURN?
        BEQ     RNUME           ;YES, EXIT
        BIC     #177760,R0      ;NO, CHANGE CHARACTER TO DIGIT
        ASL     R1              ;MULTIPLY ACCUMULATION BY 2
        ASL     R1              ;AND 2 MORE = 4
        ASL     R1              ;AND 2 MORE = 8 (DECIMAL)
        ADD     R0,R1           ;ADD NEW DIGIT TO 8 * ACCUMULATION
        BR      RNUML           ;LOOP UNTIL END OF NUMBER
RNUME:  MOV     #12,R0          ;ECHO LINE FEED
        JSR     PC,PCHAR
        MOV     R1,R0           ;PUT RESULT IN R0
        MOV     (SP)+,R1        ;RESTORE R1
        RTS     PC              ;RETURN
;RCHAR READS A SINGLE CHARACTER INTO R0
KBS=177560                      ;LOCATIONS OF STATUS AND
KBB=KBS+2                       ;BUFFER REGISTERS
RCHAR:  TSTB    KBS             ;TEST KEYBOARD STATUS
        BPL     RCHAR           ;LOOP UNTIL SOMETHING IS TYPED
        MOVB    KBB,R0          ;GET CHARACTER
        BIC     #177600,R0      ;CLEAR HIGH ORDER BITS
        JSR     PC,PCHAR        ;ECHO CHARACTER
        RTS     PC              ;RETURN
```

Read Routine   (continued from page 315)


```
;
;SUBROUTINE PNUM PRINTS OUT THE CONTENTS OF R0 IN OCTAL
;
PNUM:   MOV     R0,-(SP)        ;SAVE R0 ON THE STACK
        MOV     R1,-(SP)        ;SAVE R1 ON THE STACK
        MOV     R2,-(SP)        ;SAVE R2 ON THE STACK
        MOV     R0,R1           ;R1 HOLDS NUMBER BEING PRINTED
        MOV     #6,R2           ;R2 COUNTS DIGITS
        MOV     #30,R0          ;R0 GETS 6 ASCII CODE BITS
        BR      PNUMM           ;FIRST DIGIT HAS ONLY ONE BIT
PNUML:  MOV     #6,R0           ;R0 GETS 4 ASCII CODE BITS
        ASL     R1              ;SHIFT R1 LEFT WITH HIGH BIT
        ROL     R0              ;  GOING TO C BIT AND THEN TO R0
        ASL     R1              ;GET THE SECOND BIT
        ROL     R0
PNUMM:  ASL     R1              ;GET THE THIRD BIT
        ROL     R0
        JSR     PC,PCHAR        ;PRINT THE OCTAL DIGIT
```

Print Routine   (continued on page 317)

Figure B.2 (continued)

```
              DEC    R2              ;DECREMENT CHARACTER COUNT
              BNE    PNUML           ;AND LOOP SIX TIMES
              MOV    #15,R0          ;THEN OUTPUT CARRIAGE RETURN
              JSR    PC,PCHAR
              MOV    #12,R0          ;AND LINE FEED
              JSR    PC,PCHAR
              MOV    (SP)+,R2        ;RESTORE ALL THREE REGISTERS
              MOV    (SP)+,R1        ;FROM STACK
              MOV    (SP)+,R0
              RTS    PC              ;AND RETURN
;PCHAR PRINTS A SINGLE CHARACTER
PRS=177564                           ;LOCATION OF STATUS AND
PRB=PRS+2                            ;BUFFER REGISTERS
PCHAR:        TSTB   PRS             ;TEST PRINTER STATUS
              BPL    PCHAR           ;LOOP UNTIL READY
              MOVB   R0,PRB          ;OUTPUT CHARACTER
              RTS    PC              ;RETURN
```

Print Routine   (continued from page 316)

APPENDIX C

C.1 RUNNING ASSEMBLY LANGUAGE AND FORTRAN PROGRAMS USING RT-11 BATCH

When running programs in the RT-11 batch system, the program is punched onto Hollerith cards. Although there are no specific card columns that have to be used for the various assembly language fields, the program listings are almost impossible to read unless the fields are lined up. Employing the following list of columns will usually provide understandable listings:

    Labels   column 1
    Op codes and directives column 9
    Operands   column 17
    Comments   column 33

See Figure C.1 for an example of how to punch an assembly language program.

In addition to the assembly language, a number of control cards are needed. They tell the batch system how to sequence the program. In order to distinguish control cards, they all have a dollar sign in column 1. To avoid confusion, no other cards should have a dollar sign in column 1. The control cards you need are:

    $JOB   Indicates the beginning of your job.
    $MACRO/LIST/RUN   Indicates the beginning of your assembly language.
                         It also indicates that you want to run the program.

319

320   Appendix C

The /RUN and /LIST are optional. Thus, $MACRO/RUN would run the program, but give no listing.

$DATA   Indicates the beginning of data cards.
$EOJ   Indicates the end of the job.

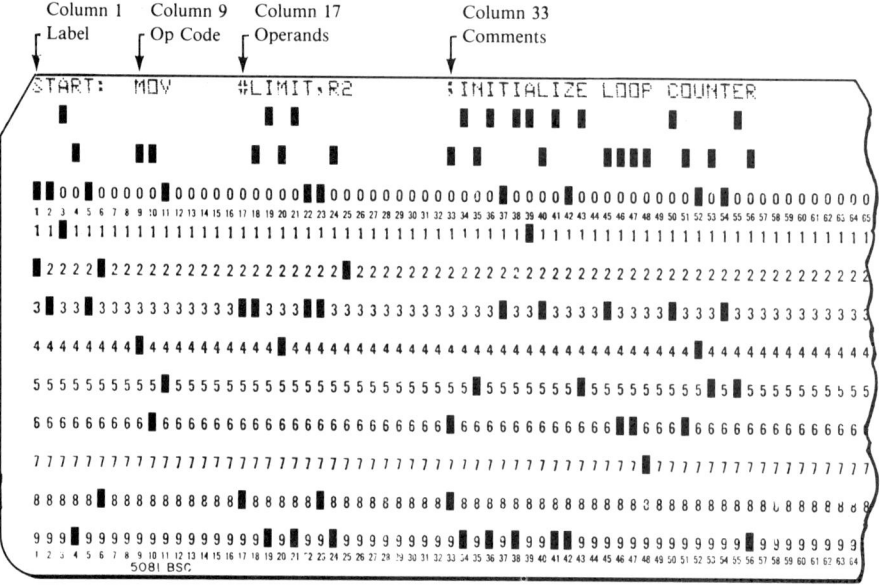

Figure C.1 *Assembly Language on a Punched Card*

In addition to the control cards, one special card called an end-of-file card is needed at the very end of your deck. This card is formed by multipunching &, -, 0, 1, 6, 7, 8, 9, all in column 1. (The symbol & represents a 12 punch and - represents an 11 punch.) Often an installation will have these prepunched and in a different color to help separate decks. Figure C.2 shows the full arrangement of a deck.

When debugging programs, it is sometimes useful to take a memory dump of your program or data areas. This can be done using the RT-11 E command. The E command is followed by two octal addresses separated by a hyphen (or minus sign). A space must follow the E. For example, the command .E 1000-1500 will cause locations 001000 through 001500 to be dumped in

Sec. C.1 *Running Assembly Language and Fortran Programs Using RT-11 Batch*

Figure C.2 Sample Batch Job

```
$JOB
$MACRO/LIST/RUN
        .TITLE   TEST PROGRAM
START:  .
        .        Macro-11 Program
        .
        .END     START
$DATA
005763
$EOJ
             End-of-file Card
```

octal. To use the E command, you must enter the RT-11 mode after your program has run. RT-11 mode commands must be preceded by a period. Figure C.3 shows how the E command can be used in a batch system.

Several assembly language programs may be independently translated and linked together. However, the previous procedures have to be modified slightly. First, each assembly language program must be preceded by a card punched $MACRO/LIST/OBJECT. Note that /OBJECT is used instead of /RUN, because the program cannot be run until all object files are generated and linked together.

Figure C.3 Use of the E Command in Batch

```
$JOB
$MACRO/LIST/RUN
        .
        .        Macro-11 Program
        .
$DATA
        .
        .        Program Data
        .
$RT11
.E 1000-1500
$EOJ
```

Then, after the last program, you must place the card $LINK/MAP/RUN before $DATA. Figure C.4 shows a job with linked programs.

The /MAP on the $LINK card requests the print out of the memory map of the programs and global symbols. Like the listing, the map is optional and the /MAP can be omitted from the $LINK card.

FORTRAN programs can be run or linked with MACRO programs by placing the card: $FORTRAN/LIST/RUN or $FORTRAN/LIST/OBJECT in front of the FORTRAN programs. Note that while one $MACRO card is needed for each assembly language program, any number of FORTRAN programs and subprograms can be placed after one $FORTRAN card.

Figure C.4 Batch Job with Three Linked MACRO Programs

```
$JOB
$MACRO/LIST/OBJECT
                .
                .  First Program
                .
$MACRO/LIST/OBJECT
                .
                .  Second Program
                .
$MACRO/LIST/OBJECT
                .
                .  Third Program
                .
$LINK/MAP/RUN
$DATA
                .
                .  Data Cards
                .
$EOJ
```

C.2 NOTES FOR THE INSTRUCTOR

Running programs in batch is perhaps the easiest way to deal with a large number of students running programs on a PDP-11. A small PDP-11* with a card reader and line printer can easily service the needs of more than 100 students per semester, using the RT-11 version of batch.

The authors encountered some problems in establishing a functional batch system in a student environment. Our solution to the problems was to use a file of job control cards (an indirect file) for bringing up the system, and a looping control file for keeping the card reader running. Figures C.5 and C.6 show the files used. Our main system has an RK05 disk that allows programs to cycle through at a rate of about one per minute.

If less throughput can be tolerated, a floppy-based system could be used. Figure C.7 shows the minimum file configuration for a system to run MACRO only. Figure C.8 shows the modified startup file. This system requires a **scratch** floppy to be placed in DX1:. This floppy will be erased every time the system iterates.

*The authors' experience is with an 11/05. An LSI-11 could be used, but DEC does not make a card reader for it. However, there are software compatible card readers available from some manufacturers.

Figure C.5 Indirect Control File for Bringing up the Batch Stream

```
SET CR: CRLF
SET CR: NOIMAGE
SET CR: CODE=29
SET CR: HANG
SET LP: HANG
SET LP: NOCTRL
SET LP: FORMO
SET LP: LC         *
SET LP: NOTAB      *
SET LP: WIDTH=132  *
SET LP: CR         *
LOAD BA:,LP:,CR:
ASSIGN LP: LOG
ASSIGN LP: LST
R BATCH
CRDSYS.CTL/T:1
```

*These choices may vary depending upon printer model.

Figure C.6 Listing of CRDSYS.CTL Batch Control File for Looping the Card Reader

```
\LLOOP \@ BATCHSTREAM STARTING.
\F\ER BATCH
\DCR:/S
\@ JOB COMPLETE
\JLOOP \@\L$$$$$$\F\ER BATCH
\D/R
\E\F
```

(*Note:* The use of spaces in this job is critical in places.)

Figure C.7 Directory of Minimum Floppy Batch System

```
28-FEB-79
DXMNSJ.SYS      86  14-AUG-77    TT     .SYS    2  14-AUG-77
NL     .SYS      2  18-SEP-78    CR     .SYS    3  18-SEP-78
LP     .SYS      2  13-MAR-78    BA     .SYS    7  30-NOV-78
PIP    .SAV     16  30-NOV-78    DIR    .SAV   17  30-NOV-78
MACRO  .SAV     45  30-NOV-78    CREF   .SAV    6  30-NOV-78
LINK   .SAV     29  30-NOV-78    DUMP   .SAV    7  30-NOV-78
BATCH  .SAV     25  30-NOV-78    DUP    .SAV   17  30-NOV-78
SYSMAC .ML      40  17-JAN-79    CRDSYS .CTL    1  05-FEB-79
STARTS .COM      1  05-FEB-79    LP     .COM    1  05-FEB-79
NOLP   .COM      1  05-FEB-79
23 FILES, 356 BLOCKS
124 FREE BLOCKS
```

Figure C.8 STARTS.COM for Minimum Floppy Batch System

```
SET TT: QUIET              SET TT: QUIET
ASSIGN DX1: DK:            ASSIGN DX1: DK:
SQUEEZE/NOQUERY DK:        SQUEEZE/NOQUERY DK:
INSTALL CR:                INSTALL CR:
SET CR: CRLF               SET CR: CRLF
SET CR: NOIMAGE            SET CR: NOIMAGE
SET CR: CODE=29            SET CR: CODE=29
SET CR: HANG               SET CR: HANG
LOAD BA:,TT:,CR:           SET LP: HANG
ASSIGN TT: LOG             SET LP: NOCTRL
ASSIGN TT: LST             SET LP: FORM0
R BATCH                    SET LP: LOC           *
SY:CRDSYS.CTL/T:1          SET LP: NOTAB         *
                           SET LP: WIDTH=132     *
                           SET LP: CR            *
                           LOAD BA:,LP:,CR:
                           ASSIGN LP: LOG
                           ASSIGN LP: LST
                           R BATCH
                           SY:CRDSYS,CTL/T:1
```

    (a) Without a Line Printer   (b) With a Line Printer
       (file NOLP.COM)   (file LP.COM)

*These choices may vary depending upon printer model.

APPENDIX D
Running Assembly Language and FORTRAN Programs from the Console Typewriter with the RT-11 System

D.1 COMMUNICATING WITH THE RT-11 SYSTEM

Before proceeding further, it is important to understand the protocol used by the RT-11 system. First, when typing into the system, you should observe a prompt character. The RT-11 system uses a period to tell you to type a system command. An asterisk is used to tell you to respond to a program. Messages are also used that ask a question. These are usually self-explanatory, such as: Are you sure? You should answer either YES or NO.

When typing commands or answers, mistakes are often made. There are two ways of correcting mistakes. The first is to type the RUB OUT or DELETE key. This erases the previous character. If you are typing at a video terminal, you may actually see the character disappear. At a hard copy terminal, a back slash is typed followed by the deleted character. You may erase all the way to the beginning of the line if you want. A second back slash is typed when you start typing again. For example, if you type:

HEXY delete delete LLO

the effect would be the same as if you typed HELLO. A video screen would display HELLO, but a hard copy terminal would have:

HEXY\YX\LLO

The second way to correct errors is to erase the entire line and start over.

To do this, hold the control key down and type U. The resulting character is called "control U" (see Chapter 8). (Note that the control key is like a shift key. It does nothing, but must be held down while a letter is typed.) The terminal will echo $\wedge$ U and then start you on a new line. You must keep on typing because you do not get another prompt character.

D.2 FILES

When using the RT-11 system, the user must deal with data and programs in terms of files. Files are blocks of information that are stored on a disk or other device. Files contain a variety of kinds of information—programs, data, and so on. This may be ASCII character information that could be printed and read by a person. It could also be binary information that contains any possible bit pattern. Binary files usually produce gibberish if sent directly to a printer. Assembled or compiled programs are in the form of binary files.

Mass storage devices such as disk or magnetic tape can contain many files. To identify these files, they must have names. RT-11 names consist of a two- or three-letter device designator, a one to six character file name, and a three-letter file type. For example:

   DXO:PROG.MAC

names a file on floppy disk zero. The name is PROG and the type is MAC, meaning that it is a MACRO assembly language program. In effect, the MAC is really part of the name, so that the same disk could contain files PROG.MAC, PROG.OBJ, and PROG.SAV. While the system merely considers these to be three different files, the intent is that they are three different forms of the same program:

   PROG.MAC   is the MACRO assembly language
   PROG.OBJ   is the relocatable object code produced by the assembler
   PROG.SAV   is the absolute core image produced by the linker

In order to copy files, there is a system command called COPY. When the system wants you to type in a system command, it will type a period. This tells you that it is ready. You may then type a command such as COPY. Each command must be followed by a carriage return before the system will react.

When you type COPY, the system will ask you where the information is coming *from*. You must then type a complete file name such as:

a. DXO:PROG.MAC
b. RK:PROG.MAC
c. PROG.MAC
d. CR:

Note in example b that there is no number after RK. Zero is always assumed, so this is the same as RK0. In example c, there is no device name. This implies the user device DK:, which is where your particular system places user files. In the last example, there is no file name, because the card reader always reads the next deck of cards as a file and names have no significance.

Next, the system will ask you where the file is copied *to*. Your answer should have the same form as before. Note, however, that you could not send a file *to* CR:, the card reader. But you could send a file to LP:, the line printer. In fact, this is one way that you could print out your program. Figure D.1 shows a list of the device names and file types that you are most likely to encounter.

When copying files onto a device, it is important to be able to see what files there are. This can be accomplished with the DIRECTORY command. Type DIRECTORY, followed by a space, and then the device name. For example, DIRECTORY DX0: would cause the names of the files on DX0: to be typed out.

Figure D.1 *Device Names and File Types*

DXn:	Floppy disk n (DX01)	MAC	Assembly language program
DYn:	Floppy disk n (DX02)	FOR	FORTRAN program
RKn:	Single platter disk n (RK01)	BAS	BASIC program
DLn:	Single platter disk n (RL01)	DAT	Data
DPn:	Multiple platter disk n	TXT	Text
CTn:	Cassette tape n	BAK	Editor backup file
MTn:	Magnetic tape n	LST	Listing
*TT:	Console teletypewriter	MAP	Memory map from linker
*PC:	Paper tape reader/punch	‡ SYS	System file
*LP:	Line printer	‡ OBJ	Object code (relocatable program)
*CR:	Card reader		
†SY:	System device	‡ SAV	Core imagine (absolute core load)
†DK:	Standard user device		
		‡ LDA	Absolute program (formatted for paper tape)

*These devices need no file name.
†These devices are usually assigned by the system to RK0:, DX0:, DX1:, and so on.
‡These files contain binary rather than ASCII information, and therefore should not be copied to a listing device (TT: or LP:).

D.3 RUNNING A PROGRAM

In order to run an assembly language program, the program should first be copied onto a multifile device, such as a disk. If your program is on cards or a punched paper tape, you could use the COPY command to produce a file on the disk. More likely than not, you want to type the program in at the typewriter. It is possible to COPY from the TT: to the disk, but this is usually awkward due to typing errors. A better method is to use the editor described in Appendix E. In any case, the program should be entered on the disk with a name of your choosing (such as PROGA) but the type should be MAC. You can then run your program by typing:

    EXECUTE PROGA   (Your program is assumed to be on DK:)

The system will see that the type of PROGA is MAC and use the MACRO assembler to translate the program to object code. The linker will then be used to relocate the object module into an absolute program that will then be loaded and executed.

If you then take a directory, you will see that two new files have been created. These are PROGA.OBJ and PROGA.SAV. These files contain your relocatable object language and absolute machine language, respectively. Now, if you want to run your program again, you need only type:

    RUN PROGA

This only works if the file PROGA.SAV is on DK:. Therefore, you must use EXECUTE once, and then you can use RUN. The advantage of RUN is that it is almost instantaneous, whereas EXECUTE involves translation and is therefore quite slow.

One thing the previous sequence lacks is that a listing of the program source code is not produced. This is easily remedied with a modified EXECUTE command. Instead of the previous, type:

    EXECUTE/LIST PROGA

A program listing will then be produced on the line printer. (If you have no line printer, control statements can be used to produce listings on the console teletypewriter.*)

If your program uses the input/output routines shown in Appendix B, then when RNUM is called, an asterisk will be typed at the teletypewriter. You should respond by typing an octal number followed by carriage return. This may be repeated as your program requires.

If your program does not work correctly, you can attempt to correct it by invoking and then using the editor (see Appendix E) and then invoking the EXECUTE command again. The old OBJ and SAV file will be replaced with new ones, and your revised program will be executed. This process can be repeated as needed.

As an aid to debugging, it is sometimes useful to see the contents of memory after your program has terminated. This can be done using console

---

*All line printer output from the system can be directed to the teletypewriter by using the command ASSIGN TT: LP:. This command could be placed in the startup command file STARTS.COM or STARTF.COM.

switches or, on an LSI-11, ODT (see Appendix A). A better method, if your program has not crashed the RT-11 system, may be to use the RT-11 E command. This will allow you to dump areas of memory. Simply type E, a space, and two octal addresses separated by a hyphen. For example, E 1000-1500 will dump locations 001000 through 001500.

If your program is hung in an endless loop, it may be necessary to type control C once or twice to get back to the RT-11 operating system. You may then use the E command to examine memory.

The EXECUTE command can also be used for independently translated programs that will communicate via global symbols. (See Chapter 7.) Each program must be in a separately named file. Then type a command such as:

```
EXECUTE/LIST/MAP MAIN,SUB1,SUB2
```

The programs MAIN, SUB1, and SUB2 will be translated to produce MAIN.OBJ, SUB1.OBJ, and SUB2.OBJ. The MACRO assembler or FORTRAN compiler will be used depending upon whether the program file types are MAC or FOR. Types may be mixed, that is, MAIN might be FORTRAN, while SUB1 and SUB2 were assembly language.

The OBJ files are then relocated and linked together along with whatever might be needed from the FORTRAN library. This produces a single SAV file called MAIN.SAV. The name of the SAV file will be the same as the first source program file in the EXECUTE command.

The /MAP on the command is optional and causes a memory map of the results of the relocation to be printed.

After the translation and linking are complete, the program is executed. Since the SAV file is MAIN.SAV, the program is rerun by typing:

```
RUN MAIN
```

Sometimes it is desirable to perform the steps of the EXECUTE command separately. There are various ways to do this, but one is to use the commands MACRO, FORTRAN, LINK, and RUN. These translate assembly language, compile FORTRAN, link object files, and run SAV files, respectively. The previous EXECUTE command could be replaced by the five following commands:

```
FORTRAN/LIST MAIN
MACRO/LIST SUB1
MACRO/LIST SUB2
LINK/MAP MAIN,SUB1,SUB2
RUN MAIN
```

APPENDIX E
Using The RT-11 Editor

E.1 FUNCTION OF THE EDITOR

As we saw in Appendix D, unless you are using the batch system, programs must reside on a file such as PROG.MAC (or FPG.FOR for FORTRAN programs). Although it is possible to create such a program using the COPY command, there are difficulties in doing so. For example, you could enter the command:

```
COPY TT: PROG.MAC
```

You would then type your entire program and signal the end by typing control Z. However, if there were any mistakes in your program, you would have no choice but to retype the entire program. The editor allows you to enter and modify programs so that correcting mistakes or adding features to programs is relatively easy.

The editor is used for creating and modifying strings of text. This text is considered to be an arbitrary string of characters. No distinction is made as to whether the text constitutes a valid MACRO program, a FORTRAN program, a nursery rhyme, or whatever. In fact, many people use the editor for dealing with English prose, such as business letters. There is a growing use of computers for this purpose coming under the general name of **word processing.** The important point to remember is that the editor does not know that you are writing

MACRO programs, therefore symbols such as .TITLE, .END, colon, semicolon, and so on, have no recognizable meaning.

E.2 CREATING A PROGRAM

In order to create a program using the editor, you must type the following RT-11 command (or its equivalent):

```
EDIT/CREATE PROG.MAC
```

PROG.MAC is the name of the file you are using for your program. Note that the full name is necessary because the editor will not assume a file type.

The editor will now respond on the console device with an asterisk. This means that the editor is expecting an edit command.† Since you are just beginning to create a program, the only useful command at this point is I for *inserting* new text. Immediately after you type I, you continue to type your entire program just as you wish it to appear. The TAB key can be used to space to the next field, and each line ends by typing the RETURN key. (Note that the system automatically adds a line feed when you type carriage return.) When you reach the end of your program (do not forget the RETURN after .END), you must get back to command mode by typing the ESC or ALT MODE key twice. In the editor, all commands are terminated by two escapes. Escape is used because carriage return is often part of the text. Figure E.1 shows a sample dialogue for creating a simple program. Note that there are some typing errors, and that the editor echoes dollar signs when you type escape. The final asterisk indicates that the editor is awaiting another command.

Figure E.1 Entering a Simple Program with Some Typing Errors

```
*I      .TITLE  EXAMP SIMPLE EXAMPLE
SSTART: MOV     A,C         THIS PROGRAM
        ADD     B,C         ;ADDS TWO PLUS TWO
        HALT                ;AND HALTS
        STOP
A       .WORD   2
B:      .BLKW   2
        .END    START
$$
*
```

†The commands described here are for the newer editor called TECO. It is assumed that the installation manager has placed SET EDIT TECO in the startup command file. For those preferring to use the older editor, EDIT, there is a correspondence table for commands at the end of this appendix.

E.3 CORRECTING ERRORS

When correcting errors, you must first point to the place the error is and then make the correction. To facilitate this, the editor has a pointer that can be moved left, right, up, and down with appropriate commands. When you finish inserting text, the pointer will always be at the end of what you inserted. Assuming that you have just finished the dialogue of Figure E.1, then the pointer will be at the very end. To move it back to the very begnning, use the J command by typing:

J   escape   escape

This would appear as:

*J$$
*

In the dialogue, the asterisks come from the editor and the dollar signs indicate escapes. To simplify illustrations, the dollar sign will be used to mean the escape key for the remainder of this appendix.

The first error we see is that the word START is misspelled by having an extra S. This mistake is at the beginning of the next line. We must therefore move the pointer down a line. This is done with the command:

1L$$

A number of lines followed by L$$ causes the pointer to move down that many lines. Negative numbers move you up so many lines.

After moving down a line, we want to delete one character. This is done with the command

1D$$

We can now see our correction by using the V command (for Verify). V$$ causes the line on which the pointer resides to be typed. In this case, the following would be typed:

```
*V$$
START:  MOV     A,C     THIS PROGRAM
*
```

The area around the pointer can be verified (typed) by putting a number, n, before the V. This will verify $n-1$ lines before and after the pointer as well. For example:

```
*2V$$
        .TITLE  EXAMP SIMPLE PROGRAM
START:  MOV     A,C     THIS PROGRAM
        ADD     B,C     ;ADDS TWO PLUS TWO
```

Another error (not the next) is that there is an unwanted line that says STOP. This is three lines down. So we can get there with 3L$$. We can then Kill one line with the command 1K$$. However, since the kill command could destroy a fair amount of typing, it is a good idea to verify the line first. The total dialogue would appear as:

```
*3L$$
*V$$
                STOP
*1K$$
*
```

E.4 INSERTING AND LOCATING THE POINTER IN A LINE

On the next line, there is another error. A colon is needed after the A. In fact, since we killed the line with STOP on it, the pointer is now at the beginning of the line with the missing colon. You may want to use V to make sure. However, we do not want to insert the colon here because it would be at the beginning of the line, *before* the A. We move the pointer one character position with the command 1C$$. We then use I (for insert), just as in the original creation:

```
*V$$
A       .WORD   2
*1C$$
*I:$$
*V$$
A:      .WORD   2
*
```

Note that there is no carriage return after the I. We only want to insert a colon. If we included a carriage return, that would be inserted also.

There is also an error on the next line. BLKW should be changed to WORD. Here, we should:

a. Go down a line

b. Go over to the BLKW

Sec. E.5   Combining Commands   335

c. Delete it
d. Insert WORD

Here, step a is 1L$$, but for step b, how far do we go across? The key to the answer is to remember that TAB is one single character; therefore we move four characters:

B   :   tab   .

Of course, this is a place where we would like to be sure. But V$$ does not help us find the pointer because it prints the entire line without any marks to indicate where the pointer is. We need the command T$$. This types the line from the *pointer* to the end of the line. The dialogue might look like this:

```
*1L$$
*4C$$
*T$$
BLKW    2
*4D$$
*IWORD$$
*V$$
B:      .WORD    2
*
```

E.5 COMBINING COMMANDS

Notice that the dialogue is getting quite lengthy. One simplification is that several commands can be combined on one line. They are simply placed one after another without escapes, except that text strings such as found after I must be followed by one escape. Note also that a count need not be expressed if it is *one*.

L is the same as 1L. Thus, the preceding dialogue could be reduced to the following:

```
*L4CT$$
BLKW    2
*4DIWORD$V$$
B:      .WORD    2
*
```

The next error is that a whole line that defines C is missing. This line should go before the .END line, and can be inserted as before, but note that we must insert a carriage return because that is part of a whole line. The following dialogue shows this:

```
                *LV$$
                            .END     START
                *IC:        .BLKW    1
                $3V$$
                B:          .WORD    2
                C:          .BLKW    1
                            .END     START
                *
```

Note that since the pointer is on the last line, the 3V can only list backward.

E.6 THE SEARCH COMMAND

The only error left is a missing semicolon on the second line. To fix this, we can go back to the beginning, go down one line, and move over to the comment. The third step is hard, because it involves careful counting. To help out, the editor has a search command which looks for a character string that indicates the right place to edit. For example, we can see that the point where we want to edit is immediately preceded by the four characters:

```
                A       ,       C       tab
```

This is a sufficiently unique combination of characters that we are unlikely to get a bogus hit. In fact, those four characters appear as a string nowhere else.

To search, use the S command followed by the string to be matched followed by at least one escape (as for insert). The following dialogue shows how this is done:

```
                *JSA,C $T$$
                THIS PROGRAM
                *I;$V$$
                START:  MOV     A,C     ;THIS PROGRAM
                *
```

Searching is useful not only for finding a place in a line, but also for finding a line or area of a large program. For example, to find the data area of a program, you could use the command S.WORD$$.

E.7 TERMINATING THE EDIT RUN

Now that you have corrected all the errors, two additional tasks probably need to be done. The first is to get a current listing of your program so that you can check to be sure that all the errors were found and corrected. The second is to exit and save the file.

In order to list a file, the command HT$$ is typed. This will type out an entire program. Then the command EX$$ can be used to terminate editing and save the program in the file you have named. It should be noted that until the EX has finished, you have not saved your program, and halting the machine or typing control C could cause everything to be lost.

Figure E.2 shows the final dialogue for listing the program and exiting. Note that when the prompt character changes from asterisk to period, it means that you are out of the editor and back in RT-11.

Figure E.2   Exiting from the Editor

```
*HT$$
        .TITLE  EXAMP SIMPLE EXAMPLE
START:  MOV     A,C         ;THIS PROGRAM
        ADD     B,C         ;ADDS TWO PLUS TWO
        HALT                ;AND HALTS
A:      .WORD   2
B:      .WORD   2
C:      .BLKW   1
        .END    START
*EX$$
```

E.8 EDITING A PREEXISTING PROGRAM

In order to edit a preexisting program, you must enter the editor without the /CREATE option. It may be necessary to type the command A$$ to make the editor read the old program. After that, editing is the same as described before. When you type EX$$, the modified program is saved with your program name. However, for safety purposes, the old version of the program is saved with the file type .BAK.

Figure E.3 shows a sequence for doing this. Your old program must originally be called PROG.MAC. After you are done, your old program is backed up as PROG.BAK, and your new program is stored as PROG.MAC.

Figure E.3   Edit Sequence for Editing Existing Program

```
.EDIT PROG.MAC
*A$$
    .
    .       Normal Edit Commands
    .
*EX$$
    .
```

E.9 IMMEDIATE MODE EDITING

If you are fortunate enough to have a system with interactive graphics or an advanced graphics terminal, editing can be greatly simplified. Such terminals include the VT-11, VT-52, and VT-100. These terminals allow various forms of **immediate mode** editing. In immediate mode, the text surrounding the pointer is continuously displayed. The pointer itself is marked as a flashing line. Whatever you type is automatically inserted, and there are special keys for erasing characters or lines, moving the pointer, and other edit functions.

It is also possible to get out of immediate mode back to the normal edit command mode, and vice versa. Consequently, the immediate mode editing does not restrict the user. As each device has its own rules for using immediate mode, they will not be discussed here. However, immediate mode can easily be related to the command mode and learned quickly with a little practice.

Summary of Edit Commands*

A	Read the old program into the editor.
nC	Move the pointer n characters to the right (left if n is negative).
nD†	Delete n characters to the right of the pointer (left if n is negative).
EX	Exit from the editor and save the program.
I*text*$	Insert *text* into program.
J	Move the pointer to the beginning.
ZJ	Move the pointer to the end.
nK	Kill n line(s) starting at the pointer.
nL	Move the pointer down n lines (up if n is negative, and to the beginning of the same line if $n = 0$).
S*text*$	Search for the string *text*.
nT	Type n lines starting at the pointer.
HT	Type the whole program.
nV	Verify $n-1$ lines either side of the line the pointer is on.

*These commands are greatly simplified here for the purpose of brevity. For more detail and for many other commands, refer to the TECO Manual distributed by Digital Equipment Corporation.

†It is possible to delete either the carriage return or the line feed at the end of a line of text. As far as the editor is concerned, these are just single characters as are any other control characters such as TAB. If you inadvertently delete a carriage return or line feed it can be reinserted, but note that the RETURN key on the console produces a carriage return/line feed pair; therefore, it is tricky to repair the damage.

Sec. E.9   *Immediate Mode Editing*

Equivalence of TECO and EDIT (old editor) Commands

TECO	EDIT	Note
A	R	
*n*C	*n*J	
*n*D	*n*D	
EX	EX	
I*text*$	I*text*$	
J	B	
ZJ	999A	Advance a large number of lines such as 999.
*n*K	*n*K	
*n*L	*n*A	
S*text*$	G*text*$	
*n*T	*n*L	
HT	/L	Pointer must be at the beginning in EDIT.
V	V	No number is allowed in EDIT.

GLOSSARY

Absolute   A value or address that is constant and does not change even if the program is relocated in memory.

Address   A number that identifies a particular word location or byte location in memory. In the PDP-11, words must have even addresses, whereas bytes may have even or odd addresses.

Address Expression   An expression the value of which is an address.

Argument   A parameter that is provided in an assembly directive or macro call.

Array   A collection of words or bytes used for a coordinated purpose.

ASCII   A standard code for representing alphabetic information. In the PDP-11, ASCII characters are represented one per byte, or two per word.

Assembly Directive   A command to the assembler to perform a certain function regarding translation. These include changing assembly modes or listing modes, allocating memory, and indicating the end of your program.

Assembly Language   A language for simplifying the process of producing machine language programs for a computer. Basically, each line of assembly language corresponds to a single machine language instruction, except that numerical op codes and addresses are replaced with symbolic names.

Auto-Increment (Decrement)   An indexing mode where the index register is automatically incremented (decremented) as the instruction is executed.

Binary A number system based upon powers of two using the digits 0 and 1. Also, describes any event that can be characterized in exactly two ways.

Boolean (Operations and Values) Operations that treat the values of 0 and 1 as meaning *falsity* and *truth*. The Boolean operations most used are AND, OR, NOT, and exclusive OR.

Borrow The deficit from subtraction that cannot be obtained from a digit (register) and must be obtained from the next digit (register).

Branch (Conditional) A branch instruction is an instruction that alters the sequence of your program by jumping to another location. A conditional branch is one that may or may not operate based upon some computed condition. In the PDP-11, branch instructions operate over a limited range of -127 to $+128$ words.

Buffer In an input or output device, the buffer is the register that contains the information to be input or output.

Byte A short sequence of bits (usually 6, 7, or 8) that is treated as a single unit of information by the processor. Bytes are often used to contain character codes. In the PDP-11, bytes are 8 bits long.

Carry The excess from addition that will not fit into a digit (register) and must be added to the next digit (register).

Code Assembly language or machine language text.

Computer A machine for performing computations. Most modern computers are automatic, and operate under control of a programmed set of instructions.

Condition Code A set of bits that indicates the state or condition of the processor at a given time. In the PDP-11, there are four condition code bits, N, Z, C, and V, which indicate the result of the previous operation.

Conditional Assembly A block of program that may be eliminated from your total program based upon some information available at assembly time.

Contents The number or data represented in a memory location or register.

CRT Cathode-ray tube, that is, a television picture tube. In computer terminology, this refers to a device for receiving messages from a computer (or teletypewriter) to be displayed on a television screen. Most CRTs also include a keyboard for data entry as well.

Decimal A number system based upon powers of 10 using the digits 0, 1, 2, 3, 4, 5, 6, 7, 8, and 9.

Deferred Address An addressing mode where the instruction does not directly locate the operand, but locates the *address* of the operand.

Glossary

Destination The location or register where the result of a computation is stored.

Device Polling A technique that may be used by the processor to determine when an input or output operation is completed. The processor continually asks the device if the input/output operation has been completed. Contrast with Interrupt.

Direct Addressing An addressing mode where the instruction contains the actual numeric value of the address of the operand.

Directive See Assembly Directive.

Effective Address An address that is computed at execution time, often by adding the contents of an index register to a base address.

Execute Cycle The period of time that the computer is executing the operation specified by an instruction. See also Fetch Cycle.

Exponent Part The part of a floating point number that indicates the position of the radix point (decimal point).

Expression A combination of symbols, numbers, and algebraic operators denoting the computation of some value. In the PDP-11 assembly language, expressions are evaluated at translation time.

Fetch Cycle The period of time that the computer is fetching an instruction from memory prior to execution. See also Execute Cycle.

Fixed Point A number representation system where the radix point (decimal point) is assumed to be at a fixed place in a word. Fixed point representation is used for integers and occasionally for fractions.

Floating Point A number representation system where the radix point (decimal point) can be placed anywhere over a wide range. Usually used for FORTRAN REAL numbers. See also Exponent Part and Fraction Part.

Fraction Part The part of a floating point number that indicates the significant digits of the number.

Global Symbol A symbol defined in one program module for use in other independently assembled program modules.

High Order The most significant digits in a number or word.

Hexadecimal A number system based upon powers of 16 using as digits: 0, 1, 2, 3, 4, 5, 6, 7, 8, 9, A, B, C, D, E, and F.

Immediate Operand An operand that is contained in an instruction, which therefore does not need to be read from memory during the execute cycle.

Index Register A register that is used to point into an array to assist with array operations.

Instruction A coded command to the processor to perform a specific operation.

Integrated Circuit An electronic circuit made of microscopic parts photographically placed on a very small die of silicon or sapphire. An integrated circuit that is only 0.04 square inches may have more than 50,000 transistors on it.

Interrupt A signal sent by an input or output device to the processor to indicate that an input/output operation has been completed. Normally, this causes the processor temporarily to suspend the execution of the currently executing program in order to execute a special program, called an interrupt routine, that services the input/output device.

Link To relocate individual program modules to their own memory space, and to insert the addresses of global locations into instructions that refer to global symbols.

Load To place a linked program into memory so that it can be executed.

Location Counter A counter in the assembler that keeps track of the memory location into which code is being assembled.

Loop A part of a program that is executed repeatedly.

Low Order The least significant digits in a number or word.

Machine Language A sequence of numeric codes that direct the operation of a processor.

Macro A named block of code with substitutable parameters that can be inserted into a program by referring to the name.

MACRO-11 The name of the PDP-11 assembler.

Mask A word where the bits are used to zero out or fill in selected portions of another word.

Memory A collection of addressable locations that contain the representations of numbers or data.

Microcomputers A computer that is extremely small and inexpensive. A microcomputer is built from one or a few integrated circuit chips, and usually has a simple instruction set and a small word size such as eight bits. As technology improves, it becomes difficult to distinguish between microcomputers and minicomputers.

Modules Main programs and subroutines that can be assembled independently, and later linked together to form a total program.

Monitor A program that controls the loading, execution, and input/output functions of user programs.

Glossary

Normalized Number A floating point number that is adjusted so that the most significant digit of the fraction part is not zero. In the PDP-11 floating point representation, all numbers are normalized.

Object Code The output of the assembler. Object Code is relocatable machine language that must be linked so it can be run. See also Link.

Octal A number system based upon powers of eight using the digits 0, 1, 2, 3, 4, 5, 6, and 7.

One's Complement A system for representing negative numbers in the binary number system. The negative of a number is formed by changing all ones in the original number to zeros, and all zeros to ones. This is also equivalent to the Boolean NOT operation on each bit.

Operand The data that an instruction operates on. This may be input data or a computed result.

Operating System The collection of programs that allows the user access to the computer. These include monitors, translators, loaders, linkers, input/output routines, editors, debugging aids, and so on. Some operating systems may have very few programs, while others are extremely sophisticated. Operating systems widely used on the PDP-11 are RT-11, RSTS, and RSX-11.

Operation Code A numeric code that indicates which instruction is to be executed by the computer. Also, a symbolic name used in assembly language to designate a machine language, numeric, operation code.

Overflow A condition that occurs when a computed result is too big to fit into a word, byte, or floating point representation.

Parity An error detection scheme where an extra bit is added to make all words or bytes have an odd (or even) number of ones.

Pass During the assembly process, the assembler reads through the input code twice in what are called *passes*. On the first pass, symbols are defined; on the second pass, the object code and the listing are generated.

PDP Programmed Data Processor, a trade name of the Digital Equipment Corporation used to identify computer models. The numbers following PDP are chronological so that the PDP-1 was the earliest, the PDP-11 is later. The size and power of the computers vary. The PDP-6 was very big and powerful, the PDP-8 was very small. Newer products have dropped the PDP nomenclature, such as the VAX 11-780 and the DEC System 20.

Peripheral Device An input or output device such as a card reader, printer, or CRT.

Processor The portion of a computer that executes instructions, performs calculations, and controls the other portions of the computer.

Processor Register The PDP-11 has eight registers located in the processor that are available to the program and can be accessed without going through memory. These are designated R0, R1, R2, R3, R4, R5, SP, and PC.

Processor Status Register A register in the processor that contains coded bits which indicate the current state of the processor. On the PDP-11, the processor status register contains the current processor priority as well as the condition code bits (the C, Z, V, and N bits).

Program A sequence of instructions for directing the operation of a computer.

Program Counter A register in the processor that contains the address of the next instruction to be executed. In the PDP-11, the program counter is one of the processor registers designated as PC.

Program Section A block of code that can be filled from various places in an assembly language program, but is eventually loaded as a contiguous block.

Q-BUS Q-BUS is a trademark of the Digital Equipment Corporation that refers to the cable and protocol for transmitting data and addresses back and forth from the processor to the memory and other peripheral devices. The Q-BUS is used on most of the LSI-11 based computers such as the PDP-11/03 and PDP-11/23. See also UNIBUS.

RAD50 In the PDP-11, a character code that allows character strings to be represented with three characters per word.

Recursive A subroutine, macro, or other process that calls itself.

Register A physical device that contains the representation of a number or piece of data. On the PDP-11, the term register usually refers to the eight processor registers R0-R5, SP, and PC. Each contains a 16-bit word.

Relative Addressing An addressing mode where the instruction contains the difference between the address of the operand and its own address. Use of relative addressing helps eliminate the need for modifying the program when it is relocated.

Relocatable A value is relocatable if it must be modified when the program is relocated.

Relocation Modifying a program if necessary so that it can be executed from a different area of memory than that assigned during assembly.

Repeat Block A block of code that is automatically repeated by the assembler.

Shift To move the digits (bits) in a word left or right.

Signed Number A number with an algebraic sign, plus or minus.

Glossary

Source The input data used by an instruction that is not modified by the operation.

Status Register In an input or output device, the status register contains various bits that indicate the status of the device. On the PDP-11, these bits may include the ready bit, the interrupt bit, the start bit, as well as error bits.

Stack An array of data that is used in such a way that the last piece of data to be added to the stack is the first to be removed.

Store The operation of modifying or replacing the contents of a memory location.

Subroutine A program segment that can be entered from various places and will return when finished.

Teletypewriter A machine resembling a typewriter for transmitting typewritten messages over an electrical connection. Often, teletypewriters are used to type messages into a computer or to receive computer printout.

Trap A forced interpretation of a program due to an error or some other condition.

Two's Complement A system for representing negative numbers in the binary number system. The negative of a number is formed by subtracting the number from zero, and ignoring the borrow that propagates off the left end of the register.

UNIBUS UNIBUS is a trademark of the Digital Equipment Corporation that refers to the cable and protocol for transmitting data and addresses back and forth from the processor to the memory and other peripheral devices. The UNIBUS is used on most of the larger PDP-11's, such as the PDP-11/34. See also Q-BUS.

Unsigned Numbers A positive number that cannot have an algebraic sign.

Word A sequence of digits that is treated as a single unit of information by the processor. In the PDP-11, words are 16 bits long.

INDEX

Absolute address, 68, 81
Absolute addressing, 156
Absolute expressions, 224
Absolute loader, 303
Absolute loader file, 290
ADC instruction, 139
ADD instruction, 40
ADD number instruction, 49
Addition, 17
   floating point, 269
Address, 34
Address assignments, 240
Address expressions, 146
Address space, 57
Address,
   absolute, 81
   relocatable, 81
Addressing mode,
   absolute, 156
   auto-decrement, 153, 156
   auto-decrement deferred, 156
   auto-increment, 152, 156
   auto-increment deferred, 156

immediate, 156
index, 147
index register, 156
index register deferred, 156
indirect, 155
register, 106, 156
register deferred, 151, 156
relative, 157
relative deferred, 157
Addressing modes, summary, 154, 156
Addressing,
   direct, 97
   relative, 97
Aiken, Howard, 2
Algorithm, 15
AND operation, 28
Argument, 68
Arithmetic, multiple precision, 137
Arrays, 143
ASCII, 165, 239
ASCII character set, 168

.ASCII directive, 176
ASCII keyboard, 169
.ASCIZ directive, 178
ASH instruction, 285
ASHC instruction, 285
ASL instruction, 130
ASR instruction, 131
Assembly directive, 68
Assembly errors, 71
Assembly language, 4, 63
   syntax, 67
Assembly passes, 71, 225, 292
Assembly process, 291
Auto-decrement addressing, 153
Auto-increment addressing, 152

BASIC to machine language conversion, 52
Batch control cards, 319
Batch system files, 320
BCC instruction, 121
BCS instruction, 121
BEQ instruction, 89, 123

349

BGE instruction, 100
BGT instruction, 100
BHI instruction, 125
BHIS instruction, 125
BIC instruction, 184
Binary arithmetic, 22
Binary counting, 21
Binary event, 21
Binary files, 296
   formatted, 297
Binary fractions, 276
Binary numbers, 20
Binary to hexadecimal conversion, 30
Binary to octal conversion, 23
BIS instruction, 184
Bit, 23
BIT instruction, 184
Bit manipulation instructions, 183
BLE instruction, 100
.BLKB directive, 177
.BLKW directive, 68, 145
BLO instruction, 125
BLOS instruction, 125
BLT instruction, 100
BMI instruction, 123
BNE instruction, 89, 123
Boolean logic, 28
Bootstrap loader, 303
Borrow, 17
BPL instruction, 123
BR instruction, 89
Branch instruction displacements, 96
Branch instructions, 87
   guidelines, 126
   machine language, 95
Buffer register, 241, 245, 249
Bus, 261
BVC instruction, 121
BVS instruction, 121
Byte, 34, 172
.BYTE directive, 175
Byte instructions, 172

C bit, 121, 139
CALL statement, 210
Calling subroutines, 111
Carriage return, 167

Carry, 17
Character files, 292
Characters, 166
Check sum, 298
Clock, 251, 255
CLR instruction, 91
CMP instruction, 98, 123
   machine language, 99
   order of operands, 101, 103
COM instruction, 185
Common block, 212
COMMON statement, 212
Compiler, 5
Computer program, 2, 34
Computers (other than the PDP-11), 56
Condition codes, 122
Conditional assembly, 232
Conditional blocks, nesting, 234
Console keyboard, 241
Console printer, 244
Console typewriter, 325
Contents of memory, 37
Control characters, 166
Conversion,
   binary to hexadecimal, 30
   bytes to words, 35
   octal to binary, 23
   octal to decimal, 20
Core image file, 290, 303
Counting, 17, 21
CRT, 170
Cursor, 170

DEC instruction, 93, 126
Decimal fractions, 266
Decimal numbers, 16
Deferred addressing, 151, 155
Destination, 49, 63
Device names, 327
Device polling, 239
Direct addressing, 97
Direct memory access, 261
Divide instruction, 284
Dividend, 129
Division, 129, 134, 283
   floating point, 272
Divisor, 129
Done bit, 243

Dot symbol, 221, 306
Double operand instructions, 188
Double-precision, 137
Doublewords, 59

EAM, 1
EBCDIC code, 192
Echoing, 182
Eckert, Presper, 2
EDIT, 339
Editing, 331
EIS option, 281
Electronic accounting machinery, 1
EMT instruction, 79, 259
.ENABL directive, 68, 156
Encoding, octal, 23
.END directive, 68
.ENDC directive, 233
.ENDM directive, 231
.ENDR directive, 220
Equal sign, 108
Equals symbol, 222, 242
Error trap, 74
.EVEN directive, 175
Exclusive OR operation, 29
.EXIT macro, 115
Exponent part, 268
Expressions, 146, 223

FADD instruction, 278
FDIV instruction, 278
Fetch operation, 33, 39
Fields, 293, 320
File types, 327
Files, 326
   binary, 296
   character, 292
FIS option, 275, 278
Fixed point numbers, 266
Floating point,
   binary, 275
   PDP-11, 277
Floating point addition, 269
Floating point division, 272
Floating point multiplication, 272
Floating point numbers, 267
Floating point subtraction, 269

Floppy disk, 13
.FLT2 directive, 279
.FLT4 directive, 280
FMUL instruction, 278
Forward reference, 291
Formatted binary files, 297
FORTRAN to machine
    language conversion, 52
Fraction part, 268
Fractions, 265
    binary, 276
    decimal, 266
FSUB instruction, 278
Full duplex, 182
Functions, FORTRAN, 213

Global symbol directory, 299
Global symbols, 206
.GLOBL directive, 207

Halfwords, 59
HALT instruction, 41
Hardware, 4
Hexadecimal, 58
Hexadecimal numbers, 30
Hexadecimal to binary conversion, 30
Hidden bit, 277
Higher-level language, 5
Hollerith code, 190
Hollerith, Herman, 1, 190

IBM card code, 192
.IF directive, 233
Immediate addressing, 156
INC instruction, 92, 126
Index addressing, 147
Index register, 147
Indexing, 146
Indexing byte instructions, 176
Indirect addressing, 155
Input device, 33
Input, no operating system, 181
Input with RT-11, 179
Instruction, 34
Instruction cycle, 304
Integrated circuit, 3
Interrupt routine, 255, 258
Interrupt vector, 254
Interrupts, 252

JMP instruction, 97
JSR instruction, 111, 197, 201
Jump instructions, 87

Keyboard, 241
Keyboard buffer register, 182
Keyboard status register, 182

Label, 66
Leader (paper tape), 248
Line clock, 251, 255
Line feed, 167
Line printer, 247
Linker, 83, 207, 300
Linking process, 300
Loader, 83, 303
Location counter, 70, 221
Looping, 88
    example of, 94, 98, 104

Machine language, 4, 42, 102
    branch instructions, 95
    CMP instruction, 99
Machine language programs, 43, 52
Macro, 109
.MACRO directive, 231
Macro definition, 229
Macro expansion, 229, 294
Macro parameters, 230
Macro-11, 64
Macros, 229
    nesting, 234
    recursive, 234
Mask, 184
Matrix, storage allocation, 160
Mauchly, John, 2
.MCALL directive, 108, 179
Memory, 33
Memory cell, 44
Memory interpretation, 47
Memory mapped input/output, 240
Memory representation, other computers, 56
Microcomputer, 57
Mnemonic operation code, 64
Mode (see Addressing mode)
Modular programs, 78
Modules, 206

MOV instruction, 41
MOV number instruction, 49
MOVB instruction, 172
MOVB with processor registers, 174
MUL instruction, 283
Multiple-precision, 137
Multiplication, 129, 133, 282
    floating point, 272
Multiply-dimensioned arrays, 160

N bit, 122
NEG instruction, 126
Negative numbers, 27
    32 bit, 284
No-op, 97
Normalized numbers, 268
NOT operation, 28
Number representation, 15
Numbers,
    binary, 20
    decimal, 16
    hexadecimal, 30
    octal, 17

Object code, 83
Object file, 290
Object module, 299
Octal counting, 17
Octal encoding, 23
Octal numbers, 17
Octal to binary conversion, 23
Octal to decimal conversion, 20
ODT, 309
One's complement, 27, 186
Operand, 45
Operating system, 11
Operation code, 42, 63
Operation codes, 102
OR operation, 28
Output device, 33
Output, no operating system, 181
Output with RT-11, 179
Overflow, 46, 120

Paper tape, 248
Parity, 186
Parity bit, 171

PC, 110, 156, 203
PCHAR subroutine, 181
PDP-11, 7, 35
Peripheral devices, 12
Phase error, 227
PNUM subroutine, 112, 116, 314
Polling loop, 244
Position independent code, 159, 305
Print operation, 33
Printer buffer register, 181
Printer status register, 181
Priority, 254
Processor, 8, 33
Processor register, 87, 105
Processor status register, 253
Program counter, 43, 110, 156, 203
Program modification, 47
Program sections, 212, 301
.PSECT directive, 212, 299
PSW, 253
Punch card, 191

Quotient, 129

RAD50 code, 193
Radix point, 266
RCHAR subroutine, 182
Read operation, 33
Ready bit, 243
Records, 296
Recursive macros, 234
Recursive subroutines, 200, 214
.REGDEF macro, 108
Register, 26
Register 6 (see Stack pointer)
Register 7 (see Program counter)
Register addressing, 106
Register deferred addressing, 151
Register symbols, 107
Register, index, 147
Relative addressing, 97, 158
Relocatable address, 81
Relocatable expressions, 224
Relocation, 79
Relocation directories, 300

Remainder, 129
Repeat blocks, 220
.REPT directive, 220
RETURN statement, 210
Returning from subroutines, 111
RNUM subroutine, 112, 116, 313
ROL instruction, 132
ROR instruction, 132
Rotate instructions, 132, 285
Round off, 131
Routine, interrupt, 255, 258
RSTS, 12
RSX-11, 12
RT-11, 12, 79
   defining registers, 108
   exiting, 115
   input and output, 179
RT-11 commands, 325
RTI instruction, 255
RTS instruction, 111, 198, 201
Running a program, 319, 325

SBC instruction, 139
Scaling, numbers, 266
Scientific notations, 267
Scrolling, 170
Selection sort, 143
Sentinel value, 177
Shift instructions, 130, 285
Shifting, multiple-precision, 140
Signed branch, example of, 124
Signed conditional branch instructions, 100
Signed numbers, 45, 119
Signed overflow, 120
Signed vs. unsigned instructions, 126
Single operand instructions, 94, 188
Software, 11
Sorting, 143
Source, 49, 63
Source code, 290
SP, 109, 198
Stack, 153, 198
   illustration, 199
   use of, 200
Stack pointer, 109, 198

Status register, 243, 245, 249, 251
Storage allocation, arrays, 145
Store operation, 33, 39
Stored program, 2
SUB instruction, 41
SUB number instruction, 49
Subroutine libraries, 302
Subroutines, 111, 197
   argument passing, 203
   example of, 113
   FORTRAN, 209
   recursive, 211, 200
Subtraction, 17
   floating point, 269
Symbol table, 65, 70
Symbolic address, 53, 65
Symbolic name, 63, 66
Syntax errors, 71
Syntax of assembly language, 67

TECO, 332
Teletypewriters, 166
.TITLE directive, 68
Transfer address, 303
Trap bit, 260
TRAP instruction, 260
Traps, 74, 259
TST instruction, 89, 93, 123
.TTYIN macro, 179
.TTYOUT macro, 179
Two's complement, 26, 186
Two's complement numbers, 120

Undefined symbols, 71
UNIBUS, 9
Unit of addressable storage, 56
Unsigned branch instructions, 125
Unsigned numbers, 45, 119
Unsigned overflow, 120
Unsigned vs. signed instructions, 126

V bit, 121
VAX-11/780, 9
Vector, interrupt, 254
von Neumann, John, 2

Word, 35, 57
.WORD directive, 69, 175
Word size, 8

XOR instruction, 282

Z bit, 122
029 code, 192

Summary of Edit Commands

A	Read the old program into the editor.
nC	Move the pointer n characters to the right (left if n is negative).
nD	Delete n characters to the right of the pointer (left if n is negative).
EX	Exit from the editor and save the program.
I*text*$	Insert *text* into program.
J	Move the pointer to the beginning.
ZJ	Move the pointer to the end.
nK	Kill n line(s) starting at the pointer.
nL	Move the pointer down n lines (up if n is negative, and to the beginning of the same line if $n = 0$).
S*text*$	Search for the string *text*.
nT	Type n lines starting at the pointer.
HT	Type the whole program.
nV	Verify $n-1$ lines either side of the line the pointer is on.

Equivalence of TECO and EDIT (old editor) Commands

TECO	EDIT	Note
A	R	
nC	nJ	
nD	nD	
EX	EX	
I*text*$	I*text*$	
J	B	
ZJ	999A	Advance a large number of lines such as 999.
nK	nK	
nL	nA	
S*text*$	G*text*$	
nT	nL	
HT	/L	Pointer must be at the beginning in EDIT.
V	V	No number is allowed in EDIT.